DYNAMICS OF BEHAVIOR

DYNAMICS

OF BEHAVIOR

ROBERT S. WOODWORTH

Professor Emeritus of Psychology
Columbia University

HENRY HOLT AND COMPANY, NEW YORK

Preface

Although the present book, in its chapter headings and detailed contents, is far from being a revision of my *Dynamic Psychology* of 1918, it does preserve the same fundamental point of view. At that time the controversy between the introspective psychology of conscious experience and the objective psychology of behavior was new and keen; and yet both parties, it seemed to me, had a common interest in dynamics, in the study of cause and effect, motives and processes, or in the questions "Why?" and "How?" focused on human activities and achievements. A dynamic psychology, I felt, could not allow itself to be fettered by the methodological restrictions of either introspectionism or behaviorism; it must be free to scrutinize and utilize both sorts of data.

I myself was much interested in the drive-mechanism relationship and tried to show that the drive was not necessarily an instinct or biological need but could be any active function that was geared to subordinate functions—any active goal-seeking that had access to subgoals. " 'Drive' is not essentially distinct from 'mechanism.' The drive is a mechanism already aroused and thus in a position to furnish stimulation to other mechanisms. Any mechanism might be a drive. But it is the mechanisms directed toward consummatory reactions . . . that are most likely to act as drives." I was not too successful in making this relationship clear; many readers assumed that I must be talking of the motive power of habit.

During the ensuing forty years my books had quite other aims than the development of a theoretical system, though I could not altogether refrain from harping on a few pet ideas such as preparatory set, objective interests, and "dealing with the environment." For most of these same years a lecture course bore the name of "Dynamic Psychology," the subject matter sometimes including heredity and environment, brain localization, and the theory of emotion, but tending more and more to concentrate on motivation, perception, and learning—as in the present book.

The old title for the lectures or for the book became rather misleading. "Dynamic psychology" came generally to mean the study of motivation, especially unconscious motivation. If I assert that the dynamic interactions of motivation, learning, perception, and problem solving are real and important, no one is likely to raise any objections. These considerations led me to change the title of my lectures, and now of this book, to "Dynamics of Behavior." The point of view is not behavioristic, however, though most of the recent experimental material cited is objective rather than introspective.

In the last few years, even since my fortunate collaboration with Harold Schlosberg in the revised *Experimental Psychology,* quite a large array of relevant experiments have appeared in the literature. The present volume is supplementary to the *Experimental* in two respects: in general theory and in coverage of this literature.

As a text for the lecture course mentioned I have used the relevant chapters of the *Experimental,* along with a preliminary mimeographed edition of the present book. This book corresponds in general to the second half of the *Experimental,* Chapters 14-26. The reading assignments I have found satisfactory are about as follows:

Dynamics of Behavior	*Experimental Psychology*
Chapter 1. The point of view	Pages 1-7
2. Behavioral dynamics	8-10, 28-32, 43-50
3. Motives in operation	107-110, 133-136, 655-679
4. Outgoing motivation	679-694
5. Theories of motivation	———
6. Control of muscular movement	———

Very important assistance has been received from Mrs. Enrica Tunnell, both in the conduct of the lecture course for many years and in the preparation and especially the indexing of the present volume.

The theories of motivation, perception, and learning herein offered may not be entirely new and original but they have at least some novel features, as suggested by the phrases, "behavior-primacy theory of motivation," "stimulus decoding and response encoding," and "question-and-answer process in learning," which are all in accord with the orientation of behavior toward the objective environment.

R.S.W.

Columbia University
October 17, 1957

Contents

1

The Point of View

Without being in doubt as to what he wished to say in this book, the author has hesitated considerably over the title. For many years the lecture course on which the book is largely based was entitled "dynamic psychology," an attractive name which has, however, come to have a rather restricted meaning. It has come to mean a study of motivation almost exclusively and is sometimes further restricted to the "unconscious springs of human behavior" and the maladjustments resulting from unconscious conflicts. Not being qualified to approach the subject from this angle, the author has thought it only fair to forestall misunderstanding by a change of title. Besides, from his point of view the subject ought not to be limited to motivation. Motives do not operate in a vacuum, and the behavior in which they do operate is affected by the processes of perception, learning, and thinking. Not only are these processes motivated, but motives themselves depend on how a situation is perceived and understood and on habits and ways of meeting a situation that have been previously learned. Theories of motivation (and there are many theories to be considered) ought to be related to theories of learning and perception. It is even desirable not to limit the study to human behavior, since much relevant information has been obtained from studies of animal learning and animal drives. This is

the view of an experimental psychologist who believes that his field
of activity will eventually prove to be of immense value to the students of human motives and maladjustments.

What lines of investigation are suggested by the title, "Dynamics of Behavior"?

A student seeking means of self-improvement might hope for
some light on the question, "How can I make my behavior more
dynamic, i.e., more forceful and effective?" He is thinking of his
own behavior as a force exerted on other people rather than of
forces operating in himself to influence his own behavior. This
more comprehensive question would suggest itself to a psychologist
who would think of a person's behavior as influenced not only by
other people but also by personal needs and drives. At any rate,
"dynamics" suggests a study of forces. In physics it includes also the
study of motions. Force is what causes motion—better, a change of
motion. Suppose that a body is moving in a straight line with a constant speed but at a certain moment it changes direction or speed.
It must have been acted on at that moment by a force, and the
strength and direction of the force can be inferred from the change
of motion. The motion is directly observed, but the force is not observed. It is inferred from the observed motion and the basic assumption that there must be an adequate cause or causes for the
observed effect. If we had to infer a separate force for every change
of motion, we should be making no progress in physical dynamics;
but since the force of gravitation, for example, acts in various situations so that we can infer from it the law of falling bodies and the
law of revolution of the planets around the sun, the assumed force
of gravitation reduces to order a vast array of observed facts. Moreover, mankind has learned how to produce certain forces and how
to apply them so as to get desired effects. Man knows several ways
of producing heat—fire, friction, electric current through a wire—
and several controllable effects of heat, and this whole mass of
knowledge and control is organized around the concept of heat.

Can we hope to derive any similar advantage from the use of
dynamic concepts in psychology? The older "functional" psychology
used such concepts freely though not very systematically or critically.
With the advent about 1900 of the more critical schools of "structural" psychology and behaviorism, the attempt was made to make

psychology a purely descriptive science. (For some account of these schools reference may be made to Woodworth, 1948.) Explanatory theories might best be left to physiology, it was thought. For example, the well-known curve of forgetting is purely descriptive; it is a summary statement of systematically observed facts. The retention of what has been learned, however, must depend on some sort of "trace" in the brain, and the forces that cause retention to decrease gradually along this peculiar curve must operate physiologically. Psychologists have not been wholly satisfied with this division of labor. Not trying to be really physiological themselves, they have conceived of certain factors or forces that might cause forgetting—one such being "interference"—and have designed psychological experiments to put these hypothetical forces to the test. Without being directly observed, interference of one action tendency with another offers an explanation of forgetting and of several other psychological phenomena; it could operate physiologically, but exactly how it acts is a question for physiology.

INTERVENING VARIABLES

For justification of these conceived though unobserved factors in behavior we are most indebted to the work of Edward Chace Tolman (1932, 1938, 1955), long an active investigator of animal behavior at the University of California. Let an organism (O) receive at a certain moment an input of stimuli (S) from the environment and respond by making a certain movement (R). The S and R are observed by the experimenter (E). He varies S and notes the resulting variation in R. But he finds that the variation in R does not depend exclusively on the variation in S. There must be variable factors operating inside O between the input and the output, and these are the O-variables or "intervening variables." Since they cannot be observed, they must be conjectured at first and then tried out experimentally to see if they have any explanatory and predictive value. The standard example of an intervening variable is hunger for food. On a certain occasion an animal does not eat the food that is offered him. We wonder why and come up with a hunch, based no doubt on our own experience, that he is not hungry. This suggestion may quiet our momentary curiosity, but it has no value as a scientific theory or hypothesis until tried out under different conditions. We must compare the animal's response to food when he is hungry and when not hungry; or since our hunch is that the animal can be more or less hungry, we must compare his response to food under different degrees of hunger. The observable response variable may be the amount eaten or the speed of eating. Since we cannot control hunger directly we must find some antecedent operation (A-variable) that can be depended on to control it indirectly. The most obvious A-variable is elapsed time since the last feeding. We try out the following tentative predictions: Immediately after a full meal the animal will eat none of the test meal; an hour later he will eat a small amount; and the amount eaten will increase with the time of deprivation, probably up to some limit which must be determined empirically. The curve or "function" relating the amount eaten to the length of the deprivation period will also have to be worked out empirically. If the tentative predictions are verified and if the curve has some regularity and uniformity, the intervening variable, hunger, is a usable concept for purposes of scientific investigation. It is firmly tied to an A-variable on one side and to a response variable on the other side.

Let us pause to notice what the experimenter has done. He started with a common-sense notion of hunger as a demand for food, but he concluded with a procedure for controlling how much an animal will eat. For control purposes he has *defined* degree of hunger as *time since* a full meal. He has pruned away from his common-sense notion of hunger everything except deprivation time. He is not entitled to say that an animal eats because it is feeling hungry or because it is getting low in internal food supply. Hunger, thus far, is simply a name for the dependence of amount eaten on time since last feeding. It seems a very meager concept, but it is adequate for learning experiments in which food is used as the reward for success in finding the food box or manipulating a food-vending machine. (Of course, there is an underlying assumption that the animals are in good health.) The meager concept can be enriched somewhat if *E* can find another way of controlling the amount eaten, as by an intelligent assortment of appetizers. Hunger, therefore, would have to be both that which is generated by food deprivation and that which is stimulated or depressed by certain known drugs.

If we appeal to physiology for information on what actually goes on in the organism during food deprivation, our concept of hunger will become more "substantive"; hunger will be more than a hypothetical force known only as having certain causes and certain effects. But physiology provides no similar information at present on other intervening variables which seem to be operating in behavior. An animal's response to the presence of food depends not only on the degree of his hunger, but also on the palatability of the food. He will eat greedily of some foods but little or none of others. Food preferences are dependable in a given species of animals (pp. 120f) and constitute an important intervening variable. They depend partly on taste, but why a sweet taste should be preferred to bitter is not yet explained physiologically. Another important class of factors influencing an animal's behavior in the presence of food was called by Tolman the *cognitive* intervening variables; they might be called abilities, and they depend on previous learning. The animal may avoid a food of unfamiliar appearance, not perceiving it to be food. Or the food may be behind a wire screen, only to be reached by a detour which the animal has not yet found. Looking at the animal in a given situation, you cannot observe any habit, skill, or acquaintance with the situation that he has previously acquired and is now carrying around with him. You can observe its effect on his response to the situation, and you may know how to control his acquisition of these abilities. Ability, like hunger, therefore, can be tied to antecedent variables on one side and to response variables on the other.

Another influential behavior theory, that of Clark L. Hull, long of Yale University (1943, 1952), makes fully as much use of intervening variables as Tolman does. Any ability factor he designates by the symbol H for "habit strength"; any demand, need or drive factor he labels D; the appeal to the animal of the food or other incentive offered as reward is labeled K; the inhibitory factor of work necessary for obtaining the reward is labeled I; and some minor factors have to be postulated in order to cover the ground. Hull's ideal was a system of postulates from which quantitative inferences could be drawn and tested. The system of interrelated factors would be perfectly abstract but it would yield inferences applicable to concrete situations. Over the years Hull and his adherents tested out and improved his postulates, but as yet no one has claimed attainment of a perfect system. Meanwhile, parts of the system have given rise to a large amount of more or less fruitful investigation. Tolman (1955) has discussed the similarities and differences between his own system and Hull's. The principal difference is Tolman's use of "expectancy" in place of Hull's "habit." What has been learned, according to Hull, is the ability to make a certain response to a certain stimulus (or stimulus complex). According to Tolman what has been learned is the ability to make a certain response to a certain stimulus and thereby obtain a certain incentive. For Hull what has been learned is simply an S–R, but for Tolman it is an S–R–K. Or, we may state instead that for Tolman the S has become a signal of a K to be obtained by making R. We shall have more to say on this difference when we discuss theories of learning (pp. 239ff).

For the present our concern is with the value of intervening variables in the prediction and control of behavior, and on this question we shall turn to another prominent student of behavior, Professor B. F. Skinner of Harvard (1938, p. 24; 1953, pp. 27-35). In the earlier book Skinner made sparing and critical use of intervening variables, finding them convenient in such examples as hunger, thirst, and anxiety, each of which can be induced by certain antecedent operations. A man can be made to drink a lot of water either by depriving him of water for a long time or by feeding him salty food; in both cases, the physiologists tell us, the body fluids become too salty. We thus know more about thirst than merely that it intervenes between an antecedent operation and a consequent form of behavior. To quote from Skinner's later book (pp. 31-35):

> The practice of looking inside the organism for an explanation of behavior has tended to obscure the variables which are immediately available for scientific analysis. These variables lie outside the organism, in its immediate environment and in its environmental history. . . . To what extent is it helpful to be told, "He drinks because he is thirsty"? If to be thirsty means nothing more than to have a tendency to drink, this is mere redundancy. If it means that he drinks because of a state of thirst, an inner causal event is invoked. If this state is purely inferential . . . it cannot serve as an explanation. But if it has physiological . . . properties, what role can it play in a science of behavior?
>
> . . . We have a causal chain consisting of three links: (1) an operation performed upon the organism from without—for example, water deprivation; (2) an inner condition—for example, physiological . . . thirst; and (3) a kind of behavior—for example, drinking. Independent information about the second link would obviously permit us to predict the third without recourse to the first. . . . Direct information about the second link is, however, seldom, if ever available. . . .

The second link is useless in the *control* of behavior unless we can manipulate it. . . . We usually set up the second link through the first. . . . In that case, the second link obviously does not permit us to dispense with the first. . . . If we must always go back beyond the second link for prediction and control, we may avoid many tiresome and exhausting digressions by examining the third link as a function of the first.

Skinner is saying that the seeming convenience of inferred inner processes conceals a pitfall for the behavior student or the human engineer, who cannot deal directly with intervening variables but has to go back to A-variables and S-variables for discovering valid laws of behavior or for utilizing such laws in the control of behavior. The physiological psychologist, on the contrary, takes an inferred intervening process as a start toward investigation. He wishes to find out what this process is, physiologically. He may try to "see into" the organism by physiological methods; or he may set up hypotheses to be tested by suitable A-variables. He may test the hypothesis that thirst results from overconcentration of salt in the body fluids by feeding salt and observing the effect on the amount of water drunk. Any competent psychologist, we may argue, will be alive to the pitfall pointed out by Skinner and still find it more than merely convenient to conceive of intervening variables. It is necessary to bear in mind that antecedent operations have produced effects on the organism which persist in some form and only so can be factors in present behavior. At the present time they are O-factors and no longer A-factors. Following either Hull or Tolman, we can say that a drive was built up by one antecedent operation and an ability by another, but both operations were applied to the same organism, so that they now interact in determining that organism's behavior.

BEHAVIOR SCIENCE VERSUS BEHAVIORISM

A student of behavior is not necessarily a behaviorist. A loyal adherent of the behavioristic school is subject to certain restrictions: he must not make any use of introspective data; he must not speak of "mental" processes; he must regard animal behavior as better suited for fundamental research than the more complicated human behavior.

When the behavioristic movement was started by John B. Watson

(1913, 1914), it had to compete with the structural and functional schools, both of which were accustomed to define psychology as the scientific study of conscious processes or of mental processes. The structuralists aimed to work out a systematic description of conscious experience, beginning with sensory experience, and their basic method was called introspection; the only possible observer of a person's sensations and feelings being the person himself. This sort of psychology was probably legitimate but of limited scope. The functionalists (in a broad sense) were investigating perception, learning, memory, thinking, and other activities which could be regarded as "mental" in distinction from such physiological functions as digestion, circulation, and respiration. They used introspection to some extent, since they believed that a person could often observe and report something of his processes of learning and thinking; but they relied mostly on objective data, i.e., on observations made by E of O's responses to known situations. These prebehavioristic functionalists were certainly students of behavior; they had even made significant progress in the study of animal behavior. And there is no reason why the functionalists of today, in their attempts to throw some light on the dynamics of human behavior, should avoid introspection as a matter of principle. They should check, of course, on the accuracy of introspective reports—check them against objective data where possible.

Using our scheme of S-variables, A-variables, and intervening or O-variables, let us ask how far we can depend on our subject, O, to observe and report these factors. In one large field of investigation O's report on the *stimuli* supplies essential data; that is the field of sense perception. Stimuli applied to different spots on the skin give sensations of warmth, cold, pain, or simple touch. How do we know this? Because O so reports. Stimulus thresholds are measured by E's applying a range of stimulus intensities and finding how weak a stimulus (of a given kind) O can perceive and report, and difference thresholds are similarly measured by E's applying two stimuli and finding whether O can tell which is the stronger. Physical sounds exist which are too low or too high in pitch (vibration frequency) to be heard by the human ear. The limits, about 20 and 20,000 vibrations per second, are found by similar methods. It is possible to make threshold determinations on animals by other methods, but with human subjects the quickest and most reliable method utilizes O's verbal report on the stimuli received (Woodworth & Schlosberg, 1954, pp. 192-194, 273-277, 330-332). In other types of experiments, as those for learning, it is unnecessary to obtain O's report on the stimuli since they are perfectly perceptible and easily discriminable.

But it is often important to obtain O's report on certain *A-variables*. One such variable consists of the advance "instructions" given to O, informing him what task he has to perform. Usually E will ask, "Do you understand what you have to do? Are there any questions?" Unless O reports that he knows what he has to do, the experiment cannot proceed. In a learning experiment it may be important to have O tell whether he has had any previous experience with the poem to be learned or the performance to be practiced; if so, his learning curve evidently cannot start from scratch. In clinical psychology O's present problem may have its roots in his past experience and he may be asked to report what he can remember that seems relevant. .

But how about the *intervening variables?* Can O observe and report anything that will make them more substantial? We were speaking of thirst as an intervening variable having no more substance than that of an unobservable link between water deprivation and the act of drinking. If we ask a person why he is going out, he may report, "Because I feel thirsty and I know where I can get a drink." He is reporting a motive for his "instrumental act" of going to a certain place. There is usually no reason for rejecting this introspective report as untrustworthy. And can we say that he is ascribing his act to a "mental" cause in the sense that is so objectionable to the behaviorists, i.e., a nonphysical cause that lies outside the field of natural cause and effect? On the contrary, this thirsty feeling of his is an indication of his physiological state. Without perceiving the physiological details, he perceives the familiar bodily state as a whole. He may not remember with any exactness the A-variable of long deprivation of water, but he reports an intervening variable of considerable substance.

Pain is distinctly subjective in that it occurs in the organism and not in the environment. It is not imaginary by any means. Let radiant heat be applied to an area of the skin and gradually increased in intensity. At low intensities O reports warmth or heat, but at a fairly definite threshold he begins to report pain which is mild at first but increases to the limit of his tolerance (Hardy, Wolff, & Goodell, 1947). The pain threshold as measured by this method of

verbal report agrees closely with a physiological measure, the galvanic skin response (Clausen, Gjesvik, & Urdal, 1953). Another way
of producing graduated intensities of pain is by the application of
weak alternating currents to a tooth filling. It is found that "there
is a one-to-one relationship between the intensity of the stimulus
and the estimation of its painfulness" (Swartz, 1953). Toothache as
reported by the victim is a reliable indicator of something wrong,
though he may not be able to locate the trouble exactly without
some help from the dentist. There are many cases of reportable internal pain which serves as an indicator of something going on in
the organism that requires attention. If you ask a person why he
is limping, he may say that his foot hurts; or if you ask him why
he is not eating his dinner, he may report a stomachache. Medically,
pains reported by a patient are of sufficient importance to justify
extensive treatises devoted to diagnostic methods for locating the
source of the trouble and to control measures for the relief of pain
(White & Sweet, 1955). Our own theoretical interest in pain can be
summed up in three statements: (1) a person's report of pain is a
reasonably dependable indicator of a bodily state which is often a
factor in his behavior; (2) pain belongs squarely in the realm of
natural cause and effect, even "psychic pain," which cannot be
stopped by transection of peripheral pain nerves, often being allevi-
ated by certain brain operations in the region of the thalamus and
frontal lobes; and (3) pain is best studied in human beings. Animals
given electric shocks or injured in accidents often do behave in ways
that would be symptomatic of pain in human beings, but behaviorists and other psychologists have insisted or admitted that we have
no logical justification for inferring conscious pain or any consciousness in animals—or for inferring an absence of consciousness, either.

Lustful states of the organism, no less than painful ones, are in-
trospectively observable and function as important intervening variables—intervening, for example, between such a stimulus as the
sight of an attractive partner and such a response as overt sex behavior. Human sex desire, to be sure, is more than a peripheral
bodily state. Like psychic pain it depends on the brain, but that is
no reason for denying it the status of a natural event with natural
causes and effects. It is subject to enhancement or inhibition from
such "mental" factors as memories and anticipations and considerations of prudence and of right and wrong, but all these factors in

human behavior belong in the realm of natural processes, as far as the psychologist can judge.

In addition to painful and pleasurable states of his organism, *O* can report his likes and dislikes for certain objects. He may not remember all the past experiences or A-variables which gave rise to these likes and dislikes, but the present likes and dislikes are reportable intervening variables in his responses to these objects. He can report to a considerable extent, though not always perfectly because of mixed motives, what he is trying to do at the present moment, what he aims to accomplish in the future, and what are his long-range purposes, hopes, and fears. It may seem a strained interpretation to regard all these O-factors as states of the organism (including the brain), but where could one draw the line between natural processes in the organism and "mental" processes in a transcendental sense?

Let us approach the question of the validity of introspection from another angle. A person's report of internal pain might be called introspective because it is a report of something inside him and not in the world outside. If you place an object in a good light before the person reporting and he says, "I see it," that report could certainly not be called introspective. If it could, all scientific observation would be introspective. And yet he reported not only the presence of the object, but also his own experience of seeing. If you now turn the light down gradually, he will finally say, "I don't see it but I know it is still there because I can touch it." (There are many similar ways by which a child can be taught what it means for him to "see.") Your subject has now certainly reported a fact about himself, a fact which under accurate control of the light would be called his stimulus threshold for light intensity. If you leave the light on at a low intensity, after a while he may say, "Now I can see the object again, though very dimly." The dark adaptation which he has now reported is a process occurring in him and not in the environment.

The next day your subject may say, "I remember your showing me an object which I saw plainly at first, then not at all when you turned down the light, and then again dimly in the faint light." This memory of a past experience is a present event in himself, and the human ability to report present memories of past events affords the psychologist a "look-in" on certain important O-factors in behavior. (The child probably learns through social reinforcements

and corrections to use the word "remember" with some discrimination, since he finds that events must have occurred which he cannot remember and even that events never occurred which he seems
to remember.)

The difficulty of drawing any sharp line between introspective
and nonintrospective observation makes it seem rather ridiculous to
exclude all introspective data from the study of behavior, as if such
exclusion were required by scientific morality. The requirement is,
rather, to separate the introspective sheep from the goats, for undoubtedly much goes on in a person's learning, thinking, and de-
ciding that he cannot observe accurately. Often the most promising
line of attack on a problem is to use introspective results as suggestive of hypotheses which can be put to the test of quantitative objective experiments.

Some psychologists would say that a proposed law should be put
to the test of animal experiments before being accepted as fundamental. As between rats and college students, the two most-used
classes of experimental subjects, rats certainly offer some advantages.
They can be subjected to closer control in respect to heredity, previous experience, and present environment and activities. They are
more uniform than the students, so that results can be obtained
from them with less variability and greater reliability. Fundamental
laws of learning and motivation have been obtained from the animal laboratory. In the equally important field of perception, however, work with animals is a slow process because they cannot be
told what they are supposed to do; consequently, the most fundamental results have been obtained from human subjects. As far as
possible, results obtained from rats should be tried out on students,
and results from students should be tried out on rats. It is not
wholly safe to extrapolate in either direction. Other animals, especially cats, dogs, and the primates, are not to be left out of the picture if we are to do justice to the source of some of our most
important findings in psychology. Human children of different ages
are important in the study of mental development, and for some
experiments they make the best subjects of all.

If the questions we have considered in this section were thrown
open to discussion in a group of psychologists, some would certainly
take one side and some the other. Some would argue for quantitative objective experiments, insisting that only in such a manner can
definite and permanent contributions be made to our knowledge.

Others would argue that in their zeal for quantitative results many psychologists have chosen problems that lend themselves to such treatment, to the neglect of more important fields for investigation.

THE DYNAMICS OF "DEALING WITH THE ENVIRONMENT"

A distinctive emphasis of this book is on interaction between the organism and the environment, physical and social. Besides objects of many sizes, shapes, and weights, located at various distances and moving in different directions, there are other organisms with drives and abilities, known or unknown to O, to be dealt with, and there are social groups with their customs, laws and institutions. Some of this total environment is not "effective" for the individual; he does not interact with it in any important way; some of it is too far away or hidden from him; some of it has no interest for him, either positive or negative. The same physical environment, such as a forest, is a different effective environment for the herbivorous deer and for the carnivorous wolf. The same social environment is a different effective environment for the adult and for the little child.

We may speak of past, present, and future environments, though only the present environment can be dealt with at the present time. Yet the past and future influence present behavior. The past environment has supplied the A-variables for O's present drives and abilities, as we have seen. He "generalizes" from the past to the present, tacitly assuming that the environment is practically the same as it was and usually profiting from that assumption, though sometimes coming to grief because the environment has changed in some important respect. As to the future, there is another tacit assumption to consider. Much behavior is based on the assumption that there is going to be a future environment which can be controlled to some extent by present action. The baseball fielder running to intercept a fly, the student preparing for tomorrow's examination, are typical human examples of dealing with the future—or, better, of dealing with the present in such a way as to be ready to deal with a situation still to come. And some of this anticipatory behavior, at least over a short time span, can be observed in animals. We shall return to this orientation of behavior toward the future under several heads: preparatory set, purpose, the timing of skilled movements, etc. (pp. 40, 45, 145). We have touched here on two dynamic factors in behavior: (1) the carry-over from the past to the present of what has been previously learned and (2) the preparation in the present for what is probably going to happen in the future—retention and anticipation. These characteristics of human and animal behavior are certainly remarkable.

Dealing with the present environment, however, is still more remarkable. It may not seem remarkable at all from an external point of view. As external observers, we view the organism in the presence of an environment. Here is O, and before him is the environment. What is to prevent his dealing with it? It acts on him by stimuli to his sense organs (receptors), and he acts on it by his muscular activity. His nerves, conducting excitation from the receptors to the nerve centers and from them to the muscles (and sometimes to other effectors such as glands and electric organs), make it inevitable that adequate sensory stimuli will elicit muscular activity with external effects. So what is there particularly puzzling about O's interaction with the present environment?

The puzzle emerges when we try to shift the point of view in order to take the picture from the organism's standpoint instead of from that of an external observer. The environment is no longer in the picture, since everything that happens is inside the organism or on its surface. The stimuli received are not external objects but excitations of the receptors, and the muscular contractions are not external effects but intraorganic activities. In order to bring the environment into the organism's picture, we have to credit the organism with something more than receptors and effectors and connecting nerves. It must have the capacity to utilize the stimuli as indicators of objects and happenings outside and to utilize the muscles for producing environmental results.

If we can imagine an organism without the just-mentioned capacity, reporting its experience in the presence of an environment, the report would sound very strange: "I admit receiving stimuli or at least having a lot of sensations—patterns of light, shade and color, sounds, odors, tastes, warmth, cold, pain, and pressure sensations— and I admit making muscular movements; but I have no evidence of any environment, of receiving any information from an environment or of doing anything to an environment." Very different is the testimony which we actually obtain on asking a person to report an experience. He will speak of green grass, of a small shiny object lying in the grass, and of approaching the object and picking it up.

Or he will speak of hearing an airplane, of getting a whiff of ammonia, of tasting "something bitter," or of lifting "something smooth, cold, and heavy, probably metallic." He speaks of objects and happenings in the physical environment; or he may speak of the social environment, as of persons recognized and communicated with by speech. He may say nothing at all about stimuli or muscular actions.

A confirmed behaviorist may object to this introspective testimony which he feels bound to regard as untrustworthy. In its defense we can state: (1) that there is no disagreement among observers such as to cast any doubt on their reports; (2) that this kind of reporting is made by all scientific observers including the behaviorists who describe the environmental situation in which they place an animal and the objective effects of the animal's behavior; (3) that the introspective reports check very well with observable behavior. A person reports seeing a small object lying in the grass, and he goes to the right place and reaches down with his hand in proper position for grasping a small object. If he reports seeing a larger object on top of a wall farther away, he advances to a greater distance, reaches up, and uses both hands. A dog's behavior shows a similar adjustment to objects in space. Undoubtedly much previous learning has contributed to such skillful dealing with the environment. The human introspective testimony, however, shows that what is learned is more than a lot of motor responses. The learning has been perceptual-motor rather than purely motor. A person is aware of a continuous spatial environment before and around him and of objects of various sizes and shapes situated at various distances. He perceives many other characteristics of objects, such as their color, odor, temperature, weight, and roughness or smoothness. Of course, he depends on stimuli for all this information, but the point is that he utilizes the stimuli as information about the environment and that his motor behavior is guided by this objectified information.

The perceptual utilization of stimuli is an intervening variable between the reception of the stimuli and the motor performance. It is more than a mere X, defined only by the stimuli on one side and the muscular action on the other. The introspective testimony gives it considerable substance. There is a translation of stimuli and stimulus combinations into information about the environment. To mention one example among many which will be considered in the chapters on perception (pp. 162ff): a cue of the distance of an object is the size of its retinal image which increases as one approaches the object; this stimulus dimension of size is translated into the altogether different dimension of distance. "Translation" is a better word here than the frequently used "transformation"; the stimuli themselves are not changed, just as a French word is not transformed when you translate it into English. The English word is your response to the French word, and seen distance is some sort of internal response to the size of the retinal image. We can call it a perceptual response.

The perception of space is tied up with the perception of objects. Approach is approach toward an object; distance is the distance of an object. Now the object is no more "given" than its distance. The retinal image of an object is decidedly not the object itself. The retinal image shrinks as the object moves away, but the object does not appear to O to lose its identity; it appears to be the same object and it even appears to maintain its size in spite of the shrinkage of its picture on the retina (size constancy, pp. 208f). Seeing an object is a perceptual response to the retinal stimuli. The same can be said of the process of getting acquainted with an object by the senses of touch and kinesthesis, i.e., by feeling of the object and manipulating it. The stimuli (and the tactile and kinesthetic sensations) change from moment to moment, but the object appears to O to maintain its identity. He assumes that he is exploring a real object and uses the stimuli as indicators of its size, shape, weight, and other properties.

"Translation" as a cerebral response

It seems then that we must credit the organism, or at least some organisms including man, with the capacity for utilizing stimuli as indicators of objects in a spatial environment. It must be a native capacity which is basic to an immense amount of learning. Some equipment for seeing objects in space is present in the eye itself, i.e., in its mechanism for focusing on objects at different distances, but much more equipment is required for the "translation" of stimuli into information concerning objects in space and concerning the environment in general—such information as will enable the organism to deal effectively with the environment. The physiological process is surely going to be very difficult to discover. However, there is already some reliable evidence as to *where* the process takes place. In man and the primates, at least, it takes place largely in the cerebral cortex and is thrown out of gear by lesions of the cortex inflicted by gunshot wounds, by tumors, or by cerebral hemorrhages. The various losses of cerebral function classified by the neurologists as agnosia, apraxia, and aphasia result from such lesions.

The cortical areas involved are those called the "association areas" in distinction from the "projection areas." The retinas are connected by incoming nerve fibers to a certain part of the occipital lobe, the area striata. This is the visual projection area, and there are also projection areas for the other senses—for audition in the temporal lobe, for touch and kinesthesis in the parietal lobe just behind the central fissure and so adjacent to the motor projection area just in front of the same fissure. The postcentral strip of cortex has incoming connections with all parts of the body, and the precentral strip has outgoing connections with the lower motor centers in the spinal cord and brain stem. Microscopically examined, the projection areas are very extensive since the area striata, for example, contains great numbers of nerve cells, of incoming fibers connecting it with all parts of the retina, and of outgoing fibers connecting it with the lower motor center for the eye muscles and also with other parts of the cortex. Yet the projection areas occupy only a relatively small part of the whole cortex, especially in the human brain.

The projection areas are separated by the much more extensive association areas (except that there is no such separation between the body sense area and the motor area). In front of the motor area is the large frontal association area, and lying between the three large sensory areas (visual, auditory, and body-sense) is the parieto-temporo-occipital association area. These nonsensory areas are called association areas because they afford opportunity for psychological associations between the different senses, as between the visual appearance and the sound of a violin, or because of the immense number of "association fibers" interconnecting the sensory and motor areas and various parts of the association areas themselves. They do have fiber connections with the thalamus, cerebellum, and other subcortical centers, but they are especially rich in long and short fibers connecting different parts of the cortex.

Our theory is that a major function of the association areas is to enable the organism to deal effectively with the environment (1) by translating sensory stimuli into information about the environment and (2) by organizing muscular movements into combinations that will conform to the environment and produce specific environmental effects.

The evidence for this theory is found in the losses of function resulting from relatively small brain injuries which do not paralyze or blind or deafen the patient but do impair his behavior. The exact localization of different functions within the association areas is difficult and largely uncertain; we need not bother with that problem.

Visual agnosia covers such defects as the following: The patient sees a familiar object and can tell its color and size, but he cannot tell what it is. An oldish man just after a slight cerebral hemorrhage went for a walk and failed to recognize his own daughter on the street. He also had difficulty in finding his way home, the latter symptom being an example of what is called spatial agnosia. A patient who cannot recognize a familiar object on sight may recognize it instantly if it is put into his hands. There are also instances of failure to recognize a familiar object by touch though it is known at once on sight. In one case the perceptual response is disconnected from visual data, in the other case from tactile data. Other varieties of spatial agnosia are the inability to point to a seen object, to reach out and grasp it, and to walk past without colliding with it. A patient may be unable to draw a floor plan of his own house, or to make a consistent drawing of a bicycle from memory, or to solve a simple jigsaw puzzle such as the "manikin test." He may be unable to follow a map of the route he should take between spots clearly marked on the floor (Holmes, 1947; McFie, *et al.*, 1950; Semmes, *et al.*, 1955).

Auditory agnosia merges into a form of aphasia. A woman came under observation because of "word deafness." She could hear well enough, but understood nothing that was said to her, though she could talk sensibly and read understandingly. Although she was something of a musician and was still able to read music, she no longer could recognize familiar tunes or imitate a heard rhythm. With her eyes closed she was unable to identify the noises made by keys rattling, paper being crumpled, the clock ticking, or the telephone ringing. Here there was a disconnection between auditory stimuli and their previously well-known objective meanings (Reinhold, 1950).

In exploring the environment the organism learns not only the spatial and other strictly physical properties of objects but also their value, positive or negative—for example, their edibility or inedibility. The normal monkey, an eminently visual organism, discriminates quickly between edible and inedible objects strewn before him and, if hungry, picks up only the edible ones. Monkeys subjected to an operation which disconnects the visual area from the "hippocampal" region lying deep in or under the temporal lobe behave quite differently. They are as active as ever visually and perceive the size, shape, and distance of objects, but they pick them all up indiscriminately, nails, sticks, and even bits of feces, as well as pieces of apple or carrot. They bring each object to the mouth and examine it orally before discarding the inedible and swallowing the edible bits. This behavior shows one form of visual agnosia. The visual data can no longer be translated into value (Klüver & Bucy, 1939; Bucy and Klüver, 1955).

Apraxia is said to be "the motor counterpart of agnosia" (Holmes, 1947). It is not always easy to distinguish from agnosia, and it seems usually to result from injury to the same broad posterior association area, though sometimes from injury to the frontal area. The patient, though still able to recognize objects, is unable to put them together so as to accomplish a desired result. If handed a cigarette and a box of matches, he flounders around and may get a match between his lips while scratching the cigarette on the box. He "cannot translate an aim or purpose into the desired action." The intact brain evidently provides a system for translating stimuli into objects and for translating the intention to accomplish certain objective results into the appropriate combination of muscular actions.

Aphasia or loss, usually partial, of speech is another result of lesions in the association areas. It has several varieties which are allied to agnosia and apraxia. In fact word deafness is a kind of auditory agnosia; word blindness, or inability to make out the configuration of a word so as to read it, is a kind of visual agnosia; and motor aphasia, or inability to organize a sequence of speech movements so as to pronounce a word or rattle off a sentence, is a kind of apraxia. Another form of aphasia consists in loss of memory for words; the patient may be able to read seen words, to understand

heard words, and to pronounce words, but he cannot get hold of
the words he needs; he may speak any words that occur to him so
that his talk, while perhaps fluent and grammatical, makes no sense
to the hearer. Can we regard aphasia as a loss of an ability to deal
with the environment—so different as it is from the other agnosias
and apraxias? Can we regard the speech functions as ways of dealing
with the environment on a par with space perception and the manipulation of objects? Apart from the perceptual skill required to
grasp the intricate configurations of audible speech, and the motor
skill required to manipulate the expired air so as to produce the
variegated flow of speech, language is distinctly a way of dealing
with an important part of the environment, the social environment.
And we may draw a moral to our story: just as the human being has
the native capacity for learning and using a language, so he has the
capacity for perceiving the physical environment and for acting
effectively upon it.

He has also the capacity for perceiving his social environment
and for acting effectively on other people. He perceives another
person not simply as an object of a certain size and shape moving
about in space, but also as an object having desires and emotions,
friendly or hostile, an object to play with or to avoid, an object to
question with the expectation of receiving information about the
environment. He learns that he himself is an object somewhat like
those other persons. He learns something of the interrelations of
persons within a group and of the relations between different
groups. He learns something of the customs and rules of conduct
current in the group and the cultural environment in general. He
gets acquainted with the social environment by means of sensory
stimuli which he translates into objective social facts, and his social
behavior consists of muscular activity directed toward objective
results.

What is "behavior"?

Even before the advent of behaviorism about 1912, psychologists
were beginning to regard the word *behavior* as a good term for the
subject matter of their science, a better term for the purpose than
consciousness or *mind* or even *mental processes*. One reason was
the obvious fact that mental processes became of practical or social
importance when they gave rise to overt activity, including, of

course, spoken or written language. Another reason was the increasing emphasis on objective rather than introspective methods in psychology, though many psychologists who liked the word *behavior* refused to join Watson in his attempt to eliminate introspection altogether. Probably the main reason was that *behavior* was a more comprehensive term. It could include motor activity, often regarded as different from mental activity, and it could include unconscious processes and factors. William McDougall in 1905 had offered a new definition of psychology: "Psychology may be best and most comprehensively defined as the positive science . . . of the activities by which any creature maintains its relations with other creatures and with the world of physical things." Other psychologists offered similar comprehensive definitions.

Such definitions are, however, almost *too* comprehensive. They do not distinguish psychology from physiology. If we define "psychological behavior" as the organism's external activity which interacts with the environment, as distinguished from the internal processes of growth and maintenance, we seem perhaps to be on firm ground. Maintenance processes belong under the head of "homeostasis," an example being the maintenance of a constant composition of the blood. When the blood sugar starts to be scarce as the result of muscular exercise, some of the glycogen stored in the liver is converted into glucose and taken into the blood. Thus the sugar concentration of the blood is kept nearly constant. Other examples of purely internal processes could be mentioned. But what shall we say of the homeostasis of oxygen and carbon dioxide in the blood? It is maintained by interchange between the blood and the air in the lungs, a genuine interaction between the organism and the environment. The air spaces of the lungs are obviously part of the environment, not of the living organism, and the same is true of the inside of the mouth, stomach, and intestines. The digestive juices secreted into these cavities act on the contained food and fit it for absorption into the body proper. Therefore, the process of digestion is an action of the organism upon the environment. If we define behavior as organismic activity that is in give-and-take relations with the environment, we cannot exclude completely the physiological processes of digestion and respiration. Actually, psychological investigation has often had to concern itself with these processes as component parts of behavior. Salivary secretion has been important in studies of learning (conditioning), digestion is found to be inhibited in certain emotions, and the respiratory movements play a part in talking and other clear examples of behavior. Certainly psychology is not directly concerned with the biochemistry of these processes, nor with the electrochemistry of muscular activity. Any sort of behavior can be studied physiologically.

The muscles, especially the striped muscles, play a large part in behavior, but it would be a mistake to define "psychological behavior" as the activity of the striped muscles. We should have to include the environmental effects of the muscular activity (which lie beyond the primary interests of physiology), and we should have to take account of the physiological fact that the striped muscles act only when stimulated by their motor nerves, that these nerves depend on the nerve centers for stimulation, and that the nerve centers depend quite largely on stimulation coming from the sense organs by way of the sensory nerves. Behavior is thus sensori-neuro-muscular rather than merely muscular. It is cerebral as well, for the brain certainly takes part in behavior that depends on learning or on perception of the environment.

Tolman, whose concept of intervening variables we have already found useful, in 1932 also introduced a distinction between *molar* and *molecular* behavior which is acceptable to many and perhaps all psychologists. By analogy with the meaning of these words in physics, behavior is molar when considered in masses or relatively large units, but molecular when analyzed into small components. The distinction is really not between two kinds of behavior, for the same behavior can be taken either way; it is a distinction between two kinds of description, a psychological description being always molar and a physiological description being often though not always molecular. Tolman's main point was that the molar description could bring to light characteristics of behavior that would not be shown by a molecular description. "I see a friend and attract his attention by calling out his name." A minutely physiological description of this bit of behavior would make a long story, but it would not bring out the essential psychological facts contained in the molar description. It would not tell what I saw or what I tried to accomplish. Seen in the large, Tolman urged, animal as well as human behavior shows cognition and purpose or at least suggests these as intervening variables.

The distinction between molar and molecular descriptions, or between different "levels of description," (Woodworth, 1908; 1929, pp. 547-550) is not limited to behavior studies. Flying at a low level you would see many details of a landscape which would be invisible at a high level, but at the high level you could see general features of the country—mountain ranges, river courses, the relative location of cities—which would not stand out at the low level. It is the same with maps. A large-scale map shows detail which cannot be included in a small map. Shall we say, then, that the large-scale map tells the truth about the country, while the small map is only a makeshift or approximation? No, for the small map shows the shape of the whole country better than the large map. (The detail map may be so large that it is printed in quadrangles which you have to piece together and view from a distance in order to see the general features of the country.) It would be a mistake for psychologists to concede that physiology, as far as it has gone, tells the truth about behavior, psychology being only a temporary makeshift. Psychology, as far as it has gone, tells quite a lot of truth, and there is no apparent reason why it should fail to unearth much more truth, using its distinctive "molar" methods.

2

Behavioral Dynamics at the Molar Level

The question is whether dynamic concepts have any rightful place in psychology or whether all study of cause and effect should be left to physiology. When anyone attempts to give a scientific explanation of a given phenomenon, he is apt to describe it in detail. If he attempts to explain *seeing,* he says that light entering the pupil of the eye strikes the retina and stimulates the rods and cones which in turn stimulate the optic nerve and so start nerve conduction to the brain. This physiological analysis of the process would not satisfy the biochemist, who would ask how light can stimulate the rods and cones and would offer a more minute description in terms of photosensitive pigments in the retina which are chemically broken down by the light, the cleavage products being the actual stimuli which excite the rods and cones. Much knowledge is available at this biochemical level, but it is not the bottom level by any means, for one may ask what goes on electronically in the pigments. the rods and cones, and the nerve fibers. There may be no absolutely bottom level, nor any absolutely fundamental explanation of any phenomenon.

Even if you know the physiology and photochemistry of seeing, you do not have to make use of this knowledge every time you try to explain behavior which involves seeing. If, while you are observing a person, he looks in a certain direction and immediately starts to run away, it would be rather absurd for you to explain this behavior by dipping into the biochemistry of seeing and the physiology of running. You want to know what he has seen. Your explanation will remain at a molar level. There are causes and effects to be discovered at the psychological level, without going down to the physiological level. It is the same in some other sciences. The geologist will explain the shape of a certain valley as a result of glacial action, not of simple erosion. The physical analysis of these two land-shaping forces is not reviewed every time the geological concepts are put to use. Such continual review would be a great waste of time in geological investigation or teaching. Just so it would be a needless waste of time for the psychologist to pause at every juncture for a dip into physiology.

Some psychologists insist on remaining rigidly at the molar level and disregarding physiology altogether. Others are attempting to work out a physiological psychology which shall provide a physiological analysis of the facts of behavior and so contribute to psychological theory. At the least, psychological theories should be scrutinized for assumptions that run counter to physiological knowledge or probability. There is much behavior that is internal and not observable from outside, as in thinking and silent speech and reading, but a theory of such "implicit" or covert behavior that assumes it to consist entirely or essentially of slight contractions of the striped muscles runs counter to the physiological fact that these muscles contract only when stimulated from the nerve centers. Consequently, thinking must consist of brain processes as well as of muscle activity.

It may be a long time before convincing physiological theories of thinking, of learning and retention, and of behavior in general can be achieved. Meanwhile we wish not only to assemble miscellaneous behavioral facts but also to interrelate them dynamically. It can be done at the molar level. And it is probable that molar psychological dynamics will be more serviceable in the understanding, prediction, and control of behavior than even well-developed physiological theories.

An intervening variable may be known physiologically, as in the case of hunger (p. 4). In many instances though, we know nothing about its physiology but do have some psychological knowledge of it. You meet an old acquaintance and speak to him. He hesitates for a moment and then smiles and calls you by name. The intervening variable here is recognition.

THE STIMULUS–RESPONSE FORMULA, DESCRIPTIVE AND DYNAMIC

Behavior occurs in an environment and usually in response to the environment. The environment acts on the organism by stimuli to the receptors, and the organism responds by muscular contractions which produce environmental effects. Often behavior is satisfactorily described without any attempt to specify the exact stimuli received or the exact muscular activity executed, what is described being the objective situation and the results accomplished by the organism. In reporting an experiment on animal learning, E will carefully describe the maze to be learned and record the blind alleys entered on each trial and the number of trials required for mastery of the problem, but there will be no mention of the receptors and muscles involved. The interest is in the process of learning, in the improvement from trial to trial. But if E wishes to discover the "cues" (stimuli) utilized by the animal in traversing the maze, he will conduct the experiment in darkness or compare the success of blind, deaf, or anosmic rats with that of the normals. He has no doubt that some kind of stimuli are necessary, as well as some muscular activity, even though in much of his work he has no special use for the familiar S–R formula.

In certain other fields of psychology the S–R formula comes into use very directly and constantly, as in studies of the senses and of space perception. Stimulus thresholds are measured, or the visual cues of size and distance are discovered and evaluated. There are other examples of use of the S–R formula—reaction times, esthetic preferences for colors or tones or odors. It is relatively easy for E to control and vary the stimulus and observe O's verbal or other responses. It is more difficult to control muscular activity or even to observe it directly, and for that reason we know more about O's utilization of stimuli than about his management of his muscles (but see Chapter 6). We do know such important facts as this one: if a man or animal is temporarily lame in one foot, he alters his muscular action so as to spare his foot, but he still can follow the usual path and reach a desired destination.

The S—R formula can be given a purely descriptive meaning. The stimulus can be observed, the response likewise, and also the fact that the response *follows* the stimulus; in addition, the reaction time or S—R interval is an observed fact. The dash between S and R can be regarded as standing for this interval or sequence. But the formula, including the dash (often replaced by an arrow pointing toward R), can be given a dynamic meaning, too, as when we say that the stimulus elicits, evokes, arouses, instigates the response —these words apparently all meaning the same, namely, that S stands in a causal relation to R. We do not necessarily mean that the stimulus "initiates" the response, for the response may be prepared in advance and only wait for the proper stimulus to trigger it off. The stimulus is *a* cause, not *the* cause of the response.

How much shall we include in the response—the whole internal process leading to the muscular activity (nerve conduction into and out of the centers and whatever brain activity may be required) or only the muscular activity itself? Logically, we have our choice; but if we limit *response* to the muscular activity, we have to recognize that there are intervening processes which may be quite elaborate, especially when they take considerable time as shown by a long reaction time. An effect cannot be separated from its cause by a blank time interval.

The behaviorists have disliked to regard anything but a muscular activity or its outer effects as a genuine "response." If anything important intervenes between the stimulus and the environmentally effective response, they insist that the intervening process must consist of internal muscular actions, along with the necessary nerve conduction into and out of the brain. Thus Watson (1914, 1919) regarded silent thought as consisting of muscular action, the muscles concerned being largely those of the speech organs; and Hull (1943, 1952), recognizing the dynamic importance of anticipation of a goal, regarded it as made up of anticipatory movements so slight as not to interfere with the overt activity of going to the goal. There is some physiological improbability in these assumptions, since the slight internal muscular activities are very likely too weak to serve as kinesthetic stimuli which could keep thought moving along or hold the series of overt movements in line to the goal. If the silent thought, "I haven't written home this week," suggests the further thought, "I'd better do it now," which in turn makes one get out writing materials, can we assume that the two series of little speech movements feed back nerve currents to the brain that are strong enough (and definite enough) to carry the whole process along? More likely it seems that any continued thought process would fade away from lack of kinesthesis. The only obvious behavioristic motive for insisting on the little muscular intermediaries (which may not always occur) is a fear that the cerebral electrochemical processes (which are always occurring while one is awake) may be contaminated with mentalism and not solidly physical. Or it may be merely the fear that cerebral action is not well enough known to justify any reference to it in psychological theory. Now that more is becoming known about brain activity, the physiological psychologists are taking heart and offering cerebral theories of thought, set, and anticipation (Hebb, 1949).

How much should be included in the stimulus? If we say that we showed a baby a doll as a *stimulus,* the baby's *response* being to move toward the doll, neither term is used accurately, though the S—R relation is properly indicated. To be accurate, the stimulus should be distinguished from any external object. We can accurately speak of a seen object as a stimulus object, but we should reserve the name *stimulus* for the light entering the eye from the object. Of course the light entering the eye and striking many rods and cones is a collection of stimuli rather than a single stimulus, though this refinement of nomenclature is often unnecessary. It is decidedly inaccurate, however, to speak of an objective situation as "nothing but a collection of stimuli." The stimuli change from moment to moment as O looks around and moves around, while the objective situation remains the same. The objective situation is something for O to work out by the utilization of the stimuli obtained.

If you have ceased to notice the steady, uniform ticking of a clock and "wake up" with a start when it stops, the cessation of the sound acts as a stimulus. In reaction-time experiments the response to the sudden cessation of a light or sound is found to be as quick as the response to the onset of the same light or sound. Steady pressure on the skin, like that of a tight glove on a motionless hand, is not felt for very long. It ceases to be a tactile stimulus, but if the pressure is increased or decreased, the change is a stimulus. Physical light is not a visual stimulus except within the range of the visible spectrum and sound vibrations are not an auditory stimulus except within the range of audible frequencies. Any physical energy, to be a stimulus, must arouse some receptor to at least minimal activity.

Objections to the S—R formula

Two objections have already been suggested. One is that in many experiments on learning and problem solving, objects are presented and motor results observed, and it is unnecessary and pedantic to inquire into the exact stimuli and muscular responses. The more serious objection is that the habit of speaking of stimulus objects as stimuli, and of motor results as responses, by-passes two large problems of psychology and so gives rise to very incomplete theories of how the organism deals with the environment. It by-passes the question, how stimuli are used in the perception of objects in space, and the question, how the muscles are used in the accomplishment of objective results. Much work has been done on the first of these questions, not so much on the second.

The severest critics of the S—R formula have been the Gestalt psychologists, especially Köhler and Koffka.

Köhler's criticism can be seen in a few sentences from his 1947 book (pp. 164-166):

> The stimulus-response formula, which sounds at first so attractive, is actually quite misleading. In fact, it has so far appeared acceptable solely because Behaviorists use the term "stimulus" in such a loose fashion. . . . How often have "a mouse," "a door," "the experimenter," and so on, been called "stimuli." . . . When the term is taken in its strict sense, it is not generally "a stimulus" which elicits a response. In vision, for instance, the organism tends to respond to millions of stimuli at once; and the first stage of this response is organization within a correspondingly large field. . . . A man's actions are commonly related to a well-structured field, most often to particular thing-units. The right psychological formula is therefore: *pattern of stimulation—organization—response to the products of organization.*

The "organization" so strongly emphasized by Köhler is not muscular coordination but a *seeing* of objects in the environment. In the total response to a collection of stimuli, there is a stage of perceptual organization preceding the motor stage. The behaviorists of course have preferred to disregard human reports of "seeing" objects in the environment, but objective experiments can be designed to show whether animals respond appropriately to the size and distance of objects (pp. 301ff).

Koffka (1935, pp. 27ff) offers the same objection in a different form: the S—R formula seems to mean that the response to a momentary stimulus is governed by that stimulus. Actually O has already been receiving stimuli from the environment and has used these previous stimuli for perceiving the environment more or less adequately and for adjusting motor behavior to the perceived environment. It is against this background that the momentary stimulus has its effect upon behavior. The previous stimuli may have been deceptive and led to a false perception and adjustment, and accordingly O's response to the present stimulus may be unsuited to the real environment (which Koffka called the "geographical environment") and yet entirely suited to the apparent environment (the "behavioral environment"). The geographical environment may be a lake, frozen over, covered with snow, and seen by a horseback traveler at dusk during a snowstorm. In his behavioral environment this level surface is a field, and he proceeds to ride across it. His behavior, moment by moment, is governed by his behavioral environment.

These trenchant criticisms do not destroy the validity of the S—R formula. It still embodies a fundamental fact of behavior and integrates psychology with biology. Though not entirely governed by the momentary stimulus, any response depends on stimuli for its contact with the environment. Without stimuli behavior would be "all at sea."

An organism has its own response potentialities, dependent on its anatomical structure, physiological characteristics such as body temperature, and previous learning. When a stimulus elicits a response, the response is distinctly the organism's own activity. The energy of the response is not obtained from the stimulus. The physical energy of the light entering the eye is very little in comparison with the energy of any strong muscular response. The stimulus releases some of the stored energy of the muscle.

The response is a new event, altogether different in kind from the stimulus. The contraction of a muscle is quite unlike the light or sound or odor of the stimulus. One of the earliest statements of the S—R formula, long antedating behaviorism, had to do with this difference between S and R. In his great work on the physiology and psychology of hearing (1863) Helmholtz pointed out to the physicists that their studies of objective sound vibrations did not convey much information on the process of hearing and the sensations of tone and noise. He began by saying:

> Sensations result from the action of an external stimulus on the sensitive apparatus of our nerves. Sensations differ in kind, partly with the organ of sense excited, and partly with the nature of the stimulus employed. . . . The sensation of sound is therefore a species of reaction to the external stimulation.

The tonal sensation is a reaction (or response, the two words meaning the same) aroused by the air vibrations; if a peculiar tone is recognized as a steamboat whistle, this recognition is a learned response to the tonal sensation; if the recognized tone is named, the naming is a further response. The series of three responses may be so rapid as to seem but a single response, or there may be some hesitation and clear separation of the stages. If we call the recognition of the tone a response to the tonal sensation, ought we not to call the tonal sensation a stimulus eliciting the recognition? It would be only logical but contrary to general psychological usage which speaks of stimuli as acting on receptors.

The objections raised to the S—R formula mean that it is too limited. It seems to imply that nothing important occurs between the stimulus and the motor response. Or it seems to imply that the sensory stimulus is the only causative factor in the arousal of a response. These limitations can be avoided by the addition of another symbol to stand for the organism.

The S—O—R formula

The O inserted between S and R makes explicit the obvious role of the living and active organism in the process; O receives the stimulus and makes the response. This formula suggests that psychologists should not limit their investigations to the input of stimuli and the output of motor responses. They should ask how the input can possibly give rise to the output; they should observe intervening processes if possible or at least hypothesize them and devise experiments for testing the hypotheses.

For example, the reaction time of a practiced adult to light is a little less than one fifth of a second (or 200 milliseconds); a very short time it may seem, and yet much longer than the time required for nerve conduction from the eye to the brain and from the brain to the finger muscles. Some of the time is consumed by the photochemical action in the retina and some by the muscles in mustering sufficient tension to move the fingers. About half of the whole reaction time, however, is taken up by brain processes, not well understood as yet. Hypotheses, at least molar ones, regarding the brain processes are necessary.

The $R = f(S, O)$ formula

This formula indicates that the response is a "function" of both the stimulus and the organism; in other words, it depends on both. Does it depend on anything else? It would seem not; all the factors which contribute to produce a particular response must be included in two classes which we may call S-factors and O-factors. The S-factors are present in the momentary stimulus (or combination of stimuli), and the O-factors are present in the organism when the stimulus arrives. The S-factors are present in the *momentary* stimulus. Previous stimuli and responses have left aftereffects in the organism, but these aftereffects are now O-factors—not S-factors. Previous experience has made certain objects familiar and certain performances skillful, but the familiarity and skill are now O-factors. Other O-factors are numerous and of many kinds. The individual's size and strength and his present state of health or illness, freshness or fatigue, confidence or anxiety make a difference in his response to a stimulus. One potent O-factor is his on-going activity; he is likely to disregard even strong stimuli that are irrelevant at the moment, while responding energetically to some faint stimulus which indicates the next step to be taken in his work or play.

The reaction time—for a simple example—depends on both S-factors and O-factors. It depends on the intensity of the stimulus, being shorter for the stronger stimuli; and it depends on the "modality" of the stimulus, being shorter for an auditory or a tactile than for a visual stimulus. Among O-factors are the subject's age (the reaction time being shorter in the twenties than in the teens or in the sixties) and also his previous practice and the incentives offered him for quick reaction. Among retarding O-factors may be mentioned drowsiness and large quantities of alcohol circulating in the blood.

The $R = f(S, A)$ formula

In this formula A stands for antecedent stimuli or conditions that have left effects on the organism and so are responsible for the present O-factors. An experimenter, or anyone who wishes to influence the behavior of an organism, cannot get at the O-factors directly but can often control them by appropriate antecedent operations. Examples were given in the discussion of "intervening variables" in the preceding chapter (pp. 3ff). There is no concrete difference between A-factors and A-variables—one term referring to the effectiveness of antecedent operations on present ability and motivation and the other to the scientific procedure which varies the operations and takes note of the resulting variations of O's behavior.

THE RETROFLEX OR SENSORY FEEDBACK

One more term, and a very important one, must be added to our formula. Any of the formulas, such as S—O—R, is likely to give the impression that the unit of behavior terminates in R, the motor response. Actually R itself produces some effect, and this effect is not usually lost in the environment without any back-action on the organism. The effect stimulates the organism; the motor response generates new stimuli; and these, rather than the muscular act, are the terminus, the destination, the goal of the S—R unit. You slap your hand on the table, and the unit terminates, not in the muscular contractions, but in the impact with its sound and cutaneous stimuli. You turn your eyes to look at an object, and this bit of behavior terminates not in the movement of the eye muscles but in the clear view of the object. To complete the formula for any bit of behavior, we must add a symbol for the retroflex, such as "Rx." We can then write S—O—R—Rx, to be read that a stimulus, acting on the organism, elicits a response and that the response generates new stimuli which feed back into the organism. The term, *retroflex,* to identify sensory feedback, was introduced by Troland in 1928.

The Rx is often of decisive importance. It may be painful, pleasurable, or indifferent. If painful, it tends to inhibit the further progress of the motor response and to prevent its immediate repetition; the opposite occurs if it is pleasurable. The act of inhaling an odor is prolonged if the Rx is agreeable, but checked if it is offensive. So O quickly learns which bottle to smell. If the Rx is

neither pleasurable nor painful, it may still convey important information. When a movement is purely exploratory, as in the eye-
movement example, the retroflex reveals a segment of the
environment. The exploratory movement amounts to a behavorial
question, and the retroflex supplies the answer. When a movement
is aimed at a target, the retroflex supplies a check on success or failure; the same is true with any type of goal.

Though the retroflex consists of stimuli, these stimuli are apt to
serve as cues of environmental facts. You lift a ping-pong ball, and
it comes up so easily that you say, "How light it is!" A heavy object
would come up slowly or not at all. Many characteristics of objects
are discovered by manipulating them and getting the retroflex.

Even in setting-up exercises and other free bodily movements
which produce no noticeable external effects, the resulting kinesthetic stimuli have much to do with the coordination and smoothness of the movements (p. 139).

Another important fact about the retroflex is that often it can
be controlled by E or by anyone who wishes to control a person's
behavior. Prompt feedback of reward or punishment for a certain
response to a situation is likely to have an aftereffect when the person meets the same situation again. The success or failure of an
attempt has a similar aftereffect. In this connection the retroflex (or
at least a favorable one) is called a *reinforcement*.

The operant—is it actually a response not elicited by a stimulus?

In Skinner's important book on *The behavior of organisms*
(1938) a distinction is made between *respondents* which are elicited
by known momentary stimuli and *operants* which are not so elicited
but are "emitted" by the organism. The typical example of a respondent is the flow of saliva elicited by food put into a dog's
mouth at a certain moment, as in Pavlov's well-known conditioning
experiment (1927). The typical example of an operant is the pressing of a bar by a rat in the Skinner box. When placed for the first
time in this small, mostly bare and empty box, the rat is likely to
remain motionless, which is what he does in other unfamiliar surroundings. After a while his exploring tendency asserts itself, and
he starts to move around the box. When he comes to the bar, he is
likely to place his forepaws on it and exert some downward pressure

and so operate a mechanism which drops a pellet of food into a pan. The rat goes to the food pan and eats the pellet. If left in the box, he will find the bar again sooner or later, and after a few rewarded bar pressings he will show a regular sequence of movements: press bar, run to pan, take pellet, eat it, go back to bar, and so on. He goes through this sequence more rapidly as he becomes more thoroughly "conditioned" and then more slowly as he becomes satiated with the food. The repetition rate measures the progress of conditioning and of satiation and also the progress of extinction when the supply of pellets is discontinued.

The rat certainly responds to the bar each time he presses it. The presence of the bar is a necessary condition for the pressing movement. In a modified form of the experiment the bar is withdrawn through the side of the box after each pressing response and reinserted from time to time. A rat that has learned the trick will promptly press the bar whenever it is introduced, so long as he is hungry. In this form of the experiment *E* certainly applies known stimuli at definite moments. Why then should we not say that these stimuli "elicit" the bar-pressing response? Apparently because these stimuli, though necessary, are not a sufficient condition for securing the response. The rat must be exploring, or he must be hungry and have learned the press-eat sequence which we described. That is, favorable O-factors must be present along with the S-factor. Probably this is always the case; probably no stimulus *forces* a response from an organism without regard to intraorganic conditions. Even that typical respondent, salivation elicited by food put into the mouth, does not occur if the animal is satiated for food. Another clear example of a respondent is the knee jerk elicited by a sharp tap on the patellar tendon; it occurs only when the organism is in a suitable state of muscular tension, neither too slack nor too tense. This distinction between respondents and operants, between elicited and emitted behavior, is not perfectly sharp.

Another distinction suggested is that an operant operates on the environment and produces results there, often securing food or other good things or avoiding injury. The respondent is said not to produce environmental results, though it may service the organism itself. Consequently, the salivary reflex   said to prepare the organism for food in the mouth. Actually, saliva and the gastric juices as well act on a certain important part of the environment, the contents of the mouth and stomach (p. 21).

The foregoing discussion is not intended in the least to belittle the productive experimental work of the Skinnerian or "operational" group of behaviorists. Rather, it is intended to show that this work belongs within the framework of a stimulus-response psychology. Thurstone in 1923 published a challenging paper on the "stimulus-response fallacy in psychology," later incorporated in his book on the *Nature of intelligence* (1924). The "fallacy" lay in the picture of an organism remaining inactive until set in motion by a stimulus. On the contrary, Thurstone pointed out, the organism is ordinarily engaged in some incomplete on-going activity and encounters stimuli while so engaged. The stimuli are responded to or disregarded according as they are relevant or irrelevant to O's ongoing activity. Thurstone said, therefore, "Let us dethrone the stimulus," relegating it to a subordinate place in our theory. The introduction of the S—O—R formula by Dashiell (1928) accomplished the necessary reform by recognizing the importance of O-factors. Although "dethroned," stimuli from the environment are essential in any effective dealing with the environment. Without them responses "emitted" by O would be wild and unrealistic. Stimuli are needed as cues of the situation with which O has to deal. "Emitted" responses to the environment include what we ordinarily call voluntary behavior. Thus the animal experiments on operants may find abundant application to human behavior (Keller & Schoenfeld, 1950; Verplanck, 1955). For voluntary action on the environment O-factors are especially decisive in the motivation and preparation of a response, but stimuli are still essential if the response is to act effectively upon the environment.

THE INTEGRATION OF BEHAVIOR IN TIME

This rather formidable heading is intended to point to the obvious fact that behavior does not ordinarily consist of separate S—R units. Usually a series of different movements—a short series at least —is necessary to produce any significant result. A series of movements occurs when you walk across the room, when you pick up an object, or when you speak a word or sentence. Some motor sequences are well-integrated units, initiated as wholes and aimed at results which are accomplished only at the end of a sequence. Some such units are provided in the native equipment of an organism; many others are built up by a process of learning. In general, integrated sequences of movement seem to be characteristic and even essential in the behavior of organisms, whether high or low in the animal scale. They may have a bearing on the much-debated question of purposiveness in animal behavior.

Two-phase motor units

The first phase is preparatory, the second effective or consummatory. The second phase accomplishes some result; the first phase makes the second phase possible. Jumping is a good example. First you flex the hips and knees, then you extend them strongly, so pushing down on the ground and throwing the body upward. The preliminary flexion is necessary to afford scope for the extensor muscles. If you are standing erect, you cannot jump without the preparatory crouch. The crouching is useless except as a *preparation* for the effective extensor movement.

There are dozens of similar examples. If you wish to grasp an object, you first open your hand sufficiently and then close it around the object. Here, in contrast to jumping, the first phase is extension, the second flexion. If you wish to bite something, you first open your jaws and then close them. If you would slap your hand down on the table, the first phase of this act is a lifting of the hand. If you would strike a golf ball, or bat a baseball, or kick a football, you first "haul off" in order to give the effective muscles scope for action. The same is done in punching or throwing. The way the body is built, with antagonistic muscles available at every joint for movement in opposite directions, such two-phase motor units are a fundamental characteristic of behavior. If you are inclined to say that all this is a matter of reflex physiology and out of place in behavior study, you should note that these preparatory movements can be made also as end movements. You can crouch without preparing to jump, open your jaws without preparing to bite, pull back your elbow to nudge someone behind you and not in preparation for punching someone in front of you. But when you make one movement simply in preparation for the opposite movement, the two-phase combination is certainly a behavior unit with a single end result. It may be obviously initiated as a unit, as shown by the absence of any pause between the two phases and by the smooth transition between the first and the second (p. 137).

Some two-phase motor units are provided in the baby's native equipment. He can sneeze within a few hours after birth, and certainly he has had no chance to practice sneezing before birth. To sneeze he inhales a volume of air and then expels it forcibly. The expelled air does the work, but the preparatory inspiration is necessary to provide the air. Strong inspiration plays a similar role in coughing, straining, yelling, and later in shouting, laughing, and singing. Many two-phase units are undoubtedly learned or at least perfected by learning; yet they have a good start in the basic sequential character of muscular action. Interesting examples could be cited from animal behavior. The upstroke of a bird's wing does no good in the way of supporting or propelling the bird in the air, but without it the effective downstroke could not occur. We can hardly believe that the young bird has to learn to put together the two phases. (For other examples see Weisz, 1954, pp. 180ff)

Polyphase motor units

Two-phase units are often repeated without interruption until some end result is reached, as in the examples of creeping, walking, running, swimming, or flying to a certain destination. Other familiar examples include chewing, drinking, hammering, sweeping, knitting. (The effective phase of a reciprocating mechanism cannot be repeated until the backstroke has intervened.) There are also units composed of more than two kinds of movement. You may reach for a sweetmeat, grasp it, carry it to the mouth while opening the mouth, and close the mouth—all as an integrated series with a single end result. When a bird flies from a tree to a water trough on the ground, he takes off, makes a few wing strokes, glides, brakes with his wings, thrusts his feet forward, and lands beside the trough. Like other polyphase units, this one is adaptable to the direction and distance of the goal. It is not a stereotyped unit, but it shows considerable unity in the smooth succession of the different phases and in the single result accomplished.

Much longer sequences of movements have some unity, being initiated as units with single destinations. You leave your room and walk to a shop to make a certain purchase. You may start out in the morning and drive the whole day to reach a certain house. These extensive units are easily divided into smaller units. They are not so closely integrated as the momentary two-phase and polyphase units which we have been considering. The small but highly integrated units reveal a fundamental characteristic of organisms: their ability to integrate their behavior into time sequences. In order to accomplish anything in the environment, they have to make movements that accomplish nothing except to prepare for other movements that produce significant results. They may have to learn most of these behavior sequences, but they do not have to learn "from scratch," for their ability and tendency to integrate their behavior over time gives them a running start.

From an adult human standpoint, the purposiveness of behavior seems to originate in long-range goals and to spread downward to subordinate goals. The student takes a certain course as a step toward his professional goal. He buys a textbook because it is needed in the course. He goes to the book store to buy the book. He leaves his room to go to the store. He turns the doorknob so as to leave the room. But the child's developing purposiveness spreads in the opposite direction. It is visible first in the little two-phase and polyphase acts, their time span being only a few seconds. Long-range purpose calls for experience and intellectual grasp.

Readiness for a coming stimulus

When a sequence of stimuli, S_1-S_2, occurs repeatedly, S_1 can serve as a signal that S_2 is coming, and O may respond to S_1 by getting ready for S_2. There are many human examples of the "Ready—Go!" type, but it is especially worth while to know whether this sort of integration-over-time is within the capability of animals. In Pavlov's conditioning experiments on dogs, the signal or "conditioned stimulus" was sometimes the sounding of a whistle. When the whistle had sounded for 10 seconds, meat powder was put into the dog's mouth. After a few repetitions of this sequence, the dog showed readiness for the meat powder by an advance flow of saliva at the sound of the whistle. This advance flow was the "conditioned response." For our purposes Pavlov's experiments on the "delayed conditioned response" (1927, pp. 89, 101) are the most significant. The giving of meat powder was progressively delayed day by day, until the whistle was finally sounded for a full 3 minutes in advance. The flow of saliva, which began immediately after the whistle began to sound in the early stages of this long conditioning process, was progressively delayed until it occurred only in the last minute before the meat powder was offered. The dog had become adjusted to the timing. Similar experiments on human conditioning have given similar results (Switzer, 1934).

In "operant conditioning" (Skinner, 1938) a somewhat similar procedure is that of periodic reinforcement. Bar pressing obtains a pellet only once every 3 minutes. When the rat has obtained his first pellet, he must wait 3 minutes before obtaining the second, and so on. Naturally, the rat does not wait; he keeps on pressing until finally the second pellet comes. But with many repetitions of the procedure he becomes fairly well adjusted to the timing and waits for a minute or two after each pellet before beginning again to press the bar.

If S_2 in our paradigm is an electric shock or some other offensive stimulus, S_1 becomes a danger signal; the response to S_1 may take several forms, all of which show some degree of readiness for what is coming. The preparatory response may avoid the shock altogether. If the shock is unavoidable, O may be ready to "take it" as well as possible; or O may be thrown into the emotional state of "anxiety" which lasts until the shock arrives and then ceases. This last form of "integration over time" was shown by the rats in an experiment of Estes & Skinner (1941; see also Figure 3 on our p. 68). While a rat was engaged in pressing the bar and eating the pellets, a tone sounded for 3 minutes at the end of which a single shock was administred from wires in the floor of the box. The rat was not disturbed by the tone and only momentarily by the shock. After a few repetitions, however, he slowed down or even ceased his pressing-and-eating during the tone, but resumed speed as soon as the shock had occurred. This prompt resumption of speed showed that the shock was what the animal was waiting for. Any sort of readiness for something particular to happen shows an adjustment of present behavior to future requirements. The "future" may be only a few seconds away, but in human behavior it may be very far away; and the readiness may be aroused not only by the conditioning procedures used with animals but also in many other ways, including verbal warnings and promises.

PREPARATORY SET, "PRESET"

Just as an alarm clock can be "set" to wake a sleeper at a certain time, and as an adjustable machine can be set to do different kinds of work, so the organism can become preadjusted for meeting anticipated demands; it can be differently adjusted for different demands. This concept of preparatory set is useful and even essential in the description of human behavior. Whether it belongs among the fundamentals of animal behavior is a question to be considered later. The word "set" has so many common meanings that the coined word "preset" may sometimes be useful. The suggested word points up the fact that the adjustment is for something not present at the moment but likely to occur in the immediate future.

For a formal definition we may say that preparatory set is a state of readiness to receive a stimulus that has not yet arrived or a state of readiness to make a movement that cannot be done until a preliminary movement has been made. Looking toward the spot where an object will appear, listening for an expected sound, and other sense-organ adjustments are examples of the preset for stimuli; the two-phase and polyphase motor units considered earlier in the chapter can furnish examples of motor readiness. The reality of preset is most obvious when some delay occurs between the getting ready to do something and the actual doing of it.

The "state of readiness" is an O-factor in the ensuing behavior. Can this state of the organism be observed and described, or must it be regarded merely as an unobservable and hypothetical inner state, an "intervening variable" which we assume in order to account for observable behavior? When there is a delay of a second or two after the ready signal and before the actual performance, the state of readiness is often visible as a *posture* of some kind. The ready posture of the runner awaiting the pistol shot on the starting line of a race is a classic example, but looking and listening postures are also perfectly observable. Since these striped-muscle activities are wholly controlled by the nervous system, we know—not merely assume—that states of readiness exist in the nerve centers, even though at the present time we cannot do much in the way of describing what goes on in the brain. Less intense muscular postures can often be revealed by electronic recording apparatus applied, for example, to the forearm so as to lead off and amplify the little electric currents in the muscles that are about to execute a hand movement (Davis, 1940). Probably brain readiness more than the muscular tension is responsible for the contributions of this O-factor to efficient behavior.

Even when we cannot give any adequate description of a preparatory set as a state of the organism, we can investigate its causes and effects. We can treat it as an intervening variable and tie it to observable stimuli and A-factors on the input side and to observable results on the output side. In human psychological experiments the subject (O) is almost always told in advance what materials he will deal with and what he has to do with them. The cooperative subject accepts these "instructions" and "gets set" to act accordingly. Outside the laboratory there are similar ways of assigning a task to a person and inducing him to undertake it. The task need not be assigned by another person; it may be induced by the present situation, either because of some kind of emergency or because of an opportunity to do something worth while. O has lost something and gets set to look for it; or he thinks of an old acquaintance and tries to remember that person's name; or he hears a strain of familiar music and tries to identify it. The fact that preset can be generated in various ways does not spoil the concept for scientific or practical use.

On the output side preset is selective. It facilitates responses for which O is set and inhibits other activities. If the runner on the mark were not selective, he would be likely to respond to some stimulus other than the pistol shot and to make some other movement instead of a forward-leaping step followed by other rapid steps. In the reaction-time experiment, with O instructed to make a certain finger movement in response to a certain flash of light, the response is much quicker than if O were not ready in advance. In a discrimination experiment, with O instructed to notice which of two lights is the brighter, he reports very small differences correctly if he is well set for this particular task; otherwise he makes errors or may not attend to the brightness at all. In an experiment on "controlled association" E may tell O, "I will pronounce a word, and you are to respond by giving a synonym. . . . *feeble.*" The subject gives a familiar synonym quickly. A little later E may say, "Now I will give you a word and you are to respond by naming the opposite. . . . *feeble.*" The subject now gives a different response quickly and correctly. The two associations, feeble-weak and feeble-strong, have both been established in O's previous use of language. Which one shall be elicited by the stimulus word depends on something other than associative strength. It is remarkable how efficiently the preset selects the desired response. A set is a handicap instead of a help if it is not suited to the present situation or to the problem in hand. A set that is biased against a certain person prevents you from giving a fair hearing; it overemphasizes his bad qualities and blinds you to his good ones. The reality of set shows up as strongly in these unfortunate cases as in the favorable examples. (A fuller discussion of set with many other examples can be found in Woodworth & Schlosberg, 1954, pp. 28ff, 48, 830ff; and in Johnson, 1955, pp. 64ff, 147ff.)

Though preset, as we have seen, is a manageable and really indispensable factor in the description, prediction, and control of human behavior, it may not be an indispensable or specially convenient concept in the study of animal behavior. It is convenient enough in some familiar cases, like that of a dog engaged in playing the game of ball catching; he takes an eager ready posture while waiting for the ball to be thrown. In general, not being able to use verbal instructions, we apply a motive such as hunger and place the animal in a situation where food can be obtained. If the food is right in sight, the animal goes straight to it, and the earlier steps in this polyphase motor unit are obviously preparatory to the end phase of eating. If the food, while visible, is behind a wire barrier, rats will work hard to get through; or, if a detour is available, they will eventually find it and use it consistently. If the food is only accessible by a maze of passages, the rats will apply themselves vigorously to this problem after once finding the food in the goal box, and they will eventually keep out of the blind alleys, take the corners in a running curve, and reach the food with no lost time. Such behavior certainly seems to be goal-directed or, as Tolman called it in a famous book (1932), "purposive" at the animal level. Perhaps the word "purpose" is better reserved for the human level; but at any rate such behavior as we have described shows "integration over time," with the high point at the end and the earlier phases distinctly preliminary to the end result. The preliminary phases or some of them may come to serve as landmarks or subgoals and so acquire derived reward value (secondary reinforcement). That is, the reinforcement or reward value of an end result such as eating, instead of remaining concentrated at the end, spreads back toward the beginning of the sequence.

When a behavior sequence, such as the rat's run through a maze, has been thoroughly learned, it may seem to operate automatically as a firm chain of S–R units. Each response in the sequence produces retroflex stimuli, external and internal, which are now able to elicit the following response, and so on until the end result is attained. To be sure, the chain of action does not occur unless the rat is hungry, and it does not maintain its strength unless reinforcement is sometimes given. But is an integrating factor of preset necessary in addition to the hunger drive, the S—R—Rx linkages, and the secondary reinforcement obtained when each correct movement has been made? A "No" answer is given by Keller & Schoenfeld (1950, pp. 239-240).

Hull, a behaviorist with a somewhat different slant, thought it better to introduce an additional directive factor (1952, pp. 101ff, 151, 287, 296). He sometimes called it the "fractional anticipatory goal reaction." It was a behavioral substitute for the older "idea of the result to be achieved" by purposive action. It was suggested by Pavlov's conditioning experiments (as interpreted by Hull). The conditioned response was regarded not as a preparatory response but as a premature consummatory (unconditioned) response. By becoming attached to the sound of a whistle or metronome, the dog's flow of saliva came to antedate its normal stimulus which was food in the mouth. Other parts of the complex goal reaction, such as approach to a food pan, thrusting the muzzle into it, opening the mouth and chewing, tended to occur prematurely at first and to drop out because of the superfluous exertion and interference involved. But the salivation persisted as the fractional anticipatory goal reaction. It could play a useful role by keeping the animal oriented toward the soon-to-come food.

Similarly, a rat reaching the end of a certain maze makes a correct left turn into the food box and receives immediate reinforcement. This ' goal reaction" becomes conditioned to stimuli received earlier in the maze, and so the left turn tends to be made prematurely and land the rat in left-leading blind alleys along the through course to the goal. But even after these overt left turns are eliminated, an inner leftward posture may perhaps remain which does not interfere with overt movements but maintains an orientation toward the goal (but see p. 309).

Hull's theory accounts nicely for *premature* reactions, including the "anticipatory errors" which are extremely hard for a rat to eliminate in traversing certain peculiar mazes (Spragg, 1933, 1934; Jones & Taylor, 1938). The difference between a premature response and a preparatory response can be seen in Figure 1. The premature left turn is an error and interferes with the orderly progress through the maze; though if such "anticipatory goal reactions" can be kept "fractional," they serve for orientation toward the goal. The *preparatory* response, on the contrary, is a help and not an interference in progress toward the goal. It is not derived from the goal reaction but is a direct adjustment to the corner which is about to be turned at high speed. Hull had nothing to say about preparatory responses or about the two-phase and polyphase motor units which

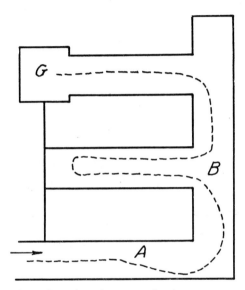

Fig. 1. A small section of a maze, showing a premature goal reaction and also a preparatory reaction. A = preparatory swing-out for taking a corner, B = premature goal reaction with retrace, G = goal.

Hull did once mention the A-type reaction under the head of "anticipatory movements": "when an animal is approaching a familiar 90-degree turn in a maze, he quite generally begins his turning movements some time before he reaches the corner" (1932, p. 488). The animal, however, instead of turning left prematurely in this case first swings to the *right*, thus beginning a wide, rapid turn to the left.

In the paper cited, as well as in his later books (1943, 1952), Hull works out an S—R picture of goal anticipation (or idea of the goal), which has appealed strongly to many psychologists, but he does not tackle the problem of truly preparatory movements. Perhaps this problem is best tackled first in cases where the goal is straight ahead so that no idea of an unseen goal is necessary and the preparatory phase of the behavior is a straightforward approach (pp. 36ff).

seem to us fundamental in the integration of behavior over time. Preparatory reactions are often perfectly observable facts. The goal reaction, transposed to the entrance of a maze, would be interfering unless kept fractional, and a preparatory response, transposed to the goal, would be interfering or impossible. The preparatory response can therefore not be a derivative of the consummatory response. Two dear friends spy each other at a little distance and rush together with arms outspread—very different motor behavior from the ensuing embrace! In general, a preparatory movement is some form of approach which would be impossible or absurd when the goal is reached.

What we have been calling "preset" is sometimes called "situation-and-goal set," and adjustment to the situation is an important part of it. The runner on the mark has not only an intense set for the quick movement he is about to make, but also a background adjustment to the spatial and social situation—the field, the track, the spectators and especially his competitors. When you wake out of a sound sleep, but not at the usual time and place, it may take you a few moments to get your bearings, to realize where you are and what you have to do. When you become drowsy, you lose track of what is going on around you; your situation set becomes vague. When you enter a novel situation—perhaps a strange room full of unknown people—you build up a situation set by degrees, looking and listening, observing the place, the people present, and what seems to be going on. These momentary observations are not immediately lost; the gist of them is retained in the set which gradually takes shape. Finally, you may feel ready to take part in the proceedings. Your situation set has come to a focus in a goal set.

As an "intervening variable" a situation set is identified by its antecedents and its consequences, by the observations of the situation which shape it up and the well-oriented behavior which follows. If we ask a person to introspect his present situation set, he is likely to be puzzled. To be adjusted to the present situation is so much a matter of course, ordinarily, that he scarcely sees what there can be to report—except, of course, the situation itself. A clear example of a situation set is the reader's set for the context of a story; the context gives definite meanings to the words and sentences. If you try to break into the middle of a story, the names you encounter—Jack and Jim and Lena—mean no one in particular, and the action is entirely blind, at least for a few pages.

Situation-and-goal set makes the difference in human behavior between responding to a momentary stimulus alone and responding to it with account taken of what has gone before to reveal the circumstances and what is expected to follow (Woodworth, 1937).

Much material bearing on the discussions of this chapter can be found in Chapters 1 and 2, pages 1-42, of Woodworth & Schlosberg's *Experimental psychology* (1954).

Motives in Operation

Of two main topics in the psychology of motivation, one is concerned with the origin and classification of motives, and the other with their operation. Without regard to the underlying motives, the immediate goal of a specific action is often perfectly clear. The laws of goal-directed behavior can be worked out to some extent without any comprehensive prior knowledge of a system of primary and secondary motives.

Ability and motivation seem to be two necessary factors in any performance. They are complementary factors; if both are present, the performance will occur, but not if either one is lacking. Of course a third factor is necessary—opportunity, which we often designate as the "stimulus," meaning an environmental situation capable of eliciting the performance. Let the stimulus-object be a fence beside the sidewalk in front of a house. Does a boy on the sidewalk vault over the fence? Not unless he has acquired the ability to vault, and not unless he has some motive. In the boy's case the motive may be purely of a playful or mischievous nature; a few years later, even if he has still maintained the ability to vault, a more serious motive would be necessary to call forth this action.

IS ALL BEHAVIOR MOTIVATED?

In spite of the innumerable examples that could be cited to prove the necessity of motivation for any sort of human or animal activity, and the difficulty of citing any clear cases to the contrary, the assertion that all behavior is motivated is too fundamental to be accepted without careful consideration. It seems contrary to the S—R formula, which suggests that a strong bond from S to R should guarantee the R whenever the S is given. To be sure, the amplified formulas such as S—O—R recognize the importance of O-factors; and motive as well as ability is an O-factor present in the organism when the stimulus arrives. But the formula might imply only a possible, not a necessary, participation of O-factors.

The law of association, as usually stated, implies that motivation is *not* necessary in recall. If A and B have become associated, A will call up B. When you have associated a person's face with his name, will not the sight of the person make you think of his name—no motivation being necessary? Perhaps not! If you are working or playing with a person, you do not necessarily think of his name every time you see his face. If you are listening to a speech or lecture, you do not have to recall the speaker's name every time you look at him. Again, though your friend's first and last names are strongly associated so that you can use his whole name whenever you wish, this strong association does not force you to think of his last name whenever you call him by his first name. Numerous instances of this sort, along with experiments on the "force" of association, led Kurt Lewin (1922, 1935) to liken associations to the couplings between the adjacent cars of a railroad train. The couplings have no force of their own; they are not sources of energy but merely transmitters of energy. Lewin wrote (1935, p. 44):

> The experimental investigation of habits (association) has shown that the couplings created by habit are never, as such, the motor of a psychical event. . . . Rather, certain psychical energies, that is, tense psychical systems which derive, as a rule, from the pressure of will or of a need, are always the necessary condition of the occurrence . . . of the psychical event.

Lewin admitted that a sensory stimulus could supply sufficient energy for purely sensory activity, but any significant motor behavior, he thought, must have motivation other than the momentary stimulus.

Lewin was not the first psychologist to insist strongly on the necessity of motivation for all behavior. One of the first was William McDougall in his *Introduction to social psychology* (1908), a book devoted to the study of motivation. McDougall attached immense importance to what he called the "instincts" (later "native propensities") of men and animals. He wrote (1908, end of Chapter II):

> Directly or indirectly the instincts are the prime movers of all human activity. . . . The instinctive impulses determine the ends of all activities and supply the driving power. . . . Take away these instinctive dispositions with their powerful impulses, and the organism would become incapable of activity of any kind; it would lie inert and motionless like a wonderful clockwork whose mainspring had been removed or a steam-engine whose fires had been drawn.

Among the native propensities which supplied the driving forces of human behavior were hunger, sex desire, fear, anger, and curiosity. McDougall was considering behavior in the large and regarding specific motives as derived from the great driving forces of life.

Much the same view was taken by Woodworth in his *Dynamic psychology* (1918). He was trying to base psychology on the investigation of the "how" and "why" of behavior. He did not believe that all human motives could be traced back to McDougall's instincts—a question which we shall consider in the next chapter—but he agreed that motivation was always necessary. He wrote (1918, pp. 36, 37, 41):

> Once the point of view of a dynamic psychology is gained, two general problems come into sight, which may be named the problem of "mechanism" and the problem of "drive." One is the problem, how we do a thing, and the other is the problem of what induces us to do it. Take the case of the pitcher in a baseball game. The problem of mechanism is the problem how he aims, gauges distance and amount of curve, and coordinates his movements to produce the desired end. The problem of drive includes such questions as: why he is engaged in this exercise at all, why he pitches better on one day than on another, why he rouses himself more against one than against another batter, and many similar questions. . . . This distinction between drive and mech-

anism may become clearer if we consider it in the case of a machine. The drive here is the power applied to make the mechanism go; the mechanism is made to go, and is relatively passive. . . . The sight of prey . . . arouses a trend toward the consummatory reaction of devouring it. But this consummatory reaction cannot at once take place; what does take place is the preparatory reaction of stalking or pursuing the prey. The series of preparatory reactions may be very complicated, and it is evidently driven by the trend toward the consummatory reaction.

Sigmund Freud is certainly to be counted among those who have insisted that all behavior is motivated. His psychological theories were almost entirely concerned with motivation, especially with the unconscious emotional motives underlying abnormal behavior and maladjustments. In his *Interpretation of dreams* (first German edition, 1900) he tried to show that dreams were attempts of the dreamer to gratify wishes that had gone ungratified in waking life, and in his *Psychopathology of everyday life* (first German edition, 1901) he gave a similar analysis of slips of the tongue and other lapses. A person is consciously motivated to say a certain word, but the intrusion of an unconscious motive causes him to mispronounce the word. Freud here goes beyond the statement that all our actions are motivated and asserts that the exact way in which the actions are performed is also motivated. This last assertion would certainly be very difficult to prove. Freud seems to assume a perfect mechanism for any act which we can perform and wish to perform, so that any slip-up in the performance must be due to the intrusion of disturbing motives. Actually, memory is often imperfect, and skill is imperfect and subject to momentary variations. Drive is not everything; mechanism (ability) is equally essential.

In Hull's system (1943, 1952) motivation is treated as necessary for the occurrence of any behavior. Ability is represented by Hull's "habit strength," which he designates by the letter H—more completely by the symbol, $_sH_R$, which means the same as $S \rightarrow R$ with the H taking the place of the arrow. H stands for the strength of the bond or coupling between S and R. This habit strength depends on previous learning. But present motivation is necessary to make the ability or habit ready for action. Readiness for action is a product of habit strength and motivation strength; if either of these factors is lacking, the product is zero and the R in question will not be made to the S in question. Motivation itself is regarded as the product of several factors, the most important being drive (D) and incentive (K). If the active drive is hunger, the appropriate incentive is food. D and K are quantitative variables; for example, D depends on the length of time since the last feeding, and K depends on the amount of food given as reward for the S—R performance. If either D or K is zero, motivation is zero; thus the response ceases when the drive declines to zero (satiation) or when the reward is withheld time after time (extinction).

It will be seen that D and K are regarded as O-factors, controllable (in simple cases) by appropriate A-factors. But is not incentive more properly an S-factor? It would be if the incentive were in plain sight and well known from past experience. In a typical animal experiment, like the maze or Skinner box, the food incentive is not present to the senses until the instrumental act, S—R, has been performed. As a stimulus, the incentive comes after the response and cannot be a factor in eliciting that same response. But it can be a factor in making the animal ready to make a similar response on the next trial. The presence of food in the maze is registered in one or a very few trials, and what is thus learned becomes a motivating O-factor in later trials. (See pp. 246f.)

Unmotivated activity

If a response is sufficiently accounted for by a stimulus, there is no room for a motive—no sense in assuming a motive. Suppose your hand unexpectedly comes in contact with a hot object, and you instantly pull your hand away. This flexion reflex is sufficiently accounted for by a native S—R connection. But now you want to get rid of the continued burning sensation in your hand. If you run to the washbowl and immerse the hand in water, this instrumental act is a series of responses to guiding stimuli from the room, door, washbowl, etc.; but all these responses are motivated by the burning sensation and the set to get rid of it.

The development of a motivated act is shown by a well-known animal experiment (Warner, 1932; Miller, 1948). The floor of a small compartment is wired so as to deliver a series of shocks when the current is turned on. A rat getting these shocks for the first time jumps repeatedly up into the air and makes other excited responses; but if there is a low wall at one side of the compartment, the rat is likely to find it and jump over into the adjacent, safe compartment, thus *escaping* from the shocks. After a number of trials he jumps the wall as soon as the shocks begin; and if a warning signal is given a few seconds before the shocks begin, he will probably learn to jump the wall in time to *avoid* the shocks altogether. The instrumental act of jumping the wall is of course a response to stimuli from the wall, for without those stimuli the jump would not

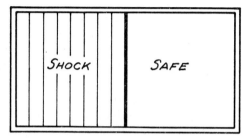

Fig. 2. Floor plan of a two-compartment box used by Warner (1932) and by many later experimenters. The floor of one or both compartments contains a grid through which electric shocks can be sent. When one compartment is electrified, the other is safe. For further use of this "shuttle box" see pages 69, 247.

occur at the right place; but these stimuli would not elicit the jump without the escape motivation. The original excited jumping of the rat was not motivated—at least, an assumed motive would be redundant—but the instrumental act cannot be accounted for without the assumption of a drive or set for escape. We shall have more to say of this experiment later.

Many similar examples could be found of direct, unmotivated responses to noxious stimuli and of motivated instrumental acts for avoiding such stimuli; and similar examples abound in the realm of positive responses to pleasant stimuli. When the baby sucks a bit of candy, that is mere S–R behavior, but when he cries for another piece, that act is motivated. In general we can say that when anything looks good, the tendency to approach it is a motive, and the approach movements are motivated. Or if a thing looks bad or in some way promises harm, the tendency to avoid it is a motive, and the avoidance movements are motivated. In the sensory-perceptual field, the response of the retina to light or of the inner ear to sound is an unmotivated activity, but when you "look sharp" or listen closely so as to identify an object or recognize a voice, such behavior is clearly motivated.

DRIVE: ITS CAUSES AND EFFECTS

In introducing the concepts of cause and effect into the study of motivation, we run some risk of bogging down in a metaphysical quagmire. The antinomy of mechanism and teleology confronts us, as it does the biologist on a larger scale. Is human and animal behavior sufficiently accounted for by antecedent causes, or must we take account also of the subsequent results of any act? Every act has results; as we said before (p. 33), every response produces retroflex stimulation so that the S—R unit is better symbolized by the sequence S—R—Rx, the Rx rather than the R being the significant termination of the unit. And we called attention to the numerous characteristic two-phase combinations such as the sneeze, the shout, the forward reach for a morsel of food, and the backward "hauling off" for a blow. In these combinations the consummatory phase would be impossible without the preparatory phase, and the preparation would be mere waste motion without the following consummation. Mechanism and teleology seem both to be involved. The question is whether one of them can be reduced to the other. To attempt a reduction of all organic processes to teleology—the circulation of the blood, the conduction along the nerves, the secretion and action of hormones—would seem hopeless and worse than useless. But to discover causal mechanisms for goal-seeking activities, along S—R lines, might be possible and would be practically useful; for if you wish to have a certain motive active in a person's behavior, you need to know what stimuli and antecedent conditions will generate and arouse the motive.

McDougall, already cited as a pioneer in advancing the claims of motivation, was also a staunch adherent of "teleological causation," which he did not believe could be reduced to mechanistic causation in any way. In 1930 (pp. 4, 10) he gave the following account of his "hormic psychology" (*hormé* being a Greek word for "urge"):

> Hormic psychology . . . asserts that active striving towards a goal is a fundamental category of psychology, and . . . cannot be mechanistically explained or resolved into mechanistic sequences. . . . Those of our activities which we can at all adequately describe . . . are activities which we undertake . . . for the sake of some result which we foresee and desire to achieve . . . and when we observe on the part of animals actions that are clearly goal-seek-

ing, we are well justified in regarding them as of the same order. . . . Psychical events, though teleological, have their conditions and their causal antecedents; but in them the foreseeing activity is a real factor. . . . To put it in other words, valuation . . . is an activity that makes a difference; applied to the foreseen possibility, it inclines our activity this way or that, to seek or accept, avoid or reject.

The characteristics of behavior which cannot be explained mechanistically appear then to be three, according to McDougall:

1. *Valuation* or the choice of goals, the determination of what should be sought or avoided.
2. *Striving* toward a goal, i.e., the performance of instrumental acts that will lead to the chosen goal.
3. *Foresight* of the results to be achieved.

Valuation

If we ask why sweet is preferred to bitter by babies and universally by animal species (Frings, 1947), we must go back in the history of the race for our answer. Since sweet substances are usually nutritious and bitter substances poisonous, this preference can be explained by evolutionary theory. Any stock that had the opposite preference would be unlikely to survive. This is a mechanistic explanation. If we ask why the child who rejects coffee comes later to relish it, our answer is that some process of learning has intervened —again a mechanistic explanation. If we wish to have an animal motivated by hunger, we take suitable antecedent measures; i.e., we deprive him of food for half a day. Not only at these primitive levels, but probably also at much higher levels, anyone's likes and dislikes, preferences, and chosen goals depend on what has gone before in inheritance and learning. Cause and effect of the ordinary, mechanistic sort appear sufficient.

Instrumental behavior

The question is whether the organism is equipped to move toward a positively valued object and away from a negatively valued one. Are instrumental acts generated mechanistically by valuations? We should have to answer, "Not by valuations—desires and aversions— alone, but very likely by these in combination with perceptual adjustment to the environmental situation." To make this statement clear we should have to anticipate later discussions of both perception and motor control (Chapters 6-8). But take a comparatively simple case: a bit of food, a short distance to the side of an animal, is sending out visual or olfactory stimuli which serve as cues indicative of food; the animal turns toward the food and advances in that direction. Such behavior is observed even in very lowly animals and is instinctive rather than learned. At a higher level both the cues and the efficient approach movements must be learned, but it still seems true that positively valued stimuli act as causes of approach movements, and negatively valued stimuli as causes of withdrawal. A hungry animal will follow a tortuous route to a feeding place, once he has learned the route. The hunger drive and the perceptual-motor mastery of the route make up an effective mechanistic combination. The only chance for teleological causation is in the process of *learning* the route. When an animal after following the correct route through a maze finds and eats the food, this final Rx (retroflex) seems at first thought to act backwards on the instrumental act just performed; but psychologists feel that it is up to them to explain this reinforcement mechanistically. Their attempts to do so will be considered in the chapters on learning.

Foresight

"Foreseeing the future" is a figure of speech. No one actually observes the future, even the immediate future. One can *predict* the future with some degree of probability, the prediction being based on previous experience. Scientific prediction is based on observations reduced to order as far as possible by aid of theory and so takes the form of laws, curves, equations. By such means astronomers are able to predict eclipses with great accuracy. They can follow the process backward as well as forward in time and infer that an eclipse of the sun must have occurred on a certain date long before the Babylonians or Egyptians made the first astronomical observations. In strict logic the equations, enabling them to reckon both forward and backward, are neither mechanistic nor teleological. In such a case mechanistic and teleological causations are merely two ways of regarding the same real process. In most cases the process is not so clear and uniform, and you cannot reckon backward with certainty. The same cause, or combination of causes, can be depended on to produce the same effect, but a given effect may have been produced by various combinations of causes.

In mundane affairs where man takes a hand and exerts some control, as in engineering, he has to think in both directions. He thinks teleologically, backward from the desired end to suitable means, in outlining his plan of action; but, since he has no magic, he must know his field mechanistically in order to select the causes that will produce the desired effects. There is no evidence of two separate kinds of real causation.

McDougall and also Freud spoke of motives, drives, and especially "instincts" as sources of energy, but this again is a figure of speech, since all the energy of an organism's activities is derived from the metabolism of food and oxygen. A drive could better be called a mobilizer of some of the organism's store of potential energy.

It should perhaps be added that a mechanistic explanation of human motives does not in the least degrade them, any more than a physical explanation of the way a violin produces its tones deprives those tones of their beauty. The nobility or ignobility of a motive depends not on its origin or physiology but on the role it plays in human behavior.

The arousal of a drive

The various terms employed in the study of motivation are likely to be confusing to the student; perhaps there are too many of them. We try to distinguish drive from need, from incentive, and from mechanism. These three are easily distinguished from one another, at least in typical cases. The need for food is a deficiency of food substances in the tissues and stores of the body; obtained food is an incentive; and any behavior that obtains or approaches the food is a mechanism or instrumental act. None of these three concepts is superfluous, but how does "drive" enter the picture? Would it not be sufficient to say that the need motivates the instrumental behavior? Given available food and the need for food, why bring in a "hunger drive"? There are cases where the individual who needs food has no appetite for it and takes little or none when it is offered—as well as cases of the reverse sort! Then there are the special food deficiencies. If the body lacks sodium chloride, a corresponding appetite for salt is shown by the individual's choice of salty foods, but vitamin-A deficiency does not lead to a preference for foods containing this vitamin; and no clear-cut motivation results from hemoglobin deficiency or from various other physiological needs. A need may remain at the physiological level and not force its way into the realm of behavior. "Drive" is conceived as belonging in the behavior realm and as directly motivating instrumental activity. This distinction is accepted by the students of animal behavior, who are the most apt to speak of drives. Stone (1932), in writing on the sexual drive, offered this general definition (p. 828):

> Aroused tendencies in animals to respond to objects of the environment which are functionally related to their biological needs are nowadays designated by the term *drive*. Occasionally, also, an author will use the term in referring to certain physiological states by which action tendencies are motivated, but the latter usage is hardly to be commended. . . . Drive, like force in the realm of physical phenomena, has conceptual as opposed to phenomenal reality.

The last sentence means in other words that drive is a "construct" rather than an observable datum in animal behavior. Human beings, however, give introspective evidence of an active drive when they report "wanting" to do something and proceed to do that very thing. Human beings thus manifest numerous drives which do not depend on any known physiological needs.

Another term which should be added to our collection is *set* (preparatory set, preset, goal set). Any fundamental difference between set and drive would be hard to find, though "set" suggests limited activities and "drive" broader fields of activity. The runner on the mark is "set" for a quick getaway, while his "drive" may be for fast running or for athletic achievement. What was said in the preceding chapter (p. 42) on ways of inducing a set bears on our present question of how drives are aroused. In human subjects the experimenter's "instructions" are often sufficient, and they are typical of many other verbal and social stimuli that put a drive into active operation.

Need as arouser of drive. Though drive is to be distinguished from need, a physiological need is likely to generate a drive—quite dependably so in animals deprived of food or water for several hours —and the intensity of the drive can be increased by prolonging the deprivation period. But how can a physiological state such as lack of water or food substances in the blood and tissues cause the organism to engage in behavioral activity dealing with the environment by means of muscles, sense organs, and the nervous system? The depleted physiological state must somehow affect the brain. There are two possible channels for this communication: by the sensory nerves and by direct chemical action of the blood on certain brain centers. Hunger pangs are evidence that the sensory channel is operating; they are due to movements of the empty stomach stimulating receptors in the stomach wall. But the periodic desire to eat still occurs in surgical cases involving transection of the stomach nerves so that no sensory communication from the stomach to the brain is possible any longer. The chemical channel is real, therefore, for hunger and it is real in thirst also (Morgan & Stellar, 1950). How blood chemistry can work on the brain has long been known in regard to respiration. The breathing center in the medulla receives sensory nerve impulses from the lungs (by way of the vagus nerves) and responds by sending motor nerve impulses to the respiratory muscles. But the rate of breathing depends on the amount of carbon dioxide in the blood circulating through the medulla. High concentration of the carbon dioxide *sensitizes* the breathing center so that it responds to weaker sensory stimuli than when the concentration is low. Probably a similar sensitizing role is played by other chemical substances, including different hormones acting on different nerve centers. These chemical agents are not "sources of energy" but act as sensitizers.

Incentive as arouser of drive. The hunger drive—perhaps better called the eating drive—may be quiescent even several hours after the last meal and become urgent at once at the sight or smell of something good to eat. A single taste of the food will often arouse a dormant appetite. There are numerous similar examples, and we really know much more about incentives than about needs, for we often see a person working for something or spending his money for something that does not gratify any known need.

The drive to escape from a noxious or obnoxious stimulus—a burn or a series of electric shocks, a bitter taste, a foul or over-pungent odor, a rasping noise, an intense flickering light—is not built up gradually by internal physiological processes, as hunger is, but is aroused by a persistent external stimulus (p. 52). Here we have an important class of cases where a drive is aroused by an incentive.

If the noxious stimulus is preceded by a dependable signal, the organism may be able to make the escape movement in advance and so *avoid* the noxious stimulus. The avoidance drive is aroused by a signal or "cue" of the coming incentive. (A *cue*, as used in psychology, is a stimulus which serves as a sign or signal of something else, the connection having been previously learned.) The eating drive also can be aroused by cues, such as the sound of the dinner bell or the sight of a good restaurant. Pavlov's "conditioned stimulus" became a cue of food soon to be given, and the aroused eating drive was manifested by advance salivation. A rat that has learned the route to the food box in a maze will start running as soon as placed at the entrance, the entrance stimuli having become cues of the incentive at the other end. Rats that are fed once a day become greatly excited when the experimenter approaches and makes his preparations for their feeding (Sheffield & Campbell, 1954).

The operation and effects of a drive

By analogy with a force in physics, a drive has two distinguishable characteristics, *intensity* and *direction*. Like a force or vector, it can be represented by an arrow, the intensity being shown by the length of the shaft and the direction by the arrow head. The direction is toward an attractive incentive or away from a repellent one. A drive has the additional characteristic of *persistence*. Once aroused, it continues to operate until a certain result is achieved, until the attractive incentive is reached or the repellent one escaped or avoided.

Drive intensity and activation or sensitization. If we disregard for the moment its direction, we can say that any drive activates the organism. (The fatigue drive is obviously an exception.) Activation is at a very low level in deep sleep; somewhat higher in dreaming; considerably higher when the fundamental drive to deal with the environment is aroused so that the sleeper awakes; and much higher when urgent tasks or exciting situations are confronted. High activation is likely to have an emotional character, especially when a drive is prevented from reaching its goal quickly. Intense hunger or thirst is not usually called an emotion, but it undeniably has an emotional character. Intense sex drive is admittedly emotional, and so is an intense drive to avoid or escape from danger. Anger is extremely emotional. Intense emotion is beneficial in situations demanding above all things a great output of muscular energy, but skill and shrewdness in escape or fighting are better served by lower degrees of general activation (Cannon, 1929; Leeper, 1948; Nissen, 1951, 1954; Woodworth & Schlosberg, 1954; Duffy, 1957).

Activation might mean that the brain was thrown into "spontaneous" activity, with resulting diffuse or random muscular movements. The movements, so conceived, would not be responses to sensory stimuli, and the stimulus-response formula would not hold good. But activation might mean something rather different, i.e., sensitization. The nerve centers might not discharge in the absence of sensory stimuli, but they might be sensitized to respond to weaker stimuli than usual and to respond more strongly than usual —as the respiratory center, when sensitized by high concentration of carbon dioxide in the blood, responds to weak sensory stimuli from the lung nerve fibers (p. 59).

It is not easy to arrange an experimental test of these two possibilities. Stimuli cannot be entirely excluded from any situation in which a man or animal is placed. Still, something can be done to reduce the stimuli and to keep them uniform so that the subject becomes negatively adapted to them. A rat in a light-tight box with the steady hum of a ventilating fan to drown out other sounds is pretty well shielded from changing stimuli; and if he is given no food hour after hour, his increasing hunger should show an increasing amount of random movement according to one theory but not according to the other. The box is arranged to tip slightly in different directions as the rat moves around, and an electrical counter records the amount of movement. During a 3-day starvation period in such an apparatus there was little progressive increase in motor activity, except in the 10 minutes per day when the light was turned on and the fan turned off. The hunger drive did not produce spontaneous movement, but it did sensitize the organism to such stimuli as occurred (Campbell & Sheffield, 1953). In a different setup, which provided an activity wheel freely accessible to the rat at all times, the result was different since the activity in the wheel increased from day to day during a period of restricted diet (Hall & Hanford, 1954). However, this result does not really contradict the other, for as soon as a rat entered the wheel and started running, he would provide himself with a good deal of proprioceptive and tactile stimulation. The evidence is still too scanty to make us certain that activation consists *entirely* in sensitization. It is too important a conclusion to be adopted hastily.

We are beginning to obtain some data on the physiology of drive, or at least of activation (Lindsley, 1951; Hebb, 1949, 1955; Gellhorn, 1954; Olds, 1958; Miller, 1957). Consider the "brain waves," electric potentials due to the discharge or "firing" of cortical nerve cells. These minute electrical potentials can be led off through the skull to electrodes placed on the intact scalp and be amplified and recorded. In sleep the waves are very slow; in a state of being awake but relaxed they are regular at the rate of about ten waves per second (the "alpha rhythm"), due probably to the synchronous firing of the cells; and in a state of attention to a particular stimulus or of expectancy, they are much faster but less regular, as if different cell groups were working separately. These levels of cortical activation seem to be controlled by that part of the interbrain called the *hypothalamus* which sends nerve fibers upward to all parts of the cortex and also downward to the autonomic system. Nerve messages coming in from the sense organs seem to have two paths to the cortex, one direct and the other by way of the hypothalamus. The direct message, we may say, carries specific information which can be utilized in the perception of objects in the environment, while the hypothalamic message is nonspecific but serves to maintain the activation of the cortex. On the efferent side the cortex has a direct motor pathway to the muscles and also a pathway through the hypothalamus by which the sympathetic system is aroused when danger is perceived.

Direction, selectivity of a drive. The two main directions of drives are approach and escape or avoidance. The specific approach or withdrawal movement differs with the object to be approached or avoided. Ridding oneself of an itch or tickle demands different movements from those appropriate for ridding oneself of a burning stimulus; and still different are the movements for getting rid of a bitter taste or a blinding light. The specific movements for voiding waste products should be mentioned here and also the reaction to danger, which differs according to the kind of danger that threatens —for example, the danger of falling, or the danger of being run over in the street.

The hunger drive and the sex drive are both clearly positive, yet they call for very different approach movements. When either of these drives is intense, the other is excluded. Both of them are best studied in animals. This is particularly true of the sex drive. Many kinds of animals have been studied to determine the role of certain hormones in sex behavior. Elimination of the natural internal source of these hormones by castration (removal of the gonads, the testes or ovaries) causes the sex drive to die out, though not instantly; and injection of a suitable gonadal extract restores sex behavior to a castrated animal (Stone, 1939; Beach, 1948). The larger the dosage of the hormone, the more readily is sex behavior aroused, and the more complete is the behavior (Beach & Holz-Tucker, 1949). The hormone alone, however, does not suffice for producing actual sex behavior. External stimulation also, largely from a sex partner, is necessary for eliciting the typical sequence of responses—mutual approach, male aggressiveness and female enticingness, copulatory position and movements, tumescence, intromission, ejaculation. "Some act by one partner evokes a complementary response on the part of the other" (Kaufman, 1953). "The most widely accepted theory purporting to explain the effects of hormones upon the nervous system . . . [is] . . . that the glandular products, instead of directly increasing or decreasing nervous activity, act upon critical nervous mechanisms in such a way as to alter their responsiveness to external stimulation . . . lower the thresholds of nervous mechanisms in which the mating patterns are organized" (Beach, 1948, p. 267).

Evidently the effect of the sex hormones on behavior is selective; the organism, including the brain, is sensitized specifically for sex stimuli and for sex responses—for cues indicative of an available partner and for responses to that partner. The hunger drive sensitizes the organism differently for cues of food and for food-getting responses. Still different is the fear drive, with adrenin as its hormone; it sensitizes the organism for signs of danger and for escape movements. Each of these drives is a selective factor in behavior. The same is true of the sets (or "presets") which were considered in the first chapter. In general, a drive has direction as well as intensity; it is selective as well as activating.

Is this conclusion consistent, however, with the drive-and-mechanism concept formulated at the outset (pp. 48, 50)? When drive is supplied to a machine, the direction of its effect and the kind of work performed depend on the structure of the machine and not on the drive. The same power can be applied to different machines and so have different effects. And if there are two sources of power, two dynamos for example, either power can be supplied to the same machine and have the same effect. In the machine shop the power is nonselective and a human operator (or an "automation" device) is present to make the necessary selections. In the organism, though, the sex drive or the hunger drive does more than supply activation; it combines activation and direction. The hunger drive cannot activate sex behavior, nor the sex drive food-getting behavior—or so it certainly seems. Yet we find the term "nondirective drive" used in theories of motivation. Here is a concept which calls for careful scrutiny. It raises two questions which should be distinguished:

1. Is there such a thing as *nondirective* drive?
2. Is it possible to *redirect* a drive so as to make the same drive activate radically different mechanisms, or so as to make different drives activate the same mechanism?

The theory of nondirective drive. Hull and some of his followers have been the principal proponents of the theory of nondirective drive. In criticizing it one encounters the danger of misrepresentation. Hull was trying to develop a purely *quantitative* theory, and he considered the factors determining the strength or probability of a particular response as purely quantitative variables. Besides S, standing for the stimulus or for the external situation confronting the organism at a certain time, the main positive factors were D, K, and H. Here D stands for drive strength, such as the strength of hunger, depending on the time since last feeding; K stands for incentive value, depending on the size of the food reward; and H stands for habit strength, depending on the amount of previous practice and reinforcement. Let a dog in a certain neighborhood have a well-established habit of going to the back door of a certain house for a bone. The probability of his going there at a certain time will depend on the strength on his hunger drive. Let him be accustomed to obtain a handout at either of two back doors; he will be more likely to go where the handout suits him better or is more likely to be given, i.e., where the incentive value is greater and surer. Thus far in our example H and K have been directive, but not D—except that after being well fed the dog may respond to the neighborhood simply by lying down in some comfortable pot. Or, being free for the time from both the hunger drive and the rest drive, but in a mood to play, he may resort to the backyard of a playful boy friend. So the direction of his behavior can depend on

D as well as on H and K. Of course, these specific directions have been learned by our subject. He has been conditioned to go to certain places when hungry, to another place when tired, and to yet another when playful. According to Hull's general S—R psychology, for a response to become conditioned, there must be some stimulus to which it can become attached. We cannot properly say that certain responses become attached to the physiological *need* for food, other responses to the physiological need for rest, and still others to a sex hormone, for these physiological conditions are not properly stimuli. But they may generate internal stimuli, known to us as hunger pangs, fatigue sensations, etc., and different responses and directions of movement can become conditioned to these different internal stimuli. If the hunger stimuli cause the dog to forage vaguely about the neighborhood and if he finds food in a certain place, his movement in that direction is reinforced and becomes attached to hunger stimuli. Other directions of movement become attached to fatigue stimuli, others to thirst stimuli, others to play-mood stimuli, and perhaps others to internal sex stimuli. Thus the specific movements in a familiar environment are determined by the habits formed under the influence of different drives.

These considerations do not prove that drives are nondirective. If the learned responses depend on distinctive internal stimuli which are generated by different drives it remains true that the different directions of behavior depend on the different drives. If C depends on B, and B on A, then C depends on A. In addition, although the specific behaviors in a given environment depend on learning, it may still be true that different drives naturally evoke different general types of behavior. Hull himself said (1950a, Postulate I):

> Organisms at birth possess receptor-effector connections which under combined stimulation (S) and drive (D) have the potentiality of evoking a hierarchy of responses that . . . are more likely to terminate the need than would be a random selection from the reactions resulting from other stimulus and drive combinations.

In other words, the instinctive responses to a new environment will differ with the drive that is active. If it is hunger, the response will be some sort of approach and foraging; but if it is fear, a response in the nature of withdrawal can be expected. Given these general directions the organism will learn the specific feeding places and safety places afforded by the environment. We can conclude that the general direction of behavior is determined by D, while the specific direction is determined by S, H and K.

Apart from drives there are drugs and procedures that are used to raise or lower the activation level in general—ways of waking you up or putting you to sleep—but whether these agents are altogether unselective in their effects on the various structures and functions of the organism is more than doubtful. A heart stimulant may be a brain depressant. In fact pharmacology provides a whole array of more or less specific stimulants and depressants, and certain drug combinations will dependably increase or decrease a man's tendency to combativeness, or anxiety, or cooperation (Nowlis, 1953, pp. 124ff).

Redirection of a drive. While absorbed in some task, you feel the pangs of hunger and are impelled to go and eat, but you may deny this impulse and stick to your task. Is it possible that the activation due to the hunger drive will drain into your task and enable you to work better than before? It seems possible; at least you may feel that you do better intellectual work while hungry than after a good meal. If so, the direction of your activity is governed by your task motive, while some of the activation is furnished by the hunger drive. There is a conflict of two motives; but one of them is suppressed as far as its direction is concerned, while its activating force is turned in the other direction. In vector language (p. 60), the two forces acting on the organism do not here combine into a resultant direction or compromise activity (as they sometimes do), but they do combine into a larger sum of activation.

Left to itself, we may say, a drive activates its own type of behavior, but if brought into competition with another drive, it may conceivably combine forces with that other drive and activate some other type of behavior. If the organism is committed to a certain task, any irrelevant drives that happen to be awake at the moment may feed into the ongoing activity and contribute additional activation to the task. Such redirection is conceivable, but whether it actually occurs is a question for the experimenter.

Clear experimental evidence on this question is scanty. We can imagine simple animal experiments of the following type: a rat learns to traverse a straight runway, 10 feet long, for example, from the entrance door at one end to the food box at the other. It is motivated by hunger which is held constant from trial to trial at a moderate degree, and its reward or incentive is held constant at a moderate amount. The rat learns this easy task and reaches a practice level of running speed. Each of the factors, H, K and D is now constant from trial to trial, and therefore the running speed is practically constant. So far thirst has been excluded, as the animal has had all the water he would drink just before each trial. But now introduce this extra drive on certain trials, by withholding water for a number of hours before each trial. The factors HKD are still held constant, and no water is present in the food box. Will the rat run faster when thirst is present, and will his speed depend on his degree of thirst?

This exact experiment has perhaps never been tried. A few similar tests with more complex setups have been given incidentally in other work (Elliott, 1929; Kendler, 1945; Kendler & Law, 1950) with results which, without being at all conclusive, suggest that moderate thirst has a positive effect and extreme thirst a negative, interfering effect. It seems likely enough that extreme thirst would dominate the organism and lead to water-seeking behavior inconsistent with a straightforward run for food.

A different though related question is whether an animal that has been placed in a certain environment (a maze or Skinner box) only while hungry and not thirsty, and has learned only to get food by running to a certain place or by pressing a bar, will continue to make the same response when thirsty but not hungry. The evidence is clear that he will generally continue, though often with some hesitation (Spence & Lippitt, 1940, 1946; Webb, 1949; Brandauer, 1953). But this result affords no evidence of nondirective drive or of redirected drive. All that the animals have learned in a given situation is to make a certain positive response; when the drive is shifted from hunger to thirst, they are still motivated to make a positive (approaching) response; accordingly they continue to make the one response which they have learned. The experiments show that an instrumental act can be carried over (transferred) from one drive to another when both drives call for similar approaching behavior.

If two simultaneous drives called for very different kinds of behavior—one for approach and the other for withdrawal—it might be difficult for the experimenter to arrange a transfer from one drive to the other or to make the two drives combine. More likely there would be an inhibition of one drive by the other as in the well-known experiment described under Figure 3.

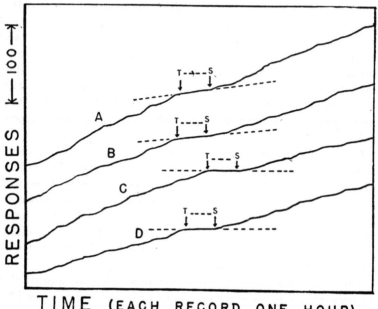

FIG. 3. (Estes & Skinner, 1941.) Anxiety counteracting the hunger drive. Rats in a Skinner box had become habituated to press the bar, when hungry, at a fairly steady rate of two to three presses per minute, as shown by the up-slope of the record lines for four successive days, A, B, C, D. The steeper the slope, the faster the rate of pressing. Near the middle of each hour a tone was sounded for 5 minutes, with a shock from wires in the floor at the termination of the tone. Preliminary tests showed that the tone by itself had no effect on the rate of bar pressing, but after it had been followed by shock several times, it began to lower the pressing rate. On the last two days shown the pressing rate was almost zero during the 5 minutes, T—S, while the tone lasted. Speed was resumed as soon as the shock was received. The curves give the average rate for six animals.

Two experiments by Amsel (1950) and Amsel & Maltzman (1950) demonstrate an inhibition of drinking by thirsty rats during a state of anxiety but the opposite effect during the emotional state generated when the rats are removed from the anxiety-generating situation. In both experiments the rats were first habituated to drinking in a definite place, and after several days they reached a practice level of water intake. Then for one group the drinking place was made an anxious place by the administration there of a series of shocks, no water being present. Finally, with no more shocks, this group was put in the same place with water present. On the first days of this test they drank almost nothing, but in successive days the anxiety wore away (as shown by a gradual decrease of defecation) and the water intake increased. In the companion experiment the shocks were administered *in a different cage;* the rats were then returned to the drinking place. These rats drank *more* than before. We may inquire what sort of emotional state would be produced by the removal from the shock cage to the water cage. It appears to be a rebound from anxiety to a positive emotion, analogous on a larger scale to Sherrington's rebound from inhibition to enhancement of a reflex (1906, pp. 195, 205ff; also Creed *et al,* 1932). If the emotional effect of escape from anxiety is positive in character, it can summate with the positive thirst drive. But anxiety itself cannot be redirected into positive channels.

Another way in which anxiety can be made to give way to a positive (approaching) drive is by the development of an efficient avoiding response to danger. You learn how to avoid harm by going promptly from a dangerous spot to a safe spot. You learn not only that one spot is "bad," but also that the other is "good." Therefore, your drive to get out of the bad place gives way to a drive to get into the good place. The anxiety that upsets you in the dangerous place while you are still unsure of avoiding harm gives way to confidence of reaching the safe place.

The "shuttle box" illustrated on page 53 was used in an elaborate series of experiments on dogs by Solomon and coworkers (Solomon & Wynne, 1953; Solomon, Kamin & Wynne, 1953; Wynne & Solomon, 1955). The procedure was as follows: a dog was put into one compartment with a screen shutting off the other compartment. After a few minutes, during which the dog explored the compartment, the light was turned off where the dog was, but the screen was raised, revealing the other, still lighted compartment and the separating wall. Ten seconds later a series of very strong electric shocks from the floor grid began, and these continued until the dog jumped over the wall into the lighted, safe compartment. It might be half a minute before the dog got over the wall and so put an end to the shocks. Meanwhile his behavior showed all the signs of intense fear: excited scrambling around the compartment, gasping, screeching, trembling, intestinal and bladder upset. This emotional behavior subsided during the three minutes of rest before the next trial, but was renewed with the onset of shocks. However, it changed in several important respects during a series of trials. (1) The dog jumped over the wall more efficiently and promptly. After a very few trials his reaction time to the onset of shocks was down to a couple of seconds; so he was taking only a little punishment before reaching safety. We might think that was as well as he could do. (2) But no—he was given a warning signal on each trial. Ten seconds before the shocks began, the compartment was darkened and the screen was raised revealing the lighted compartment beyond the wall. Within a very few trials his fear behavior anticipated the onset of shocks; it was aroused by the warning signal; the signal became a CS and fear behavior a CR. We may say that the warning signal put the dog into a state of anxiety. (3) After a few more trials the dog jumped the wall within the 10-second period before the onset of shocks, so avoiding the shocks altogether; and, once this had happened, it happened again and again; with only a few relapses most of the thirty dogs that served as subjects avoided all the shocks thereafter. (4) In further trials the symptoms of fear and anxiety diminished and disappeared completely in most of the dogs; in fact, they jumped over the wall as soon as the screen was raised, with a reaction time of 2 seconds or less, too short a time for the internal emotional state to arise. (5) The electric current was then turned off, and there were no more shocks in the first compartment; but none of the dogs discovered this fact since they continued their stereotyped prompt jumping.

This last fact, the nonextinction of efficient avoidance behavior, has long been known to experimentalists and to other people as well. If a child receives a scare in a certain place, he is apt to keep away from that place in the future and never discover that nothing dangerous is there. But the theoretical difficulty is obvious. What reinforcement is there to prevent the avoidance responses from dying out? Pavlov's law of extinction has been fully established: an established CR is extinguished if the reinforcements are discontinued. In the experiments described, however, the dog jumps over the wall hundreds of times after getting the shocks just a few times. A favorite explanation is based on the anxiety that became conditioned to the warning signal. The anxiety caused the dog to jump before the shock, and the anxiety ceased when he reached the safe compartment. The repeated reduction of anxiety would continually reinforce the instrumental response of jumping. There is a serious objection to this theory, in that the signs of anxiety disappeared while the avoidance behavior was still being maintained in full strength. As far as an observer could tell from the dog's behavior in the later trials, there was no anxiety left to be reduced, and consequently no further reinforcement was possible from this source.

We offer another explanation based upon the general theory of "learning the environment." This will be more fully presented in a later chapter. When the screen is raised, the dog's immediate environment splits into the dark compartment where he is and the light compartment over the wall. In the dark compartment the dog soon gets shocks, but in the light compartment over the wall he gets no shocks. So the dark compartment becomes a bad, dangerous place; the light compartment a good, safe place. The goodness of the light compartment is confirmed every time the animal jumps over the wall. He gets the positive reinforcement of safety instead of the negative reinforcement of anxiety reduction. He is free of anxiety so long as he continues to jump promptly into the safe place. If he delays or is delayed in the dark compartment, he becomes anxious (as his behavior shows) and so he is not likely to test out that compartment; for want of such "reality testing" he continues time after time to make the wholly unnecessary effort of jumping over the wall.

This canine behavior was "almost human." Human beings, too, display the desirable trait of shifting from anxiety in the presence of danger to confidence in their ability to reach safety. But in playing safe they often take upon themselves trouble and effort which they would find to be superfluous if only they had the courage to investigate the supposed danger. Neurotic "phobias" are striking examples. A person has somehow acquired a fear of wide streets and open squares. The open space looks dangerous to him, while the edge of the square looks safe. So long as he hugs the edge, he feels secure and comfortable, but if he ventures out into the open, he is terrified and shows some of the symptoms of anxiety that were observed in the dog.

For our present purposes the main conclusion to be drawn from the preceding experiments and considerations is that efficient avoidance is likely to be directed, not away from an active anxiety, but toward the desirable state of security. The anxiety drive is not itself redirected toward desirable results, but it gives way to a positive approach drive.

If O in repeated trials gets a shock in a white compartment and escapes into a black compartment, the white one certainly becomes a "bad" place, but does the black one acquire any positive incentive value? Preference tests, with suitable controls, provide an answer. Before and after the shock-escape training, give O a choice between a black compartment and a neutral, striped one, and his preference is found to shift decidedly to the black one. In a companion test, it shifts decidedly away from the white one. (Shocks were of course absent from the preference tests.) The results can perhaps be interpreted otherwise, but they are at least consistent with our view that a place of safety acquires positive incentive value (Goodson & Brownstein, 1955).

Anxiety in human tasks. Individuals differ in proneness to anxiety. Some appear to be always on the lookout for signs of danger, especially for "threats to the ego." They are afraid of failing. Their "feelings of inadequacy, helplessness, heightened somatic reaction, anticipations of punishment or loss of status and esteem" interfere with the work they are trying to do on such a task as an intelligence test or college course examination (Mandler & Sarason, 1952; Sarason & Mandler, 1952). If they meet with some success, their anxiety diminishes, and they can concentrate more completely on the task in hand. If they are scolded for poor work, they may go to pieces. There are other individuals who need a little scolding to arouse their energies.

This is understandable if anxiety is regarded as a drive with a direction, its direction being toward escape and self-defense. This negative drive would counteract the positive drive toward performing the task in hand and the amount of drive left for the task would not activate the individual's full ability.

But our theoretical question—also a very practical one—is whether anxiety can be *redirected* into the task in hand. The anxious person seems to be highly activated; can he direct his activation into his task? The experimenter has some difficulty in attacking this problem. He does not want to introduce extraneous sources of anxiety for fear of distracting his subjects from their assigned task. If he could identify in a large number of individuals those who are most and those who are least anxiety-prone, he could safely assume that the anxiety-prone subjects on the whole would be the more anxious during work on a task. He would have to match his high-anxiety and low-anxiety groups for the required ability. His question would then be which group did better on the task, i.e., whether the net effect of anxiety was to improve or impair the work.

First, the experimenter has to divide "the sheep from the goats"— which no psychologist would claim to do with perfect accuracy. In a psychiatric hospital, certain patients can be indicated as suffering from anxiety and others as distinctly not so suffering (Sampson & Bindra, 1954). A similar clinical division can be made by a team of psychologists with standardized interviews and observations (Buss et al., 1955). The nurses who care for hospitalized veterans can be trained to use detailed rating scales for the same purpose (Kendall, 1954).

But anxiety-proneness is not confined to hospitals; college students are likely to differ widely in this respect. Many recent experiments have been made with college students, the high-anxiety and low-anxiety groups being sorted out by aid of a printed questionnaire, the Scale of Manifest Anxiety prepared by Janet A. Taylor (1953). Most of the fifty items inquire whether the subject is troubled by worry, fatigue, nightmares, blushing, palpitation, and other symptoms which one would wish to avoid. A subject who reports a great many of these symptoms can be regarded as anxiety-prone. A few of the items suggest excitability rather than anxiety (hungry most of the time, easily distracted, too excited to get to sleep, too restless to sit still), so that a high score of symptoms reported by a person will not always mean that he or she is extremely prone to anxiety; sometimes it will mean that he or she is very responsive to either pleasant or unpleasant situations. However, the Taylor Scale gives a median score of about 13 reported symptoms from college students, as against a median of 25 to 35 symptoms in different samples of psychiatric patients (Taylor, 1953; Goodstein & Goldberger, 1955; Matarazzo et al., 1955). Therefore, it has some validity as an index of anxiety-proneness and should enable an experimenter to select a high-anxiety and a low-anxiety group from a student population. Many experimenters have used the Taylor Scale for this purpose.

The results are clear on one point at least: such reactions as the conditioned eyewink and the conditioned PGR (psychogalvanic or galvanic skin response) are most readily obtained from an anxiety-

prone group (Spence & Farber, 1953; Welch & Kubis, 1947; Bitterman & Holtzman, 1952). This result has no bearing on our problem;
it does not indicate any redirection of anxiety into positive, approaching behavior, since both the eyewink and PGR are avoiding
or defensive reactions.

In Hull's system, as explained by Brown (1953) and by Farber
(1954), the high activation of an anxious person raises the excitability of any one of his "habits" receiving a relevant stimulus from
the environment and makes it operate more strongly and frequently, provided there is no competing habit to interfere. If two
competing habits are receiving relevant stimuli, high anxiety should
raise the excitability of both of them, and the stronger habit should
continue to prevail. (If the stronger habit has a 2 to 1 advantage in
frequency under weak drive, it will have the same advantage under
strong drive, since habit strength is multiplied by drive strength to
produce the excitability or readiness for action.) In a typical "discrimination" experiment one stimulus calls for a response and an
alternative stimulus calls for no-response. The learner's problem is
largely to eliminate the false responses. High-anxiety groups are
found to give more correct responses and also more false responses,
and their discrimination, according to the most adequate method of
measuring it, is neither better nor worse than that of low-anxiety
groups (Restle & Beecroft, 1955).

Many recent experimenters have compared high-anxiety with
low-anxiety groups in a variety of tasks, including intelligence tests,
mechanical ability tests, memorizing, maze learning, etc., with results sometimes favoring the high-anxiety group but more often the
low-anxiety group. Often there is little or no difference between the
two groups. (Review and discussion by J. A. Taylor, 1956.) From
Hull's system one could not predict any decisive and regular advantage for either group. There certainly is nothing in all the work
examined to support the concept of nondirective drive or of redirected drive.

Persistence of drive. This aspect of a drive was barely mentioned
previously (p. 60), but it has been assumed in several passages. It
has been emphasized by Hebb (1949) and by Peak (1955) as an essential characteristic of motivated activity. Hebb points out (p. 180)
that animal and human activity is likely to shift its direction from
moment to moment except when some motive holds it steady (like
a rudder). Peak (pp. 159-162) says that behavior "persists to a goal

and it is this *persistence,* despite changes in stimulation, that makes it necessary to postulate" motivation. The central features of motivated behavior are "its persistence with some intensity and in some direction until a goal is reached. . . . Barriers may be encountered. Sometimes one action sequence occurs and again another. Sometimes the action and the striving continue over long periods of time until a goal is reached." Direction persists, typically, as long as a discrepancy is present between the existing state of affairs and a preferred state of affairs which can be seen in the distance or imagined. My old car is shabby and undependable, contrasting with a new car which I see or read about. Unless the new one is out of the question, the discrepancy remains with me and steers my activity persistently toward a state of affairs in which no such discrepancy remains.

Movement toward a goal is not necessarily in a straight line though that is the preferred route. There may be obstacles that must be gone around or climbed over and things that must be manipulated. Instrumental preparatory responses are learned if the same goal is approached time after time. These objects that must be dealt with on the way to the goal cease after being mastered to be merely nuisances. They become means to an end, landmarks on the way to the goal, subgoals, or preliminary goals. They are learned as preliminaries to the goal and take on some of the positive incentive value of the goal. In human beings, anyway, an instrumental act undertaken as a means to some end may become so interesting as to be an end on its own account.

Outgoing Motivation

In this work an "outgoing" motive is considered to be one that is directed toward an environmental goal, not toward the satisfaction or reduction of any organic need. Behavior servicing an organic need is necessarily directed in the first instance toward something in the environment, such as the place where food can be obtained; its ultimate goal, however, is not to be found in the environment, but within the organism. A large share of human behavior, both playful and serious, is on the face of it directed toward the accomplishment of environmental results without any ulterior intra-organic goal. Its incentives and rewards are in the field of behavior and not in the field of homeostasis. The theory that these incentives and rewards are "secondary reinforcements," derived by conditioning from association with satisfaction of the organic needs, is held in good standing among psychologists and will be considered in the following chapter, where we shall argue against it and in favor of a general behavior-primacy theory of motivation. In this chapter we shall reach only the halfway mark toward the latter theory. We call attention to behavior that deserves to be taken at its face value in almost all psychological and practical contexts, as being motivated toward results to be accomplished in the environment by the individual or social group. The most conclusive evidence for such motivation has been obtained in respect to exploratory behavior.

MOTIVATION OF EXPLORATORY BEHAVIOR

When we speak of exploration we are usually thinking of large-scale human enterprises like those of Columbus and his adventurous contemporaries, or the expeditions of Lewis and Clark in the northwestern United States, or of David Livingstone in Africa. An "explorer" is typically a man who opens up new territory for exploitation or at least makes its geography known to the public. The ulterior motives of the explorers, or of their backers, are often obvious enough—to increase the power and wealth of a government, to spread the influence of a religion—but the day-by-day goals of the explorer in the field are what we might call *invenienda*, things to be found. His immediate reward is the finding of something significant, and what shall be significant depends on what he is seeking. To a botanical explorer new species of plants are immensely rewarding; to an archeologist, old ruins, pottery, and inscriptions. Certain quests do not take the explorer far afield; his bathtub was far enough for Archimedes, and he also could proclaim, "Eureka, I've found it."

But exploratory behavior is not by any means limited to such outstanding examples.

Children as explorers

Exploration with no ulterior motive is best seen in playful examples. Place a group of boys in a new environment, and some of them will surely wander around to see what they can find. They are explorers on a small scale. If they find any novel object that they can manipulate, they put it through its paces and discover what it can do and what they can do with it. Manipulation is often necessary in exploring the characteristics of an object. The young child is a notable explorer. A little girl whose early development was studied by Harlow (1953a) insisted on being held so that she could see the room; if she "was held in any position depriving her of visual exploration of the environment, she screamed; when held in a position favorable to visual exploration of the important environment, . . . she responded positively. . . . Once she negotiated forward locomotion, exploration set in, in earnest. . . . An informal survey of neobehaviorists who are also fathers (or mothers) reveals that all have observed the intensity and omnipresence of the curiosity-investigatory motive in their own children." Exploratory behavior occurs not when the baby is hungry but when he is free from this primary drive; apparently the behavior has its own drive. It is not motivated by hunger or thirst or fatigue or by a desire for pleasurable bodily sensations. It is directed outward, toward the environment which is being investigated. Its long-range value as the means of making the child acquainted with the world he has to deal with later, and so equipping him through play for the serious business of life, can scarcely lie within the little child's horizon. His goals are more limited and direct: to see this or that object more closely, to find what is behind an obstacle, to hear the noise an object makes when it strikes the floor, to be told the name of a thing or person. He uses older people as sources of information.

As the child advances through the early years, the simple things that first engaged his attention become thoroughly familiar and require no further exploration although they are still used in more complicated activities. Building blocks are favorite playthings for several years, as observed by Guanella (1934) in a nursery school. Under two years of age the child's play with them consists of carrying them, throwing them, pounding them, and other ways of getting acquainted with blocks as units. A little later he begins to explore their structural possibilities and puts them together into piles, rows and walls, and later still into structures that have some stability, such as flat-topped "arches" of three blocks, towers that will stand, and trains that will hold together when pushed along the floor.

When a child has several toys before him, he usually shifts his play from one to another as if his interest were only fleeting. But if there is only one toy and nothing to distract him, he will concentrate on it for a long time; how long depends on how much he can do with the single toy. Moyer & Gilmer (1955) set to work to design toys that would enlist a child's attention for 15 minutes at least even if the child were only two years of age. One successful toy was a little wooden wagon with two holes in the floor for the insertion of round poles on which could be fitted fifty thin blocks of various colors. This toy was too difficult for children less than two years old and too easy for the six-year olds, but the children of each intervening age averaged half an hour in continuous play with it. A take-apart airplane averaged even longer for the four-, five-, and six-year olds. (There were twenty children in each age group.)

In older children and adults curiosity is aroused in various ways, often by a question to which the answer is unknown. An answer given *after* the question is likely to be remembered better than if curiosity had not first been aroused (Berlyne, 1954a, b). One student of human exploratory activity has remarked (Festinger, 1954):

> It would seem, at least from casual observation, that the human organism expends considerable energy just finding out about the world in which he lives. He explores, he tries things out, or is just curious about things. This kind of behavior is, of course, especially noticeable in children but is equally marked in adults who find themselves in a new situation. . . . Persons also try to find out what they can and cannot do in the environment in which they live. This represents a kind of exploration of themselves.

Animals as explorers

Unless we are interested in animal psychology for its own sake, why should we care whether monkeys or rats have the exploring drive which is so clearly present in the human species? One reason is that we cannot be sure how much of the child's exploring and manipulating activity is suggested to him by his social environment. He is given toys and encouraged to find out what he can do with them. He may even be encouraged to wander around the environment in search of what is there, though parents often restrict this sort of exploration. The baby's "visual exploration"—his strong inclination to survey the immediate environment by turning his eyes and head—can scarcely have been instilled into him by his social environment; it manifests itself too early. But the psychological theorist wishes to make sure that the apparent drive to discover what is in the environment is really a primary drive.

Psychologists inclined to be skeptical of an exploratory drive would doubtless accept certain criteria suggested by Myers & Miller (1954): "If an exploratory tendency can produce learning like other drives such as hunger, and also show a similar pattern of satiation and recovery, these functional parallels to already known drives would help to justify its classification in the same category with them, namely as a drive." Can the opportunity to explore a novel object or place, like the opportunity to eat, serve as a reward for

which animals will work and learn instrumental acts? If so, the
exploratory tendency "produces learning."

Monkey behavior has been studied very extensively by Harlow
and his associates in the psychological laboratory at the University
of Wisconsin, and special attention has been given to exploratory
rewards. Food rewards for exploration or manipulation are found
to be unnecessary; it has been found better to feed the monkeys
before rather than after the experiment. A monkey is placed in a
relatively small cage that is enclosed by an opaque box but well
lighted inside. There is not much to do in the cage, but there is an
opening in one side of the box, closed by an opaque door. The
monkey easily learns to push the door open and look out into the
laboratory. He learns this simple instrumental act and repeats it
time after time with no other reward than a half-minute view of
the laboratory (which contains no visible food or monkeys). A more
difficult task involving discrimination is then presented. When a
screen concealing the side of the box is raised by the experimenter,
the monkey is confronted by *two* doors, one marked with a yellow
card and the other with a blue card, the cards being shifted irregularly from trial to trial. Let us say that the yellow card is the positive cue and blue the negative cue; the blue door is always locked
and the yellow one is always unlocked. If the monkey pushes the
yellow door, it opens and allows him a half-minute view outside; if
he pushes the blue door, the screen is lowered, terminating the trial.
Another trial follows after a 30-second interval, and this procedure
is continued for 4 hours a day for 5 days. After 100-200 trials a
normal monkey usually begins to "catch on," and in 400 trials some
monkeys reach nearly 100-percent correct choices, always pushing
the yellow door rather than the blue. They have learned a fairly
difficult instrumental act with no reward except the opportunity for
visual exploration (Butler & Harlow, 1954). Similar results are obtained with an auditory reward, "sounds emitted by a monkey
colony," to be had whenever a certain lever is pressed (Butler, 1957).

As to satiation, the monkeys in the visual experiment just described and others at Wisconsin have shown remarkable persistence
in opening the door to look out. They showed no sign of satiation
in the 4-hour daily period or even in the whole 5-day experiment.
The lack of satiation can also be regarded here as a lack of extinction. If visual exploration were a secondary drive based on the
hunger drive, for example, it should be extinguished in a long

series of trials without occasional reinforcement by food. Since there was no satiation or extinction in the day's work, there was of course no chance to test for recovery overnight.

It has been suggested (Brown, 1953; Myers & Miller, 1954) that confinement of a monkey in an opaque box produced a state of anxiety or perhaps of boredom, which was relieved when the monkey opened the door and looked out. There are well-known behavior symptoms of anxiety in monkeys (urination and defecation, vocalizing, shaking the cage), but according to Harlow (1953b), "The monkeys at no time during the experiment demonstrated the objective behavior syndrome of anxious monkeys." In a similar experiment on eighteen young monkeys (Butler, 1954), the more naive ones were apt "to hide in the rear of the apparatus during the first several preliminary training sessions, which suggests that an anxiety state is antithetical to visual exploratory responses." The behavioral symptoms of boredom are perhaps unknown except for a tendency to go to sleep, which occurred in some prolonged experiments and put a stop to the visual exploration.

In other experiments from the same laboratory (Harlow, 1950; Harlow & McClearn, 1954) monkeys learned *manipulation* tasks without any reward beyond success in making the thing work. This result confirms those on visual exploration as indicating a drive to deal with objects in the environment.

The *anthropoid apes* are probably more quickly satiated with exploration of an object than the monkeys, but they manifest the exploratory and manipulatory drives no less clearly. No psychologist can be better acquainted with the chimpanzees than Henry Nissen of the Yerkes Laboratories of Primate Biology. Here are some of his conclusions (1954, pp. 305, 299):

W. I. Welker of the Yerkes Laboratories has been conducting a study in which chimpanzees are presented with various surfaces and objects. . . . The initial approach of the animal to the new object is usually tentative—it gives a quick poke and then quickly withdraws. After the chimp has satisfied itself that the object is not dangerous, it begins to explore and investigate it more thoroughly. The more heterogeneous or variegated the object, the more attention it gets. . . . Interest, or attention or responsiveness . . . gradually wanes. The number of contacts decreases within a session of 5 or 10 minutes and then increases again at the beginning of the next exposure to the same situation. There is, also, a session-to-session decrement of responsiveness.

Anyone who has observed mammalian behavior, and for that matter behavior of so-called lower animals also, will realize how great a proportion of activity is devoted exclusively to keeping in touch with the environment, finding out what's going on, keeping informed, getting acquainted with a strange environment or with changes and new objects in a familiar one.

Welker's own report (1956) of his chimpanzee study was devoted to satiation and recovery. In a long series of daily 6-minute sessions a pair of objects was placed before a chimpanzee until interest was lost in those particular objects. A novel pair being substituted in the following session, interest at once revived. What was satiated, then, was not the exploratory drive in general but the interest in fully explored objects. The experimenter took note during each 5-second period of a session when the chimp manipulated or inspected either of the presented objects; the maximum score was 12 positive periods per minute. In the first minute with a new pair of objects the average score of the six animals was 9.5, but by the last minute of the fifth session it was down to less than 3.5. (See Figure 4.) The score fell off during each continuous session but recovered

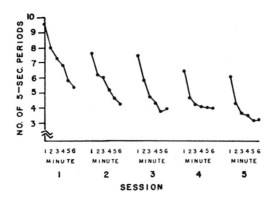

Fig. 4. (Welker, 1956.) Minute-by-minute count of amount of exploration of two or four presented objects during five successive sessions with the same objects. Each dot shows the average score in 1 minute for six chimpanzees and several pairs of objects.

partially overnight, only to sink still lower in the following session. The younger chimps (three to four years) got higher scores than the older ones (seven to eight years). The objects were so paired as to reveal exploratory *preferences;* the advantage lay with the larger or brighter or more movable object, or with the bell that could be sounded or the bulb that could be lighted. This study gives us a typical picture of exploratory behavior.

Rats as explorers. If the reader's esthetic sensibilities revolt against devoting appreciative attention to so furtive and objectionable an animal as the rat, he may be reassured to know that it is the white rat, an albino form of *rattus norvegicus,* that is most often used in the psychological laboratory. This rather attractive little animal offers the advantage for psychological purposes of having been bred and raised under scientific control so that important A-variables such as heredity, age, and previous treatment and experience are known to the experimenter. Economy of maintenance and apparatus, of course, is another advantage. And the rat is a surprisingly good learner of spatial problems like the much-used maze. So much fundamental information on learning has been obtained from rat experiments that the questions, whether the rat learns by exploring, and whether he is motivated by a primary exploratory drive, have an important bearing on learning theory. (If both questions are answered in the affirmative, we have the outlines of a theory which differs from one based entirely on need reduction or the law of effect. See pp. 239ff).

The white rat is an inveterate explorer. Placed in a maze or other enclosure he can be depended on, after some initial hesitancy and timidity, to cover the ground quite thoroughly. If there is a manipulable object present, such as the bar in the Skinner box, he can be depended on to find it sooner or later and to press or bite it from time to time even if he never obtains food, and has never obtained it, by pressing the bar (Figure 5).

Results similar to those shown in Figure 5 were obtained, without any manipulation being involved, by Berlyne (1955). The rat was placed in a rectangular enclosure tapering at one end into an alcove, and entrances into this alcove were counted for 10 minutes a day on three successive days. The exploratory activity declined during the daily periods with partial recovery overnight. On the fourth day there was a novel object, a wooden cube, in the alcove, and the recovery was complete, the amount of exploration equaling that on the first day. What becomes satiated, then, is not the exploratory tendency in general, but the exploring of a particular place or object. A previous experiment of the same author

(1950) showed the same thing; a rat's curiosity about one object may be satiated, but a different object will still receive a great deal of attention.

Another demonstration of this important fact may be added: *E* put before the rat a black-white pattern of vertical stripes. This was exposed for 10 minutes; after a two-minute rest, it was exposed

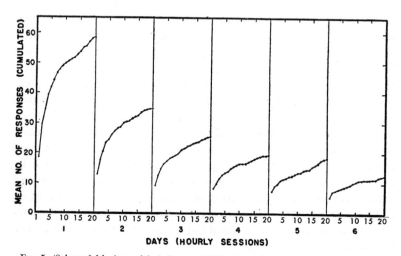

FIG. 5. (Schoenfeld, Antonitis & Bersch, 1950.) Cumulative curves of the number of bar pressings in successive periods of 3 minutes during an hour of continuous exposure to a bar in a Skinner box, without any present or previous reinforcement by food pellets. Mean results from forty rats. The curves are similar in construction to those on p. 68. The rise in a curve from each point to the next indicates the number of pressings in one period of 3 minutes. As the curve flattens out, then, the rate of pressing decreases toward zero. The curves show these effects: (1) progressive satiation during each hour; (2) partial recovery overnight, since the upward slope is steeper at the beginning of each day than at the end of the preceding day; (3) decrease from day to day in the total amount of bar pressing. These results are typical of exploratory behavior.

for 10 minutes more; the rat spent much less of the second 10 minutes looking toward the stripes. But if a radically different figure were substituted for the stripes for the second 10 minutes, the rats devoted fully as much time to this new figure as they had to the stripes originally (Thompson & Solomon, 1954).

Recovery from satiation is well brought out in an experiment of Danziger & Mainland (1954). Instead of a small box to explore, the rat was provided with an empty circular enclosure 6 feet in diameter. The floor was marked off into equal parts so that E could see how much ground was covered in each two-minute period. When these periods came one per day, the total distance covered in 20 periods was much greater than when the whole 40 minutes was continuous. With the short daily periods there was no decrease from day to day (complete recovery), but there was a large decrease from the beginning to the end of the continuous 40-minute exploration, some of the rats quitting and going to sleep before the end.

Incentive value of an opportunity to explore

Besides a law of satiation and recovery, for which we have found considerable evidence, another criterion has to be met by the exploratory tendency if it is to be classified as a drive. If an animal is shown an object or place suitable for exploration, will he work to reach it and will he learn instrumental acts for reaching it? Will an explorable object serve as the reward for an instrumental act—is exploration a consummatory activity? It seemed to be so in monkey behavior, and there is similar evidence in the case of rats.

The apparatus shown in Figure 6 afforded a choice between a relatively short blind alley and a much more adequate field for exploration (a D maze). From the choice point the rats could not see which they were choosing, but in twenty trials or less most of them learned to take the route to the D maze. Hunger or thirst reward was out of the question, since the rats had just had all they wanted to eat and drink and there was no food or water in the apparatus. When a rat reached the D maze, he proceeded to explore it rather thoroughly. It seems certain that the opportunity to explore was the reward that produced the learning.

To learn to choose the right (or the left) alley consistently when the reward is always on that side is an easy task for rats. Much more difficult is the task of choosing the white or the black alley, when the white, for example, always leads to the reward but is sometimes on one side and sometimes on the other. This discrimination task was used on rats by Montgomery & Segall (1955) with access to a D maze as the reward. The rats started, naturally, with a 50-50 choice but advanced steadily to 75-percent correct by the seventieth trial. The authors conclude: "It is apparent that a short period of exploration in a novel environment can function as a reinforcement in discrimination learning as well as in simple place learning by rats."

Confirmatory evidence is contained in the paper by Myers & Miller (1954), of which we have already made some use. Their rats, while neither hungry nor thirsty, learned to press a bar that opened the door from one compartment to the other of a "shuttle box," the

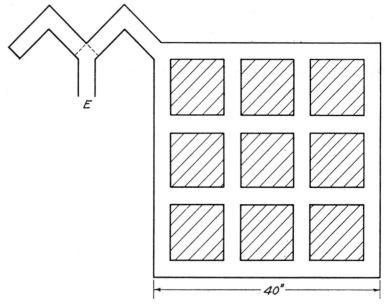

Fig. 6. (After Montgomery, 1954.) A Y maze with back-turned arms and a checkerboard maze (invented by Dashiell, 1930) at the end of one arm, the other arm being a blind alley. For each rat the D maze was always in the same position—on the right for six rats, on the left for the other six. All the alleys were 4 inches wide with walls 5 inches high. The animal was placed in the entrance and proceeded (upward in the *E* diagram) to the choice point. After he had made his choice and entered one arm of the *Y*, the sliding door was closed behind him, and he had 2 minutes either in the blind alley or in the D maze. There were four such trials with short intervals, and four more an hour later, the same procedure being repeated on the two following days.

only reward being the opportunity to poke their heads into the other compartment, sniff around, and sometimes enter. "Apparently the fact that pressing the bar is followed by the chance to observe and enter a new compartment is sufficient to produce learning." See also Sutherland (1957).

As a champion of the exploratory drive, Montgomery found it necessary to refute suggestions that it is merely a derivative of the motor-activity drive or of the anxiety drive. The activity drive finds an outlet in the activity wheel, like the wheel often attached to a squirrel cage, in which the animal can run to his heart's content without doing any exploring since this activity does not change his environment. Montgomery (1953) compared the amount of exploration in a simple Y maze (without food or water reward) of two samples of rats, one sample having been confined individually in small living cages and the other having had free access to activity wheels and often running in them the equivalent of half a mile a day. Each rat from both samples was given several 10-minute opportunities to explore the maze. If the maze simply afforded an outlet for the motor activity drive, rats that had been confined in small cages would certainly make much more use of it than rats that had had their fill of running in the activity wheel. But the amount of exploration in the maze was equal for both samples. And the exploratory pattern was the same. This pattern, discovered previously by Dennis & Sollenberger (1934) and by Montgomery (1952) is interesting in its own right. The rat tends to enter the three equal radii of the Y maze in rotation; when he returns from one arm to the choice point, he almost never goes back into the same arm; and between the other two arms he usually chooses the one less recently explored. The author's conclusion from the experiment we are considering is "that exploratory behavior is independent of the general activity drive."

In regard to the suggestion that exploratory behavior is somehow motivated by fear or anxiety, we have already noted the common observation that the rat's first reaction to a novel environment is timid or cautious and that this avoidance gives way after a while to approach and exploration. Fear appears to inhibit exploration rather than motivate it. Montgomery (1955) subjected this apparent relation to a more definite test. For 10 minutes a day for 3 days he offered his rats a chance to explore a 6-foot straight runway opening out of their individual living cages. For some of the rats this runway had sidewalls; for others it was merely a strip 4 inches wide without sidewalls, elevated 30 inches above the floor. Careless running on the open elevated strip would result in a tumble. The rats avoided it altogether at first, hesitating at the entrance and backing away, and they explored it only a little in the three 10-minute periods. Rats offered the enclosed runway showed but little hesitation and soon began to explore, and they did many times as much exploring as the other group. The author concludes that "novel stimulation may evoke the fear drive as well as the exploratory drive." The more fear, the less exploration. If the fear is not too strong, some exploration will occur and diminish the fear, so permitting more exploration to occur. If there were no exploratory drive to balance and overbalance the fear drive, an animal would be helpless in a novel situation.

Immediate rewards of exploration. The operation of an exploratory tendency has thus been demonstrated in the human child and in several animals. No doubt it could be similarly shown in other animals, certainly in birds. It is not a purely motor tendency, but might be called motor-sensory, the movement being preparatory to the reception of sensory stimuli. In visual exploration, the eye movements secure a clearer view of an object or of the environment. In locomotor exploration, approach to an object gives a better view or smell of it. In manipulatory exploration, action upon the object produces a revealing reaction of the object. In all cases, the retroflex (Rx in the formula, S—R—Rx) is the immediate goal of an exploratory response. The R in an exploratory act is a behavioral question, and the Rx is the environmental answer. The question is put to the environment and the answer indicates something in the environment. In free exploration the question amounts to "What's here?" In less free exploration, as in searching for a lost object, the question is "Where is it?" In both, the motivation is outgoing, objective, directed toward the environment. The immediate reward of exploration is acquaintance with the present environment with freedom from anxiety and readiness for action.

THE ACHIEVEMENT MOTIVES

No matter what one's ultimate motive may have been for the choice of a certain goal, the immediate motive in the actual performance is to reach that goal. As Gertrude Ederle said over television, when asked what her motive was in swimming the English Channel, "It was to get to the other side!" Her more remote motive, she said, was to demonstrate the merits of the American crawl which was supposed to be unsuited for a long, hard swim. No doubt she also hoped to win glory for herself. But these ulterior motives gave way during the performance to the immediate striving to reach the chosen goal. Perhaps it must be so; ulterior motives must retire to the background when effort is concentrated on the task in hand. Even so strong an adherent of the "instinct of self-assertion" as William McDougall (see pp. 54, 109) conceded that "If from any motive you set yourself to attain the goal" of any undertaking, from that moment you "foresee and desire" the attainment of that goal. "It is the same whenever we solve a problem. . . . The solution is the goal towards which we look forward" (1932, p. 348).

If the uncomplicated achievement motive is directed simply toward an objective goal, the ego-involved achievement motive has the ulterior goal of self-assertion, ego-enhancement, or defense of the ego against some threat. The ego-involved form is so common in human behavior, as in tests and examinations and competitive situations, that some psychologists are inclined to overlook the simpler form—the attainment of the goal. To obtain practically sure evidence of it we can examine the goal seeking of rats since in them the ego presumably is very little developed.

The rat's apparent eagerness to reach a goal increases as he gets nearer to the goal. This approach gradient was closely studied by Hull (1934). He constructed for one of his experiments a straight runway, 30 feet long, divided into 6-foot sections by light hanging doors so wired as to furnish a record of the moment when the rat passed from each section to the next. The speed gradient is shown in Figure 7.

The speed of an avoidance response, also, decreases with increasing distance from the danger region. Bugelski & Miller (1938) first shocked the rat at one end of a long alley and later placed the animal either at the shock point, but no shock being administered, or at some distance from that point. When placed at the shock point the rat started to run away almost instantly and ran away rapidly. When placed a foot away, he delayed a second or two and ran less rapidly; and when placed 3 feet away he waited 3 to 4 seconds and ran still less rapidly.

Instead of the speed of approach to a goal, the force exerted by the rat against resistance encountered near or far from the goal was studied by Brown (1948). Each rat used in his experiment wore a harness attached to a load behind, the load consisting of a spiral spring which the rat had to stretch in order to pass beyond a certain point in his approach to the food box. The strength of his

pull on the spring was measured. The rat was first accustomed to
the harness and learned to run rapidly through the 6-foot runway
to the food box, without any load. In the following test runs he
encountered the resistance either 5 feet from the food or not until
he was only a foot from it. His pull toward the goal measured 57
grams at the near point but only 41 grams at the far point (Means

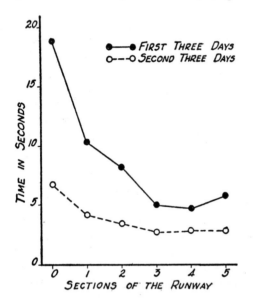

Fig. 7. (Hull, 1934, p.
394.) Running time in successive sections of a straight
runway leading to food.
The section numbered O
was the starting box, and
the long time indicated included the rat's reaction
time to E's opening of the
exit door. This starting
time was much reduced by
practice, and the speed was
increased throughout the
runway so that the gradient
flattens out though it is
still present. Average results from eleven rats, each
having fifteen trials per
day.

from twenty rats, a reliable difference). A withdrawal gradient was
found when the rats were pulling away from a point where they
had previously received a shock; they pulled away strongly when
placed near that point but only weakly when placed at a greater
distance.

These gradients of approach and withdrawal were originally explained by Hull and by Brown according to the principle of delayed
reinforcement. Responses just preceding the reward are presumably
better learned—more strongly conditioned—than responses further
back in the approach chain. The approach gradient is thus a gradient of "habit strength." This principle does not so easily explain
the withdrawal gradient since the withdrawal chain *follows* the
shock and could only be tied to it by "backward conditioning"
which is weak at the best, while the withdrawal movements are very
strong. A neater explanation would take account of "anxiety" (p.

70): the place where shocks have been received arouses strong anxiety when seen close at hand but only mild anxiety when seen at a distance. Thus the withdrawal gradient would be a gradient of anxiety, a gradient of motivation rather than of habit strength. And we can turn around and apply this reasoning to the approach gradient, for the sight of food right at hand arouses appetite more strongly than the sight of the same food at a distance. Therefore, we shift the basis of explanation from habit strength to incentive strength, from H to K. It is now well known (p. 49) that even a well-learned runway will not be run at all without some incentive and that the running speed depends on the amount of incentive. We have only to add the probable assumption that incentive value depends not only on the quantity of the reward (or punishment), but also on its nearness in space and time.

These results are a demonstration of a simple "achievement motive" uncomplicated by any ego-involvement.

The tendency to complete a half-finished task

Many ingenious studies of motivation were instigated by Kurt Lewin, already quoted (p. 49) as insisting on its important role in the activation of behavior. In his "field theory" of behavior he made much use of incentive value (which he called by the convenient name of *valence*) and of *quasi-need,* which might be derived from some more basic need but which functioned autonomously in a given total situation. An object in the environment had a positive valence if it appealed to an active quasi-need of the individual. The object then could become a goal object, and a definite intention to reach it could be aroused. A "tense system" or "force" directed toward the goal (Lewin, 1935, p. 51; 1954, p. 947) would be generated and ordinarily persist until the goal was reached.

Experiments suggested by this theory and carried out largely by Lewin's pupils are summarized and discussed in the two works of Lewin just cited.

The interrupted task. In Lewin's Berlin laboratory Maria Ovsiankina (1928) proceeded as follows. A student who has agreed to serve as subject (*O*) reports to *E* in the laboratory and is asked without further explanation to solve a certain puzzle, or to model a little dog of clay, or to perform some other task which has a definite goal though of no apparent personal significance. When *O* has become absorbed in his task, *E* interrupts the work by asking him to drop that task and switch to another. One result emerges at once: *O* is likely to rebel and insist on continuing what he is doing, but *E* persuades him to make the shift. He is allowed to complete the second task and is then left free for a short time while *E* is ostensibly busy taking notes. The unfinished first task is still lying on the table, and *O* is very likely to resume it spontaneously and carry it through to completion. In the course of a 2-hour session, *O* is given quite a number of tasks, some of which are interrupted and others not, with no reasons given. He seldom resumes work on a task that he has completed or on a task that was left unfinished by someone else; he usually resumes work only on tasks he himself has started and left unfinished.

That the tendency to resume is strong can be seen from the statistical result: with 28 *O*s and a total of 91 interrupted tasks, 72 tasks (79 percent) were resumed. Practically all were resumed after an interruption of only 2 or 3 minutes; during a longer interval there was some chance that the "tension" would leak away.

Introspective reports indicated that some *O*s became absorbed in the tasks just as interesting problems, while others regarded them as tests of their individual abilities; some were motivated by *task-interest,* others by *ego-interest.* In either case the interrupted goal-directed performance was usually resumed.

Substitute tasks and goals. A further prediction from Lewin's tension theory was tried out by Käte Lissner (1933). When one task is interrupted and another substituted, the second may be a satisfactory substitute for the first and serve to work off the tension, leaving none for the resumption of the interrupted task. A similar task will probably serve this purpose better than one that is entirely unlike the interrupted task. (Being sent out of the laboratory on some errand would be entirely unlike any of the usual tasks.) Lissner prepared pairs of very similar tasks, and pairs of very dissimilar ones, with the following results. The interrupted task was resumed:

> In 42 percent of the cases when the substitute was very similar to the interrupted task;
> In 87 percent when the two tasks were entirely unlike.

The theoretical prediction was confirmed: there was comparatively little resumption of an interrupted task after completion of a very similar one. But you could not always judge from the assigned task exactly what O's goal would be in performing it. If he was first told to model a clay dog and then interrupted and told to model a clay horse instead, the second task was an adequate substitute if his inner goal was to discover whether he could personally do such modeling (ego-interest), but inadequate if he had set his heart on producing a nice dog (task-interest).

Lissner's main result was independently confirmed in the Yale laboratory by Helen Nowlis (1941). Nowlis went ahead to study the effects on resumption of praise or dispraise for O's performance, obtaining some interesting results which, however, were not clearly predictable either by Lewin's tension theory or by the reinforcement theory current at Yale. Praise for the substitute performance should reduce the tension, but on the contrary it favored resumption of the interrupted task. The reason may be that praise tends to raise the general level of activation (p. 60), a general motivational factor that has only recently received much emphasis.

Immediate memory for interrupted tasks—the Zeigarnik effect. Another inference from Lewin's theory is that an interrupted task, if given no opportunity for resumption and completion, should remain for a short time in a state of readiness and be easily recalled, while a completed task, its tension gone, should be "laid on the shelf" for the time being. No prediction is possible as to permanent memory which may be even better for completed tasks. In the experiment of Bluma Zeigarnik (1927) the subject was given a series of twenty simple, varied tasks, each requiring a few minutes to complete; but only half of them were carried to completion, the other half (at irregular intervals) being interrupted with no opportunity for resumption. As soon as the whole series of tasks was gone through, O was asked to recall as many of them as possible. On the average a little over half were recalled, but the striking fact was that more of the unfinished than of the finished tasks could be recalled—on the average about 68 percent of the unfinished and only 43 percent of the completed tasks. A similar result has been obtained many times since, under the same conditions. But it makes a difference whether O is motivated by interest in the tasks or by concern for the ego. If he suspects that the experiment is a kind of intelligence or achievement test, and worries over the interruptions as indicative of failure on his part, he is likely to recall more of the completed than of the uncompleted tasks—a reversed Zeigarnik effect.

A somewhat fuller account of these experiments, with references to some of the later literature, is given by Woodworth & Schlosberg (1954, pp. 690-693).

Imaginative stories as indicators of the achievement motivation of their authors

The story writer may very likely "project" into his hero something of his own motivation. If the writer at the time of writing has a strong hope of some personal success, his hero should aim at some achievement and be successful. If the writer is pessimistic regarding his own success, his hero should encounter difficulties and perhaps fail in the end. Expert writers are probably less subject to this sort of self-revelation than students will be if asked to write a very short story around an enigmatical picture. The Thematic Apperception Test (TAT), devised by Murray and his coworkers (1938; see our p. 107), presents several such pictures one at a time and asks O to spend 5 minutes on each, telling who these persons may be, what they are doing and desiring, what has happened, and what will happen. The series of pictures is intended to tap the various "psychogenic needs" of young people especially. The TAT has been a favorite tool of the clinical psychologist. It is being used by the experimentalist in studies of how to stimulate motivation of different kinds.

The "need for achievement," at least in the ego-involved form, can be aroused in young male students by a series of tasks presented as being significant tests of intelligence and administrative ability, with indications that these Os are doing very poorly in the tests. This can be called the "Failure" condition and contrasted with a "Relaxed" condition in which another group of Os is given the same tasks to perform with the understanding that no personal significance will attach to the work to be done since it is simply a favor to E. Then pictures are shown, and O is asked to write a short but dramatic story around each picture, as a "test of creative imagination" (McClelland et al., 1949, 1953; Atkinson, 1954).

Though O is urged to be freely imaginative in writing a story, E must be objective and standardized in scanning it for signs of achievement motivation. If the whole story is based on an effort by any of the characters to reach a goal, that theme is one such sign. If the story contains statements to the effect that someone desires to accomplish a certain result, performs instrumental acts aimed at overcoming obstacles, looks forward to the goal, or is happy at the outcome, these items are counted toward the writer's total score in achievement motivation. The investigators found this score to be significantly higher for the group subjected to preliminary Failure than in the Relaxed condition. The stories written after Failure contained more references to long-term, career goals as compared with the completion of present tasks. Evidently the Failure preliminary aroused in the students a set for personal achievement which found an outlet in their stories. As to the Relaxed condition, it probably did not arouse any strong task set; and E might not be able to arouse in a student group an uncontaminated set for achieving results that simply ought to be done. A student is accustomed to performing tasks, at least curricular tasks, for his own self-improvement and not because they need to be done. For that reason, perhaps, a set for personal achievement is easily aroused in students.

Even within a student group the individuals differ widely in achievement motivation, and one hope of the investigators is to trace the causes of these differences. Presumably a home environment that expects young children to learn to do things for themselves and do them well favors the development of achievement motivation. Different cultures or subcultures may very likely differ in this respect. If the parents depend largely on their own initiative and achievement for making their way in life, they may instill this motivation into their children more than parents will whose income is fixed by law or by a union contract. But the individual's genes should not be disregarded; of two brothers growing up together, one is likely to show more independence than the other (McClelland, 1955; Douvan, 1956).

The desire for friends and companions

This outgoing human tendency, called by Murray the need for Affiliation, can be studied experimentally in the same way as the need for Achievement. The Aroused preliminary condition may be a gathering in the fraternity house of fellow members who are asked to consider each other's social qualities and apply to each man, anonymously, the two adjectives which best describe him from a list including such words as these: argumentative, cooperative, entertaining, friendly, intolerant, sympathetic, timid; also to pick two men as the most desirable friends. The purpose of this "socio-metric" exercise is simply to sensitize the Affiliation motives of the group. Then the members are shown a series of pictures and asked to write a 5-minute story around each picture. The pictures are not designed to suggest companionship strongly, but they do afford an opportunity for anyone whose companionable motives have been aroused to bring them into his stories. For comparison an Un-aroused group is shown the same pictures after a short exercise in anagrams (making words out of the letters of *generation*) conducted in a college classroom during a regular class period. The Aroused group put much more Affiliation into their stories than the Un-aroused do. And an important result is that the hope of good com-panionship is more in evidence than the fear of loss of companions. If the selected pictures are biased in the direction of suggesting per-sonal difficulties, to be sure, the stories run to loss of friends; but if the pictures are unbiased, the hopeful tendency prevails (Shipley & Veroff, 1952; Atkinson *et al.,* 1954).

The same conclusion was reached by French & Chadwick (1956) who used quite a different projective method. Instead of pictures they presented short descriptions of rather enigmatical behavior which *O* was asked to explain. For example: "Tom always lets the 'other fellow' win." The positive approach, "So the other fellow will feel good toward him," was more common than an avoidance, "He's afraid he'll lose a friend if he wins." But a truly negative, un-affiliative response apparently did not occur, such as this: "So the other fellow will get bored and go away."

Besides the Achievement and Affiliation motives there are in Murray's list of the "psychogenic needs" (see our Chapter 5, p. 107) many others which are "outgoing" in that they are directed toward environmental results. Individuals differ in the relative strength of these motives. The drive to dominate others is strong in some in-dividuals; some like to show off or be the center of attention; some show a strong tendency toward helpfulness. In their different ways all of them are aiming at positive environmental results. Some aims appear negative rather than positive: avoidance of injury, blame or humiliation; social aloofness; hostile aggressiveness. Perhaps "outgoing" is not the most descriptive adjective for such tendencies, and yet they all have to do with the environment in its relations to the individual. An artist or inventor who is temporarily unso-ciable because he is absorbed in his painting or invention is definitely aiming at environmental results. You cannot call him "withdrawn" from the environment as a whole but only from a part of it. A person so absorbed in thought as to be oblivious of his immediate surroundings may be trying to solve a problem that has to do with his relations to some other person. A nursery school child who takes only a halfhearted interest in the materials offered for "creative play"—blocks, crayons, paints—appears withdrawn into himself, but it is because he feels insecure, rejected, unfairly treated at home; in some such way he is concerned with the environment (Alschuler & Hattwick, 1947).

MOTIVATION OF GROUP BEHAVIOR, ESPECIALLY SOCIAL PLAY

The sociability of human beings, their tendency to come together in pairs or larger groups, motivated by something of the nature of the Affiliation need, can perhaps be explained by the principle of "secondary reinforcement" based on the primary reinforcements of food when hungry, safety when frightened, and comfort when too hot or cold. By such rewards the little child has learned to approach a fostering adult, and "stimulus generalization" can be expected to other adults and to people in general. People come to have positive valence or attraction for the child and a generalized habit is established of approaching people and snuggling up to them (or to some of them).

If social behavior consisted simply in the aggregation of individuals into groups, it could be explained rather plausibly by this theory of conditioning. But there is much more to social behavior even in the child. He engages in social play and his favorite playmates are other children, not adults. These playmates do not gain his affection by supplying his organic needs. Instead they afford him the opportunity to do something interesting in the environment. Group play develops out of individual play with objects, as in the example of block building (p. 78). The youngest nursery-school children, if two of them are placed on the floor with a supply of blocks, will make some rudimentary social contacts, but their block play is individual. At three years of age they are apt to undertake a joint project, and in the next two years the projects increase in size and complexity and in the number of children participating. In a relatively free environment with an adequate supply of materials, the children's spontaneous activities keep pace with their increasing capacity to organize their environment and their ways of dealing with it. They are attracted to organized games such as baseball which provide an opportunity for teamwork, with different players contributing different parts of the total performance. The same can be said of their dramatic play (Anderson, 1939; Biber *et al.*, 1942).

Social play is distinctly "outgoing." Its rewards include participation in the process of dealing with objects, in the results achieved, and in the interplay of skills and personal traits. People are interesting to you when they are doing something, especially if they are cooperating with you.

When an active social group is said to consist of individuals, each of whom responds to stimuli emitted by the others and acts back upon the others, something important is missing from the picture. There is the environment which is common to the members of the group. The most important stimuli often come from the environment, and the most important responses act back on the environment. The group is doing something in and to the environment. For well-integrated group activity there must be a goal common to all the members; all the members are "set" for the same situation and for the same goal. The environment of a football team consists of the field, the ball, and the opposing team, and a team becomes an active, integrated social group when it confronts this environment and starts to deal with it. When the team members discuss possible plays in the clubhouse, they are dealing symbolically with this environment as well as they can in its absence. Similarly, when a committee is devising a plan to cope with a difficult situation, the members are set for the situation and for the desired goal; the members talk back and forth, stimulating and responding to each other, but if anyone fails to "talk to the subject," he is no longer participating in the essential group activity.

Within a social group the members do certainly interact, and "interaction" may seem to be a suitable term descriptive of their activity. From what we have been saying a better term would be *coaction*. The members act together upon a situation or problem confronting the group as a whole. It is this common problem that enables the members to join forces and behave as an integrated group.

Immediate rewards of group activity

In order to participate effectively in teamwork or in any organized form of group activity, the young individual has much to learn. He has to acquire not only motor skills but also an understanding of the game. The viewer of baseball from the grandstand or from before the television screen acquires some understanding without any motor skill. He learns some of the rules and some of the strategy, so that he can anticipate what a base runner will do when the batter hits a fly ball; if he anticipates correctly, his understanding is reinforced. The actual player gets reinforcement also when one of his plays is successful; thus he learns the techniques of throwing, catching, batting, "judging the ball," making a double play, and other individual and group skills. Applause from the audience must have some reinforcing value, but more effective because more direct, immediate, and discriminating is the success of the act itself. Given the goal of a social activity, the principal reinforcement comes from attainment of the goal or from one's contribution to this result.

Though children sometimes invent a game for themselves, in the main they find that games and other forms of group activity are provided by the "culture," and in proportion as their capacity becomes adequate for understanding and performing such an activity, it turns out to have a positive attraction for most of them. Sometimes a culture is pictured as mainly an authority which prescribes norms of behavior and enforces conformity by reward and punishment. But the culture is also the provider of games, ceremonies, amusements and various forms of social activity which have a positive incentive value for the individual. The goals of these activities are such as the individual will strive to attain, and the activities are interesting while in progress so that there is plenty of reinforcement waiting to be obtained.

Competition

Among the goals provided by the culture, or at least by some cultures, is the winning of a contest between individuals or groups, especially in sports. A little boy may not see the point of a simple competitive game such as marbles, since his own success in getting his marble into the ring does not prevent his playmate from doing the same. Both can win (Piaget, 1932). When a group is walking together to some destination, the members tend to keep together, with no one trailing behind and no one trying to make a race of it by dashing ahead. Young people like to keep abreast in many ways, even in school marks, though not in sports.

In industry a piecework system of wages aims to arouse a competitive spirit in the workers, but they are apt to counter by agreeing among themselves to restrict their output. Their group code is likely to be such that the individual who turns out too much work is a "rate buster," while one who turns out too little is a "chiseler." Yet ego-involved factors are prominent in the worker's motivation, such as the holding of a preferred job, high wage scale and prospect of promotion, seniority, job security, respect of his associates inside and outside the plant, and good reputation of the plant and its products (Shaw, 1952; Viteles, 1953).

CHAPTER 5

Theories of Motivation

The operation of motives, we asserted at the beginning of this series of chapters, could be studied without any prior attempt to construct a system which should trace all the manifold human motives back to their sources. A system would introduce some order and simplification, presumably by identifying certain primary motives and relegating the rest to a secondary status. Many attempts have been made in the history of psychology to map out a system with a few primary motives, the numerous others being regarded as secondary. Usually the assumption has been that the primaries are inherited and the secondaries derived from the primaries by some process of learning.

Without going back far into the history of the subject we shall consider two opposed theories—one of which is accepted by many psychologists at the present time; the other is emerging and deserving of a radical presentation and support. The first may be called the *need-primacy* theory and the other the *behavior-primacy* theory. The need-primacy theory holds that all behavior is motivated directly or indirectly by the internal needs of the organism, such as hunger and thirst. Sex is regarded as a need to escape from certain internal tensions, and the need to escape from pain and external injury must also be included. The behavior-primacy theory holds

101

that all behavior is directed primarily toward dealing with the environment. Even eating and drinking, which certainly rid the organism of needs, can be regarded as ways of dealing with the environment and securing positive benefits and satisfactions; i.e., as forms of behavior which secure positive good rather than merely escape from harm. No matter which of these theories has the greater emotional appeal to the reader, the scientific question is which has more predictive value. Which one better covers the ground and is more systematic and parsimonious? At first sight the need-primacy theory would be the more parsimonious and systematic if it could possibly be stretched to cover the play motives of children and the absorbing interests of adults. We should have to show how these motives and interests could possibly be derived from the primary needs; thus we could "explain" the motives. But could we *predict* them for the individual or for the social group without assuming additional primaries besides the organic needs?

Two systems which clearly belong in the need-primacy class are the psychoanalytic system of Sigmund Freud and the behavioristic system of Clark Hull.

FREUD'S NEED-PRIMACY THEORY OF MOTIVATION

All fundamental "instincts" or drives in this system result from intraorganic tensions pressing for release. Such a bodily tension is not directly observable, but it is represented by a need and identified by the means taken to reduce the need. The hunger, thirst, and sex tensions manifest themselves in certain need-reducing forms of primitive behavior. These are typical positive and constructive drives. They are called erotic in a broad sense, and they are opposed by a destructive or aggressive drive which plays a prominent role in Freud's later theory. Freud sometimes spoke of the love and hate instincts. He considered all motives to be derived from these two primal forces.

The totality of drives or organic tensions is given a name, the Id, in distinction from the Ego. In this connection the Ego is not limited to self-seeking behavior but is a comprehensive concept for behavior in general, i.e., for all dealing with the environment. The sense organs, muscles, and brain are Ego organs; sense perception, motor behavior, learning, remembering, and thinking are Ego functions. The tensions that arise in the Id demand outlet into the environment, but the Ego blocks the passages. At least, the Ego is in a position to hold back the discharge of the Id as long as necessary for safety and expediency. The Ego often adopts a drive from the Id and puts the resources of intelligence and muscular strength at the service of this drive, but the Ego does not generate any drives of its own, aside from the safety motive. The Ego is mechanism, and all its drive comes from the Id.

For example, the Id tension of intense hunger demands relief and pushes the Ego to find some food, but the Ego discovers the bad aftereffects of indiscriminate gorging and regulates eating behavior accordingly. Further regulation is necessitated by social disapproval of primitive table manners. Thus the various dangers involved in satisfaction of the hunger drive are avoided. Appetizing foods and surroundings certainly belong in the province of the intelligent Ego, but no such function seems called for by the general scheme of things, since the Id tensions call for relief and not for extra stimulation. Hunger is painful; and the pleasure of eating, according to the general Freudian theory, consists in the relief of this pain. The general theory would certainly not enable us to go far in predicting human arrangements for "gracious dining" or ways and means of "working up an appetite."

The psychoanalysts have concerned themselves very little with the motivation of nutritive behavior since they do not find neuroses resulting from frustration in this sphere as they do in the sphere of sex. The sex demands of the Id are subjected to much control by the Ego from considerations of danger and social disapproval. We seem to see also a good deal of behavior directed toward stimulation of sex appetite, though this would not logically be predicted from the theory.

Sublimation

A challenging problem for any need-primacy theory of motivation is that of tracing the motives and goals of everyday life back to the organic needs. On the surface, most of our work and play does nothing to relieve these needs. Id tensions seem to be in abeyance most of the time, and yet motivation may be keen.

Freud offered two solutions of this problem; the first went under the name of sublimation. In his 1915-1917 lectures at the University of Vienna he said (quoted from the 1935 English edition, pp. 301-303):

> People fall ill of a neurosis when the possibility of satisfaction for the libido is removed from them—they fall ill in consequence of a "frustration," as I called it . . . their symptoms are actually substitutes for the missing satisfaction. This of course does not mean that every frustration in regard to libidinal satisfaction makes everyone who meets with it neurotic. . . . In general, there are very many ways by which it is possible to endure lack of libidinal satisfaction without falling ill. . . . One amongst these processes serving as protection against illness has reached a particular significance in the development of culture. It consists in . . . the adoption of a new aim—which new aim, though genetically related to the first, can no longer be regarded as sexual, but must be called social in character. We call this process *sublimation* . . . sublimation can never discharge more than a certain proportion of libido, apart from the fact that many people possess the capacity for sublimation only in a slight degree.

In this and other early works Freud explained how the frustrated sex drive might find an outlet for some people in science or art. Thus the frustrated sexual curiosity of the child might generate an interest in biology or even in physics and chemistry. And a child's "anal erotism"—his fascination with feces and the process of defecation—might be sublimated into a love for cleanliness, order, and thrift, along with obstinacy. The intense creative drive of many authors, painters, and musical composers was redirected libido, and any hobby or sport could be rather vaguely explained as motivated in this way. Many good people who were deprived of normal sex life were gratified to believe that the great energy of this drive could find an outlet in some humane social activity.

Prediction from the theory of sublimation is certainly far from precise. There are so many diverse possible outlets for blocked libido. Sublimation alone cannot say which outlet will be chosen by any individual; other selective factors must determine the choice. Besides, the theory would predict that artists and other creative workers should be prime examples of blocked libido and therefore lacking in frank sexual interest and activity—which seems *not* to be the case (Taylor, 1933; Kinsey *et al.*, 1948).

Fusion of the erotic and aggressive drives

Without ever undertaking to ferret out these selective factors in everyday interests—and without ever disavowing the importance of sublimation—Freud recognized (1923) that human activities could not be cleanly divided into those that were definitely erotic and those that were definitely aggressive and destructive. Yet the motivation of all these activities must come from the two great instincts. It followed that these opposed drives must fuse, probably in different proportions for different activities. Part of the libido must give up its sexual aim, part of the aggressive drive its destructive aim, and the fused compound must provide the motivation of various human activities. Freud did not allow that the specific nature of any activity could provide additional motivation, but he regarded the fused drive as neutral (nondirective) in aim (1923, pp. 61-63).

> We have reckoned as though there existed . . . a displaceable energy, which is in itself neutral, but is able to join forces either with an erotic or with a destructive impulse. . . . Without assuming the existence of a displaceable energy of this kind we can make no headway. . . . It is clear, incidentally, that there is a certain indifference about the path along which the discharge takes place, so long as it takes place somehow.

In particular, dammed-up aggressiveness could find a socially acceptable outlet by "enlisting in the service of Eros."

This concept of the fusion of two basic drives is maintained in Freud's later comprehensive accounts of psychoanalysis (1933, 1938). It might seem that the child's development of a conscience or Superego would introduce new drives of a social and ethical nature, but Freud did not allow any such departure from his need-primacy theory. The Superego exerted a restrictive and sometimes even cruel authority over the Ego, deriving its "energy" mostly from the aggressive instinct. The safety motive was not included among the primary needs. It was not present in the Id. Fear and anxiety arose in the Ego as it encountered the dangers of the environment, the excessive demands of the Id, and the restrictions of the Superego.

We shall not attempt to follow the fortunes of Freud's need-primacy theory in the subsequent history of psychoanalysis. Horney (1939) and other neo-Freudians have rejected the whole attempt to trace human motivation back to instinctive drives. Others, more orthodox (as Fenichel, 1945), have rejected the primary drive of aggression and have sharply limited the scope of sublimation: "It is highly improbable that a sublimation of adult genital sexuality exists. . . . Pregenital strivings are the object of sublimation."

Carl Menninger (1942) has attached great importance to sublimation, to the aggressive instinct, and especially to the sublimation of aggression (pp. 128ff):

> No sooner is a child born than . . . he begins to respond to the irritations of the outside world, meeting them first with hostility, then with tolerance, finally with affection. . . . victory of the life instinct (love) over the death instinct (hate). All aggressive energy except that small quantity necessary for self-defense against real dangers is turned into useful channels . . . This latter process constitutes *sublimation*, as I view it. . . . The connections of work with the destructive instinct are close and clear. It is easy to see that all work represents a fight against something, an attack upon the environment. . . . After work, play is the most universal method of safely disposing of our aggressions. . . . Play is a method of carrying out these aggressions in forms socially acceptable.

The very successful Menninger clinic employs work therapy and play therapy, tailored to fit the aggressive needs of the patients. Even so, it would seem that other motivating factors must be taken into account besides the universal love and hate instincts, so that prediction of results must rest on more than the bare need-primacy theory. With regard to the normal person's choice of activities, we could ask such apparently silly questions as "Does the individual like to play part of the time because play affords a fuller outlet for his aggressiveness?" or "Does he choose the work that he hates most?" The answer to the last question might be that a person's love and hate tensions have pretty well fused by the time he selects his occupation, leaving him free to choose according to other motives, if there are any.

We are not undertaking to evaluate the Freudian psychology in general. We are asking only whether this form of the need-primacy theory actually predicts the manifold motives and interests of human children and adults. The difficulty is that the theory predicts only that some behavior, represented by the Ego, will be activated, without specifying the directions which the behavior will take. The human being seeks so many goals; the theory does not indicate what these will be, aside from the primary goals of food, sex and destruction. The human individual engages eagerly in certain activities and rejects certain others; the theory does not explain these individual preferences. He might "work off his steam" by moving rocks back and forth from one pile to another, but he prefers a game of some sort, and different persons prefer different games. The person could support himself in several possible occupations, but some appeal to him and some do not. With only the needs to predict from, we could do very little in the way of predicting behavior.

The environment, with its opportunities and restrictions, steers the individual in some directions and not in others; but this "steering" is not forcing, since the individual is far from passive in relation to the environment. He accepts some opportunities and not others; he yields to some restrictions and rebels against others. Much depends on his abilities, actual and potential; some activities are too hard for him and others too easy to enlist his energies. There is a hint here of the behavior-primacy system to be followed up later in our discussion.

Murray's system of needs

A very serious and competent attempt to identify the internal "directional forces" in the lives of young men was made by the staff of the Harvard Psychological Clinic and reported by its chief investigator, Henry A. Murray (1938). He called these directional forces "needs" and distinguished two classes of needs, the viscerogenic or organic (the usually recognized list) and the psychogenic which appeared to operate in the individual's life and development, especially in his dealings with the social environment. A few of the twenty-eight psychogenic needs that were distinguished were the following:

The need for personal Achievement
  "   "   " Affiliation, friends; liking for people
  "   "   " Aggression in the Freudian sense
  "   "   " Dominance, drive to dominate people
  "   "   " Exhibition, showing off, getting attention
  "   "   " Independence, living one's own life
  "   "   " Nurturance, helpfulness
  "   "   " Succorance, being helped; dependence
  "   "   " Cognizance, exploring, asking questions
  "   "   " Exposition, giving information, lecturing

How could a group of psychologists work out such a list and come to aggreement on it? Apparently by a method of successive approximation. Starting with what seemed the probable needs or drives, the investigating group tried these out on a sample of young men, made necessary corrections and tried them on a second sample, and so on. They noticed what situations and objects were welcomed by a man, what results he aimed at and was pleased with, his expressed desires and his involuntary symptoms of desire and need. They found out whether they could agree among themselves on the needs manifested by a man and on the strength of those needs.

Evidently Murray's list of psychogenic needs was not obtained *a priori,* by prediction from the viscerogenic needs. It was obtained *a posteriori,* by examination of behavior in relation to the environment. Instead of working forward from the organic needs to predicted subneeds, the investigation worked backward from behavior to possible underlying needs. Even though the psychogenic needs were supposably derived from the viscerogenic, they operated in young adults without any obvious dependence on the viscerogenic. If so derived, it must have been in childhood and must have depended also on the home environment and on the child's abilities, as Murray says (1938, pp. 128, 129):

> What factors determine the establishment of a need as a ready reaction system of personality? This is an important problem to which only vague and uncertain answers can be given. In the first place, observation seems to show that the relative strength of needs at birth (or shortly after birth) is different in different children. Later, the strength of some needs may be attributed to intense or frequent gratifications (reinforcements), some of which rest on specific abilities. . . . Some needs may become established because of their success in furthering other more elementary needs. The gratification or frustration of a need is, of course, largely up to the parents, since they are free to reward or punish any form of behavior. . . . Certain cultures and sub-cultures to which an individual is exposed may be characterized by a predominance of certain needs. . . . There are still other factors, no doubt, that work to determine what needs become dominant.

In view of all these factors, it would be hopeless to predict an individual's psychogenic needs from the viscerogenic needs, even if the psychogenic are derived from the viscerogenic, for which derivation there is so far no evidence.

McDougall's system

William McDougall, as well as Freud, was mentioned by Murray as an important predecessor in the psychology of motivation. In 1908 McDougall attempted to work out a system of primary drives, which he called instincts then but later native propensities. McDougall's list of socially important motives was not as long as Murray's, but it included several which were later adopted by Murray, such as:

The exploring tendency
The aggressive tendency
The gregarious tendency
The dominating, self-assertive tendency
Acquisitiveness and constructiveness

McDougall did not regard these as derived from the organic needs; they were primary instincts in his system. Many more specific motives and interests were derived from them by processes of learning; and the primaries could combine and attach themselves to certain objects, as in love for a person or loyalty to a group or to a cause. The main objection raised to McDougall's system was that it assumed too many primaries. The self-assertive or dominating tendency, for example, may be acquired and not primary at all; early in life the child is likely to be praised for his little achievements and obeyed when he issues commands to his doting parents. If we expand our list of primaries to include important social motives, we of course increase the predictive power of the system, but perhaps illegitimately. McDougall himself pointed out the absurdity of postulating instincts tailored to fit the economic or political or religious behavior which a social theorist might wish to explain.

HULL'S NEED-PRIMACY THEORY OF MOTIVATION

Hull's insistence on the necessity of motivation for any behavior, his distinction between the motivational factors of drive and incentive (D and K), and his attempt to consider drive as a purely intensive, nondirective factor in behavior, with direction depending entirely on "habit" or mechanism, have been presented in a preceding chapter. For Hull, all motivation depended on organic needs. So far, his system is like Freud's. Hull's list of needs is not very different from Freud's. The aggressive drive is omitted, and the escape drive is allowed full standing as a primary factor in behavior. Hull's nondirective drive parallels Freud's "neutral, displaceable" fusion of erotic and aggressive energies, since both provide activation for behavior without giving it any direction, the direction depending on other factors. The most obvious difference between the two systems is the level or breadth of behavior which they examine. Hull focuses attention on the single act, where Freud considers the normality or neuroticism, the eroticism, aggressiveness, or sociality of the individual's behavior in the large. Without ranking one of these approaches above the other in value, we can say that the experimentalist's close examination of behavior is a psychological "must." Our question in this chapter is whether Hull's form of the need-primacy theory succeeds in predicting human behavior, motives, and interests.

Secondary reinforcement, secondary goals or incentives

Hull's system has the advantage over Freud's of taking much more account of the effects of learning. What he calls primary reinforcement is the satisfaction of a primary need such as hunger for food. More exactly, it is defined by Hull as the cessation or reduction of the need. (We shall postpone a criticism of this conception of primary reinforcement; see pp. 117ff, 258.) When an act leads promptly to such primary reinforcement, learning occurs. The act that is reinforced becomes conditioned to the need and to the external situation so that when the same need and situation occur again, the same act is likely to be made in response. Consequently, by repetition with reinforcement, a habit or mechanism is built up which deals with the situation in such a way as to satisfy or reduce the need. More than that—the mechanism itself acquires some secondary incentive value. Suppose the mechanism consists in going to a certain place where food is found; this place and the act of going there will serve as a reward for a number of trials even if no more food is found there. Or, if the drive is changed from hunger to thirst, the animal will go there for water which he has never found there. This place has become a "good" place. Similarly, a place where an animal has been shocked has become a bad place, a place to be avoided; the place to which he goes and where he gets no shocks has become a good place (pp. 71ff). (Our way of stating the facts is somewhat different from Hull's.) There are many similar results from the animal laboratories. A stimulus that just precedes the obtaining of food—like the click of the pellet-delivering machine in the Skinner box—becomes something worth working for even after the primary reward has ceased.

A striking example of secondary reinforcement in chimpanzees is the well-known food-token or poker-chip experiment of Wolfe (1936) and Cowles (1937). A vending machine was arranged to deliver a grape or raisin when a poker chip was inserted in the slot. A chimpanzee was first trained to take a poker chip from the floor and insert it for the food. Then he learned to obtain poker chips by raising the handle of another machine. Having obtained a chip, he went to the food vender and obtained his primary reward. If he were not permitted to proceed at once to the food vender, he would work on the other machine and accumulate a stock of ten or more chips which he could then use at the food vender. But when the supply of grapes or raisins was permanently discontinued, the operation of obtaining chips was extinguished. The poker chips had acquired value as tokens or promises of food; when the promise was no longer kept, the token value died out. The poker chips had not acquired permanent value in their own right. They were worth working for as means to a primary end but not as an end in themselves.

The same result has been obtained in many other cases of secondary reinforcement. In the Skinner box the click of the pellet-delivering machine could serve to maintain bar pressing for a while after the supply of pellets was discontinued, but not indefinitely. The click promised a pellet, but if the promise were no longer kept, the click lost its value and no longer served to reinforce and maintain the bar pressing (But see p. 129.)

Suppose we wished to develop in a chimpanzee a new need, not included in the list of primary needs—a need for poker chips, or a permanent willingness to work for poker chips. We would arrange to have the obtaining of a poker chip a preliminary step toward a primary goal—toward the satisfaction of a primary need. We could build up a secondary need for chips, but this need would be lost if the primary reinforcement were discontinued. We could probably maintain the secondary need without giving the primary reinforcement every time, but not if the primary reinforcement were entirely left behind in the individual's life.

The problem of "functional autonomy"

The principle of secondary reinforcement does not enable the need-primacy theory to predict the numerous interests of human beings, such interests as were called "functionally autonomous" by Gordon Allport (1937, pp. 194-207):

> The dynamic psychology proposed here regards adult motives as infinitely varied, and as self-sustaining, *contemporary* systems, growing out of antecedent systems, but functionally independent of them. . . . An ex-sailor has a craving for the sea. . . . The sailor may have first acquired his love for the sea as an incident in his struggle to earn a living. . . . But now the ex-sailor is perhaps a wealthy banker; the original motive is destroyed; and yet the hunger for the sea persists unabated. . . . The pursuit of litera-ture, the development of good taste in clothes, the use of cos-metics, the acquiring of an automobile, strolls in the public park . . . may first serve, let us say, the interests of sex. But every one of these instrumental activities may become an interest in itself. . . . Many experiments show that incompleted tasks set up ten-sions that tend to keep the individual at work until they are resolved. No hypothesis of self-assertion, rivalry, or any other basic need, is required. The completion of the task itself has be-come a quasi-need with dynamic force of its own. . . . A student who at first undertakes a field of study because it is prescribed, because it pleases his parents, or because it comes at a convenient hour, often ends by finding himself absorbed, perhaps for life, in the subject itself. . . . In brief, the principle of functional auton-omy is a declaration of independence for the psychology of personality.

Not only the adult interests emphasized by Allport, but even the motives of children in their play are apparently underivable from the organic needs. As Asch (1952, p. 298) has pointed out,

> Infants and children do not become passive or cease to act when these needs are met. On the contrary, they are active and alert when not under the pressure of biological needs. They en-gage in intense, varied, and alert explorations; they become ab-sorbed in objects and in moving, lifting, dropping, and turning. Indeed, they are most characteristically active when they are free from hunger, fatigue, or pain.

The sequence of events in a baby's nursery is likely to be food after crying, but play after feeding. There is no evidence of play as a means of getting food, or of play activity requiring any rein-forcement from prompt satisfaction of hunger or thirst or any other organic need. There is more chance for secondary reinforcement in the development of adult interests.

Hull was not unmindful of the challenge to his need-primacy theory presented by Allport's functionally autonomous motives, but he thought they could be explained by secondary reinforcement, provided lack of primary reinforcement were not always fatal to the secondary incentive. He said (1943, p. 101): "The present hy-pothesis does not imply that secondary reinforcement will neces-sarily suffer experimental extinction when the support of the primary need reduction is withdrawn. If the primary reinforcement has been sufficiently profound" during the establishment of a sec-ondary activity, anticipation of the primary reward may be intense enough to take the place of the actual reward and so resist ex-tinction indefinitely. "Here, apparently, we have the explanation of . . . functional autonomy."

The only evidence offered by Hull (1952, p. 112), and perhaps the only evidence that could be offered, in support of this daring *ad hoc* hypothesis comes from such experiments on avoidance condi-tioning as were described in the preceding chapter (p. 69). In a typical experiment a dog receiving shocks after a warning signal came to manifest anticipation of the shocks (anxiety) at the signal and to avoid the shocks by promptly leaving the danger spot for a safe spot. His anticipation of shocks was not negated, since he got away in time, and consequently extinction of the anticipation was very slow. But in a corresponding situation with a positive reward there would be no immunity from extinction; the absence of the promised food would negate the anticipation definitely.

Another curious characteristic of the anticipatory reward is that the *primary* reinforcement is anticipated. The anticipation of raisins from the slot machine would be the (internal) reinforcement preventing extinction of the chimpanzee's operation of the other machine that delivered the poker chips. Similarly, the unextin-guished liking for a picture that hung on the wall of your dining room in childhood is an anticipation of something good to eat. All acquired likes and interests must accordingly be relics of the satis-factions of primary needs. The theory does not provide for any new forms of satisfaction.

Keller & Schoenfeld (1950) make extensive use of secondary reinforcement in their explanation of human behavior. Sometimes they assume (p. 247) that "resistance to extinction of a secondary reinforcement . . . may endure for life in a man," but generally they insist (p. 241) that a secondary reinforcer "extinguishes or loses its power if separated from primary reinforcement. . . . We need not always pause to identify . . . the primary reinforcements that continue to support the power of" the numerous secondary reinforcers. "In a broad way, you may think of the supporting primary reinforcements as being such things as our daily food and drink, or relief of pain or anxiety." Such primary reinforcements, occurring frequently in everyday life, should apparently maintain the appeal of friendship, work and play, art and science, and any secondary satisfaction that we may have acquired.

Neal Miller, who has adopted and developed Hull's theory of drive and reinforcement, takes account of the fact that acquired fears are especially resistant to extinction: "One might speculate that many socially acquired drives, such as guilt, pride, the desire for power, and the need for approval, are composed of a considerable element of fear" (1951, p. 467). With reference to functional autonomy his conclusion is (p. 469):

> When generalization, higher-order reinforcement, and shifts from one reinforcing agent to another are added to this possibility, it can be seen how difficult it is in complex human situations to determine whether or not a habit actually is functionally autonomous. . . . It can be seen that the theoretical and experimental work has a long way to go before it bridges completely the gap between the fundamental biological drives and the wonderfully complex web of socially learned motives that determine adult human behavior.

Miller's conclusion amounts to saying that no definite predictions of an individual's adult interests can be based at present on the need-primacy theory alone. Some predictions could be based on the principle of learning by reinforcement. If a person is rewarded for taking a little interest in some class of objects or some line of activity, his interest is likely to increase. The reward would have to appeal to him, and it would not necessarily be any of the primary reinforcements of the Hull theory. If a person undertakes a task, success in completing that task is sufficient reward for the moment, though he would not keep on undertaking similar tasks unless there was something about them that appealed to more than the bare success motive.

Experiments on the acquisition of new interests

Edward L. Thorndike made a very serious attempt to find out how to induce and strengthen new interests in human adults. His concern was with adult education and with the question whether adults could be sufficiently interested in a new course of study to apply themselves and learn it efficiently. He applied the "law of effect" or of reinforcement, using sometimes small money rewards for success in a novel task, but sometimes only verbal approval. He found that the desire to succeed in any given task could easily be aroused, but the interest in the task itself was less open to control (1935a, pp. 29-30):

> We have made experiments to discover whether the process of selection by satisfying after-effects applies to interests and attitudes as well as to knowledges and skills. . . . Will a person who is rewarded by desired praise whenever he feels and shows liking for a certain study tend to feel and show liking for it oftener . . . than before? The answer is *Yes*. Desires, emotions, attitudes and interests seem to be . . . strengthened by repetition and reward. . . . A fundamental principle for the control of interests is then: "To attach interest to any situation (any object, study, activity, etc.), cause the person in question to have the interest in response to the situation, and reward him therefor."

In a typical experiment on the changing of esthetic likes and dislikes by approval of good taste (Thorndike, 1935b, experiments 62 and 63), a large collection of Christmas cards was rated in advance by competent artistic judges. Some cards that were definitely good, and others that were definitely poor in taste, were sorted out for the experiment. There was a pretest, followed by an hour's training and then by a posttest equivalent to the pretest. Each test contained 10 good, 10 poor, and 20 mediocre cards; the training series was similar but much longer. The individual subjects were told: "This is an experiment in appreciation. You are to tell your likes and dislikes for a series of Christmas cards. You are to look" at a card and tell quickly whether you like it, dislike it, or neither like or dislike it. "In every case express your own personal feelings." In the pretest and posttest the experimenter made no comments, but in the training series *E* expressed approval whenever *O* definitely liked an artistically good card or definitely disliked a poor one. The subjects were given no instruction in artistic principles since the purpose was not to train their intellectual judgment but to see whether their personal likes or dislikes could be changed in the direction of artistic standards by approval given only when they spontaneously met those standards. High school students (twenty of them) showed poor taste in the pretest, liking only 50 percent of the superior cards but 69 percent of the inferior ones. Their taste was somewhat improved by the training, since in the posttest they liked 68 percent of the superior and only 52 percent of the inferior. The same experiment on twenty "educated adults aged 40 to 70," showed better initial taste but the same positive effect of the training:

> *Pretest:* liked 59 percent of the good, 28 percent of the poor
> *Posttest:* liked 69 percent of the good, 10 percent of the poor

Thorndike's conclusion from these and similar experiments: "a person can be taught new attitudes and tastes as surely, though not as easily, as he can be taught facts or skills. The basic principles of learning by repetition and reward seem to operate." Whether these subjects were permanently improved in their taste for Christmas cards, or lapsed for lack of the continued "primary reinforcement" of social approval, we do not know.

What Thorndike used for primary reinforcers in his many successful experiments were not the primary needs of the Hull theory and their reduction or satisfaction. He used success, social approval, and sometimes small money rewards. Money and social approval could perhaps be regarded as previously associated with frequent primary reinforcement of organic needs and as losing their reinforcing power unless occasionally supported by prompt reduction of some organic need, though this would seem very unlikely in the case of social approval. It would take a good deal of positive evidence, and not mere speculation, to make it seem probable that the reward value of social approval had to be supported by at least an occasional further reward of food or water or sex satisfaction or relief from some anxiety. In the case of success as a primary reward, we see in young children as well as adults such behavior as this: the child undertakes to do something, persists until he succeeds, and then shows satisfaction. Whatever the goal may be that the individual undertakes to reach, he gets reinforcement on reaching the goal without any further reward. In fact, that is the way that a large share of human skill and knowledge is acquired.

With regard to Hull's form of the need-primacy theory of motivation, we can say then that much can be predicted from learning and reinforcement, but very little from satisfaction of the primary organic needs. We cannot predict human learned abilities nor the variety of human motives and interests. For prediction of human behavior something more behavioral is necessary as a basis.

Actually, Hull did not intend to predict behavior from the organic needs, for he regarded need and drive as nondirective. The direction taken by behavior, and all the details of behavior except for the reflexes and some other unlearned S—R units, he assigned to H, i.e., to learned mechanisms. Behavior in this theory had no inherent drives and apparently no acquired drives, since the anticipations resulting from secondary reinforcement were anticipations of primary reinforcement (p. 113). One could learn to work for certain goals, but not because success in reaching a goal was intrinsically rewarding; rather, because of the anticipation of some primary reward.

Hull's need-reduction theory of primary reinforcement

Hull relied mostly on the diminution or cessation of a need to establish any S—R connection. Thorndike in formulating the law of effect had spoken of "satisfaction" as the internal state which "stamped in" a rewarded performance. Hull rejected "satisfaction" for two reasons, apparently. It seemed like a *subjective* state, and therefore unacceptable to a behaviorist. One had to find out *empirically* what would give satisfaction to an animal or man; there was no independent principle from which satisfactions could be inferred. Certain needs, however, and certain ways of reducing those needs, were biologically known and perfectly objective. Needs could be taken as the primary basis of motivation and need reduction as the primary reinforcement.

There was a serious problem, or pair of problems, which perhaps could be left to the physiologists. How shall the internal need for food be communicated to the behavior system and arouse a search for food? And when food has been eaten, how shall the reduction of the organic need be communicated to the behavior system so as to reinforce the successful performance?

Hull's much-emphasized "drive stimuli' afforded a reasonable answer to the first of these questions. The need for food can be communicated to the brain by stimuli originating in the stomach, familiar to us all as hunger pangs. We are similarly familiar with thirst stimuli, sex stimuli, and stimuli from fatigued muscles; and it is reasonable to assume such drive stimuli for all urgent organic needs. Hull regarded drive stimuli as necessary to make the theory work. These internal stimuli combined with stimuli from the environment could elicit a motor response; and if the response secured food, for instance, and so reduced the need, the response would become conditioned to the stated combination of stimuli, and the animal would be likely to make the same response when hungry again in a similar environment.

The second question, apparently not considered much, is equally crucial for the theory. How can a reduction of the organic need for food be signaled promptly to the brain so as to reinforce a successful instrumental act that has just been performed? The signal would have to be prompt in order to reinforce the right response in a rapid series of varied responses such as occurs in the puzzle box. The organic need for food is not reduced by food in the mouth or even by food swallowed into the stomach but only by food that has undergone digestion in the stomach and intestine and been absorbed through the intestinal wall into the blood and lymph. Digestion takes some time; starch and sugar have to be split into the simplest sugars such as glucose, protein has to be split into the amino acids, and fat has to be split into fatty acid and glycerine—all this before absorption into the blood and lymph. We should allow several minutes, at the very least, from the eating of food to the reduction of the need for food. If the signal of need reduction be supposed to come from the intestine, which of the intervening acts will get the reinforcement? Hull recognized this difficulty (1943, p. 99): "These considerations strongly suggest that the eating of food as such brings about learning through secondary reinforcement rather than through primary reinforcement." That is, food in the mouth is followed so regularly by need reduction as to become a secondary reinforcer, a token of later need reduction. The establishment of this secondary reinforcer, however, would be virtually impossible in view of the long time interval, as Hull himself indicated (1943, p. 94): "A receptor impulse will acquire the power of acting as a reinforcing agent if it occurs consistently and repeatedly within 20 seconds or so of a functionally potent rein-forcing state of affairs." He was thinking of rats in setting the time limit so low, but rats certainly receive some sort of reinforcement from food rewards. It is probably primary reinforcement; that is, food in the mouth is best regarded as a primary goal for a hungry man or animal (Guttman, 1953). The same can be said for water in the throat for a thirsty creature, though the delay is not so great before the water reaches the blood.

Need reduction is not handicapped by any long delay in the case of escape movements. A dog gets shocks from the floor, jumps over the wall, and is free from the shocks instantly (p. 69). Here there is no question of communication from the interior of the body to the brain. The signals for the onset and cessation of the need both come from the skin and in fact belong in the realm of behavior rather than in the realm of organic processes. The emergency be-havior is supported, to be sure, by the internal sympathicoadrenal system, but is primarily a matter of response to environmental stim-ulation and fits perfectly into the behavior-primacy theory of moti-vation.

Aside from the physiological improbability of primary behavioral reinforcement by the reduction of an organic need, there is a lack of close correlation between actual reinforcement and need reduc-tion. There are cases of need reduction not giving reinforcement, and cases of actual reinforcement without need reduction.

A hungry man entering a restaurant is assailed by a disagreeable odor which quickly reduces his need or at least his drive (appetite) but notably fails to strengthen the instrumental act of entering that restaurant when again in need of food. A similar case is sex desire reduced by something repulsive in the person desired. The opposite type of exceptions deserves fuller discussion.

Reinforcement without need reduction

The facts of secondary reinforcement belong here. A token or pregoal will serve for a while as reinforcement enough for the learning of an instrumental act, though it does not satisfy or reduce hunger. The sight of a restaurant where you have eaten a good meal may motivate you to save up enough money to dine there again.

The case of saccharin is striking. This very sweet but entirely unnutritious substance has definite reinforcement value. It serves as a sufficient reward for performance in the runway or in the Skinner box. We might speculate that its reward value is merely an example of secondary reinforcement because of its similarity in taste to sugar, which has acquired reward value by repeatedly reducing the need for food. If that were the explanation, saccharin should lose its reward value if given time after time without any support from primary reinforcement; but there is no sign of such extinction in rats, and many human beings use saccharin year in, year out, to have the reward value of the sweet taste without superfluous calories (Sheffield & Roby, 1950; Sheffield, Roby & Campbell, 1954). Reinforcement, according to these authors, is exerted not by need reduction but by the vigor and excitement of the consummatory response: "correct responses would become prepotent over others because they alone would be performed with the added boost of excitement from the anticipatory arousal of the consummatory responses" (1954, p. 354). This promising theory of learning was perhaps first suggested by Margaret Floy Washburn (1936). The drive toward a goal must be most intense when the goal is visibly just within reach so that the successful act which attains the goal is done with the strongest drive and therefore becomes more firmly associated with the drive than any of the unsuccessful attempts can be. This conception of reinforcement is certainly more promising, physiologically, than the theory based on need reduction.

The case of sugar is equally convincing. Sucrose, our common food sugar, admirably supplies the need for calories when that need exists but is eagerly eaten for dessert when the nutritive needs of the individual have already been amply met. This is true for rats as well as for human beings (Young, 1948). In fact, pure sugar solutions are readily accepted by many and perhaps all animals. Frings (1947) has tried them on many species of mammals, insects, and other animals, and he reports, "I know of no animal which will refuse sucrose solutions." We can hardly suppose that each individual animal has to learn by experience that sweet substances reduce the need for food—or that bitter substances are likely to be poisonous. The chemical senses have great survival value if they provide direct incentives for acceptance or rejection. Evolution has taken care of that.

P. T. Young and his coworkers have made many studies of the food preferences of rats. Sweet substances stand at the top of the preference scale, and strong solutions of sucrose are preferred to less strong. Learning can be based on sweet taste as the only reinforcement. Place a little cup of sugar solution in the middle of a small enclosure; give a rat a few preliminary sips to acquaint him with the incentive; next day place him in the starting box, open the door and time his approach to the cup; and give him one trial each succeeding day. The typical rat takes 70 seconds to cover the distance on the first day, but only 2 seconds after a few days. He is not motivated by a need for food or water, for he has all he wants to eat and drink in his home cage. He is motivated to get the sugar solution; if it is replaced by distilled water, his run starts to slow down (Young and Shuford, 1954, 1955).

Young does not doubt that the nutritive value of foods plays an important role in the long-term feeding habits of an animal, but he believes that the taste and "palatability" of substances have more to do with preference and primary reinforcement. According to his *hedonic theory*, "primary motivation lies in the affective processes," experienced by human beings as degrees of "delight and distress," and surely having some physiological basis (1955, pp. 193, 203). We shall quote a few sentences from his paper of 1949 (pp. 103, 108, 111):

> In the present paper the writer is basing a theory of food acceptance upon the assumption that contact between head receptors and a food object produces an immediate affective arousal. When a rat tastes and touches and smells a food there is an immediate liking or disliking . . . our work leads to the view that rats accept foods which they *like* (find enjoyable) . . . It is an immediate positive affective arousal (enjoyment of food) which leads to the organization of food-seeking . . . rather than the more remote and delayed relief of gastric hunger. . . . Some day, we believe, affective arousal will be described objectively in terms of brain dynamics and the underlying biochemical processes. For the present the assumption of affective processes within the rat appears to be the simplest hypothesis for interpreting the available data upon relative food acceptance.

Some progress is actually being made on the physiology of hedonic processes, or at least on the cerebral localization of such a process as acceptance. Certain results obtained by the physiological psychologists of McGill University (Olds & Milner, 1954; Olds, 1956, 1958) came with a shock of surprise. Never giving a food pellet as the reward for bar pressing in the Skinner box, they did give the rat a brief electric stimulus at a particular part of the brain and found that this stimulus was reinforcement enough to maintain the bar pressing. The electric stimulus did not elicit the bar pressing; it followed the bar pressing as a reward. The part of the brain concerned was the "limbic" region, lying well below the surface. An insulated bipolar silver electrode was implanted at some point of this region, with a flexible lead connected outside with a source of alternating current. The connections were such that when the rat pressed the bar he received the electrical "reward" at this point in the brain, the voltage being one or two volts and the duration a second or less. A rat will keep up a good rate of bar pressing for 3 hours or more, so long as he gets this purely cerebral reward regularly (or once every few pressings, according to Sidman *et al.*, 1955, who also report similar results from cats). If the current is discontinued, the bar pressing is quickly extinguished. This limited portion of the brain seems to have a function which we may call acceptance of the result of an act and motivation for repetition of that act. No doubt much more information on this cerebral function will be forthcoming. (See also Miller, 1957; Ziegler, 1957.)

Young's hedonic factor in motivation and Sheffield's excitement factor in learning (p. 120) do not conflict, though they are different. The hedonic factor is supposed to make an object attractive or repulsive to the organism. The excitement (or activation) factor is supposed to favor the learning of one rather than another act directed toward an attractive object. Both factors lie outside the scheme of organic needs and primary reinforcement by need reduction. The hedonic factor would give behavior directions independent of organic needs, or at least not closely dependent on the needs. The excitement factor would select instrumental acts that were done with present high activation rather than with subsequent need reduction.

One advantage of the hedonic theory is that it provides for positive as well as negative motives, for appetites as well as aversions. Instead of regarding every drive as a tendency to escape from some need or tension or distress, it provides for goals that are sought for their positive value. The escape theory has been effectively criticized by Maslow (1955): "Practically all historical and contemporary theories of motivation unite in regarding needs . . . as annoying . . . something to get rid of." This view is understandable in animal psychology and in psychoanalysis which is concerned with sick people. But, for example, "if one has in general enjoyed food and if good food is now available, . . . appetite . . . is welcomed instead of dreaded." Maslow goes on to cite constructive aims that have similar positive valence.

The hedonic theory of motivation—seeking pleasure and avoiding pain—is a theory of very long standing. It was abandoned under behavioristic influence because of the subjectivity of pleasure and pain. With the now-dawning hope of some physiological basis, it is being revived. Hebb (1949), rejecting the need-reduction theory and seeking an alternative theory of motivation, points out that sustained *interest* in an activity requires some familiarity along with some novelty. Interest and motivation "are likely to be preoccupied by whatever is new in the combination of familiar events." "Many adult sports of course depend for their pleasure on the presence of some danger. . . . Similarly, problem-solving involves frustration, and many of the activities that are sources of pleasure actually depend on problem-solving. . . . Those sensory conditions are called pleasant . . . which contribute to the current development in the cerebrum, or which consist of the decline of a sensory process that interferes with development" (pp. 230-232). Hebb is clearly going beyond the intrinsic pleasantness of certain tastes, odors, and other sensations; he is seeking for a general theory of what makes activities pleasurable, interesting, and attractive.

In their investigation of the achievement motive (our p. 94) McClelland and his coworkers (1953) "decided to base motives on affective arousal, following Young's lead." They agreed largely with Hebb as to the causes of pleasure in activity. A child likes a toy if it behaves as he expects, yet not perfectly; if it always does exactly what he expects, he loses interest; but if it deviates too much from any expectation he is able to form, he acquires a dislike for it. A strong achievement motive is revealed by objective achievement *plus* evidence of joy at success and sorrow at failure; i.e., the "affective arousal" must be present in the motivation.

The hedonic theory of motivation can be combined with or incorporate into itself the need-primacy theory. It is when one needs food that eating is most enjoyable, when one needs water that a drink is most enjoyable. Some likes depend on needs, whereas others are independent of organic needs—for example, the liking for sweet tastes, odors, or tones. The combined theory has more predictive power than either theory alone. From the organic need for food you can predict that people will seek food and eat periodically; adding the hedonic theory you can do more in the way of predicting what they will eat.

The joy of achievement is certainly an important sort of pleasure and an important fact in the psychology of motivation. You engage in an activity and work toward a goal when you have some expectation of success in overcoming the obstacles and going through to the goal. To utilize this line of facts in predicting behavior you would have to know also what goals are likely to be chosen. The choice of goals would depend on the opportunities offered by the environment and also on the organism's capacities for taking advantage of those opportunities. In short: to predict human interests you have to know human capacities for dealing with the environment.

A BEHAVIOR-PRIMACY THEORY OF MOTIVATION

The main contention of this book—seemingly a perfectly obvious and innocent view—is that behavior consists in active give and take between the organism and the objective environment. This interrelationship may be called "dealing with the environment." To deal with the environment the organism must do more than merely receive stimuli and make muscular responses; it must use the stimuli as indicators of objects in space, and use the muscles for movements adapted to the objects; that is exactly what the organism does. A dog's ears receive a certain shrill tone; he turns his head in the direction of the source of the tone which is issuing from the lips of his master; immediately the dog's leg muscles begin a series of contractions which carry him over the ground to his master. Evidently the dog has done much more than receive an auditory stimulus and make a series of muscular contractions. The whole performance is geared to the objective environment—to the master as a known object, to the location of the master, to the more-or-less level ground and its unevenness, and to other demands of the situation.

In later chapters we try to show that the organism perceives and learns such objective facts as the size, shape, location and other characteristics of objects. Here we are making the claim that this direction of receptive and motor activity toward the environment is the fundamental tendency of animal and human behavior and that it is the all-pervasive primary motivation of behavior. That is what we mean by a behavior-primacy theory of motivation.

What we mean by calling the objective tendency of behavior "all-pervasive" can be brought out by comparing playful incidental activities, such as doodling, with any well-developed purposive course of action. Purposive behavior has a definite goal or end, with means adopted to reach the goal. Incidental playful behavior is not aimed at any remote goal, but it deals with the immediate environment and produces objective results. It is not random muscular activity, for it uses stimuli as indicators of objects such as the paper and pencil, and it produces immediate results which are geared to the objects. From his careful observation of the behavior of caged chimpanzees, Nissen (1954, pp. 313ff.) has reached the following conclusions:

> Our rather onesided preoccupation with the insistent demands placed on the organism to maintain those conditions which are essential for survival tends to obscure the fact that a large if not a major share of the day's activities do not, in any obvious way, contribute to the basic necessities of life. This is true of man and animal alike. . . . Observation of animals and people in "free," and even in highly "structured" situations indicates that much time . . . is taken up by brief, self-contained, often repetitive acts which are their own reason, which are autonomously motivated, and which are not to be interpreted as being small contributions to some remote, critically important aim.

This pervasive tendency to keep in touch with the environment and to be doing something with objects is clearly present when the "object" is another person. The conversation may not be aimed at any particular conclusion, but there is a constant give and take between the two people. The "goal" is simply to be engaged in social behavior.

Instead of saying that all this incidental behavior is secondarily motivated by the organic needs or other great motives, we insist that the incidental behavior represents the primary drive to deal with the environment and that large-scale purposive activities are based on this primary drive. In order to motivate food seeking, the hunger drive has to break into the on-going behavior and give it a special direction. Young boys often resist this intrusion of mealtime into their absorbing play.

Prediction from the behavior-primacy theory

Our complaint regarding the need-primacy theory, as represented either by Freud (p. 102) or by Hull (p. 109), was that it failed to predict the motives and interests of human adults or the play interests of children. Even the play of the higher animals could not be predicted from the organic needs alone. To obtain greater predictability we should have to add something closer to behavior. What we propose is that the behavioral *capacities* of any species must be added. From the bird's capacity to fly we can predict that the bird will fly and apparently like to fly or at least prefer flying to walking. If the bird is the domestic fowl *(gallus domesticus)* with slight capacity for flight, or for swimming, it will be content to walk on the ground for the most part, but if it is a pigeon or a duck, it will take to the air or to the water. Can we say that any such locomotion is merely mechanism, having no intrinsic motivation but driven by some extrinsic need? What seems to be true, rather, is that the young creature makes considerable progress in mastering its mode of locomotion before it begins to use this skill in hunting for food. Obviously, we cannot credit the young creature with so much foresight that it will exercise its flying capacity in order to be ready to fly in search of food later. The flying is done for its own sake at first, and only later in the service of organic needs. If we can say that any behavioral capacity has its own intrinsic motivation, our theory has much greater power of prediction.

A capacity-primacy theory of motivation has been proposed more than once. Does not the capacity for muscular activity demand muscular exercise, and the capacity for seeing demand the ocular activities of looking and focusing? The drive to actualize one's capacities (Goldstein, 1940) would accordingly be an important source of a great variety of human interests. This theory could be improved, so it seems to us, if we recognize that each capacity is a capacity for dealing in some way with the environment. Seeing is not simply getting visual stimuli; it quickly develops into a seeing of objects in space. Muscular activity quickly develops into a reaching for objects or locomotion toward them. Even the human capacity for recall memory and ideational thinking develops into a high-level method of dealing with the environment in the solution of problems and in planning for the future. The capacities develop, not as purely intraorganic processes, but in the "life of relation" with the environment. The motivation to deal with the environment is primary and includes the various ways of doing so which are provided by the capacities.

There is an interesting parallelism between the theory presented here and the "holistic" theory of Kurt Goldstein (1939, 1947). The organism, he insists, necessarily functions as a whole and its motivation is unitary. Its "basic drive, the only drive by which the life of the organism is determined" is the "tendency to actualize its nature, to actualize 'itself' . . . the drive of self-actualization." But since the organism has various potentialities or capacities, self-actualization includes a variety of activities which actualize its capacities. "We can say, an organism is governed by the tendency to actualize, as much as possible, its individual capacities, its 'nature' in the world" (1939, pp. 196-198). What the present theory says is that the inclusive drive is the tendency to deal with the environment, and that the capacities are capacities for dealing with the environment in various ways. Actualizing a capacity, accordingly, amounts to learning how to deal with some aspect of the environment. Goldstein seems to imply that the actualization of any capacity is strongly ego-involved, whereas we believe that O's interest can be objective and concentrated on the materials dealt with and the activity of dealing with them.

From the human child's vocal and linguistic capacities we can predict a good deal of playful behavior. Mere exercise of the vocal muscles would probably have little reward value to the child, but by combining the activity of mouth and larynx with a blast of air from the lungs he produces a variety of audible sounds which evidently are rewarding, for he produces them over and over with no extrinsic motivation. He engages in vocal give and take with favored friends and gradually learns more definite ways of communicating with them vocally. On occasion he communicates his need for food, but he acquires his speaking vocabulary in other ways for the most part. Of the hundreds of words that the child picks up before the age of three, very few are concerned with bodily needs. Most of them designate persons, animals and things that interest him or activities in which he participates. Vocalization and speech begin as autonomous play activities rather than mechanisms driven by the necessities of life.

Combination of organic need and the behavioral tendency

We are not pretending that the organic needs are derived from the tendency to deal with the environment. The organic needs are autonomous. But the behavior that is enlisted in the service of an organic need has its own rewards apart from the reduction of a need. The act of sucking appears to have rewards since not only does the infant demand more of it than is necessary (Jersild, 1954), but older people take pleasure in sucking cider through a straw or smoke through a cigarette. Adults have a sense of mastery in raising water from a cistern by a hand suction pump. In fact, they are exerting some control over nature by taking an active part in a physical process (usually without understanding it). Again, when the baby arrives at the biting and chewing stage, he devotes himself assiduously to these ways of mastering objects; and adults are known to chew gum vigorously long after they have extracted all its taste. The point is that behavior which ministers to an organic need is still behavior dealing with the environment and has its own immediate behavioral achievements, consummations, and reinforcements.

Some such immediate external rewards are well known, but they are usually regarded as secondary and not primary reinforcements. They may be both at once, for there is no reason why a stimulus that has some primary reward value should not also become a token or signal of important reinforcement to follow. The click of the pellet-delivering machine in the Skinner box is such a token and becomes a secondary reinforcement for bar pressing, as demonstrated by the extinction test (p. 111). Now even a naive rat that has never obtained food pellets by pressing the bar and obtains none during the experiment will press the bar once in a while, i.e., at a relatively slow rate called the "operant level," so manifesting his general activity level or exploratory tendency (p. 83). These foodless bar pressings are usually supposed to be getting no reinforcement. But they are sure to obtain some sensory feedback from the feel and movement of the bar. The feedback is increased if the apparatus delivers a buzz or a dim light each time the bar is pressed; and the operant level is then raised considerably. The buzz or light must be accepted as a *primary reinforcement* of the bar pressing, since neither of them has ever been followed by food in the individual animal's experience; neither of them has had any chance to become a secondary reinforcer (Kish, 1955).

Another form of apparatus (Figure 8) offers the animal a choice between a platform that moves and clicks when stepped on and another platform that gives much less sensory feedback; the platform that moves and clicks is greatly preferred. The experimenters, Kish & Antonitis (1956), reach this conclusion:

> Apparently, this stimulation, coming as a direct result of a response to the platform, was acting in a reinforcing manner and strengthening the behavior directed toward the region of the platform. . . . At the time the experiment was planned, there appeared to be no *a priori* reason for considering this class of stimuli, which have usually been considered neutral, as reinforcing. The results indicate, however, that the sensory consequences of a particular behavioral act may, under the proper conditions, reinforce that behavioral act.

This type of reinforcement, though quite out of line with Hull's insistence on need reduction as the primary reinforcement, did not escape his keen incidental observation. We have mentioned (p. 89) his 1934 experiment on speed of locomotion toward a goal. He equipped a long straight runway with a series of light hanging doors of cardboard which the rat pushed open one after another as he ran toward the food box. He noticed that these doors "seemed not to deter the animals in the least; indeed, observation even suggests that the rat, at least, may have a definite liking for such contacts."

Significance of these examples of primary behavioral motives and reinforcements

A critic might be inclined to question the importance of the examples just given. He might say that such sporadic and superficial interests in environmental happenings and results accomplished have no bearing on the practical work or deep motives of human beings. These, he might insist, depend on the basic needs of the organism, or of the psyche. We offer the counterclaim that our examples have a double significance.

1. They serve as crucial experiments, disproving the claim of the need-primacy theory to universality. No one denies that organic needs are factors in motivation, but the need-primacy theory asserts

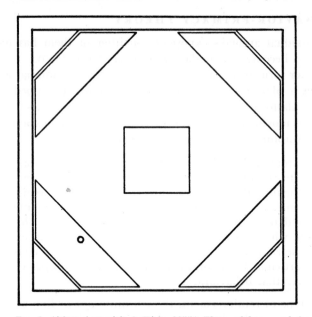

Fig. 8. (After Antonitis & Kish, 1955.) Floor of box used for testing incentives with mice as subjects. The box is 15 inches square inside, with corners screened off and a platform in front of each corner. The platforms are $\frac{1}{4}$ inch thick with three of them nailed to the floor while the fourth, a hinged recording platform, was raised slightly so that when a mouse stepped on it, it would press down on a microswitch. A record was obtained of the number of times the mouse stepped on this platform and of the total time spent there during the test period of 15 or 25 minutes. The mouse was placed on the central square and left free to move about during the test period. The corner adjacent to the recording platform could be used for visual presentation of an incentive, such as another mouse, the other three corners being blank. The question was whether the subject would spend a disproportionate time near the incentive.

In the experiment of Kish & Antonitis (1956) all four corners were blank. The mouse, however, could produce a click of the microswitch by stepping on the recording platform and could produce other noises from the recording apparatus while on the platform; he also produced a slight movement of the platform by stepping on it. These feedback or retroflex stimuli were sufficient incentive to induce the mouse to spend a disproportionate time (40 percent) on the recording platform. The box was completely dark and contained no food or water, the mice having had all they would eat or drink in their home cages just before the test. "The hypothesis that stimulation arising from platform depression was reinforcing the behavior directed toward the platform was found adequate to account for the results of the experiment."

that all primary motives are organic needs or at least basic needs of the organism. The exploratory drive may perhaps be accepted as a basic need of the organism, a need to find out what is present in the environment. But the cases cited go beyond the exploratory drive. Exploration of a cage reveals a platform in each corner, for example, but the platform that makes a noise when stepped on is stepped on most often afterwards. This preference goes beyond the goal of discovery or of novelty, for the response to the preferred object is repeated time after time. Exploration reveals things that are "good" or "bad" or indifferent. The things that are good then receive continued positive response, the bad things are avoided, and the indifferent things disregarded. But among the good things are not only such as appeal to the organic needs but also things that can be made to move or make a noise or emit a light or odor. A child on a visit, if given the run of the house, will locate not only the pantry and bathroom but also a surprising number of things that are interesting because he can do something with them. You cannot expect him to keep busy most of the time attending to his organic needs.

2. These examples point the way to a host of objects and activities which are attractive and challenging to human children or adults and which provide their own direct reinforcements. We have mentioned the child's vocalization and acquisition of speech, and we might have added his learning to read and the reinforcements he obtains when he recognizes the words and still more when he gets the story from the printed pages. We mentioned in the preceding chapter (p. 97) the skills and teamwork of adult games with their direct rewards for successful action.

Human beings have capacities for dealing with the environment in many ways that go far beyond simple manipulation and locomotion, and the culture provides opportunities for the use of these capacities. It provides tools and materials to work with, models to imitate, praise or dispraise for the results accomplished. What is the motivation of a child trying to hammer in a nail? Is it to win applause and avoid criticism? Or is not his primary goal to drive the nail straight without banging his fingers, and is not his primary reinforcer the well-driven nail? It would seem that the person with capacity for construction is motivated to construct and obtains his most direct reinforcement from the result achieved, so that the engineer who has designed and put up a fine bridge is proud of the bridge itself rather than of the money and applause received. The same can be said of any inventor; there may be large economic rewards in the offing, but he likes the material he is dealing with and his primary reward is the successful solution of a problem.

Musical capacity shows itself early, given a favorable environment. The potential musician is attracted to the piano and does much more than just pound on the keys. He does not need an adult to stand over him continually to tell him when he is striking the right notes; he can tell himself from the sound. His reinforcements come from the musical effects.

A child who makes a convincing drawing of a face, even of some particular person's face, wins applause. But where does he look while drawing? Not at the source of admiration but at his subject and at his drawing. The applause encourages him to keep on and make other drawings, but while he is engaged in any one drawing his motivation and reinforcements are concentrated right there.

The source of human interests

We have been attempting to suggest that the distinctively human interests in construction, invention, and art—and also in mathematics, science, and governmental and industrial administration—have their source, not in the organic needs, but in the human capacity to deal with the environment. They arise from the combination of human capacity with the opportunities afforded by the natural and cultural environment. The evidence for this conclusion comes partly from the way these interests emerge and develop in childhood, and partly from the marked *absorption* of the scientist or artist in the task that occupies him at any time. Mathematicians, inventors, novelists, composers are reported as doing their most creative work in periods, short or prolonged, of intense absorption in the present task. Any intrusion of extraneous economic or social motives would be distracting and defeating. Even ego-involvement retires before the intensity of task-involvement. And there is this also to be said of the ego-involvement of the creative worker. He may have high and strong personal aspirations, but they are concentrated on his line of work. He aspires to become, not an all-round good fellow, but a great painter, or composer, or chemist. His ego-interest is tied to his work and when he is engaged in some piece of work, his ego-interest has to be pushed aside for complete concentration on his task.

Predictive success of the behavior-primacy theory. If the need-primacy theory of motivation could predict the emergence of distinctively human interests, the achievement would be greatly to its credit, because it would predict so much from so little. But need primacy does not predict any greater variety of motives for humans than for animals, since the needs are the same for both. Of course, the need-primacy would have the right to assume human capacities for dealing with the environment; it could then predict the development in human societies of elaborate ways of dealing with the environment to meet the organic needs. But there would be no corresponding development of motives and interests. All the elaborate methods of meeting the needs would belong in the sphere of mechanism, not of drive.

The behavior-primacy theory regards the tendency to deal with the environment as a primary drive, and indeed as *the* primary drive in behavior. The various capacities for dealing with the environment afford outlets for the general behavior drive and give it different forms—given the necessary environmental opportunities. So the manifold human interests are predictable from the combination. It is no great credit to the behavior-primacy theory to predict so much, since the base from which it predicts is so broad. Can it be accused of assuming all that it wishes to predict? Not quite; it assumes the general drive to deal with the environment, the capacities for dealing with the environment in various ways, and the opportunities for such dealing afforded by the environment. What it predicts is that the interaction of a capacity with the environment will generate a specific interest. It predicts that an individual who engages in a task will, unless distracted, find himself absorbed in that task, interested in it and motivated to bring it to completion.

Perhaps the behavior-primacy theory, even though no great intellectual achievement, will have practical value in education, where the need-primacy theory certainly appears to be useless. Even in psychotherapy, it may be, the person who is disturbed by conflict of deep personal motives could be led to take a normal interest in some way of dealing with the environment for which he has the capacity and the opportunity. This practice has been followed on a common-sense basis even by therapists who espouse a need-primacy theory inconsistent with the practice.

The Control of Muscular Movement

To be of any value in behavior, all the psychological functions must exert some control over the muscles, directly or indirectly, and thus produce changes in the environment or in the organism's relations to the environment. Apart from the "implicit" movements that may be present in thinking, remembering, or perceiving, there must eventually be an overt movement that produces an objective result. Our knowledge of the dynamics of behavior would be a story without an ending unless we could meet this difficult challenge.

Motor abilities

Our problem would be simple if we could follow the lead of a "faculty psychology." We could then say that the other departments or functions, such as thinking and wishing, had simply to turn over their findings to the motor department and trust that department to take appropriate steps. But is there a single unitary motor ability? The modern attack on the problem of abilities is by way of tests, correlations, and factor analysis. Because of the practical importance of motor skill in industry, athletics, and the military specialties, psychologists have been conducting a great deal of this type of investigation, and they have found no single, comprehensive motor ability. The best athletes, for example, are not necessarily especially clever in hand work. There seem to be several fairly independent motor abilities. One group of ability factors has to do with the strength, speed, and coordination of large movements of the trunk and limbs, while another group has to do with dexterity. A distinction is even made between hand-and-arm dexterity and finger dexterity. Then there are factors definitely related to environmental space: eye-hand coordination, such as in aiming, and judgment of lengths and distances. Other abilities, not distinctively motor, have an important part in motor performances, such as the ability to maintain a comprehensive grasp of a complex and changing situation, the ability to visualize and keep track of what is presently out of sight, and carefulness. Individuals differ in all these respects—partly no doubt by heredity, though training will improve any of the motor skills. We shall not attempt to make much use of this line of psychological investigation. Here are a few of the important contributors to the field—Seashore, 1942; Guilford & Lacey, 1947; Anastasi & Foley, 1949; Vernon, 1951.

MUSCLE ACTION

Our approach to muscular action is by way of examining what a muscle does and asking how such action can produce the intended environmental results.

What a muscle can do

A muscle can only contract and relax, contraction being its active state and relaxation its inactive state. A skeletal muscle, being attached at one end to one bone and at the other end to another bone, pulls these two bones toward each other when it contracts and exerts no pull when it relaxes. A muscle can pull, but it cannot push. If the biceps muscle by contracting has pulled up the forearm (flexed the elbow joint), relaxation of the biceps allows the forearm to sink by its own weight, but to make the forearm extend forcibly an extensor muscle of the elbow—the triceps—must contract. Wherever there is a muscle which pulls in one direction, there is an antagonist which pulls in the opposite direction.

The contraction of a muscle can vary in force and duration and the rate of its build-up and relaxation. To see how these effects are possible we must consider the internal structure of the muscle. It is made up of little longitudinal muscle fibers, insulated from each other, each being innervated by an efferent nerve fiber which brings excitatory nerve impulses from a nerve center in the spinal cord or brain stem. These lower motor nerve centers receive stimulation from higher centers in the brain as well as from the sensory nerves. Thus the force of a muscular contraction is subject to quite a number of physiological influences.

A muscle fiber, like a nerve fiber, operates on the all-or-none principle. It gives all it has at the moment if it gives any response at all. Each pulse of its activity utilizes and consumes all the immediately available energy. How can the muscle as a whole, then, give responses of graduated strength according to the demands made upon it? There are two ways: (1) by variation of the number of muscle fibers in action—a weak contraction employing only a few fibers at a time and a strong contraction many fibers—and (2) by variation of the number of pulses per second elicited from the single fiber. As soon as a fiber has consumed all its immediately available energy, it starts to accumulate fresh energy and in a very short time is ready to respond again if it receives a strong enough stimulus from its nerve center. A muscle takes no initiative—a skeletal or striped muscle at least—for its fibers act only as they receive stimulation from the nerve centers.

Motor coordination

Seldom is a single muscle called into action; almost every movement enlists a team of muscles; and the more forcible the required movement, the larger the cooperating team. The hand muscles suffice for lifting a light weight, but the arm and shoulder muscles and even those of the back and legs get into action if the weight is moderately or extremely heavy. The muscles team up differently for different movements, as when you swing the arms together or alternately. Motor coordination is flexible enough to meet a great variety of demands, though the individual who makes the demands knows very little about the muscles and their way of acting.

Besides the muscles that directly execute a certain movement, others are brought into play and provide a suitable posture and base of support. If you double up your fist by flexing the fingers you will probably stiffen the wrist as well. You can indeed move the wrist freely while keeping the fingers flexed, but if the fist "means business," the wrist muscles cooperate. Even muscles remote from the intended movement are likely to participate slightly, as shown by the "muscle currents" (electrical changes of potential) that can be observed by aid of lead-off electrodes and amplifiers. Certain leg muscles contract slightly in arm movements and vice versa, and the masseter muscle of the jaw contracts when the hand lifts a weight. "The true unity of activity must be, not the flexing or extending of a particular muscle or limb, but an adjustmental design in which many regions of the organism participate" (Davis, 1942, 1943).

Sequential team work

It is easy to believe that a nerve can call a group of muscles into action simultaneously. What is harder to understand is how the muscles can be made to execute a movement that requires a perfectly timed series of contractions of different muscles. A familiar but highly complicated example is the movement of walking, with its smooth succession of muscular contractions and relaxations in the rump, thigh, and lower leg. You could safely defy anyone to describe this sequence from observation of his own walking. Elaborate recording methods show that the several muscles participate in regular order (Eberhart, 1951) but how the nerve centers initiate such a combination and keep it running in due order—that we do not know.

Coordination of antagonistic muscles

If the antagonistic pair of muscles at a certain joint, such as the elbow, contract simultaneously, they hold the joint fixed at any angle. The size of the angle depends on the balance of the two opposing forces. Such fixed positions are often needed. Another demand made on the antagonists is the execution of a *steady movement* from one position to another, as in carrying something that must not be spilled. Relaxation of one of the opposing muscles must keep pace with the contraction of the other. In proportion as the agonist increases its contraction, the antagonist relaxes. This principle of reciprocal inhibition was demonstrated by Sherrington (1906, 1954) in physiological experiments on the spinal cord and on the motor area of the cerebral cortex. The steady movement can be made at various speeds.

Quite different is the *ballistic movement*. One muscle exerts a quick pull on a limb and immediately relaxes, letting the limb continue by momentum. The muscle throws the limb. The limb in turn may throw a ball, wield a hammer, kick a football, or execute a great variety of quick movements, more or less forcible since the momentary impulsion from the muscle can vary in strength. Reciprocal inhibition is an important factor in ballistic movements; the antagonist by relaxing completely leaves the field clear for momentum.

Braking

The ballistic movement has to be stopped somewhere. It may be stopped by an external object, like the table on which you pound your fist. Often, however, it is stopped by the antagonist muscle which, though relaxing at the start of the ballistic movement, contracts in time to resist the movement when it has gone far enough. If an immediate return movement is made, the burst of activity in the antagonist that stops the down movement (for example) is strong enough to throw the arm back up to its initial position. The double movement in such cases is a single combined act or behavior segment, not two acts (Katz & Künnipas, 1946). When a series of oscillating movements is studied by aid of muscle currents, the burst of activity in each muscle is seen to be timed so as to bring one movement to a stop and start the reverse movement. This interesting, if very technical, line of experimentation is due largely to Stetson & Bouman (1935) and to Stetson's pupils at Oberlin, of whom Hartson, Sperry, Hibbard, and Hudgins published a series of related papers (*J genl Ps*, 1939, 20, pp. 263-338).

A long swing such as a golf drive or tennis serve is likely to begin as a ballistic movement propelled by one muscle, but it picks up additional strength from other muscles as it proceeds (Slater-Hammel, 1948, 1949).

Sensory feedback

This feedback is the same as what we called the retroflex (p. 33). A movement produces fresh stimuli which may arouse additional movements and may also affect the movement in progress. In relation to the control of movement very important feedback comes from kinesthesis; sight and hearing are also important. Kinesthesis supplies information (not always consciously perceptible) on the bodily posture and initial position of the limb that is about to execute a movement and regarding the movement as it progresses, its speed, extent, and any obstruction encountered. Without this kinesthetic information *O* may be able to execute familiar movements but hardly with his normal smoothness and precision.

The kinesthetic nerve fibers from the trunk and limbs pass up the dorsal columns of the spinal cord on their way to the brain. This is a sensory, not a motor pathway; and yet if it is severed, motor disturbances result. In man the dorsal columns may degenerate as an aftereffect of syphilis, the resulting condition being called *tabes dorsalis* or locomotor ataxia. The patient feels insecure in his movements except when he can see where his limbs are and what they are doing. He sways and staggers in walking and throws his legs out too far (lack of braking). If he stumbles in the dark, he is likely to lose his balance (lack of feedback). He cannot find the automobile pedals without looking, nor bring his forefinger neatly to the tip of his nose while his eyes are closed. These and similar manifestations of "sensory ataxia" are well known to the neurologists (Holmes, 1947; Nielson, 1951; Walshe, 1952; Wechsler, 1952).

Anyone standing on an ataxiameter with heels and toes together is likely to show some body sway, especially when his eyes are closed (Edwards, 1946). Hand movements aimed at a visible target, of course, can be executed slowly and carefully throughout their extent, but they may save time by starting as ballistic movements, with braking and slight corrections as they near the target. Visual feedback here plays an important role, affording much more precise information than is possible with kinesthesis alone. Auditory feedback plays a similar role for the singer, who often has to make slight corrective adjustments of the laryngeal muscles before hitting the desired pitch exactly.

MOTOR RESPONSES TO RAW STIMULI
AND TO THE INDICATED ENVIRONMENT

Some movements are direct responses to stimuli, but the great majority of movements are determined by what the stimuli mean as cues of objects and the location and characteristics of objects.

Good examples of direct sensorimotor action are obtained with auditory stimuli of different intensities. If a sound is very loud and sudden, like that of a pistol shot close at hand, there is a quick reflex effect, the "startle pattern" (Landis & Hunt, 1939). By the muscle-current technique, weak reflex contractions are found to occur in response to sounds of moderate and even of very weak intensity (Davis, 1935, 1950).

Of natural exploratory movements some, like sniffing and tasting, are direct responses to stimuli. The prompt turning of the head and eyes toward the source of a sound is perhaps to be classed with the direct responses, though the stimuli are the binaural time and intensity differences. The eye-turning response to the location of a light on the retina is direct; i.e., looking in the direction of an object is determined by the raw stimulus. But focusing for the distance of the object is determined by one or more of the cues of environmental distance.

Reactions to environmental space

Such innate escape movements as pulling the hand away from a painful stimulus or spitting out a bitter substance are direct responses to stimuli, but learned avoidance responses involve movement away from certain places or objects. Approach responses usually involve movement toward certain parts of the environment. Stimuli received from an object and its surroundings serve as cues of its location; often, too, there are cues of the positive or negative "valence" or present value of the object to the individual. The native basis for a great deal of behavior is the tendency to approach an object that manifests positive valence. The individual may have to learn how to approach, but he starts with a tendency to approach food when hungry or anything desired.

Reaching for an object is a characteristic form of human approach which goes through an interesting development in the first year of postnatal life. If the child is tested periodically with a small wooden cube placed on the table before him, at three months he begins to show some interest in the object by looking at it, as he does more definitely month by month. At four to five months this eye approach is joined by a rudimentary hand approach, the hand approaching at first by a wide sweep but later in a more and more direct line. With the successful approach is combined a grasping act, crude at first but refined later into a movement of thumb opposing the first two fingers. This really remarkable development of "eye-hand coordination" is the result of a combination of maturation and learning. We see the child becoming more and more responsive to the location and size of an object; he is using visual stimuli as better and better cues of objective facts—as better and better controls in his job of dealing with the environment (Halverson, 1943; Gesell, 1952).

Reactions to environmental time

Another dimension to which motor behavior becomes adjusted is the passage of time. Even a dog, as in one of Pavlov's conditioning experiments, becomes adjusted to a regular delay of 60 seconds between the preliminary signal and the presentation of food (Woodworth & Schlosberg, 1954, p. 565). If a human adult is asked to hold an electric switch closed for 15 seconds (without counting), he may not feel very sure of himself but still he is not altogether stumped. He is likely to make it 10 seconds on the first trial, with large individual differences and with considerable improvement in subsequent trials (Eson & Kafka, 1952; Falk & Bindra, 1954). Psychologists have not discovered what cues are utilized in judging the passage of time. They may be partly physiological, but somehow we are able to adjust our behavior to this dimension of environmental processes.

Reactions to environmental forces

One of the indubitable realities of our world is the pull of gravity. The baby begins at birth or even before birth to respond to this force. He does so in increasingly masterful ways: by clinging for support, by raising the head, by sitting, standing, walking, and running, as well as by lifting objects, dropping them on the floor, throwing them. There are stimuli exerted by gravity on the pressure sense of the skin and on the vestibular receptors of the inner ear; and undoubtedly there are direct responses to these stimuli. Kinesthesis also comes into play, and the child utilizes some of these stimuli as cues of many important characteristics of objects such as weight, inertia, friction, and elasticity. These "mechanical" properties of objects, along with the spatial properties, have an essential role in all manipulatory behavior.

In controlling his own movements O aims at some external result rather than at any particular muscular activity. He is likely to vary the muscular coordination while still reaching the same goal or achieving the same result. He can make movements covering the same extent, approximately, though with different muscles, as when he tries to draw two lines of the same length, one with finger-and-hand movement alone, the other with a full arm movement. He can make movements of the same duration, approximately, though of different extents and force, as in keeping time in a musical performance. But if you ask him to make movements of the same force though against different loads, he cannot do so; instead, he lifts the heavier weight with more force and keeps the two movements about equal in duration. Muscular force seems to him rather subjective and he needs some external result to aim at (Woodworth, 1899; Morgan, 1917; Buytendijk, 1947).

What comes between stimulus and response?

Any action dealing with the environment is a muscular response to sensory stimuli—certainly! But if you ask a person what he is doing, he will say nothing about sensory stimuli and muscle contractions. He will say, "I see a desirable object over there and I am going to get it." He speaks of an object and an intended objective result. *There is a chain of events* which starts with the object sending stimuli to O's receptors and ends for the moment with his arrival at the object. So described, the chain has a fatal gap in it between the sensory stimulus and the muscular response. We must bridge this gap to link the objective stimulating situation with the objective change produced by O's intervention. The objective situation and result are not present in the raw stimuli and muscle contractions; yet they are present in O's behavior and in his verbal report of what goes on in him. They are present in him as a link intervening between S and R. If you insist that this intervening link is a "construct" which you cannot observe directly, well and good!

As a construct, it is needed to show how behavior can possibly deal with the environment. It has the same status as "situation-and-goal set" for which some evidence was offered in Chapter 2.

This "central link" between S and R is more than a mere link. It has the function of organizing the stimulus input and the muscular output. It brings them into effective relations with the environment. It decodes the sensory cues into objective terms and codes the objective goal into muscular actions. The various visual and auditory cues of the third dimension are entirely dissimilar as raw stimuli, but they yield the same information regarding environmental space. The various muscular actions that result in approach to a certain goal are dissimilar except as means of reaching the same place in the environment. Thus we have an input of a large number of alternative cues and an output of a large number of alternative muscular actions. Separate linkage of each raw stimulus with each muscular action would require an enormous network of separate connections in the brain. But the environmental meaning of all these alternative stimuli and muscular responses—an object over there to be reached—greatly simplifies the linkage.

Just to illustrate the economy introduced by the objective meaning intervening between S and R, consider any letter of the alphabet, Z, for example. You are given the letter and asked to respond with the same letter. Consider the alternative possibilities on the input (sensory) side and on the output (motor) side:

Input	*Output*
Spoken letter heard	Speaking the letter
Printed letter seen	Typing the letter
Handwritten letter seen	Writing the letter
Morse signal heard, — — . .	Tapping the letter in Morse code

You may have learned to respond in any of these four ways to any-one of these four stimuli. When you hear the Morse code signal, you can respond by saying "zee," or by typing the letter, or by writing it, or by tapping it in Morse; and you can respond in any of these four ways to the spoken or printed or handwritten letter. In all, then you have formed sixteen S—R habits for every letter, and all these S—R units must be separate and unrelated, since the stimuli are all dissimilar and the responses also. But perhaps some simplification is possible. Is not Z after all the same letter, however received and however transmitted? If so, what you have learned is not sixteen direct S—R connections, but fewer less direct connections, with the "real letter Z" intervening between S and R. If "real Z" seems rather nebulous, we can say that it is the last letter of the alphabet and the initial letter of certain words, no matter how it is presented in the input or executed in the output. Similar economy on a grand scale is achieved by the spatial significance intervening between sensory cues of space and motor responses in space.

Motor skill is often better described as perceptual-motor skill, since the motor responses are governed by stimuli which have to be taken as cues with definite meanings. Quite often the operator has to be alert to a number of alternative signals in order to make the assigned response to each signal as it is received. The signals, of course, must be easily distinguished and the responses also. Further, the pairing of signals and their respective responses should be "natural" or easy to grasp. Suppose, in a laboratory experiment, a horizontal row of eight small lights on a vertical panel is the signal assembly, and a similar row of eight push buttons on the table is the response assembly. The most "natural" pairing, as anyone would agree, is between the corresponding positions in the two lines. Certainly very little work would be necessary to connect the left-end S with the left-end R, or the right-end S and R. In the middle of the rows the exact positions would be less distinct, and counting or some similar "processing" would be necessary before each S would get its correct R. If the S row were numbered from left to right, but the R row from right to left, so that the left-end S must be given the right-end R, etc., the task would certainly be more difficult, but not so difficult as one with haphazard pairing. So we could predict and so the results showed in an experiment (Morin & Grant, 1955). The haphazard pairs were gradually learned, but the direct or "natural" pairing remained much easier and quicker to use. Was it easier because of much use previously in daily life? More probably, the spatial correspondence of S and R was a favorable condition for quick work because less "processing" or transformation was required between S and R.

In a similar but more complex setup (Garvey & Knowles, 1954) there was a square assembly of 100 stimulus lights and a square assembly of 100 push buttons. It was O's task to push the button in the same position (same row and same column) as the given stimulus. O saw the stimulus assembly directly over the response assembly, so that the spatial correspondence of S and R was very good, but his response to the stimuli in the interior of the square was much slower than to those around the edges. Around the edges he could see the stimulus positions directly, but in the interior he had to count row and column to be sure and accurate—extra "processing" between S and R was required. In one form of the experiment the S and R assemblies were combined, each push button being directly underneath its S light so that the response was practically a reaching for the stimulus. This arrangement "naturally" gave the quickest reactions, and with little difference between the edges and the interior of the square.

S—R compatibility is a term introduced by Fitts and his co-workers (1953, 1954) to cover such facts as we have been considering. We have seen that the pairing of an assembly of stimuli with an assembly of responses may be such as to yield quick and accurate work or slow work with many errors. The quicker and more accurate the work, the greater is the inferred degree of S—R compatibility. If we were dealing only with a single stimulus and its assigned response, the S—R connection could be quickly learned and the question of compatibility would not arise. Hull's "habit strength" ($_sH_R$) would take care of the matter. But when we have several stimuli and assigned responses, their pairing is so important that something besides separate habit strengths must be involved. The amount of transformation or "processing" needed to convert the S system into the required R system determines the speed and accuracy of the work. Important contributors to this line of thought were Mitchell & Vince (1951) and Hick (1952).

Synchronizing in skilled work and play

What is meant by this important characteristic of skill can be observed in the playing of an orchestra, the players all keeping time with the conductor's baton and so with each other. We might suppose that each stroke of the baton was a stimulus to which the violinist responded by a movement of his bow, the flutist and trumpeter by blowing into their instruments, the drummer by striking his drum. But since their individual reaction times would certainly differ, the music would be unbearably ragged. No—what happens is quite different. The players come in on the beat—not a fifth of a second, more or less, after it. At the beginning of a piece, the conductor indicates the tempo by a few introductory strokes so that the players can time their movements to synchronize with his. From the conductor's movements and from the music sheets before them they have *advance information* of what they are to do and exactly when.

Oral reading provides another familiar example. The skilled reader pronounces the series of words smoothly and with meaningful expression. He could not do so if he saw only one word at a time and had to speak each word as soon as he saw it. Instead, he keeps his eyes moving along the page a few words ahead of his speaking voice—this "eye-voice span" being quite flexible in length —and so he has time to "process" the words before saying them. That is, he gets the connected meaning and is prepared to give it vocal expression. Perhaps it is stretching the point to say he is "synchronizing," but at least he is making use of "advance information" much as the orchestra does. The eye-voice span can be measured on simultaneous photographic records of the reader's eye movements and voice vibrations. Or a dictaphone record of the voice can be combined with a photographic record of the eye movements (Tiffin & Fairbanks, 1937; Buswell, 1920).

Advance information—stimuli received some little time before a response movement is required—is obtained in many ways. You see ahead on the page or on the road and are ready a moment later to pronounce the seen words or negotiate the sharp curve. You hear footsteps approaching your door and are ready to answer the doorbell. In innumerable other cases the distance receptors provide advance signals of danger or opportunity. When you see an object move, you can often see in what direction it is moving, and sometimes you can see how fast it is moving and even whether it is gaining or losing speed; therefore, you have the data for anticipating where the object will be a few seconds later. It is remarkable how well an expert baseball fielder can "judge" a fly ball; from the first part of its trajectory as it leaves the bat he knows where it is going to land; he runs to the spot and is ready to catch the ball. When you have learned an oft-repeated sequence of events, the early events in the sequence inform you of what to expect.

Advance information is utilized in various ways. It enables you to get set for what is coming and for what you have to do. Often it enables you to make preparatory movements. Often it gives you

time to "process" the raw stimuli and make sense out of them before you have to deal with them actively. It gives the brain time
to organize the stimuli and the muscular responses.

In man-machine combinations, so common in modern industry
and military operations, success depends on the man's being able
to forecast what is about to occur so that he can intervene at the
right times with the appropriate movements of control. If the machine goes repeatedly through the same sequence of events, the man
learns the sequence—becomes conditioned to the timing, as Pavlov's
dog became conditioned to a uniform time interval between the
conditioned and the unconditioned stimulus—and controls the machine in a routine manner. A task that keeps the operator very
much "on his toes" is that of gun pointing. The soldier must keep
the gun trained on a moving target such as an enemy plane. The
target moves along a more or less predictable course, from moment
to moment, and the gunner tries to keep pace with the target, instead of alternately falling behind and catching up. When the target
motion is too complex to be accurately anticipated, O adopts a sort
of averaging procedure which keeps his aim fairly close to the target, though mostly somewhat off. How much error he will tolerate
(without feeling obligated to do better) depends on the difficulty of
the task as well as on the individual operator (Helson, 1949).

In the air, a gunner trying to keep his gun pointed on another
airplane, presumably an attacker, is faced with complicating conditions which cannot easily be duplicated on the ground. The rudi-
ments of tracking, however, can be learned with laboratory
apparatus. O sits before a gray screen in which is a horizontal slot
6 inches long and 1 inch wide, with two markers, one moving right
and left along the upper edge of the slot, the other along the lower
edge. The upper marker may be the target and be moved by the
machine, while the lower marker is O's aim indicator or "aimer"
which he controls by turning a crank. His task is to keep the aimer
exactly under the target. If the target moves at uniform speed in
one direction, its course is easily predictable and readily followed.
If it has a regular swinging motion (a simple harmonic motion, ac-
celerating, decelerating, reversing direction, and so on), O soon
learns this stimulus pattern and adjusts his response pattern to
match. If the S pattern is more complex, it can be learned after
many repetitions, but not perfectly; and O's score of time on target

may never surpass 80 percent. Still O builds up a good deal of usable "advance information."

What has just been described is called "pursuit tracking." Another setup calls for "compensatory tracking." The target motion is impressed on O's marker, and he must compensate by bringing the marker back to center, which is indicated by the now-stationary upper marker. If to start with he has the two markers in line, and the lower one is mechanically displaced an inch to the left, he compensates by moving it an inch to the right, so getting it back on target. This would be easy, except that while he is correcting the first displacement, some additional movement is being impressed on his marker. In fact, the impressed motion is continuous and is continually being combined with his own efforts to compensate. He has to analyze the motion of his marker into its two elements— the target motion and his own corrective movements—in order to get the advance information required for synchronizing his tracking with the target's course. This difficult task can be mastered to a large extent, but compensatory tracking remains less accurate than pursuit tracking because the advance information is less directly obtained (Poulton, 1952 a, b; Chernikoff et al, 1955; Hartman & Fitts, 1955; Conklin, 1957). The sensory data received in the compensatory form of tracking require more "processing" before being fit for the control of movement; more brain work has to be done between S and R.

The target tracker and the oral reader obtain their advance information in different ways. Compare the two performers at the moment when they are initiating the definitive movement of aiming at the target or of pronouncing a certain word. The tracker cannot actually see ahead of the present position of the target, but he can tell from the direction and speed of its motion where it will be a fraction of a second later, so that if he now initiates a movement to that spot he will get there at the same instant as the target. The reader can see a few words ahead of the word to be pronounced and so discover the sentence pattern and the role of this present word; so he can initiate a speech movement of appropriate emphasis and inflection. Notice, for example, the different emphasis to be given to the word "ahead" in these two sentences:

"The eyes keep ahead of the voice which follows."
"The eyes keep ahead and the voice follows."

SKILL IN MANIPULATION

If an individual has to go through the same mechanical operation time after time, we can assume that he will improve his technique gradually, and we might expect him to approach perfection in respect to economy of muscular exertion and perhaps also in respect to speed. Economy of exertion is its own reward; whether speedy work brings any sufficient reward depends on external incentives in part, though many persons will try for speed, especially if any competition is involved. Neither eagerness nor laziness, however, will guarantee a high level of speed or economy in a complex manual operation. There are too many chances for superfluous movements, awkward and strained postures, and failure to make full use of both hands. Either the worker himself, or some one for him, has got to study the operation, break it down into a sequence of steps, and notice exactly what has to be accomplished at each step and how the steps can be smoothly combined.

Pioneers in this "motion study" of manual operations in industry were the Gilbreths, Frank and Lillian (1911, 1916). Their methods continue to be used and developed down to the present day. They identified a number of part operations which occurred in various combinations in various total operations. They called such a part operation a "therblig," a name obtained by reversing the sounds of their own family name. A simple assembly job might consist of four therbligs: moving the empty hand to a bin, picking up a piece there, carrying this piece back to the working area, placing it on top of a piece already there; this cycle being repeated time after time.

A list of therbligs (as given by Barnes, 1949, one of the chief contributors to motion study) will repay examination:

> Search
> Select
> Grasp
> Transport (move hand) empty
> Transport loaded
> Hold
> Release load
> Position (place in position)
> Preposition (place in a ready position)

Inspect
Assemble
Disassemble
Use, as a tool
Unavoidable delay
Avoidable delay
Plan
Rest from fatigue

Evidently the therbligs are not defined as specific hand movements. They are steps in an operation, *subgoals* on the way to a certain result. If the intended result is a nail driven in, the right-hand therbligs would be: transport empty hand to the tool box, search for hammer, select the tool, grasp it, transport it, preposition it by getting it right side up, position it exactly with respect to the nail, use it. Meanwhile the left hand would go through a similar series in getting the nail into position. Each hand would be subject to some "avoidable delay," until the operator had learned to work with both hands simultaneously. Much delay can be avoided if the work is so arranged that both hands can perform identical tasks by simultaneous and bilaterally symmetrical movements (Barnes & Mundel, 1939). Time is lost when a hand has to turn a sharp corner or go through a zigzag series of movements, but the work bench can be so arranged as to avoid such sources of delay. If a tool is always kept in a certain location and position, the time consumed in "search" and "preposition" is reduced greatly. The whole workroom may need rearrangement to eliminate excessive walking back and forth during an operation. By such means the motion-study expert has often cut down the time per cycle by 40 to 50 percent, nearly or quite doubling the output per hour, and this is accomplished not by speeding up the operator's movements, but by simplifying them and making them more comfortable. The workers are apt to be suspicious of a "time study" aimed primarily at increased output, unless it has been preceded by a "motion study" which simplifies the movements and improves the equipment and layout. A closely related problem is that of incentives.

The ingenious methods invented by the motion-study investigators are described from a psychological point of view by Poffenberger (1942) and from the practitioner's point of view very fully by Anne G. Shaw (1952). The method known as a "process chart" aims to present the investigator with a picture of the whole sequence of movements. "Every detail of a process is more or less affected by every other detail; therefore the entire process must be presented in such form that it can be visualized all at once." This quotation from Frank Gilbreth serves to correct any impression that the "therbligs" are to be regarded as separate units which can be inserted or omitted without any change in the rest of the operation. Gillespie (1947) has shown that any part movement is affected by its place in the sequence. "It can easily be proved that the speed of a body member movement is conditioned not only by what happens immediately before the movement but, also, by what comes after the movement." When bending to lift a heavy weight, a slower motion is employed than when bending to lift a light weight. And Simon & Smader (1955), by using an electronic timer which records the time taken by each therblig in a series, found that "transport loaded" was slowed down when the following "position" had to meet an extra demand for accuracy. This unitary character of a whole operation does not prove by any means that the analysis into therbligs is worthless. As we said previously, a therblig is not a movement: it is a result accomplished. To map out the immediate results to be accomplished will often be useful in the early stages of practice. You practice the entire operation in a series of parts, and you find the parts beginning to combine, as in the well-known "word habits" of typing and telegraphy.

Perhaps the most minute analysis of a manual skill has been made by Cox (1934). His purpose was to show—and he fully succeeded in so showing—that intelligent analysis of the mechanical and motor requirements of an operation could be made by a beginner, with help from a teacher, and that such analysis of one operation would transfer to other more or less similar operations. The operation studied was the assembly of an electric-light bulb holder. The eighteen separate pieces are first presented lying on the table, and O is asked to examine them and find out how they go together. He never succeeds in working out the complete operation without engaging in some manipulation, though he observes some characteristics of the parts and some relations between one part and another which make it possible for them to fit together. Even after he has discovered two parts that will fit, he has still to discover the motions required to put them together. He has to discover (a) what motions the parts must make and (b) what finger movements will impress the desired motions on the parts. An example: inserting a machine screw into its metal socket. The screw being picked up by the fingers of the right hand and the block by the fingers of the left hand, the next step is the accurate prepositioning of the two. They are brought together so that the screw is perpendicular to the surface of the block, with its tip at the entrance of the socket. The screw must then be pushed forward until resistance is encountered and then given a clockwise turn. But even after these necessary motions of the pieces are understood, the hand movements are not yet known kinesthetically. The learner has still to become acquainted with the resistance which is a signal to turn the screw, with the "bite" which means that the threads are properly engaged, and with the "jam" which means that the screw is not being held upright. It is in actual manipulation that he learns these signals or cues and how to respond to them. Usually the mechanics of the problem and the finger movement are mastered together, more or less, what is seen by inspection being a guide to manipulation, and what is learned by manipulation imparting additional realism to the mechanical problem and solution.

LOCOMOTION AND FINDING ONE'S WAY, ESPECIALLY IN THE AIR

It would evidently take us too far afield to consider this problem broadly enough to include what seem to human beings the almost preternatural achievements of homing pigeons, migratory birds, the salmon and the eel, the bee and the grasshopper. Investigators in biology are doing away with some of the old mystery and wild theories (a "magnetic sense," etc.) though much is still far from understood. We shall simply add a few references (Fraenkel & Gunn, 1940; Claparède, 1943; Matthews, 1951; Viaud, 1953).

Our discussion will be confined to human locomotion and mostly to the problems of the aviator. Psychologists have had some "look-in" on his problems in both World Wars. In the first war they helped to explode the plausible belief that the semicircular canals could enable the flyer to keep his bearings. In the second war they had an opportunity to make job analyses not only for the pilot but also for the navigator and other crew members. Much of this work was published in a long series of Research Reports of the Army Air Forces Aviation Psychology Program under the general

supervision of John C. Flanagan. We shall make use of several of
these Reports by different groups of investigators.

Aiming at a goal

We have already mentioned what is apparently a native tendency
to approach a desirable object. O tends to look at such an object
and to move in the direction in which he is looking. This method
of directing locomotion toward an object is fully effective only
when there is no force acting across the line of advance and de-
flecting the actual advance. In swimming across a current the swimmer's forward motion is combined (vector addition) with the
motion of the water. If he simply keeps heading toward his goal,
he continually veers downstream and must continually readjust his
aim, until finally he has to aim almost upstream. In rowing, the
same is true or in steering a motor boat. In order to maintain a
straight cross-current course, you have to "crab" into the current—
head a little upstream from your goal. How much? It depends on
the speed of the current combined with the speed of the boat. A
sure way of crabbing correctly is to sight past the goal at another
stationary object in the same line, and to keep these two objects
always in line. When you do this you have evidently progressed far
beyond the primitive tendency to go where you are looking.

The airplane pilot, too, has to correct for drift caused by a side
wind. He has to aim his plane more or less upwind. In steering for
a landing spot he has to distinguish between the aim of the airplane's nose and the real direction of his glide, since the airplane
must be kept level. Gibson (1947) and Youtz & Ericksen (in Miller,
1947) say that the pilot should keep the landing spot in the "center
of visual expansion"—though not all pilots are aware of using this
cue (Figure 9).

To understand the meaning and validity of this cue, approach a
picture on the wall, keeping your eyes fixed on a central point at
eye height so that your eyes can move straight toward this point. As
you get nearer, your view of the picture expands. Parts of the picture to the right of the central point move out to the right in your
view, parts on the left move farther to the left, parts above move
upward and parts below downward in your view. The point at
which you are looking is thus the center of expansion of the view—
provided your eyes are actually approaching this point. It is a sim-

ple matter of geometry. If the surface before your eyes is horizontal instead of vertical, something more than geometry is involved, for what is higher in your visual field appears (and is) farther away on the ground. Still it is true that the point you are directly approaching is the "center of visual expansion." What is beyond this point appears to be moving farther away, and what is this side appears to be opening out toward you.

Probably the pilot does not need this cue when he starts his downward glide from an altitude of 500 feet. The expert, knowing his altitude, speed, angle of descent, and distance from his landing

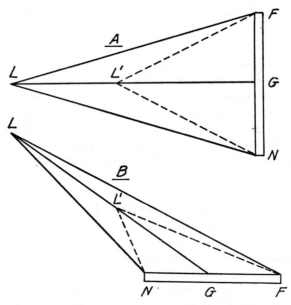

Fig. 9, *A* and *B*. *A* shows the pilot's visuosensory field or retinal image as he guides his airplane from a location L in the air directly toward a spot G on the landing strip NF, N being the near and F the far end of the strip. *B* shows his perceptual, environmental view of the strip. As the airplane moves along the line LG, his visuosensory field includes the vertical strip NGF, with the near end below G and the far end above G; and the strip expands, F moving up and N down in the visuosensory field. However, the pilot does not perceive his retinal image; he perceives the level landing strip, with N and F its near and far ends. So long as he is moving straight toward G, the forward half of the strip expands forward and the rear half expands backward, with G the center of expansion.

spot can aim pretty accurately from a mile away. He may still need
the cue just described for making a fine readjustment of his aim as
he nears the ground. He also uses visual cues of depth in leveling
off at a height of only a few feet above ground. At the same time
he must allow for drift due to any cross wind, and he must be on
the watch for other planes that may be landing or taking off. He
cannot permit his eyes to remain fixated on his proposed landing
spot, but he looks back at that spot from moment to moment.

Turning

In order to reach the destination, changes of direction may be
required en route. The automobile driver can only turn right and
left in the horizontal plane. Besides his steering wheel he needs
only one other major control, that of speed forward and back, provided by the accelerator, brake, and gear shift. The airplane pilot is
not limited to the horizontal plane. He steers in three-dimensional
space. He can turn his airplane around three axes. The airplane's
movements and turns are not much like those of an erect man; they
are more like those of a bird or fish or man swimming. Turns are
made about three axes:

Right and left around the vertical, dorsoventral axis
Nose up and down about the lateral, right-left axis
Tilt, bank, roll about the longitudinal head-tail axis

To turn right or left the pilot pushes on the right or left rudder
pedal; to nose up or down he pulls back or pushes forward on the
stick; and to bank he moves the stick to the right or left. The
stick and rudder manipulations have to be coordinated, since the
airplane must be banked to the left in making a left turn. In fact,
all three steering controls and the power throttle as well are coordinated in many maneuvers, as in the elementary task of making
a 90-degree turn without losing or gaining altitude.

The mechanics of these controls in a man-designed locomotor is a
matter of engineering knowledge. The airplane rudder, like that of
a boat, imparts in effect a right or left curvature to the longitudinal
axis as a whole so that the forward thrust of the motors against the
air resistance drives the airplane along this curve. The aerodynamics
are basically the same for the ailerons and elevator as for the rudder. No doubt the same principles of steering apply to the flight

of a bird and the swim of a fish and even to a man's swimming maneuvers. He turns right and left, ducks under and comes up from below, rolls from breast to side or back. Necessarily, he exerts these controls by muscular action, but exactly which muscles act in a given maneuver is unknown except by careful psychophysiological investigation.

An important point in the psychology of steering, whether steering an airplane or an automobile or while swimming, is the big difference between the control movements and the resulting craft movements. In the motor car there is no similarity between the driver's foot pressure on the brake pedal and the slowing down of the car—or between his foot pressure on the adjacent pedal and the acceleration of the car! You may see a beginner excitedly pull back on his steering wheel when he suddenly must stop the car—a more natural movement, certainly. You may see the beginner, with his hands along the bottom of the steering wheel, move them to the right when he means to steer to the right—another natural movement—though he soon learns to steer to the right by a clockwise turn of the wheel, no matter where he has hold of his wheel. His actions, we say, soon become "automatic," which means that he no longer thinks of his hands and feet but only of the car and the road.

As compared with the driver on a well-marked road, a pilot in the empty air is much more "on his own." He has to understand the mechanics and aerodynamics of flight in order to cope with emergencies. Yet he, too, comes to "think" in terms of his spatial environment with its altitude, wind drift, air speed, track made good over the ground, landmarks, present location over the ground, distance and direction to his destination.

Though there is no great difficulty in learning to make any control movement to produce any desired effect on the action of an airplane or of any machine, some S—R connections are more "natural" than others—more in line with everyday habit and with the spatial relations. It is natural to raise your control lever when you would produce an upward movement of anything, to make a control movement to the left when you could produce a leftward result, etc. Some such compatibilities are easily predicted from common experience, but others have to be discovered by experiment. The designer of a machine is apt to overlook such psychological factors and make his machine unnecessarily awkward for the human operator to master. This line of psychological study made some progress during World War II, as recorded by Fitts and his associates in 1947, and has been followed up since (Fitts *et al.*, 1953, 1954, and other experimenters; comprehensive treatments by Mc-Farland, 1953, and by Orlansky, 1948; also much relevant British work published largely in the *Q.J. exp.Ps*).

The pilot senses the behavior of his airplane, as the motorist senses the behavior of his car and engine (its laboring, coasting, skidding), but the pilot has a greater variety of behavior to sense and a greater variety of important cues to utilize. A good pilot has a "feel of the ship," a sensation of swaying to one side or the other as the airplane slips or skids, a sense of "sustentation" or lift as it noses upward, a looseness of control and a "shudder" premonitory of a stall. Besides such tactual and kinesthetic cues, the sight of the level or tilted wings and of the nose above or below the visible horizon are cues of the airplane's "attitude," and the hissing of the air is an auditory cue of speed (Youtz & Ericksen, 1947).

GEOGRAPHICAL CUES IN AERIAL NAVIGATION

Any human adult, if asked how he finds his way to a goal, will offer a common-sense answer. He will say that he sees or somehow knows the location of a goal and that he approaches it by walking, sailing, driving, or flying according to the available means of loco-motion. He cannot offer much information on the stimuli he uses or on how they manage to direct his movements. In driving a car he makes good use of traveled roads with their signs and maps. These symbols would not help him if he failed to get their spatial meaning. And the spatial meaning would not help unless it could generate appropriate muscular action on the steering wheel. The meaning of the road sign and the controlled behavior of the car are both in environmental terms. The stimuli are decoded in spatial terms, and the spatial terms are coded into muscular terms. The driver has learned a cue-spatial code and a spatial-muscular code.

How does the airplane pilot manage to make cross-country flights without getting lost? Sometimes he does get lost. With no help from road signs or even trails marked out in the air, his job is much more complicated than that of the motorist. Just because it is difficult, the cues and control movements and their interrelations stand out more clearly than in simpler forms of locomotion—a good reason for the psychologist's taking a special interest in the aviator's job. In a large ship, such as a bomber, the pilot in command is assisted by a crew, its most important members for our purposes being the navigator, radar observer, and radio operator, who obtain and decode the necessary geographical cues. The functions of the gunner, bombardier, and flight engineer we shall leave aside.

PLANNING THE COURSE

Before the start the proposed route is plotted on the navigator's map. Usable landmarks are located on the map and their appearance studied in aerial photographs. Air speed is prescribed, allowance is made for the expected winds, and time of arrival at the destination and at a few intermediate points is estimated. An airplane traveling from a known starting point at a certain speed in a certain direction for a certain time would reach its destination when intended. But such "dead reckoning" cannot be depended on altogether, especially because the force and direction of the wind may not be as expected; the drift and ground speed may therefore be greater or less than predicted. Besides, the heading adopted depends on the magnetic compass which requires correction from place to place. Consequently, it is up to the navigator from time to time to determine the momentary geographical location of the airplane (Carter, 1947).

LANDMARKS AND MAPS

On a clear day it should be easy for the navigator to identify a landmark which he has studied in an aerial photograph. So we might assume, but there are difficulties. He may not be getting the same view of the landmark; a town or hill presents a different appearance when viewed from a different angle. Several hills or towns may look alike unless characteristic details have been noted in advance.

The landmark must be identified on the navigator's map. A map differs radically from a view of the landscape. The map has no perspective or foreshortening; one square mile is just as large as any other on the map, whereas in the landscape view the distant areas are much smaller than the near ones. "Up" on a map is usually north, but "up" in the landscape is the direction in which the observer is looking. Even the motorist may find it difficult to translate directions on the map into directions along the road. The aerial navigator has become expert in translating map into view and visa versa, but coding and decoding are involved.

Unless the airplane passes almost directly over a landmark, the navigator has a further problem in determining his present location, i.e., in navigator's lingo, in making his "fix." When a recognized landmark lies in a certain direction ("bearing") and at a well-estimated distance ("range"), the location of the airplane is fixed. Or, if the bearings of two known landmarks can be measured at approximately the same time (one, say, lying NW and the other NE) the present location is given by the intersection of two straight lines drawn on the map.

Navigation over invisible territory

At night or above the clouds when terrestrial landmarks cannot be sighted, "celestial navigation" is still possible by aid of the sun or certain stars. The navigator's octant along with his clock and astronomical tables enables him to determine his present latitude and longitude. By making two such fixes at a known time interval while the airplane is flying straight at a known air speed, the navigator can plot the actual course over the ground, compare it with the intended course, and so compute the drift to be corrected. He feeds these data to the pilot.

In friendly territory well supplied with radio stations, the radio operator can supply fixes by taking the simultaneous bearings of two stations. When flying entirely by instruments with no direct visual cues from the ground, the pilot with his assistants "must use and interpret a new set of cues in order to know where he is going and what is happening to his airplane. The only source of these new cues is his instrument panel," with its compasses, rate-of-turn indicator, clock and artificial horizon. He has to integrate all these cues (or their meanings) into a "complete picture" (Ericksen in Miller, 1947).

Radar re-established visual contact with the ground even from above the clouds. It gave a view of the landscape, though the radar picture differed considerably from a direct view and called for interpretation of a new system of cues. Only a trained radar observer could make much sense out of them. The radar set emitted high-frequency waves which were reflected back from objects to the radar scope. "Returns on the scope differ in brightness, size and shape. Water gives practically no return. Islands . . . appear as bright areas against a dark background. Built-up areas . . . appear as bright returns against a less bright background. . . . Mountain ranges appear as long bright areas. . . . Towns, islands, rivers, lakes, etc. retain something of their shape, but details are usually lost or distorted" (Cook, 1947).

The cues utilized by the pilot of a large airplane were in large measure fed into him verbally by the navigator and other crew specialists, with another coding and decoding involved. After these men had learned their separate duties, they had to learn to cooperate as members of a harmonious team under the command of the pilot. He had to have confidence in them and they had to have confidence in him and in each other. Personality factors were important; sometimes a navigator who rated high in his specialty did not function successfully in the team (Crawford *et al.*, 1947).

Tests for crew candidates

The primary assignment of the aviation psychologists in the Army Air Forces was the development of objective tests for prediction and evaluation of success. One group of psychologists worked with paper-and-pencil tests, sifting, standardizing, validating, and trying by factor analysis to get to the fundamental abilities involved (Guilford & Lacey, 1947). Another group designed and tried out apparatus tests for perceptual-motor skill (Melton, 1947). These two and still other groups were drawn into the search for efficient methods of *training* the recruits, and their findings on the qualifications of a successful aviation instructor are not without significance for other teachers. Pilots with excellent service records were not necessarily good instructors. Some could not take a personal interest in the all-round progress of their student pilots. Some were impatient and sarcastic and inclined to "ride the controls," i.e., take over without giving the student a chance to correct his own errors. Some were unable to analyze and explain the student's errors (Galt & Grier, in Miller, 1947).

As to the success of the tests, it was considerable without being complete by any means. Miller sums up in these words (1947, p. 356): "Flying is a complex task requiring many different abilities.

The fact that the best printed tests . . . were found to predict flying ability . . . confirms the observation that perception, visualization of spatial relationships, knowledge of mechanical principles, and motivation are important factors in learning to fly. The fact that the addition of apparatus tests to this battery improved its ability to predict, suggests that motor skill and ability to perform a complex paced task are also important factors." But, he adds, we still need more knowledge of "the general structure of human perceptual, motor and intellectual abilities."

CHAPTER 7

Perceiving the Spatial Environment

The main thesis of this chapter should be rather obvious. Since the organism has to deal with the objective environment, some sort of adjustment to the environment is necessary, and this adjustment must precede the motor response and guide it. Since the environment varies from time to time and from place to place, the adjustment has to be flexible. It is exploratory and tentative until an adequate reception is obtained of the objective situation. The stimuli received do much more than trigger off motor responses, for the response must be preadjusted to the situation revealed by the whole combination of stimuli (Allport, 1955; Bartley, 1958).

What we find is a system of sensitive receptors with accessory motor apparatus suited to obtain optimum selective reception. The auditory receptors of the inner ear are served by the motor apparatus of the external ear, as is best shown when the pinna is mobile. The dog's first response to a sound consists of ear and head movements suited to secure optimum reception and locate the source of the sound. Without doing anything to the environment, this first response *prepares* the organism for effective action, i.e., for dealing with something more specific than a bare sound. The eye also has much accessory apparatus serving the photosensitive cells of the retina and making it possible for the organism to locate a visible object in distance and direction as well as to get a clear picture of the object in its surroundings. Accessory to the olfactory receptors are sniffing movements and head movements which maximize the stimulus and may lead to location and recognition of the odorous substance. Accessory to the skin receptors are, of course, the movements of handling and feeling; accessory to the kinesthetic receptors are such exploratory movements as "hefting"; and accessory to the gustatory receptors are the tongue and jaw movements of tasting, preliminary to the practical response of accepting or spewing out what is in the mouth. Perhaps we should not call this motor apparatus "accessory" as if it were of minor importance; it plays a very important role in enabling the organism to utilize its receptors for establishing contact with the objective situation.

OBJECTIVITY OF PERCEPTIONS AND INTENTIONS

In the preceding chapter (pp. 140-145) the assertion has been made and defended that, though some movements are direct responses to raw stimuli, the great majority are responses to the objective meaning of the stimuli. Stimuli come to serve as signs or *cues* of objects in the environment, of their size and shape, distance and direction, and of other characteristics including their valence and present interest to the organism. The stimuli must be "processed" before the motor response is made; the cues must be "decoded" into their objective meanings. Moreover, O's desire and intention to approach a certain object must be coded into terms of muscle action and coordination. The stimuli received are something altogether different from objects in space, and O's movements in the environment are something altogether different from muscular contractions. Yet O's movements in the environment correspond closely with the objective facts. An object of positive valence lies before O in a certain direction and at a certain distance, and his motor response is an approach movement in that direction and adjusted to the distance.

The "processing" of stimuli into objective meanings and of objective intentions into muscular coordinations might conceivably consist simply in the establishment of numerous specific associations between the receptors and the muscles, both having projection centers in the cerebral cortex, where the connections could be formed. One difficulty with this conception is the enormous number of connections that would be required—as in a telephone system consisting entirely of direct connections between every subscriber and every other one, each stimulus being connected with each response that it can elicit (p. 143). We should find it very difficult to pin ourselves down to this conception. If one should say, "When my friend comes in sight, I respond to this stimulus by approaching him," he would be breaking the rules of this game by surreptitiously assuming recognition of the person and perception of his location; the S–R connection would really be far from direct. The stimuli received from an object vary with its distance and direction, the light falling on it and other conditions, and the approach movements vary with conditions. Some more flexible system than one made up of fixed S–R connections would do better justice to actual behavior.

The objects we deal with in the environment are not usually isolated. One may be beside another, above or below it, nearer or farther away. One may be going toward or away from another. In responding to objects we take account of these spatial relations. From a common-sense point of view, there seems to be no difficulty here; we *see* one object beside another and respond accordingly. But the theory of *direct* S–R connections has no room for seeing of this sort, i.e., for perceiving objects in spatial relations.

Perception of the environment, an intervening process between S and R

We said that the theory of direct S–R connections was conceivable, but whether it can be carried through is very doubtful even in the case of animals. We found good evidence of exploratory behavior in animals (pp. 79ff), and in the present chapter we have mentioned movements connected with the sense organs which serve to provide good reception and often to locate an object in direction and distance before the animal starts to approach it. He uses the available cues to get in touch with the environment receptively before responding to it in a practical way. Though the coverage of the animal kingdom in regard to space perception is of course incomplete, there is good experimental evidence that monkeys, dogs, and rats perceive the distance and direction of objects. See, for example, page 301.

The human child's early progress in the use of his eyes has been carefully studied by Gesell and his colleagues at the Yale Institute of Child Development (Gesell *et al.*, 1949). Within the first few weeks after birth the baby is apt to stare at "some capacious distant target—a window, a ceiling, a curtain." At four weeks he seems to attend to an object that is brought within a few inches of his eyes; at twelve weeks he "fixates definitely on small objects of interest at distances ranging from one to three feet or more"; at sixteen weeks, "as he looks at an object of interest on the table top he immobilizes his eyes; presently he activates his arms and legs, but especially his arms, thus indicating that some day he will appropriate the object with hands, as well as eyes . . . ocular prehension, a forerunner of manual prehension." The baby thus builds up some acquaintance with objects in space before he is able to reach them with his hands or by creeping. His progress in eye-hand coordination was sketched in the preceding chapter (p. 141).

If an older child or adult is set before a scene of any kind and asked what he sees, he will almost certainly report seen objects, not stimuli of light. Thus he provides good evidence of the reality of perception. If we consider perception as an intervening variable (p. 3) filling a gap between stimulus and motor response, we must add that it is far from being an abstract "construct." To a large extent it is observable and reportable by human subjects whose reports are in substantial agreement to the effect that they perceive objects in spatial relations and that these perceived facts furnish practical guidance in behavior.

Objects not stimuli. The great difference between stimuli and objects can be disregarded in some parts of psychology, but it is of fundamental importance in the study of perception. The object is often some distance away while any stimulus is located right on some sense organ, such as the retina of the eye or the cochlea of the inner ear. How can we possibly see distant *objects?* The ancient Greek scientists saw the problem but offered no satisfactory solution. It seemed to some of them, since attentive looking at an object is an activity rather than a passive affair, that the observer might be sending out some sort of rays which were reflected back by the object. Others suggested that objects might continually emit replicas of themselves which came through the air and entered the observer's eyes. With increasing knowledge of the physics of light, in a much later era, the truth was learned that all which came from the object to O was reflected light, something very different from replicas of the object. When the reflected light is focused on the retina, an image of the object is produced which differs in size with the distance of the object, in shape with O's viewing angle, and in color and brightness with the illumination. The visual stimuli are obviously not stable characteristics of the object, but they serve as cues enabling O to recognize the object and also to perceive its location in the environment. More will be said presently on visual and also auditory cues for space perception.

Even when you examine objects by the sense of touch, the stimuli you get are very different from the objects you perceive. The object, for example, is a tennis ball, but the stimuli received from handling it have no spherical shape; they are simply pressures on different parts of the palm. If you explore a room in the dark, the stimuli are cutaneous and kinesthetic pressures on the palms of your hands, soles of your feet, and elbow, hip, and knee joints. You can feel these pressures if you give careful attention to the local stimuli, but ordinarily what you observe and report would be a chair, a doorknob, something like a pillow on the floor, and other objects located here and there in the room. Later, you could not remember the stimuli received, unless some of them were painful, but you could probably remember the objects. The stimuli, having no interest for themselves, served as cues of interesting objects.

In *motor behavior* the situation is much the same; that is to say that you can intend to activate a certain muscle, the "biceps" for example, but ordinarily your intention is directed toward objective results and not toward any particular muscles. Just as sensory stimuli are means for the perception of objects, so muscular contractions are means for the execution of objective intentions. Sense perception and motor intention are both directed toward the environment, and they are closely bound together. That is, you perceive a near object as within reach of the hand, a somewhat more distant object as one you can reach by walking a few steps. You perceive a chair as something to sit on, the floor as something to walk on. The facts perceived and the acts intended are "commensurate," we may say, meaning that they are both measurable in the same units, i.e., in terms of size, shape, direction, and distance, and practical value.

The perception of objective facts and the choice of objective goals belong together as a major function of the brain (p. 16ff).

A helpful analogy. We can liken the brain to the general head-quarters of an army in the field. Messages are received from the field and orders are set out into the field. The incoming messages are in code, and the orders go out in code. (The sensory and motor codes are different in the case of the brain.) The incoming messages are decoded and combined in headquarters so as to reveal what is going on in the field. And when a decision has been reached, it is coded into suitable terms for execution. We must not forget the *retroflex:* as fast as the orders are executed, the immediate results are signaled back to headquarters and decoded so as to line up with the perceived situation and the intended goal. A big problem in dynamic psychology is to try to "break" these codes—to discover (1) how the sensory stimuli are decoded into objective facts and (2) how objective goals are coded into muscular coordinations. More knowledge has been gained on (1) than on (2).

Stimulus variables and objective variables. Stimuli serve as cues of objective facts. A certain hum is a cue of an airplane in motion, and if the hum grows louder, it is a cue of the airplane coming closer. The decoding here amounts to translation of a stimulus variable, increased loudness, into the objective variable of increased nearness. A similar example is that of a retinal image becoming larger and larger; decoded it means an object coming nearer. The stimulus variable of increasing retinal size is translated into the objective variable of decreasing distance. There are many similar examples, and it seems likely that decoding will be especially easy when a continuous change or gradation in the stimulus corresponds to some movement or gradation in the environment.

In a study of perception the psychologist tries to identify the cues that are used and to discover, if possible, how they are translated into objective facts. By physical analysis of the situation possible cues are identified, and by psychological experiments these are tried out on suitable subjects so as to discover which cues are actually used. The history of the problem is long and interesting (Boring, 1942, pp. 263-288, 303-308).

VISIBLE DISTANCE

One reason why many students are not attracted to the study of perception is that they do not recognize any challenging problems to be investigated. Everything seems very simple for anyone looking at a scene. Here are objects spread out in three dimensions before his eyes—what is to prevent his seeing them so? These objects lie in such spatial relations as side by side, separated, between, around; but these relations are not fully "given" in the retinal image. The necessary data are given, but the human infant has to use his eyes for several weeks, along with his hands, before mastering even these elementary one- and two-dimensional spatial relations (Piaget & Inhelder, 1948).

But it is three-dimensional spatial perception which has presented a more obvious problem to the psychologist as well as to the painter who wishes to secure a realistic depth effect on his two-dimensional canvas. The painter's problem is to find indications of the third dimension that he can incorporate in his flat painting. One of the most important contributors to the theory and experimental work on realistic painting was Leonardo da Vinci (born 1452, died 1519). His fundamental principle was that the objects depicted should be presented to the eye in the picture as they are presented in the actual scene. They must be shown, not as they are known to be from all-round exploration, but as they are presented to the eye at one moment. To bring home to the beginner the effects of distance on the picture size and color of an object, he recommended the following exercise:

> Go into the country, select objects situated at distances of 100, 200 yards, etc.—objects such as trees, houses, men—and with regard to the nearest tree, place a sheet of glass firmly in front of you, keep the eye fixed in location, and trace the outline of the tree on the glass. Now move the glass to the side just enough to allow the tree to be seen beside its tracing, and color your drawing to duplicate the color and relief of the object, so that when examined with one eye the drawing and the tree shall be alike in color and size. Follow the same procedure in painting the second and third trees situated at the greater distances.

This exercise was intended to bring out the perspective effects: size perspective (linear), the picture size decreasing as the distance of the object increases; aerial perspective, the increasing bluishness with increased distance; and detail perspective, the loss of detail in the distance.

Stimulus correlates of distance

If the painter successfully duplicates in his picture the stimuli which the viewer would receive from the actual scene, he can trust the viewer to make the same perceptual response and to have a realistic impression of objects at their proper distances. The psychologist's first question is in what ways the stimuli received on the retina from an object can differ with the distance of the object. Size perspective gives one answer. If a man moves away from you, at 20 feet your retinal image of him is only half as tall as at 10 feet. Or consider the important case of the young child: as the mother's face approaches, it expands rapidly and enormously in his retinal image, only to shrink back to small dimensions as she moves away. When he is able to sit up in bed and move a toy back and forth on the coverlet, the optical expansion and diminution of the toy is very considerable in spite of the small area of his activity; for the toy is retinally twice as big in all dimensions at 6 inches as when pushed away to 12 inches. Evidently the individual from an early age has abundant opportunity to learn the size-distance relationship and to use the optical size of an object as a cue of its distance.

This cue by itself, however, must be of limited utility, for the object before you may be unfamiliar and stationary. How far away is a wooden stake which the psychologist has driven into the ground to test you? It may be short or tall and you are not allowed to approach it. Yet you can estimate its distance pretty well if you can see the surroundings including the ground extending from you to the object. But suppose the object to be a flat disk of light in a dark room; you look in through a peekhole and see the disk and nothing else. How far away it is you cannot tell; it might be at any distance within reason. If the disk is made to expand, most Os perceive it as coming toward them, though a few see the objective fact of change of size. With only retinal size as a cue, there is nothing to show whether the size of the object or its distance has changed; but the easiest assumption is that the object has remained constant in size and simply changed in distance (Hastorf, 1950; Ittelson, 1951). The difference between change of size and change of distance stands out clearly, however, if a clear view of the surroundings is permitted, with binocular vision and freedom to move the head from side to side. (Gogel et al, 1957.)

Retinal size seems not to be a good cue of distance unless it has some support from the surroundings. James J. Gibson (1950a) has argued with much cogency that perceived distance is primarily a matter of surfaces rather than of isolated objects. If you perceive the ground or floor as a surface extending away from you in the third dimension, anything lying or standing on this surface has a location in distance. What is there in the retinal image of the ground corresponding to its horizontal extension? The whole retinal image at any moment is a vertical projection of the external field of view. (We may properly disregard the up-down and right-left inversion of the retinal image, which is taken care of by the sensorimotor connections in the brain.) If you are looking out horizontally over the ground, it rises from near to far in your picture. Horizontal spaces on the ground are progressively foreshortened in the vertical projection (Figure 10).

You can easily verify the following statements: In your view of a room, as you look lengthwise of it, the floor rises from near to far, the ceiling descends from near to far, the sidewalls come in from near to far. If you look horizontally northward in a straight north-south street, the curb lines converge upward and inward in your picture, the cornice lines converge downward and inward, and in fact all the straight northward lines converge toward an imaginary distant point at your eye level, a "vanishing point" as it is called in perspective drawing. Such a drawing may give a fairly vivid impression of three-dimensional space, but definite lines are not necessary to give the impression of level ground, for you get that impression in looking out over a broad field or lawn. So we still have to search for the physical basis of the impression. Gibson (1950a) called attention to what he called *texture gradients* as a likely physical basis. Consider a level field plowed in long parallel furrows: if you look lengthwise of the furrows, they converge upward in your picture in the way already described; but if you look across the furrows, the more distant ones are closer and closer together upward in your picture. The visible texture of the field becomes "denser" with distance. You get similar texture gradients in looking out to sea when parallel waves are coming in, in looking over the rows of seats in an empty auditorium, or in looking over the "sea of faces" when the auditorium is well filled. Even without any such marked and regular pattern, the texture or "microstructure" of a lawn or hayfield may become denser with distance. The

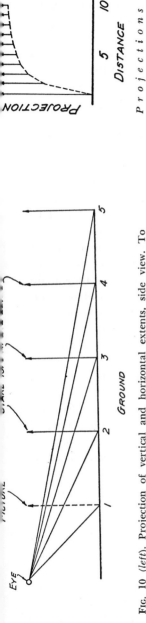

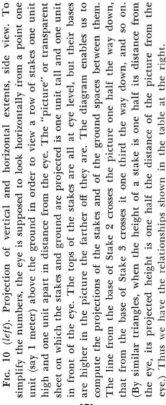

Distances from the eye	Projections of	
	Stake heights	Horizontal spaces between stake bases
Picture . . 1	1/1 = 1.000	----- 1/2 = .500
Stakes . . 2	1/2 = .500	1/2 - 1/3 = 1/6 = .167
3	1/3 = .333	1/3 - 1/4 = 1/12 = .083
4	1/4 = .250	1/4 - 1/5 = 1/20 = .050
5	1/5 = .200	1/5 - 1/6 = 1/30 = .033
6	1/6 = .167	1/6 - 1/7 = 1/42 = .024
7	1/7 = .143	1/7 - 1/8 = 1/56 = .018
8	1/8 = .125	
.	.	.
.	.	.
.	.	.

Fig. 10 (*left*). Projection of vertical and horizontal extents, side view. To simplify the numbers, the eye is supposed to look horizontally from a point one unit (say 1 meter) above the ground in order to view a row of stakes one unit high and one unit apart in distance from the eye. The "picture" or transparent sheet on which the stakes and ground are projected is one unit tall and one unit in front of the eye. The tops of the stakes are all at eye level, but their bases are higher in the picture the farther off they are. The diagram enables us to compute the projections of the stakes and of the ground spaces between them. The line from the base of Stake 2 crosses the picture one half the way down, that from the base of Stake 3 crosses it one third the way down, and so on. (By similar triangles, when the height of a stake is one half its distance from the eye, its projected height is one half the distance of the picture from the eye.) Thus we have the relationships shown in the table at the right.

To see these relations in the diagram, follow the projection lines back to the picture; for example, follow the ground space 1-2 back, the ground space 2-3, and so on. Though the actual ground spaces are horizontal, their projections on the picture are of course vertical. As the distance from the eye increases, the projections become smaller, the shrinkage being more rapid for the horizontal than for the vertical extents, as the decimal numbers show. When distance from the eye = D, the vertical stakes project in the ratio $\dfrac{1}{D}$, the horizontal lengths in the ratio $\dfrac{1}{D} - \dfrac{1}{(D+1)} = \dfrac{1}{D(D+1)}$. These projection effects occur outside the eye and have nothing to do with the inversion of the retinal image which occurs inside the eye.

The projections of the stakes all terminate above at the same level, their bases rising in the picture as their distance increases. It might seem that we were drawing them upside down; but no, they are right side up. These projection effects occur outside the eye and have nothing to do with the inversion of the retinal image which occurs inside the eye.

In the supplementary FIGURE 11 (*right*), each farther stake is supposed to be placed a little farther to the right so that their projections are side by side as seen by O. The dotted line shows the projection of successive ground spaces.

171

texture of a vertical surface, when you look at it horizontally, is uniform, without any such gradient. If the surface slants slightly forward or back, there is a slight gradient of texture, and the gradient becomes more pronounced as the slant increases, reaching its maximum when the surface is horizontal (or, more in general, when the surface is parallel to your line of sight and close to it). Instead of "texture" you can say "detail," and instead of saying that it becomes "denser" with increasing distance, you can say that detail fades out and becomes gradually invisible.

Ambiguity of cues of distance. Any stimulus correlate of distance that can be reproduced in a flat drawing or painting—whether texture or aerial perspective or even the converging lines of linear perspective—is evidently not a sure and unambiguous indicator of depth, for it may indicate nothing beyond the flat drawing or painting. If the shelves of a bookcase are more closely spaced toward the top, this vertical surface shows a gradient like that of a level sidewalk. If the nearest house is actually blue in color, the gradient of aerial perspective breaks down. If you follow the projection lines of Figure 10 out from the picture, you see that they might have originated in a sloping or curved surface instead of from the level ground. The observer's impression of flatness or depth does not always conform to the texture gradient (Gibson, Purdy & Lawrence, 1955). The ambiguity of retinal size has already been mentioned.

In spite of the ambiguity of these cues of distance, the painter can secure good depth effects by combining them in a landscape or group picture. He is limited to what are called monocular fixed-eye cues. Anyone who is looking at an actual scene, not being so limited, uses both eyes and may move his head slightly from side to side with good effects on his perception of the relative distances of the objects before him.

Parallax

The term "parallax" refers fundamentally to the obvious geometrical fact that the direction of a stationary object from an observer changes if he changes his location, and that the direction of the object changes less for a distant than for a near observer. Let there be two objects lying straight north of the observer, one farther away than the other; if he moves a little to the east, both

objects will now lie somewhat to the west of north, but the farther
one will now lie closer to the true north than the nearer one. If he
had moved to the west, both objects would have shifted toward the
east, the nearer one more than the farther one. If he had no other
cues of distance, the parallax would be a sufficient indication of
which was nearer.

Suppose that O has two photographs taken from somewhat different positions, showing the same two objects. Comparing the two
photographs, he has the necessary information to tell him which
object is the nearer, but it may give him a little trouble to utilize
the information; he has to "figure out" the spatial relationship,
since it does not stand out directly enough to be actually seen or
perceived. "Figuring out" is thinking rather than perceiving. There
are two ways of making parallax the basis of direct perception:
motion parallax and binocular parallax. In one the environment is
observed while the observer himself is moving, and in the other
advantage is taken of the fact that the two eyes view a near object
from different angles—different enough to yield a vivid impression
of depth.

Motion parallax. Any movement of an observer produces motion
in his retinal image of the scene in front of him, and the motion
affects the nearer objects more than the farther. You can bring out
this elementary geometrical relationship without rising from your
chair, if the scene before you contains objects at different distances.
As you move your head to the right, the farther objects move to
the right with you and the nearer objects relatively backward in
your picture—all because you are changing the direction of the
farther objects very little, but the direction of near objects much
more, in proportion to their nearness. The rapid motion of a railroad train makes this parallactic effect especially vivid and perceptual, as you survey the landscape from your car window: the
nearer objects rush to the rear while the distant mountains keep
pace with the train, or nearly so. An automobilist looking straight
forward gets an expanding view of the scene in front, the objects
separating to right and left, more and more rapidly as he approaches
them. The speed of this expansion in front, and of the backward
motion of objects at the sides is of course dependent on the observer's speed of locomotion as well as on the nearness of the
objects. The effects are consequently especially striking in airplane

flight, as brought out clearly by Gibson (1950a) and summarized in Figure 12.

Motion parallax is a powerful cue of distance, and not only of the relative distance from you of two objects, but also of the whole three-dimensional expanse of the environment. It combines readily with another powerful cue of relative distance, called interposition, the *covering* or partial covering of a farther by a nearer object. You can often bring the hidden object into view by a sideward movement of your own. The young child has abundant opportunity to utilize these cues in learning the important spatial relationships of behind and beyond.

Binocular parallax and disparity. With eyes placed side by side and looking forward, as in human beings, there is a chance of obtaining *simultaneous* views of an object from two positions. The two views will not differ much if the object is flat and perpendicular to the line of sight, but if it is turned so as to extend into the third dimension, its projections upon the two retinas will differ, and the disparity will increase as it is turned more and more from the frontal-parallel plane. The flat side of a ruler, held vertically at about reading distance, first in a frontal-parallel plane and then turned sidewise more or less, and viewed alternately with the two eyes, will bring out the facts mentioned. In an oblique position its picture is broader to one eye than to the other. If you look past it at the distance, you see it double; but if you focus and converge your eyes upon it, you get a single combined view with a good depth effect. The combination of the monocular views into a single binocular view occurs in the brain, corresponding parts of both retinas being connected with identical parts of the visual area. But the remarkable thing is that the two views are combined in spite of their disparity and that the combination yields a realistic depth effect. This "stereoscopic effect" is readily obtained by use of the stereoscope, an instrument which presents separate views to the eyes, corresponding to the monocular views which would be obtained of the object. If there is no disparity, the effect or perception shows a flat object in a frontal-parallel plane, but wherever horizontal disparity is present, there is a depth effect. If the disparity is too great, or if the monocular pictures are so different that they cannot be combined into a single picture, what happens is quite surprising: only one of the pictures is seen, the other being temporarily invisible but coming into view after a while and blotting

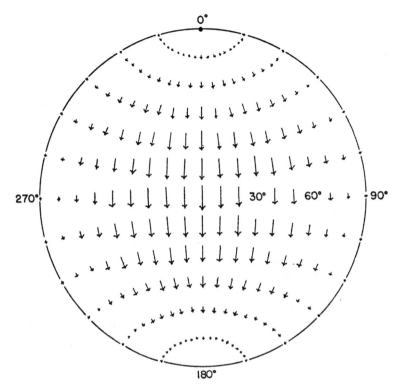

FIG. 12. (Gibson, Olum & Rosenblatt, 1955, p. 376.) Relative backward motion of points on the earth's surface in level flight. The speed of flight is represented by the central vector (arrow), the direction of flight being the reverse. This central arrow is directly underneath the airplane. All the arrows represent potential visual stimuli that would be received by an observer in the airplane who directed his eye to points along the distant horizon. For example, if he looked straight to the right (90 degrees) he would receive the stimuli represented by the right half of the figure; and if he looked at the horizon straight behind, he would receive the stimuli shown in the rear half of the figure.

If the airplane is descending obliquely toward a certain landing spot, that spot evidently will remain fixed in the picture, not moving right or left nor up or down. It will be a "center of expansion" (p. 153).

If the observer, instead of looking at the horizon, looks at some object in the foreground or middle distance, the pursuit movement of his eyes keeps the image of that object temporarily on the fovea and so motionless in the picture, while nearer points move backward and more distant points forward—a familiar visual effect which you get by looking to the side from a train or automobile.

out the one first seen. *Binocular rivalry,* this effect is called, and the alternation will continue if the eyes remain directed to the discrepant pictures.

As to the physiological dynamics of these binocular effects, little can be said, except that rivalry suggests a cycle of fatigue and recovery. Single binocular vision with its clear perception of depth is definitely rewarding and practically useful in the manipulation of objects. Certainly the binocular depth effect does not have to be learned; what the baby may have to learn is the accurate convergence which secures this reward. It is several months after birth before convergence seems to be well established; Piaget (1937) says eight months, but Gesell *et al.* (1949) say two months; no doubt individual children differ. Similarly, the reward for good accommodation of the lens for the distance of an object is distinct vision of that object; this reaction is established within the first few weeks; the saccadic and pursuit movements seem to be available right after birth. All these ocular movements show an organism well equipped for dealing with objects in space.

One thing more about *double images.* They are always present in binocular vision whenever objects at different distances are before the eyes, for when convergence is adjusted for any particular distance, all objects at other distances are projected on noncorresponding parts of the two retinas and appear double in the combined binocular view. The farther they deviate, near or far, from the convergence distance, the farther apart are their images in the binocular view. Ordinarily you do not notice these double images, but you can bring out the major facts by holding both forefingers straight in front, one a foot away from your eyes and the other two feet away. Whichever one you focus on, the other will appear double; and the farther apart the fingers are in distance, the farther apart the double images are in the combined view. Even though seldom noticed, they are dependable stimuli which probably contribute to the total impression of three-dimensional space.

Translation of retinal cues into environmental space— or of stimulus dimensions into objective dimensions

The objective or environmental dimension here in question is the third dimension, distance from the observer. We have found several stimulus dimensions or variables which serve as cues of distance. They indicate distance in spite of being altogether different from distance. As an object comes nearer, its retinal image expands in two dimensions, but what you ordinarily perceive is movement in the third dimension. Looking out over a hilly landscape, you see the bluer hills as farther away, though there is certainly no similarity between blueness and distance; there is no similarity but there is a close enough correspondence to enable the retinal color to serve as a fairly good indicator of objective distance. This also occurs in the case of motion parallax: as you move your head to the side, you make the parts of your retinal picture (the objects pictured) move from side to side in relation to each other; but what you perceive is stationary objects situated at different distances. The whole picture appears vividly as a three-dimensional environment. The disparity and double images of binocular vision are altogether different from distance and yet provide excellent indicators of the relative distance of near objects. (You know the old demonstration: with one eye shut point the forefingers toward each other and bring them as close to each other as you can without their touching; then open the shut eye also.)

The eyes can do no more than provide sensory impulses varying along *stimulus* dimensions, whereas motor behavior has to deal with the *objective* dimensions of the environment, such as distance. The brain must transform, or translate, or decode the stimulus dimensions into objective dimensions. These three words are all figures of speech, but "translate" seems more nearly literal than "transform." We can hardly say that blueness is transformed into distance, any more than that a French word is transformed into an English word in being translated. Translation suggests a collection of separate equivalents, like a French-English dictionary; "decoding" may be a shade better in allowing for *a system of dimensions,* objective variables corresponding with stimulus variables. The brain process in decoding is probably something of the stimulus-response variety: sensory impulses reaching the primary visual area arouse higher-order responses in the neighboring areas (pp. 17f); very likely a combination of stimuli is necessary to arouse the higher-order response. With the understanding that our idea of the process is extremely vague at present, we can continue to use such words as translation and decoding to indicate the perceptual result.

James J. Gibson, who has done so much to rejuvenate the psychology of space perception, with important applications to aviation, was inclined at one time (1950a) to reject the "cue theory" in favor of a "gradient theory" and to argue that any "translation" from the retinal data to objective meanings would be a superfluous intervening variable because the data correspond so directly and quantitatively to the objective facts. A cue of distance could serve the purpose when O was trying to judge the distance of a specific object or to compare the distances of two objects, but for a realistic impression of the total environment, for actually *seeing* it spread out in all directions, what O needs is the stimulus gradients corresponding to the objective gradients. However, even a gradient can be called a cue (Gibson, 1950b, p. 371). A cue is any stimulus or stimulus complex that carries a meaning, as the expansion of the retinal image of an object carries the meaning of its approach. Usually the different cues of distance agree, and O has an unquestioning perception of distance. Under special conditions they disagree, and O is reduced to a judgment of probability (Gibson, 1952). The learning required for successful use of a stimulus complex may consist in the discovery and singling out of a variable which is closely correlated with an important objective variable. "Perceptual learning, then, consists of responding to variables of physical stimulation not previously responded to. . . . The total range of physical stimulation is very rich in complex variables and these are theoretically capable of becoming cues and constituting information" (Gibson & Gibson, 1955, pp. 34-35; also Gibson, 1957; Gibson & Gibson, 1957).

VERTICAL AND HORIZONTAL

Which should be called the "third dimension"—vertical or horizontal? In pictures, the retinal image included, it is distance away from the point of observation, usually a horizontal distance. On a map, north-south and east-west—latitude and longitude—are obviously the first two dimensions, leaving altitude to be less directly indicated by contour lines. In biological importance, and in the child's development, the vertical might well be called the *first* dimension. It is all-pervasive; there is no absence of gravitation corresponding to darkness and silence. Instead of consisting like visual space of surfaces and their boundaries, gravitational space consists primarily of parallel lines filling space like streaks of rain. Secondarily there are very important gravitational surfaces, inclined planes, vertical and especially horizontal planes.

The human organism is equipped with receptors responsive to gravitational stimuli. Most curious are the otolith organs of the vestibule of the inner ear—a type of receptor found in all the vertebrates as well as in many invertebrates. When the human head is upright, the otoliths receive equal stimulation right and left, front and back; but if the head is tilted in any direction, the stimulation is unequal. Thus the vertical is distinguished from all other directions. Much the same is true of the kinesthetic receptors in the neck, which play an important role in the posture of the head and trunk. The weight of the body presses down on any supporting surface and so stimulates the touch receptors of the back or side in lying, of the rump in sitting, of the soles in standing. Always, it seems, there is some gravitational stimulation indicative of up and down, except probably in underwater swimming. In that situation the pressures on all parts of the skin are so nearly equal as to afford no clear indication of the vertical; the swimmer has to depend entirely on his otolith receptors, and if these have been incapacitated by inner ear disease, he may find himself lost under water and have to explore wildly to reach the surface.

Getting acquainted with gravitation

By neuromuscular maturation touched up with learning, the human infant makes remarkable progress during his first postnatal year in dealing with the force of gravitation. By three to four months he is able to raise his head and hold it up steadily; by seven to eight months he can raise his back and maintain a sitting position; by ten to twelve months he can straighten his whole body from head to feet and hold it vertical with no other support than the floor; and by fourteen months he can even take his feet alternately, step by step, off the floor while avoiding falls most of the time. And his acquaintance with gravitation is not limited to his own bodily sensations and motor achievements. He *sees* falling objects and *hears* them strike forcibly on the floor. Out of doors the vertical is brought home to him visually by the trunks of trees and by many other things that stand upright, and the horizontal is brought home by the sight of level ground and still bodies of water. In the house vertical and horizontal lines and planes dominate the scene and provide the spatial framework for everything. He has abundant opportunity to integrate his visual and bodily information regarding the gravitational world. He finds that a down slope and an up slope must be dealt with very differently; sliding down hill is very different from pulling his sled to the top again. Of course, the child does not readily pick up the abstract concept of gravitation. One little boy, coming home to the noon meal after an exciting morning in the snow, was asked to consider what caused his sled to slide downhill so fast, and was told that it was the force of gravitation. He said, "No, that wasn't so," and insisted that he *knew* it was not so. Being asked to explain what it was, then, that made his sled slide downhill, he hesitated and could only stammer that it was "just because it was *down*."

Tilted room and rotated room

The visual and "bodily" (otolithic-kinesthetic-tactile) indications of up and down are ordinarily in agreement. What looks vertical feels vertical. The up-and-down direction of the tree trunks or of prominent lines indoors is the same as your own up-and-down direction as you stand up straight—approximately the same at least. But it is not difficult for an experimenter, given adequate apparatus, to produce considerable discrepancy between the two sets of cues, by "doctoring" one set or the other. A tilted room in which everything is square and normal except that the whole thing is jacked up on one side to an inclination of 35 degrees, with a person inside who sees nothing outside, certainly shows that person a visual environment that is inconsistent with gravitation. Meanwhile his bodily cues remain gravitational. Let his chair inside the room be separately tilted, and let his task be to make his chair straight in spite of the continued tilt of the room (Witkin, 1949; Witkin *et al*, 1954, pp. 28ff, 44, 48ff). With eyes closed so as to have only the bodily cues, the chair was set straight with only a little error, about 3 degrees on the average and without much variation from one man to another. But when the eyes were open, the room looked normal or at least exerted a pull in its direction and increased the average error of the chair setting to about 8 degrees, with a large scatter of the individual settings, from the true vertical to over 20 degrees aslant. Some individuals were able to disregard the visual appearance and adjust the chair to the true vertical; some vacillated unhappily between the two apparent verticals, the gravitational and the visual; but the majority adopted a compromise solution without much hesitation or worry.

Though E cannot hope to modify the force of gravitation, he can compound it with another force, a "centrifugal force," caused by horizontal rotation. Compounding the downward pull of gravity with the outward thrust of rotation gives an oblique down-and-out resultant. The exact direction of this resultant depends on the speed of rotation—the faster, the farther out from the downward vertical. In an elaborate setup (Witkin, 1952; Witkin *et al.*, 1954), O's visual environment was the interior of a small room which

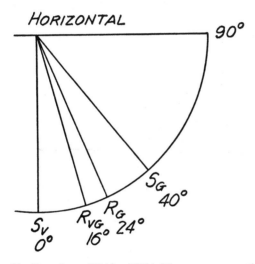

FIG. 13. (Data from Witkin, 1952.) The apparent vertical as affected by rotation, with and without a visual framework. The visual framework was an upright room in which O was firmly seated. His chair was adjusted in tilt until he accepted its position as "straight," i.e., in line with the unseen vertical lines of the building. The combined gravitational-centrifugal force acting on his body receptors called for an adjustment, S_G, 40 degrees out from the true vertical. The visual vertical, S_V, called for no deflection. The average response was R_G, a 24-degree deflection, when the eyes were closed, but only R_V, a 16-degree deflection, when the eyes were open during rotation. The subjects were forty-five college men. Their individual chair settings ranged from 11 degrees to 35 degrees with closed eyes, and from 1 degree to 32 degrees with open eyes. College women agreed closely with the men when the eyes were closed, but they were more influenced by the visual framework when it was seen.

could be propelled around a circular track at such a rate that the resultant acting on O's body was 40 degrees out from the true gravitational vertical. The chair with tight-fitting headrest could be tilted independently of the room, and it had to be tilted more or less in order to seem straight-up to O during rotation. The faster the rotation, the more the chair had to be tilted in order to seem straight. But when O's eyes were open to the upright room, this visual framework had a strong effect; without annulling the bodily effect, it forced a compromise which was generally more in favor of the visual than of the bodily cues.

The two experiments just described gave the same general result: when the visual and bodily cues of the vertical were in conflict, the resulting perception was usually a compromise, the compromise point differing considerably with individuals. In these and other related experiments there was a sex difference: on the average, the women were more responsive than the men to the visual cues, or less responsive to the bodily cues of the vertical; they were not insensitive to the bodily cues, for when the eyes were closed there was no sex difference; but with the eyes open, the visual framework exerted a stronger pull on the women. This of course was only an *average* difference, with much individual variation in both sexes. There was considerable individual consistency: those who were more responsive to the visual framework in the tilted-room test were rather likely to be so in the rotated-room test as well, the correlation r being about .60 for the men and about .70 for the women (Witkin *et al*, 1954, p. 65). In these and other conflict situations used in their extensive research, the authors consider a basic dynamic factor to be the individual's disposition to respond to the perceptual field as a whole or, on the contrary, to focus on an important element.

In free daily life, the visual cues of horizontal and other surfaces, of which so much was said earlier in the chapter, are certainly checked against the gravitational cues. An up-slope may not look much different from a down-slope, but they feel different as you negotiate them. The visual cues act as promises and the gravitational cues act as checks on these promises. The integration of these two very different sorts of cues must require a lot of experience and learning.

AUDITORY SPACE

The task of exploring the spatial environment is so important for the organism that any of the sense organs is likely to be drawn into the enterprise. The receptors located on the inner surface of the body, i.e., on the mucous membrane, may not contribute very much, though the baby does what he can with them in getting acquainted with objects. The cutaneous-kinesthetic team does an enormous amount of exploring and contributes much information on the size and shape of objects, though not on their distance and direction. The temperature and olfactory receptors can qualify to a limited degree as "distance receptors," since they can be stimulated by radiation or emanation from objects at some distance; and the distance of the source is roughly indicated by the stimulus intensity. A cautious person can avoid actual contact with the hot radiator.

Obviously the ear is the chief distance receptor, apart from the eye. Sounds are audible over a wide range of distance, their intensity at the ear falling off with the distance of the source—theoretically with the square of the distance, but often with much irregularity resulting from reflection and resonance. They are certainly useful cues of distance, even though they are not perfectly reliable. As to direction, the direction from which a sound comes, there are no obvious cues, but the behavior of men and of many animals shows that they respond quickly and often accurately to *some* cues of direction, which the psychologist has to discover. As to the size and shape of a distant object, it would seem that no auditory cues are possible; and yet some clever blind persons utilize echoes for the purpose.

The ear has one advantage over the eye as a source of information about the present environment: sounds reach the ear from all directions, bending around corners and penetrating walls in a way that is impossible for light. Consequently, the audible existence of objects in more or less definite locations enables the organism to keep in touch with the environment in a way that is often reassuring even in daylight. Though vision is certainly the major spatial sense, the contributions of audition are so distinctive, and the auditory spatial cues so different from the visual, that a dynamic psychology must certainly investigate the matter. The retinal image of a seen object has definite size and shape which serve as cues of the distance and orientation of the object. The auditory stimulus pattern provides no comparable cues, but it does provide an intensity variable and a vibration-frequency or pitch variable both of which are utilized under certain conditions as spatial cues. The crescendo of an automobile horn indicates spatial approach, and a sudden downward shift of pitch shows that that car has gone past (the Doppler effect). Hearing is also an excellent time sense; its receptors are quick to act and quick to recover from stimulation; and the slow transmission of sound through the air, compared with light, makes it possible to use auditory time intervals as cues of distance and even of direction. These time-space cues deserve our attention.

Echoes and resonance

The reflection of sound from a broad surface often makes it difficult to locate the real source of the sound since it reaches the ear directly from the reflecting surface. However, if the source is known, the reflection indicates the location of the reflecting surface. This surface can be said to be "heard" in the same way that a surface which reflects light is "seen." If you yourself are the source of the sound, the reflection from any fairly distant surface is an "echo" and serves to locate the object that sends back the echo. The pilot of a river steamboat in a fog locates cliffs and other objects along the banks by the echoes of his whistle. As the cliff is approached, the echo comes back more and more quickly.

Since sound travels through the air at a fairly constant speed (about 1130 feet per second, varying slightly with the temperature), it is possible by aid of radarlike equipment to measure the distance of an echoing object rather accurately. If a city block measures a tenth of a mile, it will take a sound approximately a second to traverse the distance and bounce back to you. We are not to suppose that echo is lacking from a near-by surface; it simply gets back so soon as to merge with the original sound. It prolongs the original sound and is heard as resonance. An empty hall resounds, a tunnel resounds as your train goes through it, or a bridge as you drive under it. When you emerge from such a locality, the cessation of resonance is a cue of relatively open space. Such *spatial hearing* plays a greater part than we realize in our moment-by-moment adjustment to the environment.

Much more expert than the human species in the use of auditory spatial cues is that night-flying mammal, the bat. How the bat manages to dodge around at high speed in the dark, catching insects and avoiding obstacles large and small, was a puzzle until their sound-producing and auditory apparatus was studied. Then it was found that their ears were sensitive to very high-frequency tones, far above the upper limit of the human ear, and that their vocal apparatus produced rapid series of very brief high tones, such as are cleanly reflected even by very small surfaces. If they were gagged to prevent the emission of these sounds, or if their ears were plugged to prevent the reception of them, the remarkable ability was gone (Griffin & Galambos, 1941; Griffin, 1953).

How the blind perceive obstacles. The bat may not be the only animal that uses reflected sounds as cues of the location of objects. Porpoises emit high-pitch tones and rapid series of clicks, and they respond to such underwater stimuli. Very likely they use the same general technique as the bats (Kellogg *et al.*, 1953). And blind human beings, those of them who show considerable facility in finding their way about without bumping into obstacles, are observed to make noises with their feet or cane, such noises as would echo back cleanly from obstacles. The blind, however, have usually been unable to tell what cues they use in detecting the nearness of a wall or, by contrast, the presence of an open door. Many of them have supposed their faces to be specially sensitive to pressure waves of some unknown kind emitted by objects. Careful experimental work was required to ferret out the cues they were using so skillfully. The hypothetical pressure waves were excluded by a heavy felt veil surrounding the head, which interfered only a little with hearing and only a little with the ability to detect the near presence of an obstacle. But when the ears were well plugged, the ability was gone. These statements were true both of ordinarily very successful blind persons and of blindfolded normal persons who had acquired some of the ability by special practice. The essential cues were sounds produced by a person approaching a wall and echoed back from the wall; the quicker the echo, the nearer the wall. Other, less dependable cues were sometimes effective, such as the heat reflected from a wall standing in warm sunshine, or the coolness in the shade of a wall (Supa, Cotzin & Dallenbach, 1944; Worchel & Dallenbach, 1947; Jerome & Proshansky, 1950; Worchel, 1951).

In a familiar environment blind persons get to know landmarks, distances, paths, ground slopes; and they produce cues for themselves by sharp sounds, made with a cane or the tongue, which echo back from walls and other objects. Vehicles moving in the street provide "audible lines" which serve as guides for the blind person walking along the sidewalk. When vehicles are scarce, he tries to remember the course of each one until another comes past. We might suppose that a wartime blackout would be a matter of indifference to a blind person. On the contrary, it was simply "devastating." With the streets mostly deserted and the windows closed, his customary reference points and "audible lines" were lacking or much reduced. The audible environment was gone, and without it he was lost. When the environment is well supplied with noise makers, the blind person is kept constantly in touch with it. It is perhaps a web rather than a continuum, but it has enough sensory substance to be worth exploring and enjoying (Mansfeld, 1940).

Auditory cues of direction

How is it possible to hear the direction from which a sound reaches the ears? Examining the internal ears we find the semicircular canals arranged in tridimensional space as if they might take care of this matter; but they are found to be concerned with body rotations and not with the sense of hearing. The movable external ears of the horse or dog turn toward the source of a sound and so doubtless secure optimal reception. The human being lacks this equipment and yet does quite well in perceiving the direction of sound. To be sure, he has two ears and it may be that binaural hearing is of some value. As binocular vision serves so well in the perception of distance, binaural hearing might serve in the perception of direction.

The right-left discrimination in hearing. In an open field or a padded room, with confusing echoes and resonance thus avoided, a blindfolded subject can tell with great certainty whether a sound is coming from his right or left. Even if it is coming from almost straight in front, he can tell if it comes from a few degrees to the right or left of his median plane extended into space. Keeping his head straight forward, he can point approximately toward the source of sound; or, more accurately, he can turn and face toward the sound. This ability, with its limitations, was demonstrated long

ago by aid of a piece of apparatus called the "sound cage." It consists of a skeleton sphere of stiff wire, say 4 feet in diameter, with a
head rest in the center and attachments for sounders at various
points of the spherical surface. O's task is to indicate the direction
from which the sound is coming on each trial. The results were
clear: O succeeds very well as far as the right-left dimension is
concerned, but only very poorly as far as the front-back and up-
down dimensions are concerned. He often confuses front and back,
and often up and down, though never right and left. A sound coming from any point in the median plane may seem to come from
above or from behind, but most often from straight in front. Moreover, the right-left discrimination is much impaired in individuals
who are deaf in one ear.

A very simple explanation might be suggested: sounds from the
right side might be heard with the right ear, sounds from the left
side with the left ear. But this is impossible physically, for the
sound waves from any point reach both ears. However, they might
and indeed must reach the nearer ear with the greater intensity.
The theory that the binaural intensity difference is the cue for
sound localization seemed acceptable until the physics of the matter
was examined more closely. Then it was seen that the intensity
difference is too slight in many cases to serve as an effective cue.
The difference results partly from the loss of intensity as the sound
radiates farther from its source, and partly from loss in bending
around the head to the farther ear. When the source is only a few
degrees to the right of the median plane, it is only a little farther
from the left ear than from the right, and the waves bend around
only a few degrees of the head to reach the left ear; therefore, the
intensity difference will be very slight. The loss in bending around
the head depends also on the frequency of the waves, being slight
for low-pitched tones and great for frequencies of 10,000 per second
or over. We should expect, then, that the binaural intensity difference would be an effective cue of direction only for high-pitched
sounds coming from far to the side; and this expectation has been
verified by experiment.

The binaural time difference as a cue of direction. Traveling
through the air at a constant speed, the sound from a source anywhere in the median plane will reach both ears simultaneously, but
from a source anywhere to the right of the median plane it will
reach the right ear first. This binaural time difference is perfectly

correlated with the angular divergence of the source from the median plane and should therefore make an excellent cue of the right-left localization of the sound, i.e., of practically all the location of which the sense of hearing is capable. Physics shows, indeed, that the binaural time difference is very small. At its maximum (when the source is close to one ear so that the sound must travel halfway around the head to reach the other ear) it cannot be as much as 1 millisecond, .001 second. For sound travels more than 1000 feet a second, and halfway around the head is less than 1 foot. If the source is only 3 degrees to the right of straight ahead—a deviation from the median plane which can often be detected—the binaural time difference is only .027 milliseconds! It seemed incredible that so small a bit of time could serve as a cue, but some hardy experimenters ventured to set up apparatus and try it out (Klemm, 1919, 1920; Von Hornbostel & Wertheimer, 1920).

The apparatus that they constructed conducts the sound from the source separately to the two ears by tubes or telephone circuits. The stimulus is made to reach one ear a little before the other, or with greater intensity. If both intensity and time are equal for both ears, O reports hearing a sound from the median plane. If the sound reaches one ear before the other, the intensity remaining the same at both ears, it is heard as coming from the side of the ear that leads in time. Thus, if the sound reaches the right ear .03 milliseconds sooner, it is heard as coming from slightly to the right; if the time difference in favor of the right ear is increased, the sound is heard as coming from farther to the right, and with a time difference of .65 millisecond the sound is heard as coming from straight out from the right ear. This experiment, which has often been repeated, proves without any doubt that binaural time difference is an effective cue of sound direction.

The experiment can be reversed with somewhat similar results. The sound is delivered simultaneously to both ears, but with greater intensity to one ear. It is heard as coming from the side of greater intensity. But a large intensity difference is required to balance even a very small time difference. In ordinary hearing, with the two binaural differences acting in the same direction, the intensity difference can do little more than confirm the localization determined by the time difference. There is one exception: the time-difference cue breaks down with steady tones of very high pitch, and the intensity difference is then large because of the weakening of the high-frequency waves in bending around the head (Stevens & Newman, 1936). The same reasoning applies to continuous swishy noises which consist largely of very high frequencies. They must be localized by the intensity cue.

An excellent cue of an environmental fact may be altogether different from the fact itself. So we have found repeatedly, and so it is here. The binaural differences have no resemblance to a location of anything in the environment. In order to make sense, the binaural cues have to be "decoded." The decoding in this case is certainly not a deliberate or inferential process. It seems to be primarily a reflex motor process, a quick turning of the head and eyes toward the source of sound, an unlearned, instinctive reaction. Much learning supervenes before the auditory cues of the spatial environment are fully utilized. A binaural difference is primarily a difference between right and left, but it can be transformed into a front-back difference by a turn of the head to either side, or into an up-down difference by a tilt of the head. Pointing the hand toward the apparent source of sound is another learned reaction. The ability to identify a seen object as the source of a sound must depend on a good deal of specific learning. There is a strong tendency to hear a sound as if it came from some object that is seen to be moving—the ventriloquism effect. Individual differences in this tendency have been measured in ingenious experiments (Witkin, Wapner & Leventhal, 1952; Jackson, 1953). In the experiments the visual and auditory cues are made to conflict and the usual result is a compromise on the observer's part. Ordinarily, of course, the different cues of location are in agreement and assist toward the individual's integrated adjustment to the combined visual-auditory world.

The Perception of Objects

The visible environment of objects is very different from the assemblage of juxtaposed areas of different sizes, shapes, and colors which make up the retinal image. If an individual tries to paint a realistic picture of a landscape, he may have considerable trouble in matching the areas in the picture with those in his retinal image, though he see the objects clearly enough. Part of the trouble comes from seeing the environment in three dimensions and having to reproduce it in two—but the retinal image which furnishes the data is also in only two dimensions. We have perhaps sufficiently wondered about this discrepancy and the organism's resources for coping with it in the preceding chapter, but how O advances from variegated retinal areas to objects in the environment is a problem still before us. We might have said, "how O gets behind the retinal areas to the objects." This achievement must depend, it seems, on several factors. Much learning must be required. Strong motivation is obviously present from infancy up, for O has usually to deal with objects rather than with retinal patches. And there must occur a perceptual activity for which we have perhaps no better general term than "discrimination," taken to mean the singling out of an object from its surroundings.

FACTORS IN FIGURAL PERCEPTION

Evidence of prior perceptual learning

If a discrimination has been made and is made more readily a second time, that is the typical evidence of perceptual learning. A face that has been dug out of a puzzle picture with much labor is found quite promptly when the picture is examined again. When you have once picked out a word or phrase from the chatter of conversation in a foreign tongue, you identify it again and again. Thus there is evidence of learning that is visual or auditory, as distinguished from motor learning and from learning to make a certain motor response to a certain stimulus. The child picks out and understands words before he can say them; perceptual learning is fundamental in his acquisition of speech. Less convincing in an argument on the theory of learning, but probably equally genuine evidence of perceptual learning, is the ability to recognize persons whom we could not call by name or to recognize objects that we could not manipulate. If we postpone learning theory to later chapters, we can rest content for the present with the certainty that the perceptions of the present make great use of previous learning.

An important characteristic of recognition is what Hollingworth called *cue reduction*. In making a person's acquaintance you notice his face, his size and figure, his manner of speaking and walking, and many other characteristic details. Later you may recognize him just from a glimpse or from the sound of his voice or even the rhythm of his footsteps. As Hollingworth said (1928, pp. 198, 262):

> Learning is typically . . . the process in which a detail becomes effective in place of the antecedent context of which it has been a constituent but partial feature. The essential fact in learning may, therefore, be described as the reduction of the stimulus leading to a response. The more complete the learning, the further does the reduction of the stimulus proceed. . . . Memory is efficient when the cues required are slight.

What Hollingworth said of learning and memory in general is notably true of recognition. Very often the recognition of a person, a thing, a place, or a social situation is the first step toward appropriate action; mistaken recognition is often the first step in a blunder. Reduced cues can lead to such mistakes. Similar statements hold good when it is not an individual person or thing, but the *kind* of person or thing before us that is rightly or wrongly recognized.

Motivation of perception

There is such a thing as wishful perceiving, seeing what you would like to find, but it is probably less common than wishful thinking (Jenkin, 1957). In the actual presence of objects, the fundamental perceptual motive asserts itself. This motive can be inferred from the ocular adjustments that secure clear vision, the movements of fixation, focusing, and convergence. These resemble reflexes that would require no motivation, but they are something more, for often the first adjustment is imperfect and is corrected by supplementary adjustments. They are goal-seeking movements, the goal being clear vision. If you ask whether clear vision is not simply a means to some biological end such as food or safety, you have an argument from the evolutionary point of view, but you must admit that the seeking of clear vision is built into the individual organism. It is an immediate drive of great potency without regard to any ulterior motivation. The evolutionary logic would go as follows: a mechanism, such as the ocular adjustments for clear vision, which serves as a means for important biological ends, is likely to have a drive of its own, a tendency to be active on its own account so as to accomplish its own direct results, clear vision in this case. At any rate, and without regard to evolutionary logic, the mechanism for clear vision is in action most of the time, provided the organism is awake and alert, even if not engaged in seeking food or safety or any other ulterior goal. All the visual mechanism requires for its activation is the presence of visible objects. Even if a person is absorbed in thought, his eyes are quite certain to be focused on some object—unless, to avoid distraction, he keeps his eyes closed. What we said in Chapter 4 in defense of an exploratory drive is pertinent here, for perception is evidently the core of exploration. The direct goal of exploration is to find or perceive "what is there."

If perception is directly motivated, it is capable of being directly rewarded—or frustrated. The direct reward of the ocular adjustments is a clear view of a certain object or scene. Frustration occurs when a clear view is not obtained. The light may be too dim, the print you are trying to read may be blurred, the handwriting may be obscure, or you may need reading glasses or a spyglass. You probably don't give up until you have done your best to see what is before you. Of course, clear vision is only the beginning of the perceptual process. What it provides is often only a cue of some objective fact, and you have still to decipher its meaning. A sound may be heard distinctly enough, but you want to know what is making the sound. You listen carefully and finally, after rejecting some possibilities, make out what the sound is to your satisfaction.

A few sentences may be quoted from an earlier discussion of the matter (Woodworth, 1947, pp. 123-124).

Perception seems like a passive affair. To the naive observer, what he sees is determined by what is there and nothing more need be said. . . . The present thesis, contrasting with these common views, is that perception is always driven by a direct, inherent motive which might be called the will to perceive. Whatever ulterior motives may be present from time to time, this direct perceptual motive is always present in any use of the senses. . . . Innumerable examples could be cited of complex or unfamiliar stimuli which are first perceived in an unsatisfactory way and then in a way that is satisfactory because it makes sense and fits into the already known situation. The well-practiced perceptions of ordinary existence are so quick and sure that no separate phase of checking and reinforcement can be detected; such perceptions create that false impression of being purely passive affairs. When a new percept is in the making—when an obscure stimulus-complex is being deciphered, or when the meaning of a cue or sign is being discovered—an elementary two-phase process is observable. It is a trial-and-check, trial-and-check process. The trial phase is a tentative reading of the sign, a tentative decipherment of the puzzle, a tentative characterization of the object; and the check phase is an acceptance or rejection, a positive or negative reinforcement of the tentative perception.

Discrimination, the singling out of objects in the visual field

A pioneer study of Wertheimer (1923) is often cited for its contribution to principles of perceptual organization, or factors in perceptual aggregation and segregation. Let us place before us for discussion a list of Wertheimer's factors:

1. *Proximity.* In a field of dots, like the starry sky, those that are

near together are spontaneously seen as a group separate from others that are farther apart.

2. *Sameness and similarity*. A cluster of bright stars stands out as a unit from the background of dimmer ones. In a dot field of several colors, those of one color are likely to stand out together, the others retiring for the moment to the background.

3. *Common movement*. If some of the dots move together in the same direction and at the same speed, they stand out from the rest which remain stationary. An important example is the parallel retinal movement of objects at a certain distance resulting from any movement of the observer himself (pp. 173f). Thus the near objects are segregated from the distant ones.

4. *Continuity*. If several of the dots lie in a straight line or fairly simple curve, this unit stands out and catches the eye. A modern example, the lights of a road as seen from an airplane at night.

5. *Closure*. This factor operates in two ways. A closed figure has an advantage over a straight line or an open curve. And if a figure, otherwise continuous, has a small discontinuity, like a small gap in a circle, the gap tends to close itself automatically. "Closing the gap" is regarded as a dynamic factor also in problem solution.

6. *Pregnance*. A figure is "pregnant" if all parts of it conform to the general character of the whole. A perfect square is more pregnant than any sort of near-square. Pregnance is regarded as so important as to be called "Wertheimer's Law," a fundamental law of field organization. Koffka (1935) endeavors to clarify it as follows: "Psychological organization will always be as 'good' as the prevailing conditions allow. In this definition the term 'good' . . . embraces such properties as regularity, symmetry, simplicity and others" (p. 110). Or again (pp. 137-138): "Organization depends upon the resulting form. Of several geometrically possible organizations that one will actually occur which possesses the best, the most stable shape." Such statements make the law of pregnance sound like the law of effect in learning. The pregnant figure, the "good" figure, must be the one that gives most satisfaction. Perhaps so, but Wertheimer regarded the perceptual tendency toward simplicity and regularity as fundamentally identical with the laws of equilibrium in physics, manifested by the symmetry of a soap bubble.

7. *Familiarity*. Previous experience has conferred a perceptual advantage on letters of the alphabet and on the profile of the hu-

man face though these configurations have very little goodness in the sense of symmetry, regularity, or simplicity.

8. *Set.* We called it "preset" (p. 40); the German term *Einstellung* is often used in English as well. We find what we are looking for; at least what we are looking for has an advantage over other figures that are equally favored by all the other factors.

The first three factors in the list, proximity, similarity, and common movement, are in a way the most fundamental, for the others cannot operate without them. In a field of many dots there are sure to be some that lie in a straight line, but this line will not stand out unless the component dots are near together, or similar in color, or moving together and separately from the rest. Some of those numerous dots certainly form a perfect circle, some form a human face, some form a letter E or any shape you may be seeking. However, they will be concealed, masked, camouflaged, by the mass of similar dots.

From another point of view the most fundamental factor is *set.* Wertheimer meant to have his *O*s take a purely receptive, passive attitude, but it is doubtful if a wide-awake subject can maintain this attitude while looking attentively at any field. He may have an esthetic attitude and look for good shapes; or, more likely, he has the ordinary matter-of-fact attitude of looking for objects. This latter attitude is inevitable when perception is functioning in the service of motor behavior. Lewin (1935, pp. 44, 49), though sympathetic with Gestalt psychology in many respects, differed with Wertheimer at this point. Wertheimer regarded his "field forces," including pregnance, as primary, with interference from set and familiarity usually playing only a minor role; but for Lewin the prime mover in any perceptual activity was some need or quasi-need, with the field forces providing guidance through the environment, but not setting the goal.

Schema with correction

If *O* is asked to reproduce a nonsense line drawing, either while it is in sight or immediately after it has been removed from sight, he almost invariably tries to find it in a resemblance to some familiar object or to some relatively simple form which he can use as a schema or ground plan or framework to guide him in perception and reproduction. The schema is simpler and more regular than the stimulus-figure and therefore requires some correction. The given figure is a near-square, for example, but there is a nick in one of the sides; O adopts a square as his schema, and notes more or less exactly the location and size of the nick; with this correction he is able to draw a fair imitation. With a more complicated stimulus figure the schema adopted may prove inadequate and have to be replaced by a better one. In his first attempts to learn a nonsense figure so as to reproduce it from memory, O may stare at it in the hope of obtaining a memory image which he can simply copy; but he finds this "photographic" attitude undependable and resorts to the more active process of schema with correction. This general result has been obtained by a long line of investigators, some of them working primarily on perception and some on memory for figures, which has at times been quite a controversial subject (Kuhlmann, 1906; Piéron, 1920; Granit, 1921; Wulf, 1922; Bartlett, 1932; Hanawalt, 1937; Vernon, 1952, 1955; more about these studies can be found in Woodworth & Schlosberg, 1954, pp. 406-416, 714-718, 773-777).

Economy of perception

The enormous mass of sensory data that is offered by the retinal picture at a single instant far exceeds what can be perceived in detail at that instant. This statement can be readily accepted if we look at a printed page and consider the multitude of letters present even within the central region of distinct vision. We should count the white interspaces as well as the black letters, and each letter or interspace consists of distinguishable parts. Even the letters that lie too far from the momentary fixation point to be read contribute nevertheless to the mottled appearance of the page. If an observer were asked to report all that he could see in a momentary exposure, he would undoubtedly feel that he perceived more than he had time to report, but he would admit that he could not possibly grasp more than a fraction of the visible detail. His description would be comparatively economical: a page of horizontal lines of 10-point type, with a few words reportable near the center and the rest illegible at the moment but certainly printed material.

Now suppose that his visible field consisted simply of a uniform green area on the right and a uniform red area on the left, vertically adjacent from top to bottom. His description could be very economical indeed, though he might specify the shades of red and green and locate the vertical division more exactly. Yet his retinal stimulation would be as multitudinous as ever, only more uniform than in the case of the printed page. It would not occur to him to report the red and green areas point by point or to follow the separation point by point, reporting that it was everywhere vertical. He would not perceive it in that detailed way; he would perceive the uniform areas and the straight vertical separation. The economy would be perceptual and not merely verbal.

The economy is possible here because the field is capable of being described by a few summary statements. The enormous mass of detailed information which it presents is mostly "redundant," to use a term of information theory. It is redundant because a few observations define the whole field. Consider the near-square again. To describe or perceive it point by point, the white interior as well as the black enclosing line, would be a never-ending job. If the figure were a perfect square, perceiving its size and position would be enough; since it has a nick in one side, the location, width and depth of the nick must be specified, but the schema and correction guarantee great economy as compared with a planless attempt to perceive and memorize the figure.

Wertheimer's field factors of proximity, similarity, common movement and continuity certainly economize the labor of perception. The starry sky is described (for ordinary purposes) more easily and economically because of the constellations, groupings based on proximity and similarity. The active process of schematization and correction makes use of the primitive field factors emphasized in Gestalt psychology. Hochberg & McAlister (1953) even suggest that a "good figure" is one that requires only a small amount of information to define it; and they find experimentally in certain cases at least that such an easily defined figure is more likely to be perceived than one which requires a larger amount of information to define it adequately. A similar conception of visual perception is proposed by Attneave (1954, 1955). "When we begin to consider perception as an information-handling process, it quickly becomes clear that much of the information received by any higher organism is *redundant*. Sensory events are highly interdependent in both space and time" (1954). "Various Gestalt-factors including symmetry, good continuation, and other forms of regularity may all be considered to constitute redundancy in visual stimulation, and quantified accordingly within a framework of information theory" (1955). Once you see that a figure is bilaterally symmetrical, careful examination of the left-hand side gives you all the information you need for reproducing the whole figure; the additional information obtainable from careful examination of the right-hand side would be redundant. Whether the esthetic effect of symmetry adds any usable information is doubtful. Information theory, developed by communication engineers, is of value to psychologists as suggesting quantitative methods for describing a presented situation and discovering how much use an observer makes of his opportunities for economical perception. It is a mathematical theory, best suited for cases where the potential information presented to O can be divided into fairly equal items such as speech sounds or printed letters of the alphabet (G. A. Miller, 1953a, 1953b).

A language as spoken or written contains much redundant "information"—not information about people and things, but merely data enabling you to repeat what you hear or read. Suppose E presents a perfectly random series of letters for O to repeat. There is no redundancy here; O has to wait for each letter to be shown before he can guess right more than one time in twenty-six on the average. He can improve his percentage considerably if he knows he is being shown a connected passage of English, letter by letter, for the context supplies advance information, sometimes exact, sometimes only more or less probable. If the letter sequence should be,

t h e w e a t h e r m a n p r e d i c t s r a i n a l o n g t
h e c o a s t b u t s n o w i n t h e m o u n t a i n s ,

some bunches of letters could be left blank and filled in correctly by O, as in a completion test. Some letter sequences, then, are redundant in this context, and the completion test indicates O's ability to perform his task economically and without dependence on the redundant information. Often, as you listen to a speaker, you could complete his sentence for him if he hesitates. He might as well just make a gesture. Still, the redundancy is not altogether waste motion. If a speaker or writer avoids all repetition and superfluous words, condensing his discourse to the limit, he gets the reputation of being hard to understand. He is feeding in information—meaningful information here—faster than his audience can assimilate and "process" it. What was said on "advance information" in reading (pp. 146ff) is relevant here.

Figure perception versus object perception

We have been considering the factors which help an observer pick out definite figures from the variegated mass of stimuli in the retinal picture or image. Stimuli that are near together in the picture, stimuli that are similar in brightness and color, stimuli that move together along the retina, stimuli that lie in a continuous line or symmetrical shape—such stimuli readily combine into units standing out from the mass. However, we ordinarily notice objects rather than even good figures. Except when we are in an esthetic mood, we are interested in objects rather than in stimulus configurations. The stretch of open sky between two buildings ought to stand out because of its compactness and uniformity and perhaps symmetry, but ordinarily we notice the buildings instead. Our objective, behavioral set dominates.

In his book on *Gestalt psychology* (1947, pp. 156ff) Wolfgang Köhler shows how the Wertheimer factors of organization tend to cause physical objects, either natural or man-made, to stand out in the visual field. An object is likely to be compact and of uniform color; the factors of proximity and similarity make it easy to see. The contour of the object in the retinal picture is likely to be smooth even if not symmetrical; and when the object moves, the parts of its retinal image are likely to move together in the same direction—though this common movement is somewhat complicated when the object turns like a wheel. In attempting to conceal a ship or a soldier the camouflage artist can take advantage of the factors of similarity and continuity, as by painting the object so as to make it similar in color and texture to its surroundings and so as to destroy its smooth contour and its internal uniformity.

PERCEPTION OF THE SIZE, SHAPE, AND "COLOR" (REFLECTANCE) OF OBJECTS

One characteristic of an object which the child must discover very early is that it changes its visual appearance while remaining the same object. What happens objectively is that the object moves or that the wide-awake child is moved; what happens in the retinal picture is that a certain patch or figure shrinks or enlarges, mean-while changing in shape. The mother's face approaches, expanding enormously and changing in shape as she turns her head. But why should the child have any other impression except that of visual change? Of course, the visual sequence is continuous rather than disjointed, with no line drawn between the earlier and later ap-pearances; it is a sequence that is repeated often and that leads to important nonvisual events of contact and feeding, so that the child learns the sequence and has his expectation confirmed and rein-forced. Perceiving the sequence as an approaching object is a good example of perceptual economy. There are similar sequences, simi-larly perceived, when the somewhat older infant creeps toward an attractive object or when he manipulates a toy, turning it this way and that and moving it toward and away from his watching eyes. To perceive the seen toy and the handled toy as the same object which changes from moment to moment, while remaining the same object through the sequence of changes, is certainly economical. How far this naive realism of the child is built up by experience and how far it is a native assumption in behavior would be hard to judge. It would seem impossible for an organism to deal with the environment on any other assumption, but it is certain that the young organism has plenty of experience verifying the assumption.

The infant's experience in his little game of rolling a ball on the floor must afford a great deal of instruction on the interdependence of visual size and distance. The visual stimuli are in continual flux; the size of the retinal image of the ball, its location in the total visual picture, the visible texture or detail, the binocular parallax, and other "cues of distance"—all are continually changing; and there is no stability anywhere, unless the ball is perceived as a real object moving on a real floor. With this core of stability given, the visual flux becomes orderly. As the ball rolls nearer along the floor, its visual size increases; as its texture widens, so does the texture of the floor over which it happens to be rolling at the moment.

Another instructive experience occurs when the child sees a novel object lying on the floor beyond his reach. Suppose he sees it as something small enough to be grasped with one hand. He ap-proaches and finds it too large for one hand. There his perception of size at a distance is corrected; or it may be confirmed and re-inforced.

Visually, a moving object is likely to change in shape as well as size. A three-dimensional object, unless a sphere, presents differently shaped surfaces to the eye as the child handles and turns it about. It also stimulates the tactile and kinesthetic senses differently, but it remains the same object and we cannot doubt that the child soon comes to treat it as the same object from moment to moment. Even a flat object changes its visual shape as it turns, a circle changing to a broad and then to a narrow ellipse, and a square or rectangle becoming an oblique-angled parallelogram. A picture on the wall gradually changes in visual shape as the little child is carried from one part of the room to another. The shape of the whole room, as we might call it, including the relative sizes and positions of the furniture, changes gradually as the infant observer moves or is carried around the room. Yet the room and its contents remain objectively the same and are doubtless perceived as remaining the same, for the continuity of these changes is very different from the visual discontinuity that occurs when the child is carried from one room to another.

As the retinal size of an object depends on the viewing distance, and the retinal shape on the viewing angle, so the retinal brightness and color of an object depend on the illumination received by the object. The retinal picture of an object is subject to great changes in brightness, some being sudden and others gradual. The light may be turned on or off; a person who is being watched may move from a bright to a dim part of the room; and even within the confines of the child's crib some parts are more brightly lighted than others so that any object the child manipulates is sure to undergo visual changes moment by moment. He may even imitate an older person who increases the brightness of an object by holding it where the illumination is strong.

Yet the retinal color of an object does not depend *entirely* on its illumination, any more than its retinal size depends wholly on viewing distance, or its retinal shape wholly on viewing angle; for under the same illumination one object is objectively white and another black; at the same distance one is larger than another in the retinal picture; and at the same angle their pictures shapes are different. The retinal size of an object depends on its momentary distance and on its inherent, stable object size; and the object size is important if one wishes to find the object and play with it. The same is true of object shape and object color. But how can one perceive the object size, given only the retinal picture of the object in its surroundings? Well, the picture gives the momentary visual size of the object, and a favorable view of the surroundings provides good cues of its distance; so the data are available for perception of object size. Similar statements can be made regarding object shape and color. The behavior of a child in the latter half of his first year after birth shows clearly that he can utilize these data and achieve these perceptions.

Very instructive to the young child, no doubt, are his numerous experiences with interposition and motion parallax (pp. 173, 177). His toy gets partially hidden behind something else, its visual size and shape being thus radically altered; yet he still sees the same toy and goes after it. Even if the toy disappears altogether, because of *E*'s covering it with a handkerchief or hiding it behind a screen, it remains a reality to the nine-month child who will remove the handkerchief or look behind the screen (Piaget, 1937; Psyche Cattell, 1940). Interest in objects, such as large plastic rings or small wooden cubes, is indicated much earlier, but the test just described is especially demonstrative. A large object can be hidden behind a small object, if the small object—perhaps the child's hand—is much closer to the eye; or a large object can be seen through a small peekhole, if the peekhole is close to the eye. The interrelations of object size, distance, and visual (retinal, projective) size are always involved in any active form of play.

Retinal size is conveniently stated in angular degrees. If you have a screen 1 foot distant from your eye, with a window in it 1 inch high, that is, one-twelfth of its distance from the eye, you have a view through the window of approximately 5 degrees in height. This "visual angle," accordingly, subtends or covers approximately 1 inch at a distance of 12 inches, 1 foot at a distance of 12 feet, 100 feet at a distance of 1200 feet. These subtended heights are the limit of what you could see through your 5 degree window. (To be more accurate, your window must be 1.05 inches high to allow a 5 degree view; it must be 2.10 inches high to allow a 10 degree view, 3.16 inches high for a 15 degree view, 4.23 inches high for a 20 degree view. If the screen were twice as far away, the window would have to be twice as tall for the same visual angle.) The retinal size and distance of an object being given, its object size is found by multiplying these two quantities together: object size = retinal size × distance. The retinal size is given whenever an object is seen; with adequate cues of distance, therefore, the data are available for perceiving the object size. Or, if the size of the object is known, the retinal size is a cue of distance, as we saw in the preceding chapter (p. 171 and Figure 10).

Objects at different distances compared in size

Young children certainly deal with a moving object as having a size of its own which remains the same during its motion or during the child's own approach to it. They must take its retinal size merely as a cue along with other cues of objective size and distance. Logically, we might expect them to see whether two objects located at different distances are equal or unequal in object size. In one case they perceive a single object to remain the same in object size while moving from one location to another. What is to prevent them in the other case from perceiving two objects in different locations as being of the same object size? The continuity of the motion experience must help to integrate the sequence of appearances. But the young child does see equal objects standing at different distances and so differing in retinal size though equal and interchangeable for behavior—equal building blocks, for example. He may be able from an early age to perceive their equality.

Perception of size and distance in the first year. From a very early age children make positive responses to an attractive object held before them within reach or somewhat beyond their reach. You cannot always tell whether the child is trying to get hold of the object, but you can usually distinguish a hand and arm movement directed toward the object from a mere expression of excitement. Seventy-three babies ranging in age from ten to fifty weeks were tested by Cruikshank (1941). While the child was lying on his back, a rattle was held out to him and note was taken as to whether he made a positive response to it within 30 seconds. In each daily test three conditions were alternated: (A) a small rattle was held 10 inches from the child's eyes; (B) the small rattle at a distance of 30 inches; (C) a large rattle at 30 inches. The large rattle was "three times as large the small rattle but of the same form and coloring." Therefore, the retinal size, shape, and color of the large rattle in C were the same as those of the small rattle in A. If determined by the retinal picture of the rattle alone, the child's response should be the same in conditions A and C; but if the abundant distance cues were utilized, positive responses to the near rattle should be much more frequent than to either the small or the large rattle at the inaccessible distance. The following table, condensed from the original, shows the percent frequency of positive responses at each age. There were twenty-two to twenty-six children tested at each age, and the number of trials on which the percents are based ranged from 154 to 230.

Frequency of positive responses

Age, weeks	(A) to near object	(B) to far object, small	(C) to far object, large
14-15	62%	31%	35%
16-17	67	26	36
18-19	78	26	35
20-21	94	24	30
22-23	99	20	20
24-25	99	13	13

Between three and six months, as the table shows, there is considerable change, positive response to the near, accessible rattle becoming practically universal while response to the distant rattles tends to drop out. This distance discrimination is perhaps somewhat disturbed by the retinal equivalence of conditions A and C (positive response in C running ahead of B), but this disturbing factor is overcome before the age of six months. "By six months of age there is evidence that . . . the equality of the gross projective sizes . . . does not lead to identical response." The objective variables of size and distance are well perceived at that age, at least within a small range of environmental space.

Matching for size of objects at different distances

With older children and adults it is possible to make a quantitative test of the following hypothesis: Objects of the same physical size but at different distances from the observer are perceived as equal in size or approximately so. The experimenter's procedure is to present objects at different distances and to ask O to match them for size. An object at one distance is designated as the "Standard" and an object at a different distance is to be adjusted until O calls it equal in size to the Standard. A good example of this procedure is given by Piaget & Lambercier (1951). Their apparatus and results

are shown in Figures 14 and 15. One match which they called for—
to adjust the far object to equal the near object in physical size—was

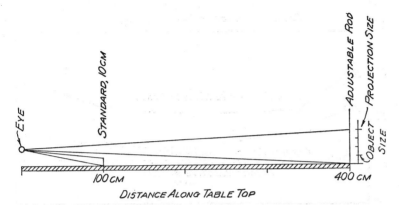

FIG. 14. (After Piaget & Lambercier, 1951, p. 86.) Setup for measurement
of objective and projective perception of visible size. By means of a head
rest the eyes are held in a constant location, 20 centimeters above one end
of the table, and at horizontal distances of 100 centimeters from the Standard rod and 400 centimeters from the adjustable rod. The latter is adjusted
in one test so as to appear of the same objective height as the Standard, and
in another test so as to appear projectively equal to the Standard. The correct
adjustments, shown at the right, are 10 centimeters and 40 centimeters
respectively. The average adjustments were approximately correct for objective equality, but much too small for projective equality (Fig. 15). Both
eyes were open in these tests; the far rod was projectively vertically over the
near rod. Children and some adults were helped to comprehend the meaning
of projective size by pretraining very much in the manner of Leonardo da
Vinci (p. 168): objects at different distances were to be painted on a sheet
of glass fixed before the eyes, and the subject's attempts were checked by
direct superposition of the painting on the distant object.

easily understood by young children, and the average match was
just about perfect for all the age groups. That is, object size was
well perceived within the range of distances employed. The other
task—to adjust the far object so as to equal the near object in
retinal or projective size—could not be made clear to children
younger than seven years and was not easily understood even by
many adults, and the matches were decidedly incorrect for all age
groups.

It seems paradoxical that projective (retinal) size should not be
judged accurately or at least as accurately as object size, for projective size is one of the essential cues for the perception of object size,

the other essential being some cue of distance. From the practical standpoint we can see that, unless O is making a picture of the

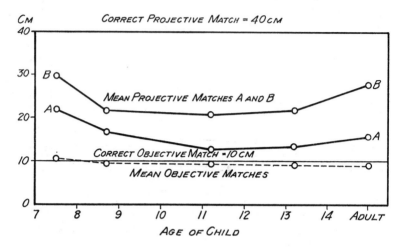

FIG. 15. (After Piaget & Lambercier, 1951, p. 91.) Objective size and projective size as perceived by younger and older children and adults; tests described under Figure 14. N (number of testees) for the age groups: 7-8 years, 36; 8-10 years, 24; 10-12 years, 24; 12-14 years, 27; adults, 42. (For the upper curve the samples were smaller, N being respectively 23, 18, 17, 27, 23 individuals.) The A curve was obtained before, the B curve after, the pretraining mentioned under Figure 14. The authors state that "the differences between the Means of the principal age groups are significant." The age differences are very small in the object-size perception, smaller than the range which is about 3 centimeters for each age group and larger for the adults. In the test for adjustment of the far rod to match the near rod projectively, nearly every individual of all age groups made the far rod too short, an error which was partially but not wholly corrected by the pretraining. This error was considerably smaller in the seven-year olds and the adults than in the intermediate age groups. Projective matching is difficult because of the intrusion of the objective appearance; the youngest children, through naïveté, and some of the adults, through reasoning, are freest from this intrusion. This is the most probable explanation of the projective curves. Joynson (1949) reached a similar conclusion.

scene before him, he is concerned with the objective size and distance and uses the cues simply as means to reach this objective goal, with no need for explicit estimates of the cues. Moreover, in the objective perceptions the size and distance cues are used in combination, not separately estimated. Looking back at Figure 10 in Chapter 7 we can see that the distance of an object is given not directly but as a projection of distance along the ground. If O were asked to reproduce the retinal projection of distance along the ground, he probably would be subject to as much error as in matching the projective size of an object. We say "probably" because the experiment has not been tried to our knowledge.

Some idea of the difficulty of projective matching can be had by aid of the painter's device: hold a pencil or other straight rod vertically at arm's length and use the thumb to mark off from the top the projective length of objects at different distances and angles, including horizontal spaces. This matching is easy and exact if the rod is superposed visually over the object, but not if the rod is held far to the right or left of the object, or far above or below.

Estimates of distance and object size in everyday situations

Believing that results obtained under the simplified laboratory conditions might not be representative of a person's ability to perceive size and distance in the home or outdoors, Brunswik (1944) obtained estimates from two young adults in a great variety of situations. The estimates were made in metric units (meters and centimeters) which these Os were accustomed to use. (It has been found, more recently, that estimates of distance on an open field are more accurate than might be expected, though subject to an individual's tendency toward over- or underestimation, which tendency is quickly reduced when O is told the true distance after each of his estimates—experiments by E. J. Gibson et al., 1954, 1955.) Even though subject to considerable error, estimates of a wide range of sizes and distances might be highly correlated with the true values. An individual might underestimate all the sizes but still rank them in their true order. Brunswik found correlations of +.99 between true and estimated object sizes and of +.99 between true and estimated distances, but considerably lower, +.85, between true and estimated projections. The Average Error for object size was 12 percent, for distance also 12 percent, but for projective size 22 percent, the two subjects agreeing closely in all these respects. Their instructions for the projective estimates went about as follows: Try to see the scene as a painter would have to see it in order to draw a perspectively correct picture, or as it would be shown in a photograph taken from where you stand; try to estimate the projections of the objects on a transparent frontal plane located one meter in front of your eyes. These subjects performed the task quite well (as compared for example with those of Piaget & Lambercier, p. 206) yet not nearly as well as the objective tasks. Physically and objectively there is an exact mathematical relationship of the three quantities: object size, distance, and projection; object size $=$ projection $\times$ distance; but we cannot expect to find the same exact equation between *perceived* object size, distance, and projection (Kilpatrick & Ittelson, 1953). The various cues of distance or size may interfere with each other in a particular case; anyway it is difficult for O to focus attention on projective size as a goal of perception, instead of using projection along with other cues as means for perceiving the objective facts of size and distance.

Could object size be perceived at all in the absence of any cues of distance? Logically, no, for the same retinal size can be produced by objects of *any* size, depending on their distance. Exclusion of all cues of distance cannot be accomplished out of doors (except perhaps if the moon were the object) but requires strict laboratory controls. Binocular parallax and disparity would furnish good cues out to a distance of 50 feet or more; hence monocular vision is necessary. Motion parallax would furnish cues; hence the head must be prevented from moving side to side. The floor, ceiling, and side walls of the experimental room must be hidden by baffles so that only the object is visible, and the object had best be a flat disk or triangle of uniform light. Even with these restrictions some slight cues may remain and yield a vague perception of distance and object size. But with all cues of distance eliminated, it is safe to say (size perception based wholly on retinal size) that objects of the same retinal size must seem somehow equal, though perhaps not really equal in objective size. Some very clever experiments have been done on this problem (Holway & Boring, 1941; Lichten & Lurie, 1950; Chalmers, 1952).

The "constancies" in object perception

One does not change the true size of an object by approaching it, nor its true shape by viewing it obliquely, nor its inherent color (reflectance) by changing the illumination. The retinal image changes, but the objective fact remains constant. The goal of perception in most of the organism's practical dealings with the environment is to get at the objective facts—to utilize the retinal size along with other cues so as to perceive the objective size and distance of an object; to utilize the retinal shape along with other cues so as to perceive the objective shape and slant of an object; and to utilize the retinal color along with other cues so as to perceive the inherent color of an object and the illumination in which it stands. In ordinary life this perceptual goal is at least roughly attained. A ball lying on the floor is seen in its true size and at its true distance; a picture on the wall is seen as a rectangle viewed at an angle; and a sheet of white paper standing in a shadow is seen as just that. So far as perception reaches these objective goals, it is said to show size constancy, shape constancy, color constancy. In laboratory tests the constancy is seldom perfect, often only moderate in degree. To measure it E needs a zero point, which is the retinal size, shape, or color, unaffected by any other cues. In a test for size constancy, if O matches a near and a far object by retinal or projective size alone, he shows zero size constancy; if he makes a correct objective match, he shows 100-percent size constancy; if his match is halfway between these points, he shows 50-percent size constancy. This "constancy ratio" has been used in a vast amount of quantitative work on what is certainly an important problem, the perception of objects and their objective characteristics.

A major contributor to this line of investigation was the late Egon Brunswik, one of whose studies has already been cited. His results on the development of objective perception are summarized

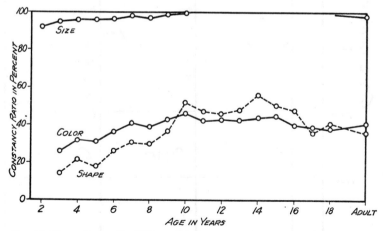

FIG. 16. (From Brunswik, 1956, p. 83.) Age curves for the perception of object size, shape, and color (whiteness). The Constancy Ratio, described in the text, provides comparable units for the three different kinds of perception.

in Figure 16. He regards the decline of the age curves toward zero constancy as a true developmental phenomenon. Zero constancy is not merely a lack of objective perception; it is the ideal result if O is set to perceive the retinal size, shape, or color. The adult will be more attentive to these stimuli if he has had any practice in drawing or painting from nature or in photographing three-dimensional scenes, or if for any reason he has become critically attentive to the cues he uses in objective perception. Animals, presumably altogether practical and objective, have, as far as tested, given very high constancy ratios (Locke, 1938).

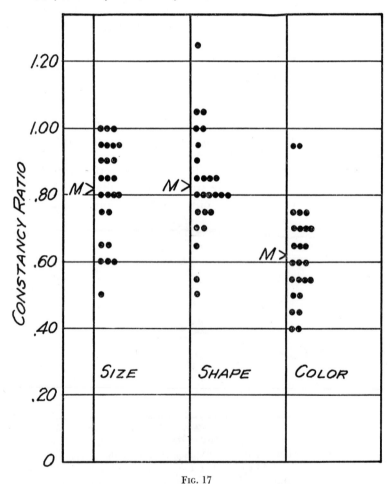

Fig. 17

Individual differences in perceptual constancy. Any theory of perception must leave considerable leeway for individual differences. Such differences have been found by all experimenters in this field and were emphasized strongly by Thouless (1932) and by Sheehan (1938). Some of Sheehan's distribution curves are shown

---

FIG. 17. (Data from Sheehan, 1938, p. 62, columns headed "Unreduced Whiteness," "Circle 150" and "45° Figure.") Distributions for size, shape, and whiteness perception. The objects to be compared were displayed on a long table in front of O.

For size matching, the Standard was a circle of 10-centimeter diameter placed in a frontal-parallel position at a distance from O of 150 centimeters (about 5 feet), and the Variable, placed at twice that distance, ranged from 8 to 22 centimeters in diameter. Being shown one of these Variables, along with the Standard, O was asked which looked larger, and a series of Variables was shown, according to the "Method of Limits," until a match was obtained. If the Variable of 10-centimeter diameter, objectively equal to the Standard, was matched with it, the Constancy Ratio was 1.00; but if the Variable of 20-centimeter diameter, projectively equal to the Standard, was the match, the Constancy Ratio was zero.

For shape matching, Standard and Variable were placed a foot apart at eye level, 5 feet in front of O. The Standard might be called a square diamond, being a square with one diagonal vertical, the other horizontal, the diagonals measuring 20 centimeters long. This Standard was projectively flattened by a backward tilt of 45 degrees. The Variables were objectively flattened diamonds shown in the frontal-parallel position. They were equal to the Standard in horizontal diagonal. One of them being shown along with the Standard, O was asked whether the Standard or the Variable looked taller. A match was determined by the Method of Limits. For a Constancy Ratio of 1.00, the tilted square diamond Standard would be matched with the frontal-parallel square Variable, but for a Constancy Ratio of zero, the projectively equal Variable (vertical diagonal = 14.14 centimeters) would be chosen. (A convenient apparatus for shape matching, with an adjustable isosceles triangle substituted for the series of diamonds, is offered by Gottheil & Bitterman, 1951.)

For whiteness matching, the illumination was provided exclusively by a single 150-watt bulb behind O. The objects to be compared for whiteness were two rotating color wheels, the Standard being twice as far from the bulb as the Variable and therefore receiving only one fourth as strong light. The Standard was a pure white paper disk while the Variable was composed of white and black sectors fused by rapid rotation into a gray, ranging from black to white according to the proportions of black and white in the mixture. One of these Variables being shown along with the Standard, O was asked which looked whiter; and a match was determined by the same general method as before. If the pure white Variable was matched with the pure white Standard, in spite of the difference in illumination, the Constancy Ratio was 1.00; but it was zero if the matched Variable was only one-fourth white, so matching the Standard in stimulus intensity on the retina.

in Figure 17. She measured the constancy ratios in a variety of tests for perception of size, shape and color (whiteness) from the same group of twenty-five college women in order to obtain correlations which would show whether the same individuals ranked consistently high or low in the different tests. A high correlation would indicate a general tendency in the individual toward objective or toward projective perception or toward a definite compromise between these two. But the obtained correlations were too low to indicate any such general tendency, except perhaps as between size and shape perception (rho = + .50). Her conclusion (1938, p. 93): "We question any use of the term constancy which implies the existence of a unit trait; and as a logical corollary, we question any suggestion that it is more characteristic of one age or intelligence level than another."

In the cases cited in Figure 17 zero constancy means a match conforming exactly to the stimulus intensity, size, or shape on the retina, while perfect constancy means a match conforming exactly to the whiteness, size, or shape of the objects compared.

We have to expect zero constancy if O receives absolutely no cues of illumination in the case of whiteness comparisons, no cues of distance in the case of size comparisons, and no cues of slant in the case of shape comparisons.

Object color is the same as reflectance, a physicochemical property of substances. Charcoal has a very low reflectance, i.e., it reflects back, diffusely, only a small fraction of the light it receives. Chalk has a high reflectance since it reflects a large fraction, perhaps 80 percent, of the light received. If charcoal is standing in a strong light and chalk in a weak light, the absolute amount of light reflected from the charcoal exceeds that reflected from the chalk, though the percentages are unchanged. A colored substance reflects the different colors (wavelengths) selectively. To some extent we can distinguish red, yellow, green, and blue objects not only in dim light but even in somewhat colored illumination. Color constancy, the perception of object color, furnishes cues for the recognition of objects so that its practical value is somewhat comparable to that of size and shape constancy.

THEORY OF OBJECTIVE PERCEPTION

Physically, as we have said, there is a definite three-way relationship of the objective size of an object (or surface), its distance from the observer, and the size of his retinal image of the object. Given any two of these, one can compute the third. Similarly with object shape and object color: given the retinal shape and the slant of the objective surface, one could compute its objective shape; or given the brightness of the retinal image and the intensity of the illumination, one could compute the reflectance of the surface.

Perception is too quick and too primitive a process to depend on computation, but it has to utilize the same data. The size, shape, and brightness of the retinal image are of course given; and O's inability to perceive them explicitly with much accuracy (pp. 206, 209) does not prevent his using them effectively as cues in the perception of objective facts. But distance, slant, and illumination are not directly given. O can perceive them if given an adequate view of the surroundings. The object itself may provide usable cues if it is familiar or shows depth or texture. If all such cues are eliminated, however, the objective facts cannot be perceived. Even if given an unobstructed view of a scene, O may get erroneous impressions: an object may appear to be nearer or farther than it is, the apparent slant of a surface may differ from the objective slant, the apparent illumination in a corner of the room may be dimmer than it seems. Such false impressions affect O's perception of an object. Logically, one would think, the resulting errors would be predictable. If an object appears farther away than it is, it should also look larger than it is (in order to produce the given retinal image); if its illumination appears dimmer than it is, the object should seem to have a higher reflectance than it has. Roughly, these predictions have been abundantly confirmed by experiments with deceptive cues of distance or illumination. The question remains, however, whether apparent size and distance are closely enough related for an exact theory or whether we must be contented with the rough relations mentioned. We shall not attempt to sift the evidence on the size-distance problem which is at present rather controversial. The factual question concerns the perception of distances from the observer. Does a physical distance of 100 feet appear to O to be more than twice 50 feet (Gilinsky, 1951), less than twice (Gruber, 1954), or almost exactly twice (Purdy & Gibson, 1955)? From our diagram of the projection of vertical stakes and the ground between them, in the preceding chapter (p. 171), the perception of size and distance might well be subject to different errors and not fit together neatly into a formula.

Attempts to reconcile shape and slant perceptions

The circles that we see are almost always ellipses projectively, for only when we view them square on, in a frontal-parallel plane, are all their diameters equal in the retinal picture. Similarly, the squares that we see are seldom retinal squares. Start with a square figure on a frontal-parallel plane surface, i.e., a surface perpendicular to your momentary line of sight. This surface can be rotated about various axes, say about three principle axes. One is the line of sight itself, the front-back axis. Turning on this axis leaves the retinal image of the square unchanged, its sides remaining equal and its angles remaining right angles. Yet when turned 45 degrees so that its diagonals are vertical and horizontal, the square looks like a diamond and no longer a square. More complex figures, letters of the alphabet, or photographed faces are unrecognizable when turned upside down, though their retinal images are unchanged except in position. However, rotation around either of the other principal axes, the vertical or the side-to-side horizontal, changes the square or any other figure, changes its proportions and angles in the retinal image or in a photograph. Of course, the objective shape remains the same. To a considerable degree the objective shape is perceived along with the slant or inclination. This approximately objective perception of shapes that are not in the frontal-parallel plane goes by the name of shape constancy. Cues of slant are essential for the perception of objective shape.

Physically there is a mathematical interrelation of the three quantities, the object shape, the inclination, and the projective or retinal shape. In a simple case, when the figure is tipped straight back from the frontal position, the vertical lines of the figure are foreshortened in the projection, according to the equation,

$$P = B \cos A,$$

where P is the projective length of a vertical line, B is the objective length of the same line, and A is the angle of inclination back from the frontal plane. See Figure 18. If the objective figure is a circle, inclined back on its horizontal diameter to 30 degrees, we have

$$P = B \cos 30° = .866 \ B,$$

so that the circle in projection is an ellipse, approximately 87 percent as tall as it is broad (since its breadth is not changed by this rotation). What the observer has given is this projective proportion, along with spatial cues of the inclination, and he does perceive a slanting circle. In a quantitative matching experiment he makes some errors, varying from trial to trial and tending to compromise between the objective circle and the projective ellipse.

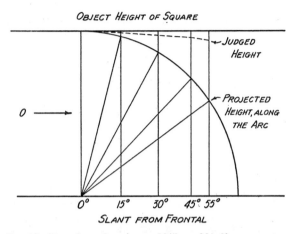

OBJECT HEIGHT OF SQUARE

←JUDGED
HEIGHT

←PROJECTED
HEIGHT, ALONG
THE ARC

O ——→

0°   15°   30°   45° 55°
SLANT FROM FRONTAL

FIG. 18. (Data from Stavrianos, 1945, p. 86.) Shape constancy: judged height of a slanting square. The radii represent the constant object height of a square presented at different inclinations from the frontal plane, the inclinations being 0 degree (frontal), 15 degrees, 30 degrees, 45 degrees, and 55 degrees. Each vertical line in the figure shows three heights: the full length of the line (always the same) is the objective height of the square; the part below the circular arc is the projection height (retinal stimulus height), and the height from the base line up to the dotted line shows the judged or "apparent" height. Though the judged height may be called a compromise between the projective and objective heights, it is much closer to the objective.

In the experiment, with free binocular vision from a fixed viewing point about 3 feet away, O was asked to pick the "best square" from a collection of near squares, some too tall and some too short, all presented at a slant. On the average of five Os, each having ten trials, the "best square," when corrected for the well-known horizontal-vertical illusion, was slightly too tall, being about 1 percent too tall at 15 degrees, 2 percent at 30 degrees, 4 percent at 45 degrees, and 6 percent at 55 degrees. Inversely, therefore, the true square was perceived too short by corresponding percents which are plotted along the dotted line. The slanted square looked shorter than when in the frontal-parallel plane, but only a very little shorter until the slant became large.

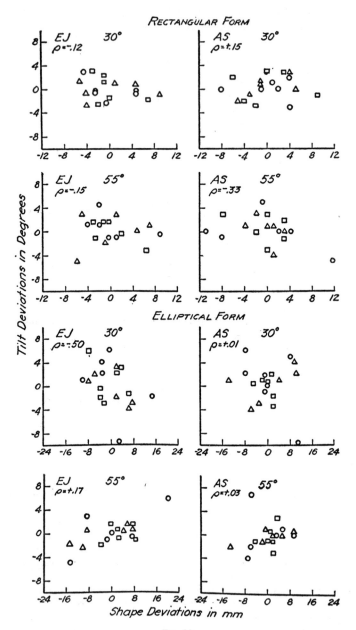

FIG. 19

We cannot expect the physical equation to hold good precisely in the perception of object shape-at-a-slant any better than in the similar case of object size-at-a-distance. The cues of inclination and even the retinal image may not be utilized precisely, and the perceptual mechanism undoubtedly has some "slack" in it, with resulting lack

---

FIG. 19 (*opposite*). (Stavrianos, 1945, p. 75.) Lack of correspondence between single judgments of shape and the accompanying judgments of inclination. Each pair of judgments is represented by a dot, circular for the first day's experiment, triangular for the second day's experiment, square for the third day's experiment. These dots would all lie in an upward-slanting diagonal if there were a firm and regular connection between apparent inclination and apparent shape. Instead, practically no correlation is shown, the Rho being slightly negative for subject EJ and slightly positive for subject AS.

What the subject saw was a gray mat-paper rectangle attached to a black surface that was inclined, top away from him, 3 feet from his eyes, at different angles in different trials. His view was monocular and limited to what he could see through a tube which cut out almost all the surroundings of the rectangle. He tried to match the inclination of the rectangle by adjusting the inclination of another surface which he saw binocularly and fully, looking back to the rectangle if necessary; and he tried to match the objective shape of the rectangle by adjusting the proportions of another, larger rectangle which was not inclined (frontal-parallel presentation). He varied somewhat from trial to trial in both of these adjustments, and the two variations did not correspond closely, as the figure shows; there was no close dependence of apparent shape upon apparent inclination.

Even allowing for some random variation in the single trials, we should expect good average correspondence of the shape with the inclination judgments if apparent shape depends on apparent inclination or if the two are closely interrelated in any way. But such correspondence as was found was not close and rigid. On the basis of several modifications of her experiment, the author was forced to conclude that a rough correspondence of judged shape and inclination was all she could demonstrate. Perhaps the normal perception of shape at a slant is disturbed by the attempt to make separate matches for shape and slant. "The perception of both tilt and shape when they are merely registered as background or as incidental parts of the total percept may differ from their perception when they occupy the observer's close attention" (Stavrianos, p. 72).

In the present experiment, as well as in that reported under Figure 18, slant matching was fairly accurate, although not as good as shape matching. The tendency was to make the match less slanting, nearer the frontal parallel, than the original. The average match for a given slant of 45 degrees, for instance, was 32 degrees in the present monocular test and 38 degrees in the binocular test. A mat surface viewed monocularly from only 3 feet away affords fair cues of slant though not so good as a binocular view from that same distance.

The important factors are texture gradient (p. 172) and binocular disparity (p. 174).

of precision in objective perception. We cannot expect the equation to hold good rigidly between projection, apparent slant, and apparent shape. On the whole, shape is better judged than slant, as seems strange since slant furnishes part of the basis for the perception of shape.

The intriguing problem presented in Figure 19 has been followed up by later ingenious experiments of Beck & Gibson (1955) and of Langdon (1953, 1955a, b). These experimenters have avoided the troublesome division into separate shape matching and slant matching, but they have not discovered any precise, rigid formula linking shape and slant perception. The mechanism operates quite well though "the hypothetical linkage between psychological shape and slant is not rigid" (Beck & Gibson, p. 130). Or, as Langdon puts it (1955a, p. 26): "In the normal process of shape perception the orientation of the object is perceived by virtue of surround cues in relation to stimuli emanating from the object itself." Instead of an "invariant relation" between perceived shape and slant, "it would seem more probable . . . that the interaction of numerous factors, some of them subjective and variable, is involved." The fundamental factor would seem to be everyone's assumption that he is dealing with a real environment in which objects can move without changing their size or shape.

The experiments cited in the last few pages have been motivated by Koffka's demand for a precise "invariant" relation between perceived shape and slant (1935, p. 229).

> The two aspects of the percept will be coupled together so that if one changes, the other changes also . . . if two equal retinal shapes give rise to two different perceived shapes, they will at the same time produce the impression that these two shapes are differently oriented. The question is whether shape and orientation are as rigidly connected as size and distance.

Besides the factors of retinal shape and cues of slant, Koffka recognizes the factor of set or attitude. "Constancy can be tremendously affected if the subjects' attitude is directed towards 'projection' rather than towards real shapes" (p. 235). This attitude, suitable for a painter, puts all the emphasis on retinal shape, as also on retinal size and color, pushing aside the cues of slant, distance, and illumination. Even the painter cannot maintain this attitude as he moves around in the environment and manipulates objects.

But it is an attitude that is more characteristic of some persons than of others and accounts in part for individual differences in the various "constancy" experiments. While studying these large individual differences in color constancy, Henneman (1935, pp. 58-59, 63-66) distinguished the painter's attitude or *photographic set* from the objective or *object-directed set,* the former favoring attention to the stimulus colors, the latter attention to the inherent color or reflectance of an object. Individuals who spontaneously adopted the photographic set got a much lower range of "constancy ratios." It was possible by intensive coaching to get many individuals to change from their spontaneous attitude to the other, at least partially and temporarily. "The evidence seems to favor the view that personal factors, probably attitudes of perception, are operative."

Situation-and-goal set in perception

This concept is of dynamic importance here as well as in the motor behavior and reading which were used before as illustrations (p. 46). While you are reading a story, your immediate *goal* at any moment is to find out what will happen next, and you are certainly set for this goal. For a momentary stimulus you have the words that are directly in view. The meaning you get out of them depends on the words already read. This context is the *situation* for which your reading mechanism is set, and without both parts of this situation-and-goal set you would not be getting on with your story.

Reading is a special kind of perception which we shall not pause to analyze further. In ordinary perception with an object-directed attitude, your immediate goal is to examine an object and perhaps to make out its size, shape, or color. Your focal stimulus is the retinal image of that particular object. But you have to utilize its visible surroundings for cues of its distance, slant, or illumination. In order to perceive the object, you have to be set for its spatial framework. The order of events would seem to be normally as follows: first you become set for a scene that stretches out into the distance; then you focus on an object in the middle distance, for example; its visual image means an object of such and such a size because your object-perceiving mechanism is adjusted for a certain distance.

Sometimes the operation is reversed. Looking across a river you have no clear indication of its width, but you spy a man on the opposite bank and perceive his distance from the size of his retinal image or projection. You might *infer* his distance by some such process as this: you assume that he is 6 feet tall and that your outstretched arm is 1 yard long, out to the ruler which you hold up covering the man. Finding his projection to be 1 inch tall you have the data for solving a proportion: as his projective height of 1 inch is to his objective height of 72 inches, so is the projection distance of 1 yard to the real distance of 72 yards. Compared with this explicit process of reasoning, the perceptual process is much more compact; it does not use numbers or a ruler nor pretend to reach so precise a result. It may be too quick to reveal any exact order of events. In the more common case of perceiving the size, shape, or color of an object, however, there would seem to be no doubt that you start with a set for the visible environment and advance to perception of the particular object.

Otherwise expressed, the perception of objects requires the use of appropriate "codes" for translating stimuli into objective facts (pp. 16, 142). A retinal image has no objective meaning until it is decoded. Its size does not specify any size of the visible object, nor its shape any definite shape of the object, nor its color any definite object color. It is the same here as it is with printed words. Such a letter group as *main* or *ours* has no meaning until you know what language is being used. A language is a code, French being one and English another. If you are set for the particular language, you get the meaning of the letter group instantly. Retinal images are like letter groups in this respect, though the codes are based on physical facts and not on arbitrary conventions. When you are set for a particular distance in the visible environment, you are ready with a code for translating retinal size into object size—and similarly for shape and color. Ordinarily, as you look over a scene that provides good spatial cues, you soon become ready to use all these cues and to see things in their approximately true sizes, shapes, and colors.

CHAPTER 9

Learning the Environment

I: SEQUENCE LEARNING

In accordance with our general definition of behavior as a "dealing with the environment," several chapters on "learning to deal with the environment" would be expected, for certainly a great deal of learning is necessary. If, instead, this series of chapters is headed *learning the environment,* some explanation and justification are in order. Such a phrase as "learning a person or thing or place" has an unfamiliar, awkward sound, though the awkwardness is gone if we say "getting acquainted with" instead of "learning." No one can deny that getting acquainted with the environment and with the objects in it is a form of learning and should be included in any general investigation of the learning process. Our choice of chapter headings is influenced by the conviction, several times expressed already (pp. 140, 167), that the motor behavior of human beings (at least) is guided by the perception of objective facts. Accordingly, learning to deal with the environment depends on exploration and perception of the environment, with enough retention of what has been perceived to influence later behavior.

Whether *all* learned behavior, including the motor skill of the pole vaulter and the coloratura soprano, depends on the perception of appropriate objective facts and relations, is a difficult question on which one should not be dogmatic in advance. Of course other abilities are required, but the vaulter does have to keep track of the bar he is trying to clear, and the soprano of the purity and pitch of her tones. Any skilled performer keeps constant check on *results,* which are objective facts to be perceived. And if we could examine a skilled performance minutely we should probably find that constant use was made of *cues* indicative of the state of affairs with which the performer had to deal from moment to moment.

The chapter headings of this section of the text are concerned with the question, "What?" What is learned of behavioral importance about the environment? One heading asserts that cues are learned, another that places and things are learned. The present chapter, asserting that sequences are learned, is placed first because the process of sequence learning may be the key to other sorts of learning. The individual's notion of cause and effect may be vague, uncritical, and unformulated, but if a regular sequence of events, A followed by B, has impressed itself sufficiently on the individual so that A serves as a signal to get ready for B, he can make good use of this learned sequence. In such cases as the lightning-thunder sequence he gets ready to "take" what is coming; in many other cases he gets ready to do something, or makes a preparatory response of approach or avoidance. Language, whether heard, spoken, read, or written, continues in time and contains many regular temporal sequences: the sequence of sounds or letters in a word, the sequence of words in a familiar phrase or their order in the sentence structure of a familiar language. The learning of these linguistic sequences by the young child is really a large-scale achievement. Music affords further evidence of the vast amount of sequence learning that occurs in human children and adults.

Sequential learning of a very important kind occurs in the process of getting acquainted with things and persons. A stranger appears before a child and proceeds to do something pleasing to the child. The next time that person appears, the child smiles at the sight of him, anticipating the same sequence of events as before. The child has learned a characteristic of that person. The child sees a pale pink strawberry and proceeds to bite it, learning, as we say, that pale pink strawberries *are* sour. The "are" in this statement is psychologically significant; the sequence of events in the learning process has dropped out of sight, "telescoped" into a characteristic of the object. If anyone doubts the asserted characteristic of pale strawberries, you give him one to try, reverting to the original sequence. The characteristics of objects are often learned in this sequential way, and not only their permanent characteristics but also their temporary states—the crossness, for example, of a growling dog or a frowning person. Again our statement is apt to be, "The dog *is* cross" rather than "If you touch him, he will snap at you." What is discovered and checked by a sequence of experiences and stated in a conditional, "if—then," form is soon "reified" into a declarative form which asserts something about the environment. The reifying, objectifying tendency, *reification,* is undoubtedly a source of economy in behavior.

The "sequence of events, A followed by B," impinges on O as a sequence of stimuli or stimulus complexes which we shall call S_1 and S_2, the numbers indicating the order in time. If the sequence gets learned, some sort of *adjustment for S_2* is made during the S_1–S_2 interval—unless that interval is too short. The adjustment or "preset" (p. 40) does not always show in O's motor behavior. It may be only an anticipatory waiting for S_2 to occur, a readiness to "take" S_2 as we said before. But if S_2 is going to call for some definite motor response, a *preparatory response* is almost sure to be learned and evoked by S_1, so that the whole sequence becomes $S_1R_1S_2R_2$, or a longer chain of S—Rs leading to a final consummation. The preparatory response may consist in *approach* to a good thing, *avoidance* of a dangerous thing, or *disregard* of a neutral thing. If the good S_1 is a distant view of your friend, R_1 is approach, S_2 is a near view, and R_2 a hand clasp or other greeting. If S_1 is new and strange, R_1 may be cautious or exploratory. Even if S_2 is not really *produced* by R_1, it plays the part of a retroflex of R_1 so that the learned sequence could be represented by the formula, S_1R_1Rx. If S_2 is consummatory in any way, it is said to be a reinforcement of R_1. If S_2 is injurious or distressing to the organism and R_1 escapes or avoids S_2 and secures the desirable state of safety, this safety is a reinforcement of R_1 (p. 71).

Enough has been said of the importance of sequence learning. The question now, a question that may cause us some trouble, is *"How a sequence can be learned?"* Is it enough that S_1 shall be followed by S_2 at a suitable interval, neither too short nor too long? One necessary or at least favorable condition, we should judge, is that S_2 shall elicit a consummatory or somehow significant R_2 and so obtain reinforcement. Another may be that S_1 shall catch O's attention and have the quality of a signal.

Our discussion of these matters will focus on the "conditioning" experiments of Pavlov and his successors, but these experiments were not so revolutionary as they have often seemed. It may be worth while, then, to place conditioning in the context of other studies of sequence learning which were entirely independent of Pavlov's work.

Sequence learning not automatic

Memory experiments in great number and variety have presented lists of words, numbers, or nonsense syllables for O to memorize. Hard, close work has been found necessary to master any long list.

There is a well-attested incident which occurred in a Swiss psychological laboratory when a foreign student was supposed to be memorizing a list of nonsense syllables. After the list had been passed before him many times without his giving the expected signal that he was ready to recite, the experimenter remarked that he seemed to be having trouble in memorizing the syllables. "Oh! I didn't understand that I was to learn them," he said, and it was found that, in fact, he had made almost no progress toward learning the list. He had been taking careful note of the separate syllables, with no effort to connect them into a series (Meumann, 1908, pp. 24, 232).

This incidental observation was of considerable importance, if it could be verified experimentally. The use of "paired associates," instead of lists to be learned entire, is convenient for this purpose. Twenty pairs of unrelated words may be presented, such as:

$$
\begin{array}{l}
\text{omelet} \quad . \quad . \quad . \quad . \quad \text{burglar} \\
\text{freeze} \quad . \quad . \quad . \quad . \quad \text{design} \\
\text{kitchen} \quad . \quad . \quad . \quad . \quad \text{lightning} \\
\text{tiger} \quad . \quad . \quad . \quad . \quad . \quad \text{music}
\end{array}
$$

The subjects are asked to learn the pairs. But the words are so presented that the temporal contiguity of the second word of a pair with the first word of the following pair (as burglar . . . freeze) is as close as that between members of the same pair. We quote the report of a pioneer experiment of this sort (Woodworth, 1915, reprinted 1939, pp. 118-119):

I read a list of twenty pairs of unrelated words to a group of sixteen adult subjects, instructing them beforehand to learn the pairs so as to be able to respond with the second of each pair when the first should be given as stimulus. But, after reading the list three times, I told them that they should, if possible, give also the first word of the following pair on getting the second word of the preceding pair as stimulus. I then read the first word of the list, waited five seconds for the subjects to recall and write the second word; then read this second word, and waited the same time for them to recall and write the third word, namely, the first word of the second pair; and so on through the list. The results were most definite: the second members of the pairs were correctly recalled in 74 percent of all the cases, but the first members were recalled in only 7 percent of the cases. The subjects reported that this great difference was apparently due to the fact that they had examined each pair with the object of finding some character or meaning in it; whereas they had neglected the sequence of pairs as being of no moment. . . . This experiment serves to strengthen doubts that have often been raised, especially by the work on incidental memory, regarding the adequacy of contiguity in experience as an associating force. . . . Since the associations within pairs gave ten times as good a score as those between pairs, we may perhaps say that mere contiguity does not contribute more than one-tenth of the whole associating force; the remaining nine-tenths being contributed by the noting of suitable features in the material. Even the small fraction thus left to contiguity does not necessarily belong to it; for it is not improbable that the sequence and relation of successive pairs were sometimes observed.

The result just cited has been confirmed in somewhat different experiments by Reed (1918), by Huang (1944), and by Thorndike (1931, pp. 16-29; 1932, pp. 64-77, 82) in his well-known study of "belongingness" as a factor in the establishment of associations. The old law of association by contiguity should be modified to read that contiguity is a necessary but not a sufficient condition for the establishment of an association. An additional necessary condition, as we see it in human memory experiments, is an attentive noting of the combination of stimuli that are to be associated. For a sequence of stimuli, S_1-S_2, to be learned, S_1 should be taken as a signal of S_2 to follow.

The subject in one of these memory experiments is apt to start rather passively in the hope that the seen or heard list will simply impress itself on him. After a few repetitions, finding that this "photographic" process is making little headway, he takes a more active, enterprising attitude. He tries to find short *groups* in the list that he can grasp as units, so cutting down the number of separate items to be learned. He may find similarities here and there which serve to give character to the list. He notes the *position* of some items in the list as a whole, especially at or near its beginning and end which are usually mastered before the middle. So he transforms the list from an amorphous mass into a fairly well-structured sequence, and it is this sort of a sequence rather than a bare series of items that he finally masters. On a smaller scale one does something like this in memorizing a telephone number; it is more easily remembered if it can be perceived as a unified structure.

The reaction time experiment foreshadows conditioning

Reaction time (RT) is half a century older, dating from Helmholtz's work in 1850. In both procedures the subject is given an S_1-S_2 sequence, S_2 calling for a decisive response, R_2, and S_1 serving as a preliminary signal. In both O soon supplies a preparatory response, R_1, which is called the conditioned response in one case and a readiness to react quickly in the other. In both also there is first of all a *general adjustment* to the experimental situation: Pavlov's dog was habituated to the laboratory and harness and was hungry, i.e., ready in a general way for the eating response, R_2; the reaction-time subject agreed to cooperate and was given "instructions." He was told that on each trial he would be given a "Ready" signal followed shortly by a certain sound. At the ready signal he should place his forefinger on a certain telegraph key and hold the key closed until the sound came, then raise his finger as quickly as possible. (Or, he should leave the key open until the sound came and then press as quickly as possible.) Here S_1 is the ready signal, S_2 is the sound to which O is to respond by a finger movement, R_2, and the measured RT is the S_2-R_2 interval. But, what goes on in the S_1-S_2 interval, the preparatory period or "foreperiod"? Of course, O makes the obvious preparatory movement of placing his finger on the key. But something more is necessary for maximum quickness of reaction, as is shown by two regular findings in RT experiments. (1) The reaction is relatively slow at first but improves rapidly for a few trials and more slowly to a practice level; something is *learned* that makes quick reaction possible. (2) The fore-period must not be either too short or too long. If it is shorter than 1 second, O does not have time to get ready for the quickest reaction, and if it is longer than 3 to 4 seconds, his maximum readiness is not maintained. (*E* varies the foreperiod slightly from trial to trial, for if it is perfectly uniform, O will learn to synchronize with S_2 instead of reacting to it. Cf. p. 145.)

Evidently a process takes place during the foreperiod that prepares the organism for very quick response to a certain expected stimulus. In part this is a muscular preparation which can be revealed by a record of the muscle currents. If electrodes are strapped to the forearm over the finger muscles and the action potentials in these muscles led off, amplified, and recorded, the muscular activity is found to start up soon after the ready signal and increase gradually during the foreperiod. Sometimes it increases too rapidly and gives rise to a premature overt finger movement, but usually it is kept below that level until the expected stimulus arrives. The trick is to have this preparatory tension quite high when the stimulus arrives. There must be a balance between eagerness and caution. O is consciously eager and may become aware of the danger of premature reactions, but the preliminary muscular tension is involuntary. Another parallel with the conditioning experiment is the "extinction" of the preparatory muscular activity when the ready signal is repeatedly *not* followed by the expected S_2 (Davis, 1940; Fink, 1954).

The preparation for a quick reaction is not entirely in the forearm muscles (and their nerve centers). There is a sensory set for securing good reception; if the reaction stimulus is to be visual, the preparatory set includes eye fixation on the location of the expected stimulus. Many other interesting facts about RT could be mentioned. The "disjunctive" reaction requires discrimination between two or more stimuli. The ready signal is always the same, but S_2 is to be, for example, sometimes a red light and sometimes a blue light. To the red, O must respond with the right hand on one key, but to the blue with the left hand on another key. His readiness cannot be pushed up so high as in the simple RT experiment—or he will be guilty of many false reactions (Bowles, 1956).

We are not to think of the preparatory movement in the foreperiod as if it consisted entirely of preliminary tension in the muscle that is to execute the reaction. Even in the simple reaction the preparation starts with the very different movement of placing the finger on the key and pressing down if the reaction is to consist in lifting the finger. If the required response is to be forcible instead of merely quick, the preparatory movement starts with a reverse movement, a crouching down in preparation for jumping (as in the familiar picture of runners on the line awaiting the pistol shot), or a "hauling off" before a punch, or drawing in air preparatory to shouting or singing. Some such "two-phase motor units" are instinctive, as was said before (p. 38). Some are acquired or perfected by specific practice. When a sequence of stimuli of the "Ready-Go!" type has been well learned, the interval between the two stimuli is typically occupied with a two-phase preparation, a getting into position to "go" followed by tension in the muscles that execute the "go"—and often by tension in other muscles, too, indicative of a state of eagerness.

CONDITIONING AS SEQUENCE LEARNING

Pavlov's procedure (as reported in 1927 on work beginning about 1902) for conditioning a dog to salivate in preparation for the reception of food offers important suggestions as to how a sequence is learned. He made the sequence as clear cut as possible. The dog in his harness was wide awake but free from discomfort and from distracting stimuli; then a buzzer began to sound and continued until meat powder was introduced into the dog's mouth. The dog's first response to the buzzer was what Pavlov called the "investigatory reflex," or the "What is it?" reflex, a pricking up of the ears and turning the head toward the source of sound—in short, an exploratory response and a readiness for something more to happen. After a few trials, the routine being kept very uniform, the investigatory reflex faded out and gave way to an advance flow of saliva followed by a much stronger flow when the meat powder entered the mouth. Pavlov had provided apparatus for receiving and measuring the output of saliva moment by moment. The buzzer, S_1, had now become a "conditioned stimulus," called CS; the advance flow of saliva, R_1, was the "conditioned response," CR; while the meat powder, S_2, was the "unconditioned stimulus," US; and UR or R_2 was the "unconditioned response" of strong salivation and eating movements. The initial investigatory response to the buzzer is sometimes regarded as of no importance since it fades out after a few trials, but Pavlov found it to be essential or at least important for a quick establishment of the CR.

The process of sequence learning in this clear example consisted of two steps: first a readiness for *something* to follow; second, a readiness for meat powder to follow. The investigatory response was a behavioral index of the first step, the advance salivation an index of the second step. These two steps were primarily brain activities of a receptive and perceptual sort. That is, what the dog learned was primarily an environmental sequence, a signal followed by food.

This statement of what the dog learned differs from one that is often made. It is often said simply that he learned to salivate at the sound of the buzzer, no perceptual sequence learning being admitted. The meat powder is said to "reinforce" the advance flow of saliva, building it up gradually from zero to a moderate strength. But the occurrence of the meat powder is not regarded as learned. Nothing but a motor or glandular response to a stimulus can be learned, according to this view; a perceived object, event, or sequence of events cannot be learned. This strictly behavioristic theory has the merit of apparent simplicity, but it does not correspond to the observed facts. On the first trial, and usually for several trials, there is no advance salivation to be reinforced, and yet something is being learned; learning is getting its start. The food-signaling role of the buzzer is becoming more definite, and every time that food follows, the dog's impression of this definite sequence is reinforced. Or, we can say, the dog's adjustment to the sequence is being reinforced. We need not inquire whether the dog's perception of the sequence involves consciousness; we can regard perception as the organic *function* of getting acquainted with the environment, as in the perception of size and distance. For a critical discussion of the relation of conditioning and perception by a psychologist who is thoroughly acquainted with all the literature, see Razran (1955).

Pavlovian conditioning is sequence learning

Our heading is a matter of fact, though sometimes slurred over in formal statements. The question is whether the CS must precede the US, as Pavlov insisted, or whether the two could be strictly simultaneous or even occur in reverse order. Skinner (1938, p. 18) simply said that the two must be "approximately simultaneous," and Hull's "third postulate" in 1943 and 1952 said that they should occur in "close temporal contiguity" or in other words be "closely associated" in time. In spite of these formal statements, the to-be-conditioned stimulus always occurs before the US in any concrete instance. As Pavlov put the matter, CS is a signal of the coming US.

In a test for possible *backward conditioning* CS is given a little after US, and this reversed sequence is repeated time after time. Then comes a test trial with US omitted and only CS given, the question being whether anything like a normal CR will occur. The usual result is that a very few such responses are obtained. In one experiment (Spooner & Kellogg, 1947) on human subjects, the unconditioned response was the reflex withdrawal of the hand when it received an electric shock from electrodes attached to the forefinger. The CS was a short high-pitched tone. When the tone always came half a second *before* the shock, O soon came to lift the finger before the shock in 60 percent of the trials, though this movement did not avoid the shock. (It can be regarded as a preparation for "taking" the shock.) But in the group which got the tone half a second *after* the shock, the finger withdrawal occurred in only 10 percent of the test trials, and the percent decreased as the series of trials proceeded, "adapting out" instead of showing progressive conditioning. Moreover—and here is a difference that is more significant than it may seem—the latency (or reaction time) of these "backward conditioned" responses was much shorter than the latency of the regular forward-conditioned responses, being $\frac{2}{10}$ or $\frac{3}{10}$ seconds instead of $\frac{4}{10}$ seconds to over a second according to the length of the S_1-S_2 time interval in the forward order; this "delayed CR" will be considered on p. 234. The backward-conditioned response seems to be a sort of startle reflex sensitized by the series of shocks. With continuation of a shock-tone series of trials, O becomes accustomed to the innocent tone and his startle response "adapts out"; whereas with continuation of a tone-shock series, the getting-ready response "adapts in," we might say, or becomes conditioned. Both the positive and the negative forms of adaptation come under the head of sequence learning. In a simple example of negative adaptation, S_1 is a stimulus which elicits the "investigatory reflex" the first time it occurs but not being followed shortly by any significant S_2 it ceases to get any attention after a few trials. With regard to backward conditioning, a review of the whole literature by a leading authority concludes that it can sometimes be obtained under special conditions, with the US not too strong and the following CS not too weak; "the organism must not be so much preoccupied with the US as to fail to attend in some degree also to the CS" (Razran, 1956, p. 67).

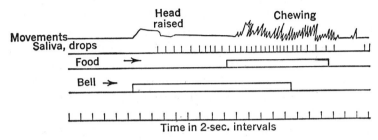

Fig. 20. (Zener & McCurdy, 1939.) Polygraph record of a dog's well-established CR and UR. S_1 was the sound of a bell, and S_2 was food presented in a pan. The conditioned response included a moderate flow of saliva and the motor response of raising the head toward the food pan. The unconditioned response was quite different, including a rapid flow of saliva along with chewing movements. Zener (1937) gives some revealing photographs of the dog's motor CR.

Backward associations in human verbal learning

In many memory experiments O memorizes a list of words, numbers, or nonsense syllables. There may be twelve items in the sequence. After enough trials he can recite the sequence perfectly, but he cannot recite it backward, not by any means, except perhaps by a slow process of reversing the order bit by bit. Nevertheless, he can learn it in reverse order in fewer trials than it took him to learn it forward. Ebbinghaus (1885) inferred that backward associations were formed incidentally in the process of forward learning, but later investigators found that they were mostly formed *inside the groups* of items, often rhythmical groups, used by O as an aid in memorizing the list. He may organize a list of twelve syllables into six two-syllable feet, trochees or iambs, and recite it with an accent in each foot. If in a later test he is given the first syllable of any foot as stimulus, he will give the second syllable as the readiest response; but if he is given the second syllable of a foot as stimulus, his readiest response is the first syllable of the same foot. The foot has become a unit, and either part of it suggests the other part (Müller & Pilzecker, 1900).

The clearest demonstration of this sort of learning is had when O's task is to memorize "paired associates," not complete lists. Let each pair consist of a nonsense syllable followed by a familiar adjective, the syllable being given as stimulus and the adjective being the required response. The stimulus is shown for 2 seconds on a "memory drum" and then the response is shown beside it for 2 seconds more. The list of seven pairs is shown again and again (in different orders) until O anticipates each R correctly when shown its S. When he has done this twice, he is shown the adjectives, one at a time, as stimuli and allowed 4 seconds to respond to each with its paired syllable; i.e., he is shown the original Rs and asked to tell the original S for each R. The students score 50 percent on the average in this backward task as compared with 100 percent forward (Feldman & Underwood, 1957; see also Murdock, 1956).

CR preparatory to UR, not identical with it

An old misstatement was that conditioning consisted in attaching the unconditioned response to a new stimulus, namely the conditioned stimulus; what was learned being accordingly the connection S_1-R_2. There was some excuse for this mistake in the case of Pavlov's salivary CR, where the only obvious difference was one of strength, the conditioned salivation being much weaker than the unconditioned. Pavlov was fully aware also of a *motor* component of the conditioned response, an approach to the food, an entirely different movement from the UR of eating elicited by the food in the mouth. See Figure 20. There are other conditioned responses which are apparently like their following unconditioned responses except in strength and quickness. One example is the withdrawal of a hand or foot in anticipation of an unavoidable shock; it is weaker and much slower than the reflex elicited by the shock itself (Hilden, 1937). A very similar example is the partial closure of the eyelids in anticipation of a puff of air against the cornea; the puff elicits the notably sharp, brief lid reflex, but the warning signal (after conditioning) gives a gradual semiclosure which typically lasts until the puff arrives (Hilgard, 1936). Respiratory conditioned responses, on the contrary, are apt to be altogether different from their following unconditioned responses: if the unconditioned stimulus calls for a yell or a squeal, an expiratory act, the preparatory conditioned response will be an inspiration or a suspension of breathing (Schlosberg, 1934).

Certain other discoveries of Pavlov should be briefly considered, with theory deferred until later in the chapter.

Extinction of a conditioned response

Suppose a CR of the Pavlovian type has been established. For example, S_1 is the ticking of a metronome which continues 15 seconds before food is given the dog, and the CR is salivation elicited by the ticking in advance of the food. The food, S_2, is called the reinforcement. Now apply S_1 without S_2, the metronome as before but without the reinforcement. Repeat S_1 at intervals of about 5 minutes, never giving S_2, and soon the salivary and motor CR begins to diminish until finally it ceases altogether. The dog has learned a new sequence, metronome followed by no food. After being a signal of food coming, S_1 has become a signal of *no* food coming.

This "extinction," however, does not erase the effect of the previous conditioning nor put the metronome back into its original state of being a novel stimulus. Its ticking is still a familiar sound but instead of being a "good" signal it has become a "bad" one. It makes the dog slump down in his harness instead of perking up and preparing to eat. It has acquired an inhibitory instead of an excitatory effect. The inhibitory effect can be deepened, even after the salivary CR has ceased, by further trials with the metronome not followed by food.

The next day put the dog back in his harness and start the metronome, and you get the salivary CR again unless the previous extinction has been very deep. You can extinguish the CR again as before, and more quickly than before, but you can then restore it by a few reinforcements. You can extinguish and restore it repeatedly by omitting reinforcement and beginning it again, and both extinction and restoration become quicker until one or two trials with reinforcement are enough to re-establish the CR, and one or two trials with no reinforcement are enough to re-extinguish it. The metronome has become a signal for eating or for slumping, and one or two trials suffice to shift it back and forth.

The discovery of extinction was perhaps Pavlov's greatest achievement. Its theory will give us a little trouble later.

The delayed CR

Pavlov customarily allowed the metronome or other S_1 to continue for 15 seconds before the reinforcement. Thus he could obtain an advance flow of saliva for measurement. He found he could
lengthen this interval (the foreperiod in RT language) to a minute
or two, making the change gradually but then sticking to a definite
routine. In a series of trials the advance salivation adjusted itself
to the interval; starting in the early trials nearly as soon as the
metronome started, it delayed progressively till near the end of the
foreperiod. More than that, the CR became a two-phase affair, a
slumping followed by a perking up and salivating, an inhibitory
phase followed by an excitatory one, in Pavlov's terms. The metronome had become a signal of the environmental sequence: no food
for a certain time followed by food.

"Generalization" of the conditioned stimulus

A CR that has been established, with a certain S_1 as its CS, will
be elicited by other similar stimuli but less strongly; and the less
similar the new S_1, the less strong the R_1. This "generalization
gradient" is not an achievement or result of learning; it might be
called a primitive failure to distinguish or differentiate similar
stimuli; the more similar two stimuli, the less chance of primitive, unlearned differentiation. If S_1 is a metronome beating 100
times per minute, a substituted beat of 60 per minute will give the
same CR, though less strongly. If S_1 is a vibratory touch stimulus
applied to a human subject's shoulder, vibrations applied nearby
will get a fairly strong and regular CR, but applied to more distant
parts of the skin only a weak and less regular CR, often after some
hesitation.

Stimulus differentiation

The fact that response to the changed stimulus was weaker than
to the regular S_1 showed that the sensory effects of the two stimuli
were somewhat different and suggested that the dog might be
taught to make different responses to them. Pavlov accomplished
this result by giving the two stimuli many times in mixed order, always reinforcing one and never the other. So he extinguished the

response to the changed stimulus while maintaining the CR to the regular CS. This differentiation was much more easily accomplished if the positive S_1 and the negative S_1, as we may call them, were a good deal different than if they differed only a little. For example, if the positive S_1, to which a salivary CR was first established, was a circle of white paper while the never-reinforced or negative S_1 was a light gray circle, a long series of trials gave no differentiation, both circles continuing to elicit the salivary response. But when a dark gray S_1 was tried, differentiation was quickly established; then the negative S_1 was made lighter, step by step, and in a relatively few trials the dog was giving the salivary CR to white and not to light gray (Pavlov, 1927, p. 122).

This dog had learned two environmental sequences, white circle followed by food, gray circle followed by no food. What he had learned was not simply to distinguish white from gray—for he had been able to do this from the start—but to take these two stimuli as signals of different events to follow. We see here a good example of "cue learning," the problem of our next chapter.

Instrumental or operant conditioning

A response is called an operant if it operates on the environment. (Whether it is "emitted" by O or elicited by a stimulus from the environment, a question discussed in our Chapter 2, can be disregarded as inconsequential here.) It is called instrumental if it secures some result of value to the organism such as food or safety. In order to be instrumental it must ordinarily operate on the environment; the two terms are practically equivalent. In a sequence, $S_1-R_1-S_2-R_2$, the preparatory response, R_1 is an operant if it is instrumental in securing the reinforcing stimulus, S_2. In Pavlovian or as also called "classical" conditioning, the conditioned response, R_1, is said to prepare the organism for the reception of S_2, the unconditioned or reinforcing stimulus; whereas in instrumental conditioning the conditioned response prepares the environment to make the unconditioned stimulus available. (This distinction is not as neat as it seems; for the advance flow of saliva does prepare a certain important part of the environment, the inside of the mouth, for the reception of food; and the motor component of the Pavlovian CR is some sort of approach to the food and clearly instrumental. There are some purely internal

CRs such as tensing the muscles or the sympathetic activity which raises the blood pressure in preparation for a sudden exertion.) Operationally, i.e., from E's point of view, there is a difference, since in Pavlovian conditioning E applies the two stimuli with a certain time between them, without regard to what O does; whereas in instrumental conditioning S_2 does not occur unless and until O makes a suitable R_1.

The typical conditioned operant is the rat's bar pressing in the *Skinner box* (p. 34), which was a simplified version of the Thorndike puzzle box. Thorndike (1898) offered his cats more than one promising lead: they could try squeezing between the slats, or shaking the door, or pulling a cord which hung down inside the box. Trial and error occurred almost inevitably. Skinner (1938) designed an environment as free as possible from alternative leads; there was nothing of a positive sort that the rat could do except to explore the box and incidentally press the bar. This instrumental act caused a food pellet to drop instantly into the box; being promptly found and eaten by the rat, the pellet reinforced the pressing response to the sight or odor of the bar. An $S_1-R_1-S_2-R_2$ sequence was learned, bar-stimulus and bar-response followed by pellet-stimulus and pellet-response. The pellet unit can be subdivided into approach and eating, or even into a larger number of steps. But the more significant fact is the close integration of the successive movements. A thoroughly conditioned rat does not press the bar tentatively and wait to hear the pellet drop; his approach to bar, press, and run to the pan that receives the falling pellet are so smooth and quick as to look like a single movement.

Another favorite setup for operant conditioning is the *straight runway* (Graham & Gagné, 1940), which amounts to a maze simplified to the limit by the omission of all blind alleys and corners. It has a starting box at one end and a food box at the other. The starting-box door is opened to begin a trial, and the rat's reaction time in leaving this box and his running time to the food are the response measures. On the first trial the rat hesitates in leaving the starting box and explores the runway in a leisurely manner, but in a few trials these delays are eliminated. The runway setup corresponds closely to a modification of the Skinner-box setup in which E removes the bar from the box after each trial and inserts it again to begin another trial, instead of following the usual Skinnerian procedure of leaving the bar in the box and measuring

O's *rate* of responding, i.e., the number of bar pressings per minute.

In an analogous experiment on *human subjects* (Verplanck, 1956), O is instructed to score a point on his score sheet whenever E says "score" or gives a tap on the table. E has previously chosen some act of O to be reinforced in this manner. It may be a hand movement, as touching one's ear, or a verbal act such as saying a number; but O is not informed what the required act will be. It should be some specific act that E can notice and reinforce instantly. Here R_1 is O's specific act, S_2 is E's tap on the table or saying "score," and R_2 is O's marking an additional point on his score sheet. The procedure called "approximation" may be necessary before O makes the required movement. For example, reinforcement is given at first for any hand movement, then limited to any hand movement that touches any part of the head, and finally limited to movements that touch the ear. In this way O can be brought up to a high rate of ear touching. When this has been accomplished, the reinforcements may be cut down to one for every five ear touchings, or to one per 15 seconds (fixed ratio or fixed interval reinforcement, as used successfully by Skinner on rats and pigeons). If the reinforcements are discontinued altogether, extinction can be obtained, either abruptly or gradually. O's motivation is to up his score, and some Os build up a good score without being able to state exactly what movement is the successful one. Much trial and error occur in this experiment, especially during the extinction series when many Os show signs of emotional disturbance.

Use of the term, "conditioning"

But why should instrumental or operant learning be called conditioning instead of simply learning? If it is called conditioning, why should maze or puzzle-box or any other learning not be called conditioning as well—as indeed it sometimes is but without general approval? The reason cannot be that the same *theory* of learning holds good for both Pavlovian and operant conditioning but not for other examples of learning, for some theorists try to apply a single theory to all learning, while others believe that the two varieties of conditioning require different explanatory theories. And Skinner, who introduced the term, "operant conditioning," insists that theories of learning are superfluous (1950). He and his adherents aim to keep their reports and discussions at the descriptive level. Accordingly, operant conditioning must be descriptively—or operationally—like the Pavlovian type in some essential respect. Now Pavlov is famous for his careful control of conditions and for his insistence that under such conditions animal behavior is regular and dependable enough to belong under the head of natural law. However, Pavlov's sampling of behavior was exceedingly limited, and Skinner undertook to show that even instrumental behavior would be "lawful" and predictable if the experimental conditions were sufficiently controlled and restricted. Since he succeeded in this undertaking, he adopted Pavlov's terms —conditioning, extinction, spontaneous recovery, stimulus generalization and differentiation—for his own parallel results obtained in operant learning.

The psychological operationist's attitude toward his animal or human subjects is much like that of the engineer toward his materials; both aim to exert efficient control. (See a quotation from Skinner, 1953, on our page 6.) That was also Pavlov's attitude toward his dogs; he found out how to make them salivate at the sound of a metronome, and how to make them stop salivating at that sound. Skinner, allowing his rats and pigeons freedom as to exactly when they would make a specific response, could still control the rate of their responding and the probability that they would respond within a certain minute. In the experiment cited from Verplanck, O was made to touch his ear at a rapid rate and then to cease doing so. O was doing this because he "wanted to," but his behavior was "nonetheless lawful and orderly as a function of the manipulations of E."

There is thus good reason for classifying the Pavlov and Skinner experiments together under the head of "conditioning." There is no good reason, however, for dividing the instrumental learning experiments into two classes, conditioning and nonconditioning. Thorndike's (1898) puzzle boxes allowed more freedom for varied reaction and his cats accordingly were more variable in the early trials than Skinner's rats, but the unrewarded variations were gradually eliminated and behavior became "lawful and orderly." Thorndike even included in this study what was probably the first experiment of the conditioned-operant type. He placed the cat in a small box and let her out to obtain a morsel of food whenever she licked herself or, in other cases, scratched herself. The cats formed the required association, though sometimes only after many trials (Thorndike, pp. 27-28). We can even go back to the memory experiments of Ebbinghaus (1885) and find strict control of conditions and results which were "lawful and orderly as a function of the manipulations of E." Many other experimenters have obtained reproducible results on learning under carefully controlled conditions, and it is impossible to make a division on this basis between conditioning and other learning experiments. Most learning experiments demand selective learning, the elimination of false leads, and in that respect are more complicated than the Pavlov and Skinner experiments. In contrasting his own work with that of Tolman who made much use of the maze, Skinner wrote (1938, p. 437):

> The maze is not a suitable instrument for the investigation of the dynamic properties of behavior. Even when we consider a single "choice-point," there remain two possible responses—turning right and turning left. No measure of the strength of either is provided by maze behavior, since a "choice" reveals only the relatively greater strength of one.

As a matter of fact, Skinner did not concern himself much with learning. Typically, his animal subject was first conditioned to press the bar and obtain a food pellet, and then the experiment proper began, concerned with extinction, discrimination, change of reinforcement schedule, and other factors in the *output* of the learned behavior—extremely important work, too.

THEORY OF SEQUENCE LEARNING

If we lay aside, for the moment at least, such learning theories as Thorndike's Law of Effect and Hull's Law of Reinforcement by Drive Reduction, and simply ask what O learns when confronted by a quick sequence of stimuli, $S_1 S_2$, and how he learns it, we find that he learns to take S_1 as a signal of the coming S_2, and to make preparations accordingly. If S_2 is something good, his preparation, R_1, is some form of approach; if S_2 is something bad, he prepares to avoid it or at least "take it"; if S_2 is something of no importance to him, he prepares to disregard it, as by continuing what he is doing. The preparation for S_2 depends on the response which will be made to S_2, that is on R_2. If R_2 is to be some form of acceptance, R_1 is an appropriate form of approach; if R_2 is to be adverse, R_1

makes ready for escape or avoidance; if R_2 is to be a disregard of S_2, R_1 is a beginning of such disregard.

Proceeding next to inquire how these sequences are learned, we can safely say that the *motor preparation depends on the sequence of stimuli,* so that what is primarily learned is the sequence S_1S_2. Must we, therefore, adopt the S—S theory of learning, supposed to be specifically applicable to Pavlovian conditioning? On the contrary, we have already seen (pp. 223ff) that stimulus contiguity is not a sufficient condition for the establishment of an association. Something more is necessary. Let us review Pavlov's conditioning experiment once more, since it is perhaps the clearest-cut and best-studied example of the learning of an S_1S_2 sequence. The signal, S_1, must not be lost in the medley of other stimuli; it must stand out and get the dog's attention, arousing the "investigatory reflex," equivalent to a question such as "What's that?" or "What next?" And the question is promptly answered by the highly significant S_2, the meat powder in many experiments—in others, the squirt of acid solution into the mouth. In both cases the preparatory CR which develops in a few trials is salivation with a motor component: an approach to the food, avoidance of the acid. But we are concerned now with the first and second trials before any conditioned response appears. The reinforcement theories are apt to by-pass these first trials, but evidently the learner could not do without them. Our theory is that *question and answer are the key* to the problem: S_1 puts the question and S_2 gives the answer; S_1 arouses a questioning set, a readiness for some unknown S_2. Consequently, when S_2 comes, it is more than merely contiguous to S_1; it belongs to it as an answer belongs to its question. Combination of the two stimuli is facilitated by the experimental arrangements, the dog being wide awake and hungry and free from distracting stimuli.

If we speak of "expectancy" here, the meaning is the same as when we speak of question and answer. The investigatory response to the novel, outstanding S_1 is an indefinite expectancy of something more to follow, and S_2 transforms the indefinite into something definite. A single trial may not go far toward making the expectation definite; several trials may be necessary before the dog takes S_1 as so definite a signal of coming food or acid that his investigatory response gives way to a definite conditioned response. If S_1, the buzzer noise, comes from the left, the investigatory response includes a turning of the head to that side; but the food comes from in front, and in a few trials the leftward turn gives way to a forward movement. The leftward turn was exploratory, but the forward movement is instrumental.

Tolman's concept of "expectancy"

The role of expectancy in learning and performance has been most fully worked out by Edward C. Tolman (1932). It has much the same role in a learned performance as Hull's "habit strength," which we have been representing by the letter H, or more completely by Hull's own symbol, $_sH_R$, an ability previously learned which is a factor in O's present performance. In comparing his own system with Hull's, Tolman (1955, p. 320) puts the difference in a nutshell: "His $_sH_R$, or habit, is an S—R connection whereas my expectancy is conceived as an activated $(S_1-R_1-S_2)$ expectation." In Pavlov's experiment S_1 is the buzz signal and S_2 food in the mouth, R_1 after conditioning being approach to the food and salivation. In the Skinner box S_1 is the bar-stimulus, R_1 is pressure on the bar, and S_2 the sound of a pellet falling into the food pan. In both experiments S_2 is also called the reinforcement, Rf. For Hull, Rf is the agency that strengthens the S—R connection, S_1-R_1 and causes the learning; yet it does not form part of what is learned. The stimulus sequence, S_1S_2, is not learned, but only the S—R connection, S_1-R_1. It seems incredible that O should adjust to the sequence without learning it, but Hull's theory requires that only S—R connections can be learned. Whether the reinforcing stimulus or "state of affairs" operates by way of satisfaction, need reduction, or vigor of consummatory response (our pp. 120ff), in any case only the S_1-R_1 connection is learned, according to Hull.

According to Tolman (1932, p. 331) "What Pavlov's dogs acquired [was an expectation] to the effect that 'waiting' in the presence of the sign-object, color or sound, would lead to the significate, food." And in the Skinner box experiment, what the rats acquired was an "expectancy . . . to the effect that if the actor responds by the 'performance' of pressing, he will get to food" (Tolman, 1955, p. 318). If "expectancy" seems to imply a subjective state (contrary to Tolman's intention as an avowed behaviorist), why not follow our own view that the *environment* is learned? We can say then that Pavlov's dog learned the sequence, buzzer—time interval—food, and that Skinner's rat learned the sequence, bar—pressure on it—pellet in the pan. Instead of using the "if—then" form, which seems too explicitly intellectual for animal processes, we can use the matter-of-fact sequential form. In the shuttle-box experiment (p. 53), with a warning signal followed 10 seconds later by shocks from the floor, we can try to state what is learned by the conditional sentences, "If I wait here very long after that buzz, I shall get a shock; but if I jump promptly over the wall, I shall get no shock." Perhaps it would be better to dodge the self-reference by substituting "one" for "I." But to get rid also of the explicit conditional form we can suppose the animal to learn the sequences, buzz—short interval—shock, and buzz—jump-over-wall—no shock.

Reification of a sequence. We can go one step farther in the objective direction. As we said earlier in the present chapter, human beings at least translate a regular sequence of stimuli into a thing-characteristic; they translate a conditional sentence into a declarative one. Instead of saying, "If you bite a pale pink strawberry, you get a sour taste," they reify the sequence by saying, "Pale pink strawberries *are* sour." Since the declarative form is the more unsophisticated and unthinking, it doubtless is the better approximation to what the animal learns. In the shuttle box, accordingly, what is learned is best expressed by such statements as, "Buzz is a shock signal," and "The wall is a way of escape," or even (p. 71), "The next compartment is safe." Or again, in the Skinner box, "The bar is a pellet-getter," and in a puzzle box, "The chain is a door-opener," whereas the spaces between the slats are "no good, too narrow." Our theory is, then, that animals learn the good or bad characteristics of the objects with which they have to deal.

Such a statement would probably not displease Tolman, though he has not expressed himself in exactly the same way, apparently preferring the conditional form. He speaks continually of objects, goal-objects, means-objects, sign-objects, and he recognizes that the three can "fuse" into a single "large object." In one passage (1932, p. 334) he says: "Whenever a given sensory sequence is actually presented very frequently by the environment, and in such a way that there is practically always the same response to be made to the whole," the sequential expectation "will in time fuse for the organism from a sign-gestalt, in which one object or part is sign for another object or part into a single 'large object.' " We would simply argue that reification does not have to be forced on the organism by very frequent and uniform sequences; rather, it is a line of least resistance and greatest economy in the organism's dealing with the environment. In general, Tolman and Woodworth are in agreement on so many essentials that Woodworth's students, after hearing his lectures, have sometimes said they could see no real difference between the two theories—certainly when both are contrasted with Hull's theory. In the theory of learning the latter contrast is marked, but there is not much controversy regarding Hull's factors in performance: D, K, J, and I (Tolman, 1955, p. 320). But Seward (1956) even finds a tendency for Hull's and Tolman's theories to converge.

Exploration as the first step in conditioning

Our temporary fascination with "expectancy" has made us digress from the question we set ourselves on p. 240, as to how the learning of a sequence got started. Something more than temporal contiguity was required. This something more, we thought, was indicated by the investigatory response of Pavlov's dog to the initial sounding of the buzzer or metronome. Exploratory behavior, whether looking, listening, or sniffing, and whether done by human or animal organisms (pp. 77ff), is a questioning process which may find a significant answer. If so, a connection is formed between the question and the answer, or between the stimulus which aroused the question and the following stimulus which gave the answer. Something more dynamic than mere temporal contiguity is present when the question, "What does the stimulus S_1 portend?" is promptly followed by the stimulus S_2 which gives an answer (Kilpatrick, 1954).

The learning of *paired associates* has already been considered twice in the present chapter, and we now consider it again briefly as an example of S_1S_2 learning, analogous to Pavlovian conditioning, and ask what goes on in the first few trials, before O can give the required R_1 which is an anticipatory saying of S_2. When he sees or hears the S_1 of a pair, O's question is, "What is coming as the S_2 of this pair?" His question is answered when he sees or hears the S_2, and he leaves that pair behind for the moment and passes on to the next pair. In addition to temporal contiguity, there is the unifying dynamics of question and answer. After a few presentations O succeeds in giving the correct responses for some pairs, and this anticipation is confirmed or reinforced. We cannot speak of reinforcement in a strict sense until O succeeds in giving the correct response to a stimulus. His response may be approximately correct a few trials before it is entirely correct; he may say "happy" when he should say "smiling"; so his anticipation of the general meaning is reinforced while his partial error is corrected. The S_2 of any pair continues to be an answer to a question as long as his response is inaccurate or hesitant. With perhaps ten or fifteen pairs to be learned in a bunch, there are many questions to be answered. The task amounts to the learning of ten or fifteen conditioned responses simultaneously.

Further steps in sequence learning

As described so far, sequence learning can be called a cognitive process rather than a motor process. It is a process of getting acquainted with a bit of the environment. The word "cognitive" has an elevated sound, but sequence learning is fundamental rather than elevated. Sometimes it is best described as a slow, gradual process of being impressed by a repeated sequence of stimuli. Sometimes, on the contrary, it is an alert perceptual process. The human subject in the eyelid conditioning experiment perceives the regular sequence of events—warning signal followed quickly by a puff of air against the eye—in a very few trials, but we do not regard him as "conditioned" until his lid begins to make a partial anticipatory wink; and that may take fifty trials. As to the gradual process of being impressed by the sequence, we can speculate that in this case it consists in a growing disagreeableness of the puffs; if so, the partial anticipatory wink would be a simple form of instrumental CR. And we could speculate similarly regarding Pavlov's experiment: an alert dog must perceive the sequence of stimuli, buzz—food, in a trial or two, and be increasingly impressed with the regularity of the sequence and with the disadvantage of getting meat powder in a dry mouth; thus his advance salivation would be instrumental. These instrumental acts would, of course, not be deliberate; rather, they would be examples of the natural tendency to prepare for what is coming, so far as one is equipped with natural preparatory responses and so far as one has become acquainted with the sequence of events.

When the S_2 of our formula is an electric shock or some other noxious stimulus, the S_1S_2 sequence is learned very quickly and the observable R_1 is at first some sort of excited emotional behavior, of which we had an example in the shuttle-box experiment on dogs (p. 70). We saw there also how the emotional behavior faded out as instrumental acts were learned for escape and then for avoidance of the shock. This shift from the emotional to the instrumental response has been observed by many other experimenters, though it does not occur in some dogs (Wolf & Kellogg, 1940), nor in most rats (Schlosberg, 1934, 1936), nor perhaps even in some people.

The emotion stirred up by a warning signal clearly results from sequence learning, since the response to S_1 is determined by the nature of S_2. We can say the same of the instrumental acts of preparing to "take" a shock that is unavoidable or to avoid one that can be avoided. They are ways of solving the problem set by the sequence of events—of solving it at the trial-and-error level, if no better. We have to admit that trial and error, with its varied responses to a problematic situation, involves something more than sequence learning, namely, a shifting from one sequence to another. Different leads are tried and the resulting sequences provide a check on them. A lead may look promising at the start but turn out a moment later to be a blind alley. In a maze, the stimuli at the entrance of a side-alley arouse the investigatory response of entering and exploring, followed quickly by the dead-end stimuli. This sequence of events, continued by the reverse movement to the alley entrance, will be "reified" in the course of a few trials so that the entrance stimuli are equivalent for the rat to the human sign, "Dead End Street."

When exploration requires manipulation rather than locomotion, the same dynamic factor in sequence learning is present. Thorndike's cat confined in a puzzle box, with food visible outside, is motivated to reach the food and explores the interior of the cage with that motivation. A chain hanging inside the cage provides an S_1 for tentative, questioning manipulation, a pull which is immediately followed by a positive answer: the door swings open and the cat goes to the food. There is a complete $S_1R_1S_2R_2$ sequence, though several trials may be necessary before the sequence is strongly enough impressed on the cat for prompt unquestioning action on every trial. There are other promising leads that must be eliminated.

To speed up the instrumental conditioning process in the Skinner box, the rat may first be taught to go to the food pan when a pellet is dropped into it. The next day there is a horizontal bar present along one wall of the box, and the rat will find no food in the pan unless he first presses the bar. An investigatory pressing of the bar is followed at once by the sound of a pellet falling into the pan and the already learned response of going to the pan. The rat learns the regular sequence of objects, bar and pan, with which he has to deal. The fact that the animal's initial investigation takes different forms in different situations—pulling a chain in the puzzle box, exploring an alley in the maze, looking at the buzzer in Pavlov's setup—need not alter our theory that sequence learning by the question-answer process is the first step in all these forms of learning.

We are obviously crediting animals such as the dog and the rat with the capacity for perceiving space and for recognizing objects. Some evidence on this matter is given in other chapters (pp. 164, 301). Any animal that has to move freely about in the environment and deal with objects would be seriously handicapped if he could not translate sensory stimuli into cues of objective facts.

Hull (1952, Chapters 8 and 9) made a valiant attempt to explain space perception and maze learning in purely motor terms, or S–R terms, without assuming any intervening variable of perception. He did not recognize sequence learning nor any tendency to make preparatory movements (our p. 44). He made much use of S generalization and of R generalization. To work our way critically through his argument would be more of a task than we care to attempt, but it does seem that in both his S generalization and his R generalization he is tacitly assuming in the animal the perception or identification of an object in a certain objective place. What else except the object can hold together the varied stimuli the animal receives from the object or the various approaches, direct and indirect, he makes in approaching the object?

Incentive learning

In a short sequence, $S_1R_1S_2R_2$, the incentive is represented by S_2, and the nature of this incentive, good, bad, or indifferent, determines the nature of the preparatory response, R_1. In a longer chain of S–R units the "primary" or fundamental incentive is the final S in the chain, but preceding stimuli acquire "secondary" or preliminary incentive value (p. 110). In all these cases the incentive value present in the situation has to be learned, for it is not usually visible or anyhow presented to O's senses at the start of a trial. It is an O-factor, built up by the A-factor of previous rewards (in most cases). Incentive learning is, therefore, an exceedingly important kind of learning. And it is apparently a very easy kind. After the rat once finds food in the goal box of a maze, his behavior takes on an urgency not present in the first trial. The dog in the shuttle box (p. 69) showed fear at the warning signal after only a very few experiences of the shocks.

In Crespi's (1942) experiment the rats had to traverse a 20-foot straight runway for a food reward, the amount of the reward differing from one group to another. The food was in small pellets, weighing .5 gram each, but the number of pellets found in the goal box differed as shown in the following table, along with the average speed attained by each group at its practice level after fifteen to twenty trials.

Amount of incentive	Average running speed
1 pellet	.53 feet per second
4	1.15
16	2.33
64	3.46
256	3.90

The bigger the incentive, the faster the rat ran to get it—a result that has been confirmed in various other experiments. But we are concerned with the *learning of a new incentive* when the rats were shifted up or down from the small or large rewards to the medium one of 16 grams. In both cases it took the rats only a single trial to shift their speed markedly up or down, as shown in Crespi's curves.

The behavior of the rats in the goal box on first finding only sixteen pellets instead of the usual much larger quantity was clear evidence that they "noticed" the change: they peered excitedly here and there in the goal box and hesitated or refused to eat. It was perceptual learning, as perhaps all incentive learning must be in the first instance. It is the learning of a *stimulus,* S_2 in our notation (see Guttman, 1953, p. 222).

Results closely paralleling Crespi's were obtained by Zeaman (1949) and by Metzger, Cotton and Lewis (1957). With a different setup Pereboom (1957) finds a much more gradual readjustment to the changed incentive.

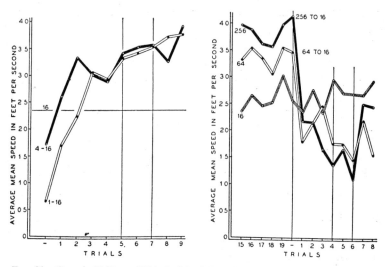

FIG. 21. (Crespi, 1942, p. 508.) Quick shifts of running speed when amount of incentive is suddenly changed. Consider first the diagram on the right which shows, as far as the first light vertical line, the high running speed of the groups receiving 256 and 64 pellets per trial and the medium speed of the group receiving 16 pellets. Beginning on this first vertical line, all three groups received 16 pellets per trial. The 16-pellet group shows no definite change, but the downward-shifted groups immediately began to run slowly, even more slowly than the 16-pellet group—apparently a contrast effect.

In the left-hand diagram, the practice level of the 16-pellet group is shown by a horizontal line, and the previous low levels of the 1-pellet and 4-pellet groups are represented by the first points on their curves, which show their speed on the first trial when they found 16 pellets in the goal box. On the very next trials their speed increased, showing that they had "learned" (noticed and remembered) the increased incentive. For all groups there was a single trial per day after 22 hours of food deprivation.

The learning of an incentive or of a change in incentive will probably not always be quick and distinctly perceptual. In the experiments cited the incentive change was large and striking. A small change would probably "impress itself" only gradually and produce only a gradual change in behavior.

Negative as well as positive incentives, drawbacks as well as appeals, are learned and retained, functioning in later trials. If one of two alternative routes to food is longer than the other, rats learn the difference in a few trials and consistently choose the shorter, as has been known since the work of De Camp (1920). If they have a choice between two food boxes, one requiring a pressure of 60 grams on a bar to obtain the food, the other a pressure of only 40 grams, they learn in a few trials to choose the smaller pressure (Thompson, 1944). If they are thoroughly adjusted to taking a weak shock from the floor grid of an obstruction box, on their way to food, a single strong shock substituted for the weak one is lesson enough to keep them off that grid permanently (Warden & Nissen, 1928). They may test the grid once or twice with their forepaws, in a gingerly manner, but they quickly convince themselves of its negative incentive value. A student consulting the bulletin board to ascertain his examination mark, and finding an "F" beside his name, certainly learns something difficult to account for on some theories of reinforcement (Allport, 1946). It is easily explained by the question-and-answer theory of sequence learning.

Probability learning

Besides the amount and quality of a reward (its incentive value or valence), O ought logically to take account of the *chances* of obtaining it by the "correct response." If the chances are slim, even a fine reward is not worth much effort. The prize offered in a contest may be a large sum of money, but many strong competitors will be working for it, and your own small chance of winning the prize makes you prefer some other way of spending your spare time. Similarly, with a negative incentive—harm of some kind that may result from an action—you will avoid this action if the harm is very probable even though small or if it would be very serious even though improbable (Hilgard, 1956, pp. 198, 390).

Several recent authors (Rotter, 1954; Peak, 1955; Tolman, 1955; Detambel & Stolurow, 1957) have recognized the importance of combining probability with incentive value in order to estimate the appeal of a project to the individual. The "probability" in question is, of course, the apparent or subjective rather than the strictly objective probability, the latter being usually unknown to the individual. A legislator, in considering whether or not to vote for a proposed law, will take account of the desirability of the results to be accomplished and of the probability, as he sees it, of accomplishing those results by the proposed law.

Our question is whether objective probabilities can be *learned* when there is no opportunity for the statistical approach of counting the positive and negative cases and striking a balance. We shall consider a strictly trial-and-error situation with two alternatives which are objectively randomized in a long series of trials, in one series in a 50:50 or 1:1 ratio, in other series in a 2:1 or a 3:1 ratio, etc. In any case, O has no way of responding in any single trial except by making a blind choice and then finding out whether his choice was correct. He cannot learn how to be correct all the time nor in any specific trial—except of course when one alternative is always correct, the 100:0 objective ratio, commonly used in maze and discrimination experiments. There are, however, two things he could conceivably learn. (1) He might learn the objective stimulus ratio and reveal this learning by a response ratio approximating, perhaps only gradually, to the stimulus ratio. (2) Without learning the stimulus ratio exactly, he might find one alternative more frequently correct and *always* choose that alternative. Such would be the behavior of a scientific gambler who knows that in the long run it yields the largest percentage of hits.

The mathematics of the simplified situation we are considering is fairly simple itself. Let the alternatives be Red and Green balls in a jar, a large number of them, thoroughly mixed. On each trial O first guesses Red or Green and then draws a ball and sees whether he has scored a hit or not. If the jar contains the same number of each color, his chances are even on each trial so that about half of his Red guesses will be correct and half of his Green guesses likewise, giving him a total score of about 50-percent correct, no matter what his response ratio may be, i.e., whether he always guesses Red, or always Green, or sometimes the one and sometimes the other.

In another jar let the objective ratio be 60-percent Red to 40-percent Green, and let O discover this ratio and make his response ratio correspond, guessing Red 60 percent of the time and Green 40 percent. In 100 trials, then, he draws 60 Reds and guesses 60 percent of them Red, so scoring 36 (60 percent of 60) on Red; and he draws 40 Greens and guesses 40 percent of them

Green, so scoring 16 on Green; his total score comes to $36+16=52$. He gets 52 percent correct by this procedure. But suppose that, after finding the Red to be more frequent than the Green, he proceeds to guess Red on every trial: he will score on all the 60 Reds though on none of the 40 Greens, and his total score will be 60 percent. If he had made the wrong decision and guessed Green every time, his score would be 40 percent. These two scores, 60 percent and 40 percent, are the maximum and minimum to be expected when the objective ratio is 60:40.

If you prefer algebraic symbols, let the objective ratio of Red to Green be $p:(1-p)$. If your O always guesses Red, his score is p, measured in "relative frequency," a p of .60 being the same as 60 percent. If he always guesses Green, his score is $(1-p)$. If he succeeds in diagnosing the objective ratio and makes his response ratio the same, his total score will be $p^2+(1-p)^2$, as illustrated above with the 60:40 ratio. Another example may help, this one in common fractions. Let two thirds of the balls be Red and one third be Green, and let O adopt the same ratio for his guesses. Then he gets two thirds of the two-thirds Reds correct, and one third of the one-third Greens, his total score coming to $\frac{4}{9}+\frac{1}{9}=\frac{5}{9}$. But if he had always guessed Red, his score would equal the Red fraction in the jar, i.e., $\frac{2}{3}=\frac{6}{9}$.

We shall cite several experiments bearing on our question whether O can learn the relative frequency of two alternatives in a random series of cases. If he had simply to *observe* the cases, he could count each alternative and make a report of his count. But in all these experiments he has to make a *guess in advance* on each trial and then find out whether his guess was correct. Our question is whether his guesses gradually deviate from the 50:50 level where he is apt to start the series toward a level corresponding to the frequency ratio of the two alternative stimuli.

When the objective frequency is either 100:0 or 0:100, as it has been in a vast number of maze and discrimination experiments, we already know that either men or rats will gravitate toward the rewarded alternative or away from the unrewarded, and we are not surprised to see that these two curves approach the 100-percent and zero levels quite rapidly. We are not much surprised to see the group dealing with the 50:50 stimulus series stick closely to the medium level in their responses; they could not improve their score by shifting either up or down. This is a typical "insoluble problem"; when tried on rats it often gives rise to a "position habit," a choice of the right-hand alternative all the time—or of the left-hand alternative—really the best solution possible since it obtains the reward half the time (all that can be obtained anyway) and saves the labor and trouble of making all those useless choices.

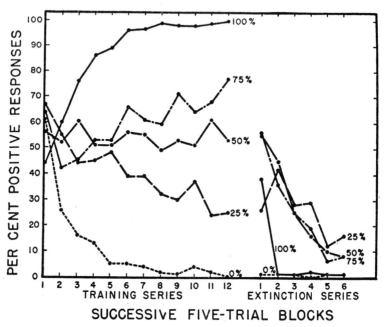

FIG. 22. (Grant, Hake & Hornseth, 1951.) Probability learning by five groups of thirty-seven students each. Two light bulbs were mounted a few feet apart on an upright screen, the one on the left serving as a warning signal followed *sometimes* by a flash from the one on the right. During this 3-second interval each subject wrote an X on his record sheet to indicate a positive guess or an O to indicate a negative guess, and he then noted whether his guess had been correct on that trial. For the different groups, as shown on the figure, the second bulb flashed on every trial, on 75 percent, 50 percent, or 25 percent of the trials in random order, or on none of the trials. In the immediately following Extinction Series, the first light continued as before but the second light never flashed; this made no difference to the 0-percent group, a striking difference to the 100-percent group, and a less abrupt difference to the three intermediate groups—least of all to the 25-percent group, since the difference between one flash in four trials, irregularly, and none at all might take a good many trials to impress itself.

In the Training Series of sixty trials, the 100-percent and 0-percent groups approach their asymptotes rapidly, as would be expected. The significant fact is that the guesses of the intermediate groups approach the frequencies of their respective stimulus series.

We are not too much surprised to see the curves of the 75-percent and 25-percent group in Figure 22 deviate gradually from the 50-percent response level toward the top and bottom of the scale. We can say that they obtain more reinforcements, i.e., score more correct guesses, by shifting their guesses toward the more frequent alternative. But are they gravitating slowly toward the 100-percent or 0-percent levels where they will score the maximum of correct guesses, and also save the hesitation and labor of many doubtful choices, or are these two groups going to settle down at the 75-percent and 25-percent response levels, corresponding to their respective stimulus levels? We cannot honestly assert that these curves are approaching asymptotes at 75 percent and 25 percent, though it looks so. Longer training series would answer our question, as we shall see in the next two figures.

We think it quite important to have this question answered, since one result would mean that the subjects were gravitating automatically toward behavior giving the maximum number of "reinforcements," whereas the other result would indicate a learning of the environmental probabilities. If we should cross-examine a subject who was drawing red and green balls from a jar and guessing Red about 75 percent of the time: "Why do you guess Red so often?" "Because I've found many more Reds than Greens in the jar." "But why, then, don't you guess Red every time?" "Simply because after all there are a good many Greens there and sometimes I catch one of them." The subject is adjusting his behavior to the objective probabilities which he has learned. Learning the environment is the primary achievement, with behavior adjustment secondary. Usually it is best to let behavior conform to the environment, so far as the environment is known, but this is not strictly true when all that can be known about the environment consists of certain probabilities.

The longer series of trials shown in Figures 23 and 24 seem to answer our question quite definitely. The response frequencies approach the stimulus frequencies and settle down there, and there is no sign of any tendency to advance toward the 100-percent level.

Any doubt as to whether some counting is not involved in all probability learning is dispelled by Brunswik's (1939) experiment on rats, which was the first experiment of this sort (Figure 25). Their choices gravitated toward 75 percent for the arm of the T maze that held food 75 percent of the time, as against the other arm which gave the reward in only 25 percent of the trials. Without any approach to counting they found one arm "better" than the other and chose the better side oftener though not exclusively. The 2:1 ratio of "goodness" did not affect their behavior reliably, though there are indications that it would do so in a longer series.

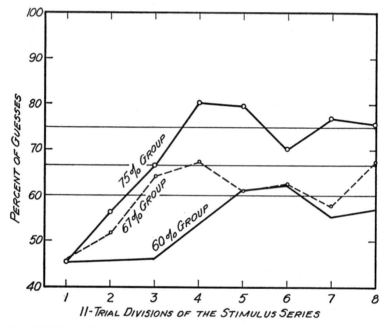

FIG. 23. (Data of Jarvik, 1951, p. 293.) Probability learning by three groups of students, twenty-one to twenty-nine in a group. The experimenter pronounced the words "Check" and "Plus" in a random series at a rate of 4 seconds per word. Each of these words was preceded by a ready signal, "Now," and the subjects had 2 seconds for making a check mark or a plus sign indicating their guess of the coming word, and 2 more seconds for noting the word actually spoken. The series pronounced to the three student groups were randomized but differed in the relative frequencies of the two stimulus words, the percent of "Checks" being 75, 67, or 60. The group percent of "Check" responses approximated, within fifty trials, to the stimulus percent. In the further continuation of the series there was no sign of a tendency to approach 100 percent of "Checks."

Brunswik urged that this type of experiment was more representative of everyday behavior than the usual laboratory study of learning in which one alternative is always rewarded and the other never. "In the natural environment of a living being, cues, means or pathways to a goal are usually neither absolutely reliable nor absolutely wrong. In most cases there is, objectively speaking, no perfect certainty that this or that will, or will not, lead to a certain end, but only a higher or lesser degree of probability" (1939, p.

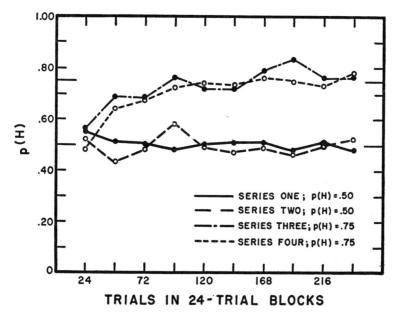

Fig. 24. (Hake & Hyman, 1953, p. 68.) Probability learning by groups of ten students each. On each trial a warning light was followed after 4.5 seconds by either a horizontal or a vertical line of small lights. During the 4.5 seconds O made a guess or prediction whether the line would be H (for horizontal) or V (for vertical); then he saw whether his guess had been correct or not. There were 240 trials, one every 9 seconds. Each group of subjects was shown a randomized series of H and V lines, a 50:50 series for two groups, and a 75:25 series for two, as indicated on the figure. In none of the series was there any recurrent pattern for O to discover and use as a partial guide for correctness in the single trial. But the groups getting the 75:25 series became gradually impressed by the preponderance of H lines and increased the frequency of their H guesses to about 75 percent. Thus, according to our $p^2 + (1-p)^2$ formula, they must have increased their score of hits to about 62.5 percent. If they had plunged for H all the time, they would have raised their score to 75 percent, but there is no indication of such a "plunge" even in these long series of trials.

175). This is perhaps especially true of animal life in the wild and of human social situations.

The human subjects in these probability-learning experiments were by no means merely passive or receptive; they took an active, experimental attitude toward their task, trying out sequential patterns which seemed to be present in a part of the stimulus series but finding them not present later on. What they did learn, besides the approximate relative frequencies of the two alternatives in their

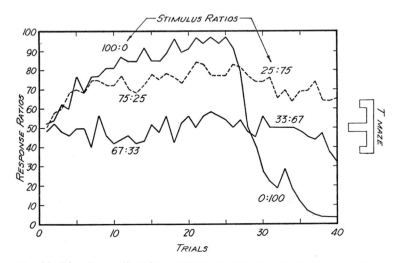

FIG. 25. (After Brunswik, 1939, p. 180.) Probability learning by groups of forty-eight rats in a single T maze. In the initial learning the food reward was always on the same side (chances 100:0) for one group; for another group it was on one side in three quarters of the trials and on the other side for one quarter (chances 75:25); and for the third group it was on one side for two thirds of the trials, and on the other side for one third (chances 67:33). Beginning immediately after twenty-four trials, marked by the vertical line in the figure, the chances were reversed for each group, so becoming 0:100, 25:75, and 33:67. Before the reversal the choices approximate closely to the 75:25 frequency as well as to the 100:0; and there is some indication that the 67:33 ratio is making an impression, though the responses of this group do not differ reliably from 50:50. Reversal of the stimulus ratio brings a quick reversal of the response ratio in the case of 100:0 and makes a slow change in the expected direction with the other groups. Another 75:25 group trained with a *penalty* for a wrong guess, i.e., with shock always present on the side opposite to the food, showed a clear reversal of the response ratio in sixteen reversed-frequency trials.

To clarify the figure, hold it sideways, top to the left, and trace upward. The Stimulus Ratio 75:25 means that the food reward was in the left end of the T maze three quarters of the time, in the right end one quarter of the time. The Response Ratio, starting at 50 percent of the responses to the left, levels off near the 75-percent level, but descends somewhat when the Stimulus Ratio is reversed to 25 left:75 right.

respective series, was the presence of *runs* of the same alternative
—more runs and longer runs of the more frequent alternative, of
course. They were apt to assume that a run could not last very
long, but they laid this assumption aside, partially, as the series
progressed. When they scored a hit with a certain guess, they were
likely to repeat that guess on the next trial (Jarvik, 1951; Hake &
Hyman, 1953). They seem to begin their attack on such a series
with two tacit assumptions: that runs of two alike are very probable, but that longer runs are less and less probable (Brown & Buel,
1940). They are likely to start with a moderate preference for one
of the alternatives, as for right as against left, or for red as against
green. Probability learning consists partly in the *unlearning* of
these assumptions and preferences. (Other experiments on probability learning: Gardner, 1957; Messick & Solley, 1957; Parducci,
1957; Solley & Messick, 1957.)

Anticipation in the service of target tracking. Once before we
considered the value of "advance information" in motor control. In
a probability situation the advance information is correct only with
a certain relative frequency; still it may be useful. In an experiment
of Wyckoff & Sidowski (1955) a small rotating target was visible
only in an arc of 90 degrees at the top of its course, but O got a signal 1.5 seconds each time before it came into sight. To score a point
he had to keep his tracker on target for half a second. If it had always moved from right to left, an advance start would have been
a great help in this difficult task. If its direction had been wholly
unpredictable, half the time from the right and half from the left
in a random series, advance starts would have gone wrong half the
time and been of no service. But when it came from one side 75
percent of the time and 25 percent from the other, he could learn
this proportion approximately and adjust his advance starts accordingly. Since, however, he was scored not for correct anticipations
but for time on target, he learned, or at least some of the subjects
learned, to go beyond the 75-percent level and plunge for 100-
percent anticipations in the more probable direction.

REINFORCEMENT IN SEQUENCE LEARNING

In this discussion we limit ourselves to the varieties of learning
mentioned in the present chapter—a broad field at that since we

have taken a look at Pavlovian and instrumental conditioning, paired associates, and the learning of incentives and of probabilities. The field of sequence learning is bound to be broad if we were anywhere near right in regarding learning the environment as fundamental and as accomplished by the question-and-answer procedure.

According to our familiar formula, $S_1R_1S_2R_2$, when the sequence occurs for the first time, the R_1 elicited by S_1 is an investigatory, questioning response, and the answer is given by S_2, which supplies the incentive. The incentive is positive, negative, or neutral and indifferent; and the R_2 elicited by S_2 is some sort of approach, or of withdrawal, or of disregard. Typically the first thing learned about the sequence is S_2, the incentive present in the situation; the second thing learned is the signal role of S_1; and the third thing is some instrumental preparatory R_1 which differs with the incentive and with the opportunities afforded by the situation. In the oft-cited experiment with the sound of a buzzer followed by shocks from the floor of the enclosure, the first sign of learning is the animal's resistance to being placed in that enclosure, the second sign is his emotional excitement at the sound of the buzzer, and the third is his instrumental act of jumping over the wall.

With repetition of the same S_1S_2 sequence, it becomes more and more strongly impressed on the organism; the signaling role of S_1 is confirmed by the regular coming of S_2; and instrumental responses are established if they succeed in securing a beneficial incentive, in avoiding a noxious one, or in making it easy to disregard one that is of no consequence one way or the other.

It is important to notice that, according to our account of sequence learning, reinforcement can occur whether S_2 is a beneficial, a noxious, or an indifferent incentive. Any of these incentives can be learned, and learned quickly; and, if the same sequence is repeated time after time, appropriate preparatory adjustments and instrumental acts get repeated reinforcement. Reinforcement is not necessarily "rewarding" in the usual sense, for it is painful in some cases. In another sense there is a reward when a painful S_2 that has been anticipated and prepared for arrives on schedule. The *preparation* is rewarded.

One advantage of our "cognitive" theory, or learning-the-environment theory, is that it allows for the learning of "bad" as well as "good" environments. Certainly both kinds of environment are learned. How could bad environments be learned if learning depended primarily on need reduction or satisfying consequences?

If our theory seems to fly in the face of the "empirical law of effect," which has so much evidence in its favor, we have only to bring into the picture an undoubted characteristic of behavior which we may call the *ameliorative* characteristic. The organism tends to better its condition. Having found a beneficial incentive in the environment, it approaches; having found a noxious incentive, it withdraws, tries to escape, avoid, or minimize the harm. If it succeeds, it gets some relative reward at least, and its preparatory instrumental acts are reinforced. The first step, however, toward any such amelioration is that of learning the incentive present in the situation.

The law of effect can be regarded as a derivative of these two characteristics of behavior: the ameliorative tendency and the tendency to explore (with the ability to learn what is found by exploration). The ameliorative tendency is responsible for the positive or negative incentive value of objects found in the environment and so for the effort to approach or withdraw. Environment learning is responsible for finding the incentive objects and for finding ways and means of approach or withdrawal. That is, environment learning covers the learning of the sequence, $S_1 S_2$, and the learning of any instrumental R_1. Successful instrumental acts are reinforced, but so also is the organism's impression of the $S_1 S_2$ sequence. Cognitive grasp and motor control of the situation are rewarded, both of them; but, if anything, cognitive grasp, at least of a primitive sort, has the priority.

For a view of behavior akin to the present one in respect to the law of effect and cognitive learning, see Nuttin (1953).

Extinction of a preparatory response

It is the preparatory CR that is lost in extinction; it is the advance salivation, or the ready posture, or the advance movement of approach or withdrawal. It is extinguished in a series of trials when the signal S_1 elicits the preparatory response R_1, but the consummatory event $S_2 R_2$ does not follow because S_2 is not given. The preparation comes to naught.

"Satiation" is something else. The food reward S_2 continues to be given but the animal stops eating, his hunger being exhausted. Consequently, both the consummatory response R_2 and the preparatory R_1 drop out. In satiation the *drive* is lacking though the incentive is still present; in extinction the drive is present but the *incentive* is lacking. Satiation is due to an internal change in the organism, but extinction is due to a change in the environment. Our theory is that extinction includes a "cognitive" learning process, i.e., a learning of the changed stimulus sequence, and an economical readjustment of behavior to the absence of incentive.

For evidence of the cognitive phase we should look closely at the first few trials of the extinction series. This series continues the acquisition series without any sign that a change is coming. However, the absence of the accustomed reward is a striking event which obviously makes an impression on the subject. A human subject will exclaim in surprise and ask if something has gone wrong with the apparatus. The rat presses the bar repeatedly when his first press fails to produce a pellet (Ratner, 1956); or, if he has learned to open a door into the food box and finds the door locked, he shows emotional excitement and attacks the door viciously. In a maze, when he first finds no food in the goal box, he proceeds to re-explore blind alleys that he has learned to pass by. Thus he is making a quick start in the learning of a changed environment. But a single trial is not enough to reveal to O whether the reward is in a new place, or permanently gone, or likely to be present again on the next trial. The following trials have an exploratory character, with gradually decreasing advance flow of saliva, decreasing rate of bar pressing, decreasing speed in the runway or maze. After a few or sometimes a good many unrewarded trials an extinction level is reached in which only widely scattered R_1 responses are made. This readjusted behavior can be taken as evidence that O has become well acquainted with the changed, no-incentive environment.

Rapid extinction. Since extinction means a readjustment to a changed environment, quick extinction is better than slow. The speed of extinction is measured by counting the unrewarded trials until the extinction level is reached; the fewer these trials, the quicker the extinction. A "trial" here means a preparatory act of salivating, pressing the bar, traversing the maze or runway, etc. In "latent extinction" experiments E tries to reduce the number of these *active* trials by taking rats that have learned to run rapidly for food in the goal box of a runway, placing them repeatedly in the now-empty goal box, and then counting the active trials to extinction. These experiments have usually given positive results, i.e., have succeeded in hastening extinction, but the interpretation has varied. We may say that the animal has learned the absence of any incentive for running. Or, since the behavioral sequence is tied to the objective situation, we may say that he has *unlearned* the "secondary" incentive value of the goal box; it is not worth running to any longer (Seward & Levy, 1949; Deese, 1951; Page, 1955; Moltz, 1955; Moltz & Maddi, 1956; Brown & Halas, 1957). One difficulty in these and other extinction experiments is the wide scatter of individual animals in number of trials to extinction. Even under the same experimental conditions some individuals are extinguished after a single active trial, whereas others keep on trying twenty times or more before giving up. The persistent ones seem not to be running for food, since after reaching the goal box they do not approach the (empty) food cup—as if the opportunity to have a run were incentive enough for lively young animals (Bugelski, Coyer & Rogers, 1952). Pavlov had noticed such individual differences (1927, p. 51):

> Under the same set of external conditions some animals will have the conditioned reflexes rapidly extinguished, while in others the whole process will be much delayed. In excitable dogs the reflexes are mostly slow of extinction, but in quiet animals extinction is rapid.

Pavlov's theory postulated two opposed cerebral states, excitation and inhibition. The inhibitory state required for extinction would be more readily produced in the quiet type of dogs. (Rats, we may surmise, are more excitable than human adults and so take more unrewarded trials in extinction experiments.)

The amount of work or effort required to execute a response should be a factor in the speed of extinction—the greater the effort, the fewer unrewarded trials to extinction. This result could be predicted whether the inhibition operates automatically like muscular fatigue or whether it is a negative incentive that has to be learned in the course of an activity and that operates as a disinclination to continue or repeat the activity. It must be admitted, though, that recent painstaking experiments have yielded discordant results. Applezweig (1951) concluded that "When habit strength is constant, the more effortful the performance of a task after reinforcement has been removed, the more rapidly will extinction occur." But from another study the conclusion is drawn that "amount of work, within the limits employed [5-, 40-, and 80-gram pressure on the bar], bears no relationship to the extinction of a molar bar-pressing response in a free-responding situation when habit strength is controlled" (Maatsch, Adelman & Denny, 1954). And from a third: "The rather complex set of relationships found in this study cannot be incorporated into any existing set of constructs dealing with inhibition alone; the problem is considerably more complicated" (Aiken, 1957). Our guess is that another important factor in extinction belongs under the head of learning the environment; O has to distinguish an extinction series from the conditioning series. (See also Lawson & Brownstein, 1957; Johdai, 1956.)

Re-extinction is quicker than first extinction. In regard to this finding there is reassuring agreement from Pavlov down. In the Aiken (1957) experiment just mentioned the following $S_1R_1S_2R_2$ sequence was learned: S_1 was E's raising of a screen in front of a little door; R_1 was the rat's push on the door; S_2 was a food pellet just behind the door; R_2 was the taking and eating of the pellet. In forty-five trials this sequence was thoroughly learned. Next day the same S_1R_1, but there was no pellet behind the door; it took forty-six of these unreinforced trials (on the average with a wide scatter of the individuals) before the rats gave up pushing the door. On the following day some "spontaneous recovery" was shown (without any further reinforcements), but extinction was reached in an average of only nine trials.

Similar results have been obtained with the bar-pressing task in several variations. In order to obtain repeated extinctions, E may depend on spontaneous recovery (Miles, 1956) or he may interpolate sessions with reinforcement (Wickens & Miles, 1954). He may begin each day's session with reinforcements which are discontinued after the positive R_1 is re-established very well (Perkins & Cacioppo, 1950). Instead of food he may apply the negative incentive of momentary shocks from the floor of a Skinner box, one shock every 20 seconds, except that bar pressure postpones the shock for 20 seconds so that by pressing at a rate of over three times a minute the rat can avoid all the shocks. When, after many hours of this experience, the rat has settled down to a fairly efficient rate of three to six presses per minute, each session begins with shock present and continues with shock absent. During the extinction period the rat occasionally delays his regular bar pressing but gets no shock, and so a start is made toward learning the changed situation. In repeated sessions the rat discriminates more and more quickly between the shock and the no-shock periods (Boren & Sidman, 1957).

We might be tempted to attribute the quicker-and-quicker extinction in all these experiments to the gradual development of some inhibitory factor. It could not be Hull's "reactive inhibition," I_R, which is supposed to dissipate rapidly and could not accumulate from day to day in the extinction sessions. But it could perhaps be something like his "conditioned inhibition," $_sI_R$, conceived as a gradually acquired tendency to "take it easy." In that case we should expect the rate of bar pressing to slow down when the incentive was present as well as during the extinction periods. Data on this point are provided by Bullock & Smith (1953). Having given their rats preliminary acquaintance with the box and food pan with pellets in it, but without the bar, they began a series of ten daily sessions with the bar present and forty pellets to be obtained by bar pressing. When these had been obtained, the pellets ceased coming but the rat remained for an hour more in the box with the bar available for pressing. The rate of bar pressing increased day by day during the reinforcement periods but decreased day by day during the extinction periods, as shown in the following extract from their data (p. 350, text and Figure 2):

Number of Bar Pressings in the First 5 Minutes

	Day 1	Day 5	Day 10
During reinforcement . . .	5	36	39
During nonreinforcement . .	19	9	8

These rats were learning concurrently to press the bar and get a pellet and to cease pressing when no pellets were forthcoming. Their cue for ceasing to press was the failure of pellets to appear when the bar was pressed, though they did not obey this cue instantly and cleanly but still pressed at intervals—about once in 10 minutes in the latter part of the hour.

Slow extinction. The difference between a situation offering an incentive and one not offering that incentive must make an impression on the organism if a start toward extinction is to be made. In the experiments no signal is given equivalent to E's saying, "Now we start an extinction series; no more pellets (or shocks)." When such a signal is given in human experiments, extinction is almost instantaneous. In the absence of any such signal there is no difference until O has made his usual preparatory response and the incentive fails to follow. This single failure, though very impressive at the moment, does not insure permanent readjustment of the organism to the changed situation. The situation looks the same, smells the same; S_1 is the same stimulus complex, and retains most of its learned signal character, being still a signal of the incentive S_2. A number of trials are necessary to change S_1 from a signal of food-behind-that-door to a signal of no-food-there—especially if the organism, being hungry, has a bias in favor of the positive signal. The organism shifts gradually from confident positive responses, first to exploratory behavior, and finally to negative responses. This learning process becomes quicker with repeated extinction series.

In the Skinner box exploratory behavior consists in bar pressing; if the bar is not pressed, no information is gained about the situation. The bar will be pressed many times before the "operant level" is reached. Extinction should be very slow, as indeed it is. By way of contrast consider shock avoidance. When a dog has learned to avoid shocks from the floor of an enclosure by leaping out at the sound of a buzzer, and the situation is changed by discontinuance of the shocks, he gets no information of this change by leaping out but only when he omits or delays his leap. Extinction should be slow—as it is.

Slow extinction after intermittent ("partial") reinforcement. It was formerly assumed that the omission of reinforcements on scattered trials during conditioning would result in slow learning and rapid extinction. This assumption was pretty well shaken by Skinner's ingenious experiments (1938 and later) with intermittent reinforcement. He obtained high rates of bar pressing and slow extinction with fixed-ratio conditioning (one pellet after a certain number of presses) or with periodic or aperiodic reinforcement (one pellet at regular or at irregular intervals). The work of Humphreys also (1939, 1940) created a stir among the theorists because it seemed to favor "expectancy" as against "reinforcement." By omitting reinforcements in an approximately random half of the trials, he was still able to obtain a good level of human eyelid and PGR (galvanic skin response) conditioning, with remarkably slow extinction following.

The learning process may be somewhat impeded by lack of reinforcement on every trial. Such is the conclusion of Jenkins & Stanley (1950) in their critical review of the literature. In regard to
extinction, however, they find the "Humphreys effect" or "Humphreys paradox" amply confirmed as a fact, on rats as well as men.
Confirmation has continued in recent studies. Perkins & Cacioppo

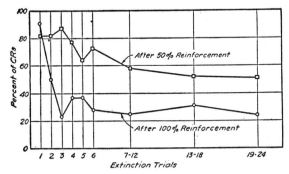

FIG. 26. (Woodworth & Schlosberg, 1954, p. 564, from Humphreys, 1939, Figs. 2 and 3 combined.) Course of extinction of the
conditioned eyelid response after intermittent (50-percent) and
100-percent reinforcements. In the first three or four extinction
trials the progress of extinction is very rapid after 100-percent
reinforcement, but almost entirely lacking after the 50-percent
reinforcement. Similar extinction curves for PGR are given by
Humphreys (1940, p. 73).

(1950) find that in repeated daily sessions in the Skinner box, with
conditioning followed immediately by extinction, the extinction becomes progressively more rapid for both the 100-percent and the
50-percent groups, but the 50-percent rats always require several
unreinforced trials before the bar pressings begin to disappear. Weinstock (1954), in a runway experiment and with only one trial a day
so as to rule out the immediate aftereffects of eating a pellet which
play a part in some theories, finds extinction quick after 100-per-
cent reinforcement, slow after 50 percent and still slower after 30
percent.

The theorists have worried a good deal over the "Humphreys
paradox," but they seem to have come around to emphasis on *discrimination* (however conceived). The shift from 100-percent reinforcement to an extinction series with no more reinforcements is
abrupt and striking so that the extinction learning process can start

with the first trial. No such sudden shift occurs after 50-percent reinforcement during which there have been runs of two or three
trials without the incentive. For the first two or three extinction
trials the situation as presented to O does not change at all, and
many trials may be necessary before the absolutely no-incentive
character of the new objective situation is learned. (Cf. Elam, Tyler
& Bitterman, 1954; Freides, 1957.)

These experiments on intermittent reinforcement are akin to
those on probability learning (p. 249ff and especially Figures 22
and 25). If we ask why a shift downward in *amount* of incentive is
so much more quickly learned than a shift from 50-percent reinforcement to zero (p. 265), the answer is that the changed *frequency*
of a reward can only be learned in a series of trials.

Our theory, then, is that extinction is primarily a process of
learning a changed environment, often requiring a considerable
number of trials because it is probability learning. We may ask why
O should not continue his habitual preparatory response after he
has learned the present absence of the accustomed incentive. The
answer would bring in an inhibitory factor, not necessarily identical
with reactive and conditioned inhibition, but more like a general
disinclination to act without any incentive.

10

Learning the Environment

II: CUE LEARNING, DISCRIMINATION LEARNING

We have already had something to say about the learning of cues—signals, conditioned stimuli—and we found that they were harder to learn than incentives but easier than efficient instrumental acts. In the sequence, $S_1R_1S_2R_2$, the presence of a positive or negative incentive, S_2, is learned very quickly (p. 247)—more quickly than the signal character of S_1 or than a successful approach or avoidance response, R_1. (The consummatory response, R_2, is usually some already-established response to the incentive, such as eating the food or jumping away from the burn.) The high point of the sequence is the consummation, S_2R_2, including of course the feedback or retroflex from R_2, such as the taste of the chewed food. This high point or goal is the most impressive part of the sequence and so is learned or "noticed" very quickly; the preparatory stages, the cue, and the instrumental act, are learned more slowly.

There is much more to be said, however, about cue learning. There is a large class of animal experiments that go under the head of "discrimination learning." For example, an animal is placed in a small enclosure with two exit doors side by side, one door white and the other black. If the animal pushes against the white door, it

opens and he finds a morsel of food inside; but if he opens the black
door, he finds nothing inside. In repeated trials the white door is
always positive and the black door always negative, but their positions are irregularly interchanged so that a position cue, right or
left, will get him food only half the time, and the only way he can
get the food every time is by using the white door as his positive
cue—or by using the black door as a negative cue and always avoiding it.

What the animal has to learn in this experiment is not the difference between black and white as *stimuli*. His eyes and visual apparatus no doubt react very differently to black and white. The
question is whether he can learn to use black and white as dependable *cues* of the location of food in a particular environment. Most
of the experimental work classed as discrimination learning would
be better called cue learning or cue differentiation. Typically, two
sequences have to be discriminated, such as:

S_1	R_1	S_2	R_2
White door	Enter	Food	Eat
Black door	Enter	No food	Not eat

The two S_1 stimuli are easily distinguished, and so are the two S_2
stimuli; yet the dependable connection of white with food and of
black with no food is not established in rats for many trials, often
100-200. The difficulty is not with the rat's learning ability, for if
the food is always behind the right-hand door, or always behind the
left-hand one, he masters this connection in a very few trials. A
suggestion comes from an experiment on kindergarten children.
They were shown four little cubical boxes, painted four quite different shades of green. A reward was secretly hidden under one of
them and the child was told to have a try at finding it. In many
trials he made no progress in using a particular shade of green as
his cue—unless he were clearly informed that *the reward would
always be under the same box*. Without this information he was
apt to take the experiment as a pure guessing game in which he
could not hope to be right more than a fraction of the time (Schaeffer & Gerjuoy, 1955). For the rat the situation may be somewhat
similar: if the food is not always in the same place, finding it half
the time is good enough.

Pretraining in discrimination of the relevant cues

If the cues are fairly similar, even though distinguishable, there is a natural tendency to disregard their differences and respond in the same way to both the positive and the negative cues. Some learning is necessary before O can consistently respond to the positive cue and abstain from responding to the negative cue—or before he can consistently make one manual response to one of the cues and another manual response to the other cue. Correct manual responses are very important in many practical situations, as in the control of a machine or the piloting of an airplane (pp. 153, 156). Therefore, preliminary practice in paying careful attention to the cues themselves may facilitate the manual performance.

The manual task in one experiment (J. H. Cantor, 1955) required the subject to move an upright rod from its central position into one of six radial slots according to a color cue. The slots were cut in the top of a box, and the rod was pivoted inside the box, below the central position, in order to be easily movable into any one of the slots. The six color cues ranged from red through orange to yellow, some of them being quite similar. One group of students received pretraining on the colors; they practiced responding to each color by a certain letter of the alphabet. Shifting then to the manual task they surpassed other groups that did not have the pretraining in discrimination of the relevant colors. Similar results have been obtained by other experimenters (Baldwin, 1954; Battig, 1956; and others).

If we ask what the subjects in this experiment carried over, "transferred" from the pretraining to the manual task, the most obvious answer is not the most certain. The most obvious is that, having learned names (letters) for the six colors, they carried over these names and used them also as names for the six slots. The letters would then be associative links between the colors and their respective slots. Or, somewhat less obviously, we might say that a name attached to a color makes the color sensation more distinctive, as the name, "orange," given to a color intermediate between red and yellow, makes that part of the spectrum stand out more distinctly than before. The most certain answer to our question, however, is that the pretraining forced the subjects to *notice* the similar colors carefully enough to make each one distinct from the others.

Without some such perceptual work the distinctive names could not be learned in the first place; but, once this work was done for the purpose of naming the colors, it would not need to be done all over again in the manual task.

Other studies justify our *emphasis on the perceptual factor.* In one experiment (Rossman & Goss, 1951) nonsense figures were used instead of colors, and the pretraining consisted in associating each figure with a nonsense syllable. The manual task was facilitated by this pretraining, and there was some silent saying of the syllables during the manual task, though subjects required to speak the syllables aloud were distracted rather than helped. "The groups with verbal learning experience used the syllables as facilitating devices to some degree during the motor learning. However, they reported that looking for identifying parts [of the figures] was more frequently employed, and as subjectively evaluated, more helpful." (Cf. Kurtz, 1955, p. 290.)

An experiment of E. J. Gibson & Walk (1956), done on rats in a discrimination box, presented a black circle and a black triangle, on white background, as the positive and negative cues of the door to food. The pretraining consisted simply of exposure of the animals from birth up to black circles and triangles on the white walls of their living cages. Two circles and two triangles were always present, but their locations on the walls were changed from time to time so as to avoid any differential secondary reinforcement of either figure through nearness to the food pan or water bottle. These changes in the location of the figures would surely elicit exploratory activity (p. 83) and good reception of the two shapes. Beginning at the age of 90 days these pretrained rats were given the discrimination test along with litter mates that had been reared under the same conditions except for the absence of the figures. The pretrained rats learned much more quickly than the controls. At the end of 15 days of testing, ten trials per day, eight out of the ten pretrained rats had mastered the task, but none of the nine litter mates—the advantage of the pretrained group being reliably established. (Whether the *early* exposure to the figures was especially important is a question for further experimentation.)

The motivation of these rats, as far as we can see, was simply the exploratory drive, whereas the human subjects in the previously-described pretraining desired to succeed in a naming task. In both cases the behavior primarily aroused was exploratory, and the primary result was increased definiteness of certain colors or figures.

VTE behavior—vicarious trial and error

What was said a few years ago about this curious form of exploration and its role in cue learning could justifiably be repeated today in spite of recent critical reviews and discussions (Taylor & Reichlin, 1951; Austin, 1953; Goss & Wischner, 1956). With two alternatives to choose from in a discrimination setup, the animal subject—especially perhaps the rat—is likely to fall into a position habit, always choosing the right-hand door or always the left-hand one. Consequently, he obtains reward in a random half of the trials and punishment in the other half. (If he is allowed to correct his errors, he will finally reach the reward on every full trial, but at the cost of many punishments.) After persisting for many trials in this position habit, he begins to show VTE. He hesitates before jumping, looks from one door to the other, sometimes looking back and forth several times, sometimes making a feint at jumping to one door and the other before his decisive jump. It is a picture of indecision. This VTE behavior increases gradually in amount, and concurrently the correct choices (as of the white door on either side) become more frequent. When he has reached the point of choosing the white door every time, his hesitation and VTE gradually disappear.

It seems clear that VTE facilitates the animal's transition from response to a place to response to white. Yet the animal cannot learn the two S_1S_2 sequences by merely looking at the two S_1 cues or making a feint at jumping. He has to follow through with an actual jump in order to experience the whole sequence. The VTE must operate by making him more receptive or attentive to the black and white. Quickly looking from one door to the other brings out the black-white "dimension" which he had not noticed so long as he was jumping routinely to one place.

We cannot say that the individual who shows the most VTE is necessarily the quickest learner of differential cues. Too much of it will slow the learning process by reducing the number of definitive choices. Besides, rapid looking back and forth confuses the S_1 phase of the S_1S_2 sequence. Hesitant behavior before making a plunge is found in human behavior, as well as in rats confronted with a gap to be jumped. It differs from VTE in that there is no choice to be made, except the choice between jumping and not jumping. With practice it decreases almost from the start (Taylor & Reichlin, 1951) instead of first increasing to a maximum as in the case of genuine VTE. These qualifying considerations do not annul the exploratory value of VTE in discrimination learning.

The animal's slow progress in differentiating the positive and negative cues has stimulated experimenters to design apparatus and forms of experiment that might yield quicker learning. This is practically important as a time saver in any elaborate research, and it is theoretically important for the light it may throw on the questions, "What" and "How"—what exactly is learned in cue differentiation, and how it is learned.

SIMULTANEOUS AND SUCCESSIVE CUES

In the experiments described thus far the positive and negative cues are presented simultaneously, and the subject has to choose between them, approaching one and avoiding or disregarding the other. In another form of experiment, only one cue is presented at once, sometimes the positive one and sometimes the negative, and successful behavior consists in advancing when the positive cue is present and not advancing for the negative one.

Simultaneous cues

Slow learning of the two sequences, such as white followed by food, black followed by no food—or equilateral triangle followed by food if pointed up, no food if inverted—could be because of delay in reaching the food. In the old "discrimination box" the rat had to traverse some distance after choosing his cue before reaching the reward. A quicker sequence would probably be more impressive and more easily learned. The arrangement of black and white doors side by side, enabling the rat to choose a door, push it open and find food or no food just inside, shortens the sequences in time and space and does in fact cut down the learning time considerably.

Lashley's (1930) *jumping-stand* apparatus was a radical departure from the old discrimination box. The two doors were filled with cards, black versus white, or bearing two figures to be discrimi-

nated. After preliminary training the rat would jump across a gap
of 7 to 10 inches from the jumping stand against his chosen door.
If his choice were correct, his jump would knock down the positive
card and admit him to the food just beyond; but if his choice were
incorrect, he bumped his nose against the locked door and fell into
a net or apron from which he was lifted by E and replaced on the
jumping stand for another try.

The sequence from choice to reward or punishment here is certainly brief and impressive to the animal. More important perhaps
is the fact that he gets *good visual perception* of a cue while making
the serious move of jumping at it. He looks before he leaps and as
he leaps. He looks at his intended landing place and gets good reception of the lower half at least of the card. Ehrenfreund (1948)
found it much better to have the triangles near the bottom than
near the top of the two doors. He also found that the element of
punishment was not very important, for his rats did not bump their
noses and fall into a net when they jumped at the negative cue;
they simply found themselves in an empty black box. Still they
learned rather quickly.

One who has adopted and developed the jumping-stand apparatus and made extensive use of it is Paul E. Fields (1935, 1953, 1954).
In his 1953 paper (p. 69) he has this to say of its advantages:

> The essential point in his [Lashley's] technique was that the
> rats were required to slow down in front of the stimulus patterns
> before they jumped across a gap to the positive figure. The extra
> attention secured in this manner plus the immediacy of reward or
> punishment was conducive to high accuracy of response.

Fields (1953) diminished the emotional disturbance for the rat of
falling into the apron and being picked up by E and placed back
on the jumping platform; he provided a little ladder enabling the
rat to climb back himself. He introduced other ways of facilitating
the learning and increasing the reliability of the learned performance under normal conditions, in preparation for a test on rats of
the effects on skilled performance of drugs, high altitude, radiation
dosage, etc.

Instead of two doors, Harlow (1949) has extensively used *two
small wells in a table top* covered with two different objects which
are interchanged in position in random order; the reward is always
under the same object for a series of trials, after which two new

objects are presented, again with food always under a certain object. In a long succession of such problems a monkey learns very gradually to take the result of his first trial as an index of the positive and negative cues for the current problem: if he lifts object A on the first trial and finds food in the well beneath, he sticks to A as his positive cue for the later trials of that problem; but if first choice of A uncovers an empty well, he shifts to B as the positive cue. The cue objects can be wooden blocks of different shapes, but they can just as well be household objects of suitable size; hundreds of variegated objects have been used in long investigations. This form of simultaneous-cue problem has been used also on preschool children and on marmosets, cats, canaries, and probably other animals besides the numerous rhesus monkeys of Harlow's "learning-set" experiments. We shall have more to say of the results.

One result which may be more significant than it seems at first has been obtained with the Harlow apparatus. If the positive and negative cue objects, instead of being placed directly on the wells, are displayed a few inches vertically over the white covers which now have to be displaced for inspection of the wells, the learning of a very simple discrimination is much retarded, and the establishment of a learning set is impossible (McClearn & Harlow, 1954; Murphy & Miller, 1955). Here there is no delay of reward; the raisin is obtained just as quickly by lifting the white covers as by lifting the cue objects in the usual setup. It is the *spatial separation of the cue* from the manipulandum that causes the difficulty. The cue does not *belong* to the manipulandum when it is separate from it. The "manipulandum" here is the object which *O* must move to obtain the reward. The cue, in a simple problem, is the white block a few inches above the manipulandum; it *points to* the correct manipulandum, we may say, without being a *property* of the manipulandum itself, as it is when the white block covers the well and has to be displaced. If *O* were responding to "raw stimuli" (p. 140), it would make no difference whether the white cue were right on the manipulandum or a few inches above it. But if he is dealing with objects in space, he has two objects to deal with in the case of the pointer cue and only one in the case of the object-property cue. The white block "gets more attention" when it is a manipulandum as well as a cue than when it is only a pointer.

Even when the cue object is directly over the well, in these experiments, it is not the object of primary interest to the animal.

Primary interest attaches to the morsel of food in the well. When the wells are covered with squares of plywood, painted red and green, with red the positive cue, we might expect monkeys or chimpanzees, known to possess adequate color sense, to learn the discrimination in a very few trials. Actually, it usually takes them 50 to 100 trials. Jarvik (1953) tried out the effect of eliminating the colored squares. He colored pieces of bread red and green with tasteless vegetable dyes, but also flavored the green ones with quinine. On each trial he placed a red piece and a green piece a few inches apart on the table and gave the animal his choice. After sampling once or twice the red and green bread, monkeys and chimpanzees always chose the red (or the green if the red samples were the bitter ones). They learned the red-green discrimination in one or two trials.

In a second test Jarvik (1956) used halves of peanuts, the shells being stained red or green, and the kernels being removed from the green ones. Again the chimpanzees (monkeys not tried) learned in one or two trials to use the positive cue.

In terms of objects dealt with, there are three of them when the cue object is separate from the cover concealing the reward; two of them when the cue object is also the cover; and only one when the cue color is *a directly visible property of the reward itself.* Cue learning is slowest when three objects are involved and much the quickest when only a single object is involved.

A similar result has been obtained with the jumping stand (Wodinsky, Varley & Bitterman, 1954). There were four doors in a semicircular arrangement about the stand. The rats were first taught to jump only to the end doors. If the positive and negative cues (as horizontal and vertical black stripes on white doors) were on the two middle doors, the rat's progress in using them as "pointers" to the adjacent end doors was very slow. But if the cues were on the end doors to which the jumps were made, learning was relatively rapid.

Human beings make much use of pointer cues, like the red and green lights on the road, the large plus sign of an intersection ahead, the arrows pointing right and left, straight up or obliquely downward—besides the signs that use printed words. It would be troublesome to learn these cues by trial and error, and we usually depend on information from some source for their meaning. Human beings, however, also make much use of the visible and audible properties of objects as cues of those objects. We distinguish one person from another by their faces and even by the sound of their voices over the telephone. We identify metals and dress goods by color and sheen. We recognize places and buildings by their visual patterns. Such cues we learn by direct experience rather than from outside information, and only a little experience may be needed.

Successive cue differentiation

When the positive and negative visual cues are present simultaneously, so that *O* can look back and forth from one to the other, conditions would seem most favorable for getting different impressions from the two and so making a start toward using them practically. Conditions would seem quite unfavorable if only one cue were present at a time. In ordinary life, to be sure, we recognize many persons by their faces though we never had the opportunity of placing them side by side and making a simultaneous comparison. We might like to do so when two brothers or sisters have a strong family resemblance, but most people we know are different enough to render close simultaneous comparison unnecessary for later recognition.

For careful laboratory proof that animals can learn differential cues when only the positive or the negative cue is present at the same time we go back to Pavlov. Some of his experiments on "stimulus generalization and differentiation" were done in 1909-1911 (Pavlov, 1927, Lecture VII). During this same period the "discrimination box" for simultaneous presentation of both cues was being developed by Yerkes and Watson (Yerkes, 1907; Yerkes & Watson, 1911). Both the simultaneous and the successive cues were differentiated very slowly, neither offering the animal learner any great advantage. Both types of experiment have something to tell of the learning process.

Pavlov's procedure has often been summarized without mention of one significant point in the dog's behavior. After establishing by regular reinforcement a positive salivary response to the positive cue, Pavlov proceeded to throw in his negative cue. The first time that he did so, the dog's reaction was the *"investigatory reflex"* which we judged (p. 228) to be very important in getting the simple CR started. Pavlov says (1927, p. 112):

It is obvious that the investigatory reflex can be used to determine the degree to which the nervous system of a given animal is capable of discriminating between various stimuli. If, for example, . . . there is present a definite musical tone, any even slight alteration of its pitch will suffice to evoke an investigatory reflex in the form of a definite orientation of the ears and maybe of the whole body of the animal in relation to the tone. The same is true even of slight changes in various other elementary or compound stimuli. The investigatory reflex, of course, takes place only provided that the structure of the analyzing [sensory] apparatus is sufficiently delicate to register the change in the environment.

Since the dog noticed the changed stimulus on the first trial, what he had to learn was not to distinguish the positive and negative cues *as stimuli.* He had to learn them *as signals* of food and no food. What he had to unlearn and overcome was not "stimulus generalization" in a strict sense, but cue generalization. The two tones did not sound alike, but their different *meanings* had to be learned by following through the two sequences, such as

Higher Tone—Food, Lower Tone—No Food;
or
Luminous Circle—Food; Luminous Square—No Food.

The positive and negative cues, with food and no food, were presented in irregular succession at intervals of several minutes, a few trials per day. Good differentiation was established in twenty trials or less.

When Pavlov wished to utilize this technique for determining a difference threshold—the smallest difference in pitch or shape or brightness that the dog could perceive—he found it necessary to approach the threshold gradually. To determine the darkest gray that could be distinguished from black, he used a black screen as his positive cue, then introduced a white screen as the negative cue and secured differentiation of these two. Then, keeping black positive and always reinforced, he put in light gray, then medium gray, and darker and darker grays as negative cues. He actually used all the available grays without breaking down the dog's discrimination (Pavlov, 1927, p. 132).

Pavlov explained cue differentiation by the extinction of the negative cue through nonreinforcement while the positive cue was being maintained by continued reinforcement. No doubt some puzzling questions remain. Why should it be necessary to have the negative cue very different at first from the positive, in spite of the fact that even a small change of stimulus gives the "investigatory reflex"? Why should the transfer be so successful from a wide positive-negative difference to a smaller one? And is it safe to say that only the responses to the positive cue are reinforced? A mouth free from surplus saliva when there is no food coming seems like a reward. The negative side of the differentiation, instead of being a pure state of inhibition and unresponsiveness, may be a learned adaptation to the sequence of events signaled by the negative cue (p. 266).

At any rate, Pavlov demonstrated one procedure for establishing cue differentiation without having the positive and negative cues present at the same time. His response measure was the quantity of saliva secreted in response to the respective cues.

A favorite measure in eyelid conditioning is the frequency of responses, the number per block of (say) twelve trials; this percent increases in conditioning and decreases in extinction. In cue dif-

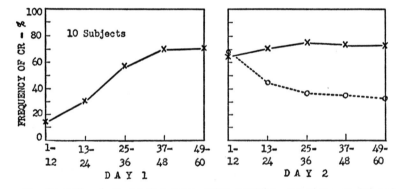

Fig. 27. (Hilgard, Campbell & Sears, 1938.) Establishment of the conditioned eyelid response to a positive cue (Day 1), followed on Day 2 by further strengthening of this CR and partial extinction of the eyelid response to the negative cue. The reinforcing or unconditional stimulus was a puff of air against the open eye. For the positive and negative cues there were two windows in the screen before O; either of them could be lighted up. Light in the left-hand window was a signal of air-puff to follow half a second later, but light in the right-hand window was never followed by the puff. On Day 1 only the left-hand light was used; Day 2 both lights were used in irregular order.

Cue generalization is shown by the fact that lid responses to the light in the right-hand window (never reinforced) appeared at the very beginning of Day 2.

ferentiation the response frequency increases for the positive cue and diminishes for the negative cue, as shown in Figure 27. The positive and negative cues are given in succession, never simultaneously. Yet differentiation is established rather quickly.

Should we expect cue differentiation to be *retained?* No doubt response to the positive cue would be well retained (according to many results showing good retention of conditioned responses). But the extinction of response to the negative cue ought to be followed by spontaneous recovery during a period of disuse (p. 233). The response to the negative cue would then reappear after a rest, and be as frequent as at the start of the experiment. In a follow-up of the results shown in Figure 27, retention was tested after 4 to 10 months of disuse (Hilgard & Humphreys, 1938). The percents were as follows:

	Lid response to positive cue	*Lid response to negative cue*
At start of Day 2	65%	65%
At end of Day 2	73	33
At end of Day 3 (an additional day of differential training)	64	21
Retest after 4-10 months	73	53

The final difference of 73-percent response to the positive cue, as against only 53-percent response to the negative cue, is not by itself statistically reliable, but it is confirmed by the retention scores of three other groups in the same investigation so that the authors were justified in concluding (p. 122): "Discrimination is long retained . . . the retention is selective, so that more responses appear to the positive than to the negative stimuli."

Successive discrimination succeeds, not only with the conditioned type of response such as the salivary or the eyelid CR, but also with the jumping-stand and the runway experiments. A rat on the *jumping stand* is confronted by a single door bearing either the positive or the negative cue. If he jumps against the positive cue, he gets through to the reward; but if he jumps against the negative cue, he falls into the net. Cue differentiation is quickly achieved (Solomon, 1943). A rat in the starting box of a *runway* is confronted by either a white or a black floor leading to the goal box. When the floor is white, there is food in the goal box—but not when the floor is black. Here, too, cue differentiation is achieved rather quickly (Verplanck, 1942). In these experiments with the jumping stand or the runway time measures of the animal's response are possible and convenient: the *latency or starting time and the running time* (or the speed of running). The progress of cue differentiation is shown by the gradual slowing down of the responses to the negative cue along with the gradual speeding up of the responses to the positive cue (Raben, 1949). A pretty double time curve is obtained, similar to the frequency curve shown in our Figure 27, p. 278.

Instead of the time of single responses Skinner (1938) used as his measure the *rate* of responding, i.e., the number of responses per minute. For positive and negative cues he lighted and darkened the Skinner box, providing pellets for bar pressure during the light periods but not during the dark periods. In this form of the successive-cue experiments, also, some discrimination is rather quickly in evidence.

The experimenters have provided plenty of examples of simultaneous and successive cue differentiation. Both kinds are perfectly feasible. If we wish to know whether either kind is essentially *easier* to learn, we shall have some trouble in keeping all other conditions constant while we make the same cues simultaneous for one group and successive for another. The jumping stand before a single door, or the two-well apparatus reduced to one well, would lend themselves to this problem.

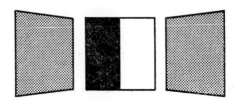

FIG. 28. (Bitterman & Wodinsky, 1953.) View from the jumping stand of two gray doors at the sides and a middle door used only for the cues to be differentiated. The three doors were in a semicircle centered on the jumping stand. As shown, the middle door displays the *simultaneous* cues, the task being to jump to the gray door next to the white cue which was sometimes on the right and sometimes on the left. For *successive* cues, the middle door was all white or all black, and the task was to jump to the right-hand door when the middle door was white but to the left when the cue was black.

A plan for presenting either simultaneous or successive cues, much used by Bitterman and his associates, is illustrated in Figure 28. When the cues are simultaneous, one is positive and the other negative, as in most experiments on discrimination learning. The animal could conceivably learn to approach the door on the white side or to avoid the door on the black side. When the cues are successive, both are equally positive, one calling for the choice of the right-hand door, the other for choice of the left-hand door. The two tasks are after all *not the same except* for the matter of simultaneity or succession. The successive task may seem too blind to be learned at all. Still, the rat makes a choice and jumps on every trial and so has a chance to differentiate the sequences, some of which lead to reinforcement and others to a fall into the net. At any rate, rats do master both of these tasks; and in this particular experiment the successive task was mastered in 80 trials as against 140 for the simultaneous task. (We could regard both tasks as successive, the black-white patterns being taken as units and differing much less than the all-white and all-black.)

The *advantage* shown in this experiment *for successive cues is exceptional.* Many variations of the experiment have been tried and usually the simultaneous cues have been more quickly differentiated than the successive. For one example consider Spence's use (1952) of the T maze. Advancing through the stem of the T the rat comes to the junction of the side arms, one being white and one black for simultaneous cues, but both being white or both black for successive cues. In one case he must learn to take the white side arm for food; in the other case he must take the right side when both are white, the left side when both are black. The simultaneous task was learned in an average of 59 trials, the successive in an average of 143 trials.

Are the results of these two experiments as flatly contradictory as they appear at first sight? We may ask in particular why the simultaneous cues were so much easier to differentiate in the T maze than in the situation pictured in Figure 28. Well, the contrast in the T maze between white path on one side and black on the other must have been quite striking, especially as the animal had to respond in a direct manner by entering one of the paths. The white and black are properties of the "manipulanda," i.e., of the two alternative paths. In the other case the white half of the cue display is a "pointer" and not a property of either manipulandum, i.e., of either door. So we can explain the relative ease of the simultaneous task in the T maze. The relative difficulty of the successive task in the T maze is something we shall not attempt to explain.

Instead of two doors or two paths two covered wells can be used (p. 273) in this general design for comparing the differentiation of simultaneous and successive cues. Warren & Baron (1956b) found that cats easily learned to push aside the object covering a well and take the reward if successful. For simultaneous cues, dissimilar objects covered the two wells and the cats learned quickly to displace the positive object. For successive cues, both wells were covered with identical objects, the reward being in the right-hand well for one cue object, in the left-hand well for the other cue. This successive problem was much more difficult for the cats. An analogous experiment on fourth- and fifth-grade children revealed the same disadvantage of successive cues (Perkins, Banks & Calvin, 1954).

More successful than the experiments we have been considering in presenting simultaneous and successive cues under strictly comparable conditions is a test of the matter on college students by Loess & Duncan (1952). The stimuli were squares and circles on white and gray cards, one square or circle to a card, Class A consisting of circles on white and squares on gray, Class B of circles on gray and squares on white. This arbitrary classification had to be discovered by O. There were two sizes of circles and two sizes of squares, but size was irrelevant. The subject responded by pressing one of two keys. When two cards were shown simultaneously, he pressed the key on the side of an A card; when only one card was shown, he pressed the left-hand key for an A card, the right-hand key for a B card. He might take several seconds to reach a decision; when correct, he was so informed by a buzz. This relatively easy task was mastered as quickly by the successive group of subjects as by the simultaneous group. A more difficult task used the same figures and the same rules, but each figure was complicated by a superfluous triangle, pointing up or down. This task was mastered much more quickly by a simultaneous than by a successive group, i.e., by subjects who saw an A specimen and a B specimen together than by those who saw only one at a time. "It may be that when the discrimination is relatively easy . . . , it will make little difference whether or not direct comparison is possible. . . . As the discrimination is made more difficult the method of simultaneous presentation, with its greater opportunity for direct comparison of the positive and negative stimuli, may prove advantageous." This hypothesis of the authors was supported by their results and also by the results of other experiments (MacCaslin, 1954).

THEORIES OF DISCRIMINATION LEARNING

We have already examined the *How* of the process of learning to differentiate positive and negative cues or cues for alternative responses. We have spoken of cue differentiation as a process of sequence learning, of O's being impressed with the contrast between the alternative S_1S_2 sequences. We have emphasized the role of exploratory behavior such as the dog's "investigatory reflex" elicited by the intrusion of a novel cue into the established routine of a conditioning experiment, and such as the "VTE" which helps the rat to break away from a position habit (pp. 271, 276). We have seen that a "set" for the regularity to be expected in a specific laboratory situation could be an essential guide for a monkey or a human child (pp. 268, 273). And with human adults we have found language to be an aid, since pretraining in the task of naming the separate cues insured close attention to the cues themselves (p. 269).

All this emphasis on a perceptual factor in cue learning amounts perhaps to a theory, but the well-known theories of discrimination learning are concerned with the *What* rather than the How. What has O learned when he responds differently to different stimuli? What are the cues he has learned to differentiate? Three theories have been offered in answer to the latter question.

1. *A configurational or total-figure theory.* Although the Gestalt psychologists might favor this theory, they have apparently not done much on this particular problem (see, however, a suggestion of Köhler's, 1947, pp. 274-275). We present it simply as a common-sense theory which would square with much ordinary experience. When we distinguish people by their faces, we certainly take each face as a whole and do not attempt to pick out the identifying characteristics; the same is true with many other objects. In fact, two objects may differ in total appearance much more surely than in color, shape, or size so that it would be foolish to attempt to state exactly how they differ if all we want is to be sure that they are different. (This configurational theory is not the same as one proposed by Gulliksen & Wolfle, 1938, and cogently criticized by Lashley, 1942. They were thinking of the compound configuration

of the positive and negative cues presented simultaneously—circle on one door and triangle on the other, for example—whereas we are thinking of the circle as one configuration and of the triangle as another, the two being distinguishable as wholes.)

2. *A selective or single-aspect-at-a-time theory.* Let the two simultaneous cues be a white circle on one black door and a white triangle on the other black door. The two total configurations differ in several aspects which could serve as differential cues. The white figures differ in shape, the black areas under the figures differ in size, and the two doors differ in location. If the animal subject adopts a position habit at first, he seems to be using the location cue for the time being to the neglect of the figures. If he learns after a while to choose the door with a circle on it, he seems to be using the shape cues, but he might be responding only to the black areas. We could find out by transfer tests in which only parts of the door configurations were presented. At any rate, the theory is that difficult discriminations are mastered by selection of some distinctive part or aspect as a dependable cue. The "selection" need not be deliberate; something about one door catches the animal's eye and so becomes his S_1 for the moment. If he responds and obtains the reward, he is on the way to mastery of the problem. This theory leans heavily on "attention" as a function of the organism: in the presence of a plurality of stimuli, it is possible for the organism, and even unavoidable, to respond selectively. Some stimuli, some aspects of the objects present, will be perceived more definitely than others—color (white or black) more definitely than size or shape, for example. Among the proponents of this theory, Krechevsky (1938) and Lashley (1942) have been prominent.

3. *A summative, nonselective theory.* Without denying the selectivity of the animal's response to a complex of stimuli—for example, that he may respond at one time to the location of a door, at another time to the white color of a door—this theory lays no special weight on selectivity. While the animal is always jumping to the right-hand door and getting reinforcement only when that door is white, the connection of white door with food is gradually being strengthened in spite of the animal's inattention to the white and black. Meanwhile the connection of black with food is not being strengthened and may even be weakened. Therefore, the white-food connection is gaining an advantage over the black-food connection, even while the animal is dominated by the position habit.

How the white-food connection ever becomes stronger than the position habit is not so clear, since in the usual procedure the position habit is reinforced on half of the trials. But if we assume that a very strong position habit cannot be further strengthened by rewards though it can be weakened by nonreinforcement, this habit may eventually be reduced to a moderate strength and be surpassed by the white-food connection; i.e., the preference for right over left may be surpassed by the acquired preference for white over black (Spence, 1936; 1951, p. 719).

This nonselective theory of discrimination learning is also called the *"continuity theory,"* and the selective theory, by contrast, is a "noncontinuity theory." What seemed like a logical deduction from the selective theory was that the animal would make no progress toward consistent response to the white door as long as he was dominated by the position habit. He would be paying no attention to the white and black and not exploring the $S_1 S_2$ sequences that start with white and black. Therefore, it should make no difference to the animal whether white or black were the positive cue during the early (perhaps forty) trials while the position habit was dominant. Have black positive during these early trials and then shift to white positive: the animal should learn white positive just as quickly as if white had been positive from the beginning. According to the continuity theory such a shift from black to white positive should handicap the animal considerably, since the only decisive factor is the balance (from the beginning) of reinforcements and nonreinforcements for the different $S_1 S_2$ sequences—without regard to the animal's attention and explorations.

Here was a clear opportunity for experimental testing of the opposed predictions. The test was made several times by different experimenters and the *results were definitely in favor of continuity*. Perhaps, however, the selective theorists were too bold in their deductions; maybe they should have allowed for some *incidental learning* and simply predicted that a rat, like a man, could learn a sequence more quickly and efficiently by attentively exploring it than by letting it "roll over him" while going through his right-side routine. This possibility might be hard to put to a crucial test. But there are other facts—VTE especially—indicative of active exploration during the process of cue differentiation.

According to Lashley (1938) and Dodwell (1957) the cues actually learned are not total configurations nor sums of all their parts, but some one part or aspect serves to distinguish the two doors. A rat has learned to respond differentially to a white square and a diamond-shaped white figure; test him now with parts or modifications of those figures. In this transfer test some parts or aspects prove to be "equivalent" to the whole figures in maintaining the learned cue differentiation, but other parts or aspects will not serve. The bottom halves are likely to be equivalent to the whole figures, but the top halves are not. In jumping the rat has probably fixated the lower parts of the two figures, since they are near his landing place (p. 273). But visual fixation is not the whole story; if the more distinctive cues are on the upper halves of the doors, the rat will find and use them. Wide black and white stripes, horizontal on one door and vertical on the other, are known to be an easy pair of cues for the rat to differentiate—much easier than upright and inverted triangles. In one experiment (Mahut, 1954) the rats required 160 trials to differentiate the triangles, only 70 to differentiate the stripes. But if each door had a triangle below and a set of stripes above, seventy trials were enough; the rats evidently had no trouble in finding the stripes.

It seems, then, that even though we grant to the continuity or nonselective theory their contention that all the stimuli receiving a balance of reinforcement are becoming gradually connected to the positive response, we must also grant to the selective theory that some stimuli (parts or aspects of the discriminanda) are being connected more rapidly. *Some parts or aspects stand out* and are noticed more quickly than others. How much initiative the rat has in this selection we cannot say; human subjects will actively look for cues and try out their hunches till they find some cue that is dependable (Prentice, 1949).

There are some other *facts which seem inconsistent with a strict continuity theory.* Though learning of the correct cues is going on during the dominance of a position habit, it is supposed to consist only in the gradual strengthening of an S—R connection. Nothing is said of any perceptual differentiation preceding the appearance of the correct motor response. The position habit remains dominant until the balance of reinforcements begins to favor the correct cue, as white versus black. If the motor responses are *timed,* however, they are found to become quicker to the correct positive than to the negative cue. The jumps are still made all to the right, but they are quicker when the right-hand door is white than when it is black (Mahut, 1954).

"Abortive jumping" is a curious bit of rat behavior often observed on the jumping stand during the dominance of a position habit, with rewards half of the time and falls into the net the other half. The rat breaks the force of a bump against a locked door by turning somewhat to one side. He does so mostly when jumping to the negative cue. With white positive and black negative and the rat jumping always to the right, abortive jumps occur mostly when black is on the right, so revealing a dawning differentiation of the cues though the overt choices would indicate no learning as yet (Maier, 1956; Maier & Ellen, 1956).

Another fact suggestive of a selective factor in the learning of complex cues is brought out by transfer tests such as we have mentioned: individuals that are about equal in the number of trials they take to learn the correct choice are found to use different parts or aspects of the large and small white squares, for example, that E has provided as cues; one rat goes by size, another by total amount of light, a third by the black stripe beneath the squares. The animals, some species more than others, seem to do some "shopping around" in search of an easy, dependable cue (Lashley, 1938; Dewdney & McCall, 1954; Towe, 1955).

We must not get the impression that the *continuity theory* is outdated. As a part of the Hull system (so intended by Spence, 1936, and accepted by Hull, 1950b), it is still very much alive and *used in the design of experiments*. We will cite one or two examples.

Eninger (1952) begins his report by saying:

> One of the numerous empirical implications which are derivable from Hull's behavior theory (1943) is that a compound discriminandum involving two sense modalities will result in more rapid learning than a simple discriminandum involving only one or the other of these two sense modalities. . . . This follows from the theoretical assumptions that (*a*) each . . . component . . . becomes separately associated with a response . . . , and (*b*) the separate associative strengths summate . . .

The experiment made use of a simple T maze, the stem from the entrance to the choice point being either white, black, or gray. The Visual Group of rats learned to choose the left arm of the T when the stem was white, but the right arm when the stem was black. The Auditory Group approached the choice point through the gray stem and learned to choose the left arm during silence, but the right arm when a high-pitched tone was sounding. The Auditory-Visual Group had both cues combined; they learned to turn left from a white stem during silence, but to turn right from a black stem when the tone was sounding. This group learned much more quickly than either of the other two, thus verifying the summation effect.

An experiment of Church (1957) is especially interesting because it shows a mechanism for the social handing down of behavior from a leader to a follower. It was again an experiment on rats by the use of a T maze. The rats were thirsty and obtained water as their reward for going to the correct arm of the maze. First some leaders learned to run always to the left arm for their reward, and other leaders to run always to the right arm. Then a follower learned to obtain his *reward by following a leader* either to the left or to the right, the leader being changed from trial to trial in a random series such as LRLLRRLRRL, with no other cue except to follow the leader. At the end of 150 trials (ten per day) the six followers were following the leader perfectly. Then an incidental cue was added, a light in one arm of the T, so that in following the leader a rat was incidentally going always to the lighted arm (or always to the dark arm for half of the followers). Finally came a test without leaders, to see whether the followers would use the incidental cue alone. In twenty test trials per rat, not 100 percent by any means, but at least 77 percent, well above chance, agreed with the incidental cue. "According to the continuity theory, a set to respond to one aspect of the stimulus situation does not interfere with the learning of other effective cues preceding the reward."

We could classify this result also under the head of secondary reinforcement (p. 110). Finding the reward always in a lighted alley would attach secondary incentive value to a lighted alley.

Of other recent experiments on "continuity," some favor the theory and others dispute it (Babb, 1956; F. H. Boring, 1955; Goodwin, 1955; Goodwin & Lawrence, 1955). One difficulty with the theory is *our lack of quantitative knowledge about the effect of non-reinforcement.* Is the weakening effect of one trial without reinforcement equal to the strengthening effect of one trial with reinforcement? This assumption is favored by Wickens (1954) and works well in explaining some results of Babb (1956). It apparently would not explain the elimination of a position habit by a 50:50 random reinforcement of that habit during the establishment of a white-black discrimination. To explain such elimination, which often occurs, Spence (1936) assumed that a strong existing habit would be more weakened by one nonreinforcement than strengthened by one reinforcement, as we have already noted (p. 285). Correspondingly, Spence assumed that a weak S—R connection would be more strengthened by a reinforcement than weakened by a nonreinforcement. Only at a medium strength of the existing S—R connection would the two effects balance each other. Spence sometimes (1937) disregarded this refinement, however, and treated all reinforcements as equal in potency. He also equated the potency of reinforcements and nonreinforcements, except early in a learning series.

An implication of this denial of inhibitory potency of nonreinforcement in the early trials was perhaps unintended. It is that a rat, or even a chimpanzee, learns nothing about the *location* of the food from not finding it inside one of the doors. There are reasons for doubting this implication. We noticed before (p. 246) that incentive learning was rapid; after finding food once or twice in a maze, the rat's behavior in subsequent trials shows that he is searching for the food, his question being, "Where?" At the start of an experiment on discrimination learning—so as to minimize position habits—E usually gives the rat a few forced trials, with the food sometimes on one side and sometimes on the other; the rat then starts his free runs with the implicit question, "Where?" When the "correction method" is employed, he corrects each error by running across from the empty door to the other one; therefore, his initial nonreinforcement answers his question for that one trial, and indeed conveys the same "information" as a reinforcement. When correction is not allowed, a nonreinforcement still tells where the food is, and this information often has a visible effect on the rat's next choice, which is apt to repeat a success and shift to the other side after an error. In the one-door, successive form of discrimination, nonreinforcement is as important as reinforcement Figure 27, p. 278); in the two-door, simultaneous discrimination it certainly has some potency, though we cannot say how much on the basis of any current theory.

Rules of the game

Let us regard any one of these experiments in discrimination learning (cue differentiation) as a game with certain rules which must be discovered by *O*, the subject. Consider a two-door (or two-path) setup with simultaneous presentation of the positive and negative cues. We ask what *sources of information* regarding the rules are available to *O*, and we see that there are *two sources:* the *stimuli* presented by the two doors or paths; and the *retroflex*, reinforcement or nonreinforcement, resulting from *O*'s choice of a door. The presented stimuli always differ in at least one respect (dimension) which is their location, usually right and left (R and L). The stimuli must also be either alike or different in other respects, such as color. If they are both white or both black (W or B), that dimension is irrelevant, so much information being conveyed by the stimuli alone. If the doors are alike in all respects except location, location must be the only relevant dimension. If choice of the left-hand door brings reinforcement, that door is shown to be correct; if it brings nonreinforcement, the other door must be correct. Complete utilization of the available information in this simplest case would result in one-trial learning, which sometimes occurs in a simple T-maze.

But there are certain underlying rules of the game which may be taken for granted by some individuals but may have to be learned in the course of many trials: (1) reward is always present behind one door or the other, (2) but never behind both doors at once, and (3) a rule holds good throughout the game or at least for a series of trials. Information on these points is not provided by a single trial.

With these general rules adopted by *O*, his problem is to fix on the relevant cue dimension and on the particular cue that is positive. *E* can provide information on an *irrelevant* dimension by making both doors alike in a certain respect, both white or both black, for example. *E* cannot rule out location so directly when there are two doors to choose from, since he cannot make them alike in location. With successive cues on the same door, the location cue is ruled out and position habits are prevented. A left-door position habit in a two-door setup can be broken up by several consecutive nonreinforcements, but then *O* is apt to shift to a right-door position habit. He is receiving no direct information of the irrelevance of location.

Now let us consider a two-door setup with *three* cue dimensions: location—R versus L; color—W versus B; and a third—X versus Y. Let X and Y stand for hurdles across the alleys to the food wells, X for high and Y for low hurdles, the hurdles being plainly visible from the choice point, as are also the white and black interiors of the alleys—but not the food wells (Lawrence & Mason, 1955; Goodwin & Lawrence, 1955). Aside from location there are four kinds of alleys, WX, WY, BX, and BY. If E wishes to establish a W versus B discrimination, with X and Y irrelevant, he can present two X alleys to choose from or two Y alleys, one being W and the other B, rewarding always the choice of W (or else always the choice of B). Similarly, if he wishes to show the irrelevance of the WB dimension, he can present two W or two B alleys, one being X and the other Y. If he does not wish to offer such definite information, he will always make his two alleys different in *both* dimensions, WX versus BY or WY versus BX, still always rewarding O's choice of one particular aspect, W, B, X, or Y. Such problems are by no means beyond the learning capacity of rats, and they can be made to shift without excessive difficulty from one cue dimension to another, from use of the WB cues to the XY cues, and vice versa. If called upon to make such shifts repeatedly, back and forth, they readjust their choices more and more quickly. Similarly, if called upon to reverse cues within a single dimension, as from white positive to black positive, they do so more and more quickly in repeated reversals.

HIGHER-ORDER CUES

The black and white doors which serve as positive and negative cues in many discrimination-learning tasks can be called cues of the first or lowest order. The subject learns to approach the positive door, so establishing a habit of the first order. In a well-known experiment E then proceeds to reverse the cues, placing the reward always inside the white door instead of inside the black door as before. Since O has no warning of this change, he carries over his habit of choosing the black door but gradually learns to choose the white one. This new habit is on the same level as the old one, a habit of the first order, and the reversed cues are still cues of the first order. Now let the cues be re-reversed, black being again positive and white negative, and let them be reversed back and forth many times—and we obtain the remarkable result that fewer and fewer trials are needed to reverse the habits. We obtain a learning curve of the second order, a curve of the first order being shown by the learning of each separate habit. Early studies of learning to reverse were by Buytendijk (1930) on rats and by Harlow (1944) on monkeys.

The existence of curves like that in Figure 30, of which a large number have been obtained by different experimenters, presents

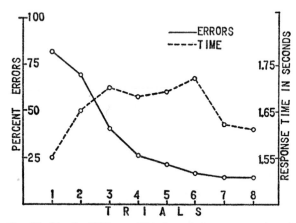

FIG. 29. (North, 1950b, p. 468.) A typical or average learning curve for a single reversal. The error curve shows the gradually decreasing percent of rats that chose the now incorrect arm of the T maze, which was correct just before the reversal. Therefore, the high percent of errors on Trial 1 really shows the degree of mastery of the preceding task. Without warning the food had been shifted from one arm to the other, and the rats learned rather quickly to shift their choice accordingly, though a few of them did not accomplish the shift during the eight trials shown in the graph.

The time curve shows the changes in time taken to reach the goal from the starting box. The rapid running of Trial 1 slowed down as soon as errors were encountered. Hesitation and VTE (p. 271) occurred until the errors were mostly eliminated.

This is a learning curve of the "first order." To obtain one of the second order, showing improvement through a series of back-and-forth reversals, E counted each O's errors on Trials 2 to 6 of each successive reversal and constructed a graph of the changing group Mean Frequency, as shown in Figure 30.

a challenge to the theorists. A curve like the first one (Figure 29) could be explained in the usual way by the gradually shifting balance of reinforcements and nonreinforcements from one to the other of the alternatives. When the cues are reversed (without warning), the existing balance is strongly in favor of the previously positive alternative which has been receiving all the reinforcements so that the choices have come to be practically all on its side. Suddenly the previously correct choice is not reinforced, and if *O* persists in making the old correct choice, he gets no reinforcements. When he tries the previously incorrect alternative, he gets some

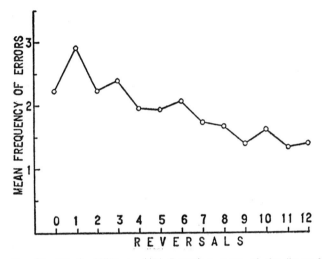

FIG. 30. (North, 1950a, p. 448.) Learning curve of the "second order," showing gradual decrease of errors made by thirty-six rats in a series of reversals. The discrimination required was one of position. The original task (marked 0) required the animals to take the left arm of a T maze for food. When this task was fairly well learned, the reward was shifted without warning to the right arm; for Reversal 2 it was shifted back to the left arm; and so on. The count of errors in Trials 2 to 6 combined was found on the average to decrease from about 3 on the first Reversal to what appears to be a level of 1.5 on Reversals 9 to 12.

food. So the balance shifts gradually to the new positive alternative.

But *why should the choices shift more and more quickly*, with fewer and fewer of the old correct choices, as the series of reversals back and forth continues? The balance in favor of each new positive alternative does not shift any more quickly. If anything, it must shift more and more slowly because of the increasingly heavy load of all the previous reinforcements and nonreinforcements that has to be carried along. Indeed, the old prediction was that in such a series as we are considering the reversals would become slower and slower, instead of quicker as is the fact.

Another challenging fact is that reversal is quicker if the previous habit has been learned to the *high criterion* of eighteen correct choices out of the last twenty trials, and even if it has been *over-learned* by many additional trials, practically all of which have been correct, so that the balance in favor of the old positive alternative is truly enormous. Yet when the reinforcements are shifted the subject follows suit very quickly (Reid, 1953; Warren, 1954b; Pubols, 1956).

It seems certain that in a series of reversals the subject is *learning to reverse*. He is *learning something besides the separate habits*. He is learning to shift from one to the other when he gets the proper cue. This cue must be the nonreinforcement of the previously correct choice. When *E* suddenly shifts the reward to the other alternative so that *O*, following his previous habit, finds no reward, he gets a jolt which serves as a cue of some change in the environment. In the special routine of these reversal experiments it is a change to a regular series with reversed cues, and *O* readjusts his choices accordingly. Reversal after a well-earned habit is quick because the "jolt" is so striking. The change is impressive and easily noticed, like the shift from 100-percent reinforcement to zero reinforcement of a conditioned response, as compared with the shift from intermittent to zero reinforcement (p. 264).

If our interpretation of the reversal experiments is on the right track, it should be possible to achieve *one-trial reversals* in rats, as was done with monkeys some years ago (Harlow, 1944). For the rats, an easy discrimination would be desirable, with training in each successive reversal carried to a high criterion. The discrimination box used by Dufort, Guttman & Kimble (1954) presented two doors side by side and differing in appearance, the one on the left displaying a large white circle and the one on the right a small white circle. In the first task food was always obtained by going to the left-hand, large circle; never by going to the right-hand, small circle. It was definitely an easy discrimination and was learned to the high criterion of eleven correct trials out of the last twelve, and with only four trials per day so that the habit had to be carried over from day to day. When this criterion was reached, the cues were reversed, food now being obtained only by going to the right-hand, small circle. When the reverse choice was learned to the same criterion as before, re-reversal occurred, and so on.

The first reversal was learned rather slowly, the previously established left-hand choice tending to persist for a good many trials, but the later reversals were learned more and more quickly until, from the seventh reversal on, all the nine rats showed one-trial learning. They shifted their choice after a single nonreinforcement of the old choice. Their cue for making the shift was obviously the nonreinforcement of a well-established choice; nothing else happened to elicit the shift of response. Prompt shifting was rewarded; with the noncorrection method used, it was the only sure way to secure food without any more unreinforced trials; so in a series of reversals the choice was shifted in fewer and fewer trials. A similar result was obtained by Capaldi & Stevenson (1957).

We call this nonreinforcement of a previously established choice a *cue of the second order*. Cues of the first order would be the left and right locations of the doors, the large and small white circles, and, in other discrimination-learning experiments, black and white doors and any other contrasting stimuli, figures or objects which elicit approach or avoidance after sufficient learning. This cue of the second order cannot directly elicit a revised choice when correction is not allowed; its effects appear in the following trials. What happens immediately is a *change of set*. Before a reversal the animal has acquired a set to go unhesitatingly to the left for his reward; now nonreinforcement disturbs this set; after sufficient experience, a single nonreinforcement may produce an immediate reversal of the set, and the new set can be retained and put to work on the next trial.

A different type of second-order cue is used in the Skinner box, when bar pressing is reinforced during bright illumination, but not during dim illumination. The first-order cues here are stimuli from the bar itself, which are the stimuli to which the rat directly responds. The bright illumination, "setting the occasion" during which the bar pressing will be reinforced, is a cue of the second order. There are other varieties of second-order cues; for example, the factory whistles which cause the operatives to start and stop responding to the first-order stimuli from the machines.

Learning sets

Besides the routine of repeated reversals there is another routine which monkeys at least can learn and master (Harlow, 1949; Harlow & Hicks, 1957). *E* gives *O* a series of tasks, each task presenting two easily distinguishable objects placed over two food wells, one and only one of which contains a raisin or some similar reward. The monkey displaces one of the objects and takes the raisin if his choice is correct. Correction of the first choice is not permitted. The two objects are located right and left in random order, but for the same task the reward is always beneath the same object. The outcome of the first trial thus shows which object is the positive cue for the duration of that particular task. Such is the rule of the game—simple enough we might suppose, but difficult for the monkey because of his strong tendency to vary his response. He settles down after a number of trials on the first task to consistent choice of the positive object. The next task presents two other objects with the reward always concealed under the same one of these two. In a long series of such tasks the monkey gradually adopts the rule of the game and masters each task in a single trial. The first trial in a new task is necessarily blind, but if it proves to be correct and so reveal the positive object, that object will be chosen for each later trial of the task. If the first choice proves to be incorrect, the monkey switches on the second trial to the other object which he continues to choose for the duration of that task.

In Harlow's terms the monkey has acquired a "learning set," a set for tackling each new problem of the same sort in a certain standard manner, eliminating the spontaneous variation that occurs in the earlier tasks of a series. In the series as a whole the monkey is *learning how to learn* this kind of task. The number of trials per task can be reduced to six or four since the monkey is choosing the positive object from the second trial on.

If we ask just how, if at all, this "learning to learn" breaks out of the narrow bounds of continuity theory and the balance of reinforcements and nonreinforcements, we can answer that the exploratory, *trial-and-error* attack of an animal on a new problem is *reduced to a single trial*. Instead of gradually building up a balance of reinforcements in favor of one alternative object, the animal has learned to take the positive or negative outcome of his first choice as sufficient. He has learned to disregard the right-and-left location of the two objects and their relative attractiveness—in the early tasks of a series a monkey often shows a preference for one of the two objects—and to pin himself down to the outcome of his first choice.

It is not necessary to present both the positive and negative objects on the first trial of a new task (Harlow & Hicks, 1957). Place a raisin in one well and cover it with the positive object: on the second and later trials the monkey disregards the other object that is introduced and chooses the object shown to be positive on the first trial. Or, on the first trial cover an empty well with the negative object: on the second and later trials the monkey avoids this object and chooses the other object that is introduced. Progress is gradual in a long series of tasks. (The exploratory tendency may account for the different heights of the two curves in Figure 31; it is more natural to try out both objects than to adhere consistently to the object shown to be correct on the first trial.)

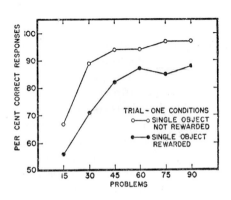

FIG. 31. (Harlow & Hicks, 1957.) Increased correctness of Trial 2 during a series of ninety discrimination tasks or problems. On Trial 1 of each task a single object was presented; displacement of this object revealed an empty food well and so was not rewarded; or, in other tasks, reward was found. A correct response on Trial 2 consisted in choice or avoidance of this object according as it had been rewarded or not on Trial 1.

In a series of learning tasks we, of course, look for evidences of *transfer,* and in the learning-set experiments there is an abundance of positive transfer effect. If we ask what "habits" can be carried over from one task to another, we must admit that the particular object choices are not carried over, since new objects are used in each successive task. Stimulus generalization would be as likely to cause interference as positive effect. What is transferred must be techniques such as disregard of locations and of object preferences, along with the helpful factors of close attention to the stimulus objects and prompt adoption of the positive and negative cues for a given task. Cue *reversal* after mastery of a task becomes increasingly successful as a series of tasks proceeds; like other examples of successful reversal it seems impossible to explain by the balance of reinforcements and nonreinforcements. One element of technique that develops in the course of a series of similar problems with changing materials is the *inhibition of transfer* by a *fresh start* at the beginning of each new task (Riopelle, 1953, 1955; Warren, 1954a).

That different discrimination habits involving the same first-order cues can be kept going independently, at least by chimpanzees, is shown by an experiment of Thompson (1953). The first-order cues were three easily distinguishable figures which we may call A, B, and C; and the three habits were A+ versus B−, B+ versus C−, and C+ versus A−. When these had all been mastered and relearned concurrently, any one of them could be thrown into action by presentation of the two relevant figures; thus, figures A and B presented together activated the set for choosing A, etc. Each pair of figures was a second-order cue for activating a different set.

The second-order cue may also be called a *set cue,* since it is the *cue that activates a set.* It can be a color signal, as in an experiment of Riopelle & Copelan (1954). The cue for the monkey to reverse cues was a change in background color. The two cue objects stood on a *green* tray, but when the monkey had learned to choose the positive object, finding reward in the well underneath, a *yellow* tray was substituted and the cue values were reversed. In a series of such problems with different pairs of cue objects, the five monkey subjects learned to reverse their choices instantly when the color changed. With further training they learned to accept *any change of tray color* as a signal for reversing choices.

"Oddity" is another second-order cue. Three or more objects stand in a row, all but one of them being duplicates and choice of the odd one being rewarded. The odd one stands in different parts of the row in the trials constituting a single task, location being irrelevant. In successive tasks different objects are presented, but there is always an odd one which is the positive cue. In a series of such tasks the monkey learns to look at once for the odd object and take that one for his positive cue.

These learning-set tests have been tried on species below and above the rhesus monkey in the animal scale:

  on the marmoset by Miles & Meyer (1956; see our Figure 32);
  on the house cat by Warren & Baron (1956a);
  on the rat by Koronakos & Arnold (1957);
  on the canary by Pastore (1954, 1955);
  on the chimpanzee by Hayes, Thompson & Hayes (1953)

on the young human child by Harlow (1949), by Hayes, Thompson & Hayes (1953), and by Shepard (1957).

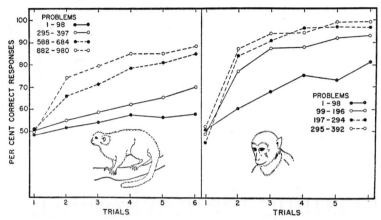

FIG. 32. (Miles & Meyer, 1956.) Progress of marmosets (left side) and of rhesus monkeys (right side) in the acquisition of learning sets. Average results from three marmosets and five rhesus. The first trial on each task (problem) is necessarily near the chance or 50-percent level. The rise from this level to the second trial becomes increasingly steep as the series of tasks progresses, and it is always much steeper for the rhesus than for the marmoset. "The dullest macacque (rhesus) was at all times better than the brightest marmoset." Yet the marmosets did learn very gradually to take the outcome of the first trial on each problem as the key to the whole problem. Each problem presented two novel objects to choose from, and the outcome of the first choice revealed the winner for the remaining trials of that problem.

In general, the ability to identify and utilize second-order cues is more or less proportional to the phylogenetic status of a species, though more work needs to be done on the psychologically-so-important rat, and more work needs to be done on young children in relation to their mental age. Hayes, Thompson & Hayes suggest that "man, chimpanzee, and rhesus monkey differ very little in their ability to acquire sets for object-discrimination learning . . . it seems fairly certain that all three groups will overlap." The children's spontaneous comments sometimes revealed their progress in learning the "rules of the game." Naming the objects was not a strong factor since they had no names for many of the objects. Some children, however, reported early in the series of tasks that the reward was always under the same object in the same task, and a few reported later on that they could pick the winner only after one blind guess.

CHAPTER 11

Learning the Environment

III: PLACES AND THINGS

If behavior consists in an active dealing with the environment, and if it depends very largely on learning, it must depend on what we can properly call "learning the environment." If we said, "learning *about* the environment," we should imply the sort of information that can be picked in conversation and reading. What we mean is a *direct acquaintance* with persons, places, and things—the kind of learning that occurs when we see a person, hear him talk, watch him act, and participate with him in social activity; and that occurs also when we feel of a rough or smooth surface, lift a light or heavy object, taste a sweet or sour apple, smell of a rose or a cheese. It is the learning that occurs in exploration and manipulation.

Some of this learning might be called purely *sensory* or a getting acquainted with the direct sensory effects of salient *stimuli* that impinge on the receptors, such as sweet and sour, warm and cold. However, most of it is better called *perceptual*, a getting acquainted with *objects* by means of the stimuli received from them. By sequence learning the color of an apple has become a cue of its taste so that an adult, utilizing his past experience and the present appearance of the apple, can warn a child that "It's still sour." He decodes the present stimuli, processes them, and comes up with a statement of certain characteristics of an object in the environment.

Many characteristics of an object, such as size, shape, weight, and object color or reflectance, are quite obviously perceptual because they are dependent on the decoding of a combination of stimuli. The size of the retinal image of an object must be combined with cues of its distance in order to reveal the size of the object itself (p. 201).

In getting acquainted with a new place, person, or thing, the stimuli that O works with are ordinarily not "raw" by any means (p. 140). They are decoded stimuli, cues of objects and objective facts. If O talked to himself while exploring a town, he would speak of streets, corners, up and down slopes, houses and stores. He is getting acquainted with objects in their spatial relations. He is learning the spatial framework of the town and the location of different objects in the framework. On reaching home he could perhaps draw a rough map of the town or at least *recall* some of the objects and spatial relations he has perceived. Even if his recall memory is rather sketchy, he would *recognize* many objects and places on going into town again. His recognition memory is almost certain to be better than his recall memory.

It would be very difficult, probably impossible, for a human adult or child to suppress his object-perceiving processes and take in only raw stimuli. In a drowsy or absent-minded state his perceptions could be vague and faulty, but in the state of alert responsiveness to the environment his learning is based on objective perception. That is the main point which we are trying to make.

Can we assume objective perception in animals?

We raise this question here because of the vast amount of work on learning that has used animal subjects, especially the rat, in the learning of spatial layouts such as simple and complicated mazes. This work has proved to have important bearings on the dynamics of learning. Does the rat find his way about by motor responses to raw stimuli, or are his motor responses governed by perceived objects in spatial relations? We need tests specifically directed to spatial perception in the rat, and fortunately such tests have recently been tried.

In a discrimination test (Greenhut, 1954) there were two white alleys extending forward from the choice point, each of them showing an upright black peg. The rat was rewarded for choosing the alley containing the peg which was nearer to the choice point, sometimes the right-hand alley and sometimes the left-hand one. When so much had been learned, the near peg was gradually moved farther away and the far peg brought nearer. The discrimination still held good. Then a regular psychophysical test was given, a middle distance of 10 inches being paired with other distances ranging from four to twenty-four inches, choice of the nearer being still rewarded. The regular psychophysical result was obtained: the smaller the difference in distance, the larger the percent of errors; and a difference threshold could be computed. The threshold was rather large, indicating rather coarse distance perception of distance for the white rat, but the regularity of the results showed that distance was certainly being perceived. The available cues of distance were the retinal size of the peg and its location on the floor of the alley (p. 170).

Another study is based on the fact that a rat will step down readily from a low platform to the floor, but not from a high platform. He evidently judges distance but possibly has learned the cues by much previous trial and error. A test was made on 90-day-old rats (fairly mature at that age), one group having been reared in the light, another group in the dark. The "floor" was objectively a transparent sheet of glass, only 3 inches below the narrow platform which extended across the middle of the floor. As far as visual cues were available, the floor on one side of the platform was only 3 inches down, but 53 inches down on the other side, these visual cues being provided by sheets of patterned wallpaper under the glass, facing upward at those two distances. The rats of both groups agreed in stepping down almost exclusively to the visually near surface and avoiding the visual "cliff." The authors comment, "These results suggest two conclusions. First, hooded rats, 90 days of age, do discriminate visual depth or distance. . . . Second, such discrimination seems to be independent of previous visual experience, since dark-reared adult animals behaved like their light-reared litter mates only 20 minutes after being exposed to the light" (Walk, Gibson & Tighe, 1957).

"Hooded rats," used in this last experiment, are known to be visually superior to the albinos. Greenhut found them so in her distance-discrimination test cited above. However, the difference is only one of degree so that we are justified in regarding space perception as a factor in the maze learning of the albino or "white rat," much used in maze experiments. We are also justified in crediting this animal with some ability to perceive the *size* of an object at different distances, though definite tests for "size constancy" (p. 208) have perhaps not been tried. Without this ability, an animal could scarcely approach an object as decisively as he does, for the object would be constantly changing in visual size. A door, seen from the jumping stand, is visually much too small to jump at with any chance of getting through. In general, the rat's behavior is such as we could expect from an animal able to perceive sizes and distances objectively, not at all what we could expect from an animal forced to make motor responses to raw stimuli.

Blind rats, like blind persons (p. 185), locate an obstacle by making noises, largely with their feet, and hearing these noises reflected back from the obstacle (Riley & Rosenzweig, 1957).

Evidence for perception in maze learning

By perception we mean the use of stimuli as cues of objects and their sizes, distances, and other objective properties. An animal that has the ability to perceive the distance of a seen object will certainly do so when he has good visual cues of distance. To judge from ourselves, a wide-awake animal could not help seeing objects in space. Sense perception is not a high-level intellectual process. It is very concrete and directly responsive to stimuli, though it does involve a decoding or processing of the stimuli. It is also very practical and necessary for the direction of even the simplest movements of approach. From such considerations we could reasonably infer object perception in animals that are actively dealing with the environment and that are known to have the ability of space perception. But we should like experimental evidence obtained in the study of animal maze learning, for example.

It will be worth while to re-examine from this point of view John B. Watson's pioneer attempt (1907) to identify the stimuli which enable a white rat to find his way through a maze—slowly and exploringly on the first trial, rapidly and unhesitatingly after learning a particular maze. Watson's behavioristic program, as he said a few years later (1914, p. 10), was to "take as its starting point, first, the observable fact that organisms, man and animal alike, do adjust themselves to their environment . . . secondly, certain stimuli lead the organisms to make the responses. In a system of psychology completely worked out, given the responses the stimuli can be predicted; given the stimuli the responses can be predicted." Watson did not insist that every response must be a *direct* consequence of its stimulus; he allowed for "implicit behavior," especially in the form of subvocal speech movements intervening between a stimulus and a thought-out response. But perception was not an admissible process; it was so badly contaminated with introspective attempts to describe and explain the conscious states involved. Therefore, nothing could be said of the rat's responding to *objects* and their distances and sizes; only the raw stimuli and the motor responses could be considered.

A normal rat traversing a maze receives a variety of stimuli: visual from the alley walls and floor and perhaps from outside the maze; auditory from the sound of his footsteps and from resonance of the blind alleys; olfactory from the floor boards; tactual from his feet on the floor and from his vibrissae touching the walls; and kinesthetic feedback from his own muscles and joints as he walks, runs, and turns. Perhaps some of these stimuli are superfluous. Watson found that blind rats learned the maze about as quickly as normals; consequently, he ruled out the visual stimuli. He found that anosmic rats learned about as well as normals; therefore, he ruled out the olfactory stimuli. He found that blocking the ears had little effect, and even that cutting off the vibrissae and anesthetizing the soles of the feet had little effect. He concluded that kinesthetic stimuli, which he could not very well eliminate, must be the essential ones and the only essential ones. He supported this conclusion by some transfer tests: after learning a maze in the light, rats could still run it correctly in the dark; or after learning it while in possession of their vibrissae, they could still run it correctly when deprived of them. What could they be carrying over from the normal to the deprived condition? Direct S—R connections from eye to legs or from vibrissae to legs could not be carried over to an eyeless or vibrissaless condition. Only the kinesthetic S—Rs were available for transfer from the normal to all of the deprived conditions. Watson concluded that maze learning by the rat consisted in the establishment of kinesthetic-motor connections.

This apparently cogent reasoning had to be rejected later when a variety of other experiments gave results adverse to the claims of kinesthesis. The leg and trunk kinesthetic pathways to the brain were severed in rats that had learned a maze, with the result that the rats moved awkwardly but still followed the correct path (Lashley & Ball, 1929). And rats deprived of sight, smell, and hearing—all three—were unable to master a maze or to make any appreciable progress in learning it (Honzik, 1936). Kinesthesis, though important in the smooth functioning of the motor system, was shown to be neither necessary nor sufficient for following the correct path in a complicated maze. What, then, could have been carried over in Watson's transfer tests, from the normal condition to the blind or deaf or anosmic condition? Grant the rat the ability to perceive objects in space; then he could learn the layout of the maze, the arrangement of correct and blind alleys, and the approximate location of the food box. Carrying over this acquaintance with the objective maze from the normal to a deprived condition, he could use such cues as were still available for finding his way through this familiar locale. See also Restle (1957).

Motor variation in maze running

Is it possible that running the correct path through a maze becomes so automatic as to require no cues at all? One may get that impression from watching a rat that is well-practiced in running a particular maze—he runs so rapidly, turns the corners so smoothly, and reaches the goal so surely. All he needs, one might think, is to be placed at the entrance, and his internal clockwork will carry him around to the goal without any cues on the way. But no! Careful observation shows that his movements vary from trial to trial, too much for a motor automatism. If something novel is placed somewhere along the correct path, he pauses to sniff at it. If the alley walls are removed, he cuts across the open space to the goal. Many experiments of this general sort have been tried, the most dramatic being the transfer test of Macfarlane (1930). He flooded a large maze with shallow water; when the rats had pretty well learned to wade through the correct path, he deepened the water so that they had to swim. They entered a few blind alleys after the shift but on the whole continued to follow the correct path in spite of the radical change in their motor behavior. What was carried over from wading to swimming could not have been a motor automatism; it must have been an acquaintance with the objective maze.

Swimming under water is quite a different performance, even for rats, from swimming on the surface. Mason & Stone (1953) forced rats to swim under water by placing a transparent ceiling a little below the surface. The rats first learned to do this on a straight course terminating in an exit ramp. Then a couple of blind alleys were introduced. The rats seemed rather panicky but they managed to learn the maze. In a transfer test the ceiling was absent, and the rats swam on the surface. They carried over much of what they had learned under water. This was proved by the fact that they made only half as many errors as a companion group that learned the surface maze from scratch.

PLACE LEARNING IN THE MAZE

Compared with a town, a farm, or an animal's home territory, the maze is certainly a very meager environment. All that is required of a maze learner is to proceed by the most direct route available from the entrance to the goal box, without straying into any of the blind alleys. A human being, and probably an animal, already well acquainted with an ordinary locale, can find his way easily *from any part of it to any other part*. If we were studying animal behavior in natural environments, the hypothesis of fixed motor habits would probably never suggest itself as an answer to the question, "What does an animal learn in exploring the environment?" Well-worn paths of approach to a water hole and the home burrow betray a certain amount of motor routine, but elsewhere the animal seems to "follow his nose" in any direction without getting lost. The maze has been used so much because it enables the experimenter to study the animal's learning process quantitatively, by timing each successive run from entrance to goal, by counting the blind alleys entered, and by counting the trials required to reach such a "criterion" as five or ten errorless runs in succession. So the effects of different cues, drives, and incentives can be measured. There is some danger, however, of the psychologist's losing sight of the elementary questions, "What does the rat learn in a maze?" and "How does he learn it?"

The hypothesis of place learning

"Since neither chain reflex nor motor pattern accounts for the rat's behavior in the maze, we ask once more what it is that the animal learns. The most obvious answer . . . is simply that the rat learns the place. By place we mean a concrete situation containing *objects in spatial relations*. . . . He observes the food-containing character of the food box, the dead-end character of a blind alley, the particular odor of a bit of floor—and the *location* of these parts in relation to each other" (Woodworth, 1938, p. 135). This formula needs some revision so far as concerns the definition of the place which the rat actually learns when he is intent on reaching the food box. He does not observe and learn the entire "concrete situation," but limits himself to such extramaze and intramaze cues as will guide him to the goal. Brown & Humphrey (1955, p. 405) say, "We cannot . . . agree with Woodworth in his definition of place-learning . . . a definite concrete situation is not required in spatial learning." They base this criticism on transfer tests. They set up duplicate mazes in two very different concrete situations, one being a square laboratory room well lighted through its windows, the other being a circular room or dome, uniform on all sides and rather dimly lighted from the ceiling. In each room the maze was placed in several positions but always so that the food box was in the center of the room. When a group of rats had mastered this task in one room, they were tested in the other room, and strong positive transfer effects were obtained. What the animals learned in one room and carried over to the other was the location of food in the center of the room or the habit of always going away from the wall of the room. "Inasmuch as the only common factor in the two environments was the relation of the choice-points to the walls, it would seem that what had appeared to be place-learning of a finite location in space was in reality a learning of the food position in relation to a nonspecific wall" (p. 406). Other rats learned to go *toward* a nonspecific wall for food and in other experiments to go toward a light, or away from a light into the darker part of a room. (To allow for transfer or generalization we might say: "The rat learns the place or some of its characteristics.")

Organismic versus environmental space. The organism has a right-left dimension, a front-back dimension, and (if a four-footed animal in the standing and walking position) a dorsal-ventral or back-belly dimension. The dorsal-ventral dimension (or the head-foot dimension in man) corresponds to the vertical dimension of the environment, but the right-left and front-back dimensions of the organism evidently do not correspond to any fixed directions of environmental space, since the organism may face north or south or in any environmental direction. The distinction is sometimes important in the study of maze learning because the question arises whether the animal is learning to step forward and turn right and left in a certain rhythm or learning to approach a certain object by following certain pathways for certain distances. Objects, pathways, and distances are environmental affairs and have no meaning in organismic space. In terms of stimulus, response, and reinforcement (without any learning of the spatial environment) we could say that what O learns is to execute that series of forward steps and right and left turns which secures food in the shortest time and with the least effort. In environmental terms we should say that he learns the location of the food and the most direct path to it. His visible behavior might be the same in either case; decision between the two possibilities could perhaps be reached by a detailed study of his behavior during learning or by some sort of transfer test.

Goal pointing

After a few trials in a particular maze, and long before it is fully mastered, the rat tends to steer in the general direction of the food box, as is shown by his entering blind alleys that start off in that

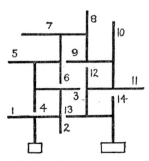

Fig. 33. (Tolman & Honzik, 1930.) Floor plan of a 14-unit T maze used in a study of goal pointing. It was a large maze, the blind alleys being mostly 15 inches long. The rectangular food box was located at the southeast corner of the maze, so that the five blinds that extended to the south or east were goal pointing. These five accounted for 63 percent of all the blind-alley entrances, the remaining nine blinds accounting for only 37 percent. The thirty-six rats in the group made a total of 2286 "errors," i.e., blind-alley entrances.

If O's choices were governed by organismic and not by environmental direction, his set would be to turn right rather than left at each choice point, since the goal is to the right of the entrance. The figure shows that a turn to the right would also be a turn toward the southeast at many choice points, the organismic and the environmental directions coinciding at these points. Where they do not coincide, at choice points 4, 9, 11, 12, and 13, the south or east blind alleys are entered much oftener than the right-turn blinds, as computed from Figure 6 (p. 250) in the original article.

direction much more than blinds which lead in the opposite direction. This result has been obtained by several authors, including Tolman & Honzik (1930). It may seem strange that Hull (1952, p. 290) took pains to check over these data and verify Tolman & Honzik—Hull was so strongly a motor theorist and so little inclined to admit a perceptual intervening variable. Hull, it appears, was not bent on denying cognitive and purposive factors as much as on showing that they could be conceived as direct S–R processes going on inside the organism. Here he speaks of "directional movements such as those of the eyes." This theory of space perception may or may not have permanent value. At any rate, it implies the functional reality of some learning of environmental space. (A "directional movement of the eyes" could refer to organismic directions such as right and left, but a continued deviation of the eyes to the right could not steer the animal through a complex maze toward the goal. Hull must have been assuming a tendency to turn the eyes, not right or left, but toward an object in the environment.)

Location learning versus motor learning

The location of food or water or any incentive in the environment is a matter of importance to an animal. When he goes to the right place, he obtains reward, and this reinforcement is a factor in his learning to go there. Another factor comprises the cues available for guiding him to the goal. Kinesthetic feedback from his own movements is always available, but the earlier studies with complex mazes showed that kinesthesis alone did not enable a rat to master the winding route to the food box. Some cues from outside the organism—visual, auditory, olfactory—were necessary for adjustment of the animal's movements to the environment. But if the maze were simplified to the limit, with a single choice point, as in the one-unit T maze, perhaps the animal could learn to make a left turn to food without regard to the environment, or at least without regard to the extramaze environment.

Instead of rotating the simple T maze, E may provide a cross maze or T maze with a demountable stem which can be attached to either side of the choice point. If for convenience we say that the top of the T extends east and west, the stem can be attached so that the rat enters from either the north or the south. To teach him a *location, E* puts the food always in the east end box so that the rat must turn right from the south entrance, but left from the north. To teach him the trick of always *turning left* at the choice point, *E* enters him at the north when the food is in the east end box, but from the south when it is in the west end box.

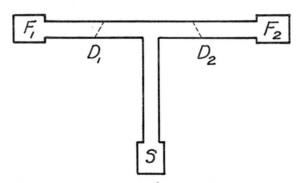

FIG. 34. A single-unit T maze. S is the starting box, F_1 and F_2 are the food boxes or end boxes, only one of which contains food on a given trial. The passages may be walled alleys, or they may be wooden strips 1 or 2 inches wide, 2 to 3 feet long, elevated perhaps 2 feet above the floor. The end boxes may be just alike, or they may differ in color, shape, flooring, or any respect that would make them easily distinguishable from the inside, though concealed from the choice point by doors or curtains, D_1 and D_2.

The cross maze was introduced by Tolman, Ritchie & Kalish (1946), who found location learning to be very easy for rats and left-turn learning much more difficult.

The cross-maze experiment was repeated on very young rats by Waddell, Gans, Kempner & Williams (1955). The rats were twenty-four days old when the learning began; their eyes had been open for about a week, during which they had been weaned and also tamed to overcome timidity in the maze. Again it was found that a location was much more easily learned than a fixed turning habit. Evidently no prolonged visual experience is necessary to enable the rat to utilize a view of the surroundings for identifying the regular location of food.

The visible extramaze environment in these experiments was nothing like the uniform expanse of cheesecloth mentioned above. Rather, it was an ordinary laboratory scene, with ceiling lights and various objects in different parts of the room, though without any definite landmark designed for the guidance of the location learners.

For so simple a piece of apparatus, the T maze or the cross maze has been adapted to a surprising variety of problems, many of

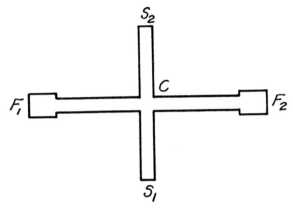

FIG. 35. Diagram of a cross maze, S_1 and S_2 being the possible starting points, F_1 and F_2 the possible food locations. Variations in size and construction as in the T maze in Figure 34. Often only one of the entrances is present at the same time. (C = choice point.)

them concerned with the question of location learning. We shall not review the older work again but shall confine our comments to some of the newer experiments.

In an experiment of Scharlock (1955) a cross maze was inclosed in a good-sized "muslin room," intended to make the extramaze environment uniform in all directions, except for a small electric bulb just beyond each of the end boxes. For one group only the east bulb was lighted and the food was always in the east box; these rats had a good cue of the location of food, and they learned to go to the east whether entering from the north or the south. A control group was treated in the same way, except that both bulbs, east and west, were always burning so that there were no visual cues distinguishing east and west, and there were no kinesthetic cues either, with entrance sometimes from the north and sometimes from the south. This control group did not learn to go consistently to the east; they made no progress in twenty-eight trials (four per day).

That the difference between a fully visible environment and a very restricted environment is important in location learning was demonstrated by Galanter & Shaw (1954). With a fully visible environment, it is easy to learn to go to the same location for food —much easier than to learn always to turn left for food—just as originally stated by Tolman and his coworkers. In both cases there is a conflict to be adjusted—the conflict between always going to the same location and always executing the same movement. There is no conflict when the animal starts always from the same entrance and finds food always in the same location—as when, for example, he starts always from the south entrance and finds food always in the east end box. This problem, in a fully visible environment, is mastered in two trials as compared with eight trials for place learning and forty for turn learning. Probably these findings would hold good also of human spatial learning, the visual cues of location being the most important, but the kinesthetic also making some contribution. Auditory cues can be important, too, as in the case of the blind (p. 186).

Locating two different incentives in the same maze

Can an animal learn the locations of a drinking place and of another eating place within the same environment, so that he goes regularly to one when thirsty and to the other when hungry? Common sense would have a ready answer, but the psychologist would prefer an experimental test. The question has to do partly with the drives and partly with learning. Do the hunger and thirst conditions produce internal stimuli that are different enough to elicit different behaviors? And can they lead to the learning of different goal locations? The way to answer the first question is to experiment on the second, as was done by Hull (1933) and independently by Leeper (1935), their methods being apparently much alike and yet different enough to produce a large difference in speed of learning. Leeper's maze was suitably designed for location learning; it was a simple T maze with food always in one end box and water always in the other. Hull's maze was so designed as to exclude location learning, for it had only one end box which contained water on the days when the rat was thirsty but food on the hungry days. The rat had to take one route to the goal box for water and another route to the same box for food. If he started on the hungry route while thirsty, or vice versa, he encountered a barrier near the goal box and had to retrace and take the other route to the same destination. Hull's rationale for such a setup (1933, p. 255) was "that the drive stimulus will be associated with . . . the successive movements involved in the running of a maze" —with the "movements involved" in securing the reward, not with the location of the reward.

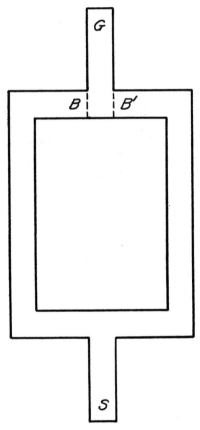

Fig. 36. (After Hull, 1933, p. 260.) Floor plan of alley maze offering two routes from S to G, one route to be taken whenever the rat was hungry, the other whenever thirsty. A barrier inserted at B or B′ prevented his reaching the goal by the wrong route. The alleys were 5 inches wide.

Hull's rats made very slow progress in learning to take one route while thirsty and the other while hungry, reaching the level of 70-percent correct choices in about 600 trials, the level of 80-percent correct choices in about 1000 trials, and not much further in 1200 trials. Leeper's rats reached the 70-percent level in about 25 trials, the 80-percent level in about 50 trials, and approximate perfection in 100 trials. Location learning was much easier than pure motor learning, just as in the simpler problem involving only a single drive and a single correct choice. Several later experimenters have obtained results similar to Leeper's (Kendler, 1946; Rethlingshafer, Eschenbach & Stone, 1951; Manning, 1956).

Hull's experiment was repeated by Seeman & Williams (1952) but with a modification intended to make the eating and drinking situations more distinct though identical in location. The maze was painted black inside, but water was served in a white goal box with a white approach alley (BB' to G in Figure 36), and food in the black goal box with black approach alley. So the goal anticipation on hunger and thirst days would be more distinct, and the secondary (preliminary) reinforcement also. Learning, therefore, should be facilitated, quite in line with Hull's system. The results justified this predictive reasoning, the 70-percent level being reached in about 200 trials, and the 80-percent level in about 250 trials—much more quickly than in Hull's original experiment but much more slowly than in Leeper's location-learning experiment. There was no disproof of "cognitive" learning, as the authors agree.

THE "HOW" OF PLACE LEARNING

We have been concerned with a "What" question and trying to show that the location of objects in environmental space is learned. It is the environment that is learned rather than a motor habit or than a chain of forward and backward movements and right and left turns in organismic space. Coming now to the question of *how* the spatial environment is learned—of how we learn a locality so as to find our way about in it—we may think at once of maps which can be studied in advance of any actual exploration. From a town map a visitor can learn much about the arrangement of streets and the location of important buildings before venturing out of his hotel room. He can do this if he knows how to use a map—how to decode the map symbols into distances and directions on the ground. A translation or decoding is necessary, as we mentioned in connection with aviation (p. 158). Often the organismic directions, right and left, are useful intermediaries between the map and the streets of the town, though there are no fixed right and left either on the map or in the town. The visitor, sitting in his hotel room and planning a route to follow in the town, can use his finger to trace the route and take note of corners where he must turn right or left. He can put the information so obtained into words: "On leaving the hotel I turn left, pass two streets and turn left on the third," and so on. Out in the town, however, he does well to take note of landmarks in environmental space; otherwise he may be unable to find his way back to his hotel. The organismic directions cease to play a major role when he has become acquainted with the actual surroundings.

More primitive methods of place learning have been of theoretical interest to psychologists—such methods as are available to a rat in a maze. This animal does a lot of free exploring in a strange maze and a lot of goal-directed exploring once he has found such an incentive as food somewhere in the maze. He learns where the food is located and after a number of trials runs unerringly from the entrance to the food box. The theoretical question of *how* he has learned opens up two main possibilities: learning by exploration and learning by reinforcement or reward. Learning by exploration would be a "cognitive" or perceptual process, a noticing of objects such as paths, corners, blind alleys, and the food box and remembering them well enough to recognize them later and use them in finding the way. The reinforcement theory can be conceived (though not necessarily) as noncognitive. The reinforcement learning process consists in a "stamping in" or strengthening of S–R units that are quickly followed by reward. The prompter the reinforcement, the greater the strengthening; thus the last part of the maze is likely to be learned first, and a blind alley is eliminated because it delays reinforcement. This theory is complicated—and improved—by the admission of secondary reinforcement (or preliminary reinforcement, p. 110): landmarks along the way to the goal acquire reinforcing properties of their own. (With this admission, reinforcement theory apparently ceases to be entirely noncognitive, for the landmarks are objects which are perceived, identified, located in the maze—in short, the landmarks are learned, as in the exploration theory. What spreads back from the goal box towards the entrance need not be primarily a strengthening of S—R connections. The goal box becomes a "good place," and the goodness spreads back to the approach landmarks. This we suggest in accordance with a theory which incorporates the positive claims of both theories, cognitive and reinforcement.

Place learning by exploration

As a test for cognitive learning, allow the animal a few minutes or hours for preliminary exploration of a complex maze that includes a number of paths, corners, and blind alleys, and a goal box which for the time being is empty. Then place food in the goal box, let him find and eat it, take him out and place him at the entrance. The question is whether he will now find his way to the food box in less time and fewer blind-alley entrances than a control animal that has not explored this particular maze. We shall not review again the many experiments of this general type from the work of Lashley (1918) and Blodgett (1929) down to recent years. The results have been positive though the interpretation has been subjected to much debate. The debate seems to have quieted down, leaving a general agreement that preliminary exploration of an empty maze does enable an animal to master the route to food quickly and with relatively little wandering.

Place learning by reinforcement

We must not infer from the results just cited that an animal's learning of an empty maze is learning without any reinforcement. If the animal were a pet dog, placed repeatedly at the entrance of a maze, and taken out by a friendly hand when he reached the goal box, petting for his success would be reinforcement enough to keep him performing and improving. Young white rats, too, take kindly to gentle handling and petting, and those accustomed to such treatment from E and receiving it as an extra reward, in addition to food, learn a maze much more quickly than those receiving only food as reinforcement (Bernstein, 1957). When, therefore, rats that have received advance taming and gentling from an experimenter (as is customary in maze experiments) are repeatedly placed at the entrance of an empty maze and taken out when they reach the goal box, they are receiving some reinforcement for avoiding the blind alleys and running to the goal box. No such distinctive reinforcement will be attached to the goal box if care is taken to lift the rats out of the maze sometimes at one place and sometimes at another, but even so preliminary exploration of the empty maze facilitates the later learning of the route to the food box (Buxton, 1940). However, the exploratory drive of the rat (which must certainly be admitted, p. 83) can function without extraneous rewards. Finding "what is there" is reinforcement enough to produce some learning, and a complex maze will include parts having some incentive value for a rat, such as straight paths to run in and blind alleys to serve as cubbyholes. Therefore, the fact that a rat learns by free exploration, "cognitively," is no proof that he learns without reinforcement.

Place learning by the question-and-answer process

A maze, or any place that is being explored, affords much opportunity for *sequence learning* (p. 223). We saw before that the mere temporal contiguity of two events, S_1 and S_2, was not enough to establish an association between the two. But if S_1 evokes the "investigatory reflex" or any kind of questioning response, R_1, and if S_2 gives an answer to the question, these conditions favor some degree of learning of the S_1S_2 sequence.

The difference between mere temporal contiguity and a question-and-answer process is illustrated by the experiences of the passenger and the driver during a motoring trip. The passenger takes the sequence of turns as they come, while the driver is on the watch for cues of where to turn. Consequently, the driver learns and remembers the route much better than the passenger.

Within a complex maze there are many short S_1S_2 sequences which the rat encounters during free exploration. He comes to a corner in the path, receiving certain stimuli, S_1, as he approaches. He turns the corner tentatively and receives stimuli, S_2, from a long straight stretch, his response, R_2, being to advance rapidly. Later in his continued explorations he approaches the same corner many times, and S_1 becomes a definite cue of a long runnable stretch around the corner. A preparatory response, R_1, takes shape; he starts running before he reaches the turning point and takes the corner with an outward swing (Figure 1, p. 45). The steps in this learning process are: first, incentive learning; second, cue learning; third, instrumental or preparatory-response learning. Other parts of the maze present different sequences and give rise to different bits of maze learning. Some parts may have positive incentive value, other parts being negative or neutral; and preparatory responses of approach, avoidance, and disregard are learned (p. 239). All these bits of learning are included in what we call "getting acquainted with a locality."

When the powerful incentive of food has been found in the goal box, integration of these bits of learning will develop, as far as they contribute to reaching the goal box quickly and easily. The incentive values of parts of the maze are likely to change; the long straight stretch acquires additional positive value and is run at top speed. A *blind alley* which has had some positive value as a resting place now acquires negative value as a place of frustration and delay. As soon as the dead end is perceived or as soon as a blind alley is recognized, the animal will turn around and try another alley. His penetration of the blind alley is likely to decrease from trial to trial, since he needs to go less far before getting adequate cues of its dead-end character.

Hull's original explanation (1932) of the elimination of a blind alley was based on his principle of *goal gradient,* or promptness of reinforcement. Of two alternative routes to a goal, the shorter brings quicker reinforcement and comes to be chosen more and more. A blind alley amounts to a detour and gives way gradually to the through route at any choice point. In his last book (1952, p. 298) he offers an explanation more in line with place learning, though he admits only S–R conditioning. The rat's U turn at the dead end becomes conditioned to the traces of stimuli, external and kinesthetic, received part way down the alley and is made earlier and earlier in repeated trials. In our terms, the U turn part way down the blind alley is a preparatory phase of the act of leaving that alley and going elsewhere; it is an R_1 evoked by mid-alley cues and preparatory to S_2R_2, the cues of the through route with the response of taking that route. The two hypothetical descriptions are alike in referring to concrete behavior as related to local characteristics, instead of merely to delay of reinforcement. Detailed study of the rat's behavior in blind alleys might show one description to be more tenable than the other; for example, hesitation after the U turn before starting outwards would be inconsistent with our description.

Incidental incentive learning

This heading can be used to identify a problem which has given rise to much debate and experimentation. If a hungry but not thirsty animal, while seeking the food in the goal box, comes across water in another part of the maze but does not drink, will there be any incidental learning of the location of water? For a behavioral test, put him in the maze on another day when he is thirsty and not hungry, and see whether he goes to the water location. This simple test gives negative results: a rat continues to go to the well-learned food box. We shall not review again the older studies that followed the discovery of this fact by Spence & Lippitt (1940) but will cite some recent work. First let us consider what our question-and-answer theory of sequence learning has to say on the problem. A hungry but not thirsty rat is seeking an answer to the question, "Where is the food?" When he finds the food, he has an answer, so that the conditions favor learning the sequence of stimuli and responses that has led to the food. But when he incidentally comes across water in the maze, it answers no present question and its location has little chance of being learned. Mere temporal contiguity is not a sufficient condition for the establishment of associations (p. 224). Some incidental curiosity might be aroused by the presence of a little pan in one part of the maze; the question, "What's that?" might be aroused and lead to momentary investigation, but the answer obtained would be to the effect that there was no food there, only unwanted water; no tendency to return to that part of the maze would be established; if anything, the tendency would be to avoid that spot as undesirable and wasteful of precious time, for the rat is putting on speed toward the food.

The experimenter may use "forced runs" in order to make sure that the nonthirsty rat has adequate opportunity to perceive the location of water; i.e., E locks the door to the food box of a T maze and so forces the rat to go across to the water box before being taken out. Presumably these forced runs increase the rat's resistance to the frustrating water box. Accordingly, the negative results of the reversed-drive experiment afford no evidence against the perceptual theory of location learning. A human subject, however hungry and however stuffed with water, could incidentally take note of a drinking place for future use; the rat apparently does not have so much forethought, but his choosing a place that has always been "good" in preference to one that has been "bad" is perfectly consistent with Tolman's perceptual theory of place learning and with our question-and-answer theory.

When a hungry rat is focusing his activity upon finding and eating food, this preoccupation with food would prevent his paying any attention to water and its location. It would be a strong inhibitory factor. A *double-satiation* experiment might give somewhat more positive results. Let the rat be satiated for both food and water, let one end box of a T maze contain food and the other water, and by forced runs make sure of ample opportunity to perceive both locations; then test him on one day when he is hungry but not thirsty and on another day when he is thirsty but not hungry, and see whether he shows any signs of knowing the two locations. During the training period this rat would be free from the inhibitory factor mentioned and be reduced practically to the state of "free exploration." Accordingly, we could expect some location learning, though perhaps not such. The double-satiation experiment, also originated by Spence & Lippitt in 1940, has been repeated many times with variations and has given moderately positive results: not 100-percent choice of the appropriate end boxes, but reliably above chance.

The role of reinforcement in perceptual learning

Sometimes the controversy between the cognitive and reinforcement theories of learning has led to the supposition that perceptual learning is entirely independent of rewards. Our question-and-answer theory would *not* lead to any such supposition. Let a hungry animal be exploring a maze. Even during "free" exploration, his hunger drive generates an underlying question as to whether there is any food present. When he perceives food in a certain spot, this perceived location is much more impressive than anything else in the maze. His activity is visibly raised to a higher level, his exploration becomes goal-directed, his question becomes a definite "Where?" and the answer he receives every time that he reaches the goal strengthens his mastery of the correct sequence of paths. Incidental perception of unwanted water will be much less impressive at the best.

However, "primary" reinforcement, in the sense of need reduction or the somewhat broader sense of consummatory activity such as eating, is not necessary for location learning. In an experiment of Schlosberg & Pratt (1956) rats learned to go to food which they could see and smell but not touch or eat because it was covered with a mesh screen. Both end boxes of the simple T maze contained screened-off cups, always baited in the left-hand box and empty in the right-hand one. The first question was whether hungry rats would show any preference for the food box; the result was that they learned in a few trials (one free trial per day) to choose the food box about 80 percent of the time. The next question was whether the same preference would be shown by food-satiated rats. The answer was "No"; they did not choose the food box more than half the time. After 12 days of this the drive conditions were interchanged: the previously hungry group was run while satiated and lost their preference for the food box in a couple of days; the previously satiated group was run while hungry and in a few days began to show a preference for the food box. The results obtained during hunger "can be described neatly in terms of secondary reinforcement. The smell of the food had long been associated with the ingestion of it . . . the secondary reward lost its motivating value when the relevant drive was removed . . . the secondary reinforcer did not produce learning in the absence of the relevant drive" (p. 151). The authors say further:

> But the fact that we can handle the present results in terms of secondary reinforcement doesn't lend any support to a strict S—R theory, especially one based on drive reduction. It is true that this type of theory is becoming increasingly dependent on the concept of secondary reinforcement, but it might be argued that this very dependence is a weakness. Indeed, the concept of secondary reinforcement seems more at home in an expectancy theory than in an S—R drive reduction theory. (P. 151.)
>
> But . . . we must explain the fact that the satiated rats aren't very effective at learning the location of food . . . some one functional system is dominant at a given time, and . . . determines what we do, what we see, and what we learn. So a satiated rat . . . will learn little, if anything, related to food *qua* food, i.e., something to eat. (P. 152.)

The important point in the present context is that an animal in search of food can learn its location without eating it, simply by seeing and smelling it in its environmental location, i.e., by a *perceptual* process activated by the hunger drive.

Another thing that a hungry animal can learn much better than a satiated animal can is the *absence* of food from a spot where food should be. An experiment of Levine (1953, Experiment II, Second Study), though designed for a somewhat different purpose, bears directly on this matter. In the first stage of the experiment the left-hand end box of a simple T maze contained water while the other box was empty; in the second stage, the left-hand box was empty while the other contained food. Rats that were thirsty in the first stage and hungry in the second stage easily learned to make the switch. But rats that were both thirsty *and hungry* in the first stage had a great deal of difficulty in making the switch because, no doubt, they had searched for food in the first stage and thoroughly learned the foodlessness of the right-hand box. What they had thus learned in the first stage interfered with what they had to learn in the second stage. Meanwhile the rats that were merely thirsty in the first stage, not searching for food, were not impressed with the foodlessness of the empty end box. Even a human being would be unlikely to notice the absence of eating places along a city block, unless he were hungry or unless he were planning for a future meal.

Another example of perceptual learning of an absence of food occurs in the experiments on "latent extinction" cited under the head of "rapid extinction," page 260ff. After rats have regularly found food in a characteristic goal box, some latent extinction is produced if they are merely *placed* several times in that same goal box, now empty—provided they are hungry during their stay in the empty goal box, but not if they are satiated during this stay (Moltz & Maddi, 1956). In our terms, the hungry rats perceived the absence of food more keenly than other rats could that were entirely indifferent to the presence or absence of food.

THING LEARNING, TOOL LEARNING

The "things" that human beings learn are likely to have the role of *tools*, i.e., to be used as means for accomplishing certain ends. Just as a path is a means of reaching a goal by locomotion, a hammer is a means of accomplishing a result by manipulation. A hammer is "explored" by handling it and noticing how it behaves and what you can do with it. The tridimensional movement of the hammer is more difficult for psychologists to observe than the route taken by an animal in a maze; for that reason, in part, we have less information to report on hammer learning than on maze learning. Machines, as distinguished from ordinary hand tools, can be made to furnish records of the accuracy and speed of the human manipulator with learning curves of his quantitative improvement. Good research use has thus been made of the typewriter and more recently of the pursuit or tracking apparatus (p. 147).

Let us first consider whether our "question-and-answer theory" of sequence learning can be applied in simple examples of thing learning. In the classical puzzle-box experiment of Thorndike (1898) a hungry cat was placed in a slatted cage with a bit of fish lying just outside. The cat tried to squeeze between two slats but found the space too narrow. He soon learned this narrowness and "no-goodness" as shown by his desisting from this line of attack. Clawing at one object after another, he finally came to the door button. It yielded to his touch and he persisted in clawing at it, showing that the motion made an impression on him. Our theory is that this sequence—seeing the button, clawing it, and getting the retroflex of button moving—yields a momentary acquaintance with that object, an acquaintance which can be strengthened by repetition. We have our familiar sequence, $S_1R_1S_2R_2$, with S_1 the visual stimuli from the button, R_1 the questioning response of clawing at it, S_2 the button's movement, and R_2 the persistent clawing. When he had turned the button far enough, the door opened and he went out and ate the fish. This longer sequence required several trials to master but could be learned by an extension of the same process. No additional dynamic factors need be assumed, except the drive toward the food activating the process as a whole. If the cat were incapable of perceiving and learning the narrow space between the slats and the motion of the door button, he could not learn the entire sequence or gain effective acquaintance with this bit of environment.

The theory provides for learning without any reward beyond acquaintance with the thing manipulated. You have no immediate use for your new hammer, but you would like to "get the feel of it" so as to be prepared to use it later. To take a still simpler case, you see a small object which "looks heavy"; when you lift it, however, so little force is required that you say, "How light it is!" and the next time you adjust your lift to the perceived weight of the object. This adjustment proves that you have learned something.

What have you learned from lifting the object? There are three theories:

1. *The motor theory* (or S–R theory with no intervening perceptual variable). You learn to respond to the sight of this object by lifting it with a small amount of force.
2. *The expectancy theory.* You learn to expect the object to come up easily if you lift it with a small amount of force.
3. *The object-learning theory.* You learn a property of the object, namely its lightness.

The three theories are not so much alike as they seem when expressed in common-sense language which speaks in objective terms—of seeing and lifting the same object, for example. The motor theory, in order to speak only of stimuli and motor responses, would have to cut out all reference to an object and say only that you learn to respond to a certain combination of stimuli by making certain muscular contractions. It would be difficult or impossible to conduct an experiment in these terms, for E could scarcely give O the necessary instructions without identifying the object and designating the act of lifting and the question to be answered (regarding "weight," which means the weight of an object). The motor theory, in spite of its apparent down-to-earth concreteness, is actually far removed from any operational test.

The expectancy theory also is forced to refer to the object: "If I lift *this object* again gently, I expect it will again come up easily." The *if-then* form of statement is suitable when you retest your first impression, but it does not fairly represent the impression itself, which was an impression of a light object ("reification," p. 242).

The object-learning theory seems to be left in possession of the field since it is tacitly assumed by the other two theories. Hull's attempt to explain expectancy and object learning in S–R terms (p. 44) can be hailed as an ingenious achievement at the speculative level, but it obviously admits the facts which it attempts to explain.

In getting acquainted with a pistol you would examine it visually and manually. If you had a blank cartridge, you would proceed to fire the pistol; to the intense auditory feedback your R_2 would be a characteristic pattern of muscular action. With repetition, as you became habituated to the noise, the startled movement would diminish (Landis & Hunt, 1939; Davis, 1956). You learn the pistol, or any tool which you use, as an object in relation to yourself in a man-tool combination. You operate with the tool on other objects so that learning a hammer includes learning nails and boards. In hammering you focus on the part of the environment where results are to be accomplished, i.e., on the nail and board more than on the movement of the hammer, and much more than on the triceps and other muscles that perform the physical work. It is the psychologist's job, rather than yours, to work out the patterns of muscle action which produce the environmental results (Guthrie, 1952; Davis, 1957).

Athletic and industrial skills

A coach may be able to utilize a knowledge of muscle patterns in helping the athlete. He is more likely to find some use for the industrial "motion study" which analyzes a complex operation into a series of steps or "therbligs" (p. 149). Such a step is described, not as a hand or body movement, but as a subgoal, a result to be reached on the way to the end-result of the operation. Under the guidance of a trainer even a beginner can do fairly well in working out the necessary steps and acquiring some elements of skill (p. 151). At an early stage of such analytical practice the performance will be jerky, each subgoal being checked off before the next step is taken; but with mastery of the steps, a remarkable process of synthesis begins. While executing the first step, the performer "looks ahead" and makes ready for the second step. So the pauses between steps are eliminated, and the whole performance becomes smooth and continuous.

The acquisition of skill in typewriting

The analytic-synthetic learning process just mentioned is well shown by the extensive experiment of Book (1908) which followed up the classical studies on telegraphy by Bryan & Harter (1897, 1899) and obtained comparable results. Book wired the machine to record the time of every response, the type itself furnishing a record of the typist's accuracy. The stages in learning to typewrite by the "touch method," with the keyboard concealed by a screen, were about as follows.

1. *O* either first memorized the keyboard or had a diagram of it

before him. Striking a letter was at first a complicated process. Looking at the material he was to copy, he picked out the first letter, located this letter on the diagram or from memory, then felt on the actual keyboard for the corresponding location, struck, and checked his correctness or error.

2. After a few hours of practice he could hit each letter by a single stroke; he had acquired dependable "letter habits" and could increase his speed.

3. Further practice changed the performance in unexpected ways. While striking one letter, O was able to make ready for the next one. He found himself anticipating the sequence of finger movements in any short familiar word or in a suffix such as -ing. The single movements could be trusted at this stage, but care was necessary to keep them in the right order; by degrees the order, too, became dependable. This was the stage of "word habits."

4. Similar habits developed for familiar phrases, and the whole performance became quite flexible, phrase habits, word habits, and even the separate letter habits being thrown into action according to the exigencies of the copy. The expert was able to keep his eyes on the copy a couple of words ahead of his fingers on the keys.

The gist of this study is conveyed by the terms, *higher units* and *overlap*. A "word habit" is a higher unit built up by synthesis of letter habits, and the synthesis depends on overlap, a preparation for the second step while executing the first, much as in oral reading (p. 146). While the fingers are typing one word, or while the speech apparatus is saying it, the eyes are taking in words ahead, "advance information" which reaches the motor organs only after the intervening processes of decoding and recoding have taken place in the brain (p. 17).

Acquisition of skill in the task of tracking a moving target

The requirement in this task is to keep your gun or aimer pointed directly at the target. To do so you must utilize "advance information," as we noted in the chapter on control of movement (p. 146ff). The simple pursuit rotor provides a target which moves in a horizontal circle at a uniform speed such as 54 or 60 rpm (revolutions per minute). You can see the circular disk in which the small metal target is imbedded, and you can see the circular movement of the target. Your aimer is a stylus with a hinge in it making it impossible to keep the point steady by pressure on the target. Your visual acquaintance with this apparatus is not

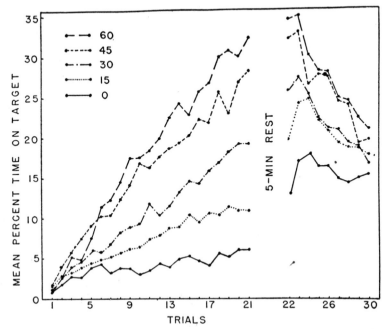

FIG. 37. (Bourne & Archer, 1956.) Practice curves in a simple pursuit task. The trials were 30 seconds long with intervening rests of 60, 45, 30, 15, and 0 seconds, the lowest curve showing the relatively slow improvement of subjects who were allowed no rests in the course of the first twenty-one trials. The rests gave more rapid improvement, and apparently a whole minute's rest after each half-minute of work was the most favorable. The work itself calls for unremitting attention. After the 5-minute rest all groups worked for nine more trials, which were "massed" trials, without any rest intervals. The performance improved immediately after the long rest and declined during the continuous work period. These results are very "reproducible"; see a similar study and curves by Ammons & Willig (1956).

For much longer curves obtained from practice in more difficult tracking tasks, see Archer, Kent & Mote (1956); also Battig, Nagel, Voss & Brogden (1957).

sufficient, as you discover as soon as you try to keep the stylus on the target. You can hit the target, but you cannot stay on it for as long as a second, if you are a beginner. The target gets away from you, and your pursuit around the circle is jerky and jagged. But you learn to get back more easily and to stay on longer at a time. You are less panicky when you lose the target, and you aim not merely to reach the momentary position of the target but rather to pick up its circular course so as to keep pace with it for some distance. You are learning how to utilize the advance information afforded by the predictable movement of the target.

Are you really learning the "thing," the environmental object, in these experiments and practical tasks, or are you learning your own capabilities and limitations? Best stated, perhaps, you are *learning the man-machine combination*. You learn what to expect from the machine in the way of stimuli and of feedback from your intervention. If the target oscillates about its main path, you learn that it is impossible to follow the oscillations but that you can do fairly well by following the average course (Briggs, Fitts & Bahrick, 1957). If your task is simply to turn a crank at a constant speed and if you are given visual feedback from a stationary target on a screen, with your aimer showing when you are turning too fast or too slowly, you learn that some oscillations in your speed are unavoidable but that you can maintain a good average by centering your oscillations close to the target (Lincoln, 1954, p. 200). If you have to follow a zigzag course without seeing ahead, you learn in a series of similar courses to utilize the "statistical properties" of these courses, such as the relative frequency of long and short movements and of "runs," and you learn also your own proneness to overshoot or to stop short of the mark (Poulton, 1957). If you have to make a long series of responses at irregular intervals, but are allowed some freedom, you learn to adjust the timing to greater uniformity and so to work more smoothly and achieve a higher score of hits (Conrad, 1956). These thumbnail sketches of some recent elaborate experiments may serve at least to show that tool learning is really man-tool learning. A hammer, as a young child would define it, is "Something to pound with." An older child would go further by describing some of the shape and material of a hammer, but he could not omit the function of hammering from his definition. He would not feel called upon to mention the biceps and triceps muscles, but a human hammerer would certainly be implied—even if the definition were made broad enough to include drop hammers and pile drivers—and even if these machines were controlled by automation. To return to the hand hammer, the point is that neither a description of the object apart from the human operator, nor a description of his movements apart from the object, could yield an adequate account of what is learned in this typical example of tool learning. We might go on to consider the learning of things that are not tools or manipulable in any strict sense but which do have useful properties for those people who deal with them, like the properties of the North Star for the navigator or those of the summer moon for the lover. Any sort of thing can be dealt with in some way, and the $S_1R_1S_2R_2$ sequence can be detected in the learning process.

Some further problems in learning

In concluding these chapters on learning the environment we shall briefly raise two questions on which there is little definite to say: (1) the question of pure motor learning and (2) the question of learning that cannot be reduced in any way to the formula of sequence learning.

Is there any pure motor learning, not geared in any way to objects in the environment? How about free setting-up exercises that make no use of dumbbells or any other tools? There is more "gearing" than appears on the surface, for a free arm movement is geared to the body posture, and the posture is geared to the floor. Every movement has to deal with gravity. As for an "object" to be dealt with, the trunk or a leg, an arm, or a finger can be treated as an object, as when you throw back your shoulders or cross your fingers.

Is there any nonsequential learning? This possibility is suggested by the facts of recognition. You recognize a human face as a simultaneous whole and apparently you learn a face as a whole and need not examine it part by part, sequentially, in order to recognize it later. If you were planning to reproduce its configuration by a drawing from memory, then you *would* examine it sequentially and attempt to tie the parts to each other and to the whole by a question-and-answer procedure. Such, anyway, is the procedure of a subject attempting to memorize a nonsense figure so as to reproduce it by a pencil drawing. Such detailed study may not be needed for later recognition of a characteristic figure or face or landscape—or color or tone or odor. The question is important because recognition is often easy when reproduction or recall is impossible. Recognition seems to be a fundamental form of memory. (Cf. Deutsch, 1955.)

Concept Learning and Problem Solving

A concept, as the term is used in psychology, does not refer to any particular sort of experience or behavior. It refers, typically, to a characteristic of the environment which can be learned by the individual. In the environment are found objects which can be classed together because they are alike in certain respects, while differing in these respects from other objects. An inquisitive child on first going to church notices people sitting, not on separate chairs, but in parallel rows on long benches with backs; and on asking for the name of these long seats, he is told to call them "pews" in church. He has then made the acquaintance of a certain class of objects, with the class name and a usable definition; therefore, he has added a new concept—new to him—to his already considerable stock of concepts.

Often a child or adult makes the acquaintance of a concept in the reverse order, first the class name and then its meaning. He wants to know the difference between a horse's trotting and galloping. There are two ways of trying to teach him the difference: by showing him horses in action and by describing the two modes of locomotion. The first way is the method of *denotation,* i.e., of pointing to instances of the concept; and the second is the method of *connotation,* i.e., of stating the characteristics of any object to which the concept properly applies. (In the terminology of logic, "extension" is equivalent to denotation, and "intention" to connotation.) Similarly, in testing a person for his mastery of a concept, you could ask him to point to instances of it (and not to any objects that do not belong), or you could ask for a definition. You might find his performance satisfactory in denotation, but vague and incomplete in connotation.

For the psychologist, then, a concept is an objective fact (or system of facts) for the individual to discover, learn, and use. It is analogous in these respects to the through route in a maze. Just as we insisted that maze learning was an example of getting acquainted with the environment rather than the establishment of a pattern of bodily movements, so we argue now that there is something in the environment to be learned. Is it absurd to speak of a concept as present in the environment? It may not be any more absurd than it is to speak of the through route to the food box as being present in the maze before the rat has learned it. If a route is defined as something traversed, it cannot be present in the maze until the rat has found and traversed it. It is not present in a lonely maze; it is present only in the rat-maze combination. The experimenter puts a rat in the maze and watches to see whether the through route will develop. Although it is possible to speak in this sophisticated manner, the fact remains that E incorporated a through route in the maze—a "potential" through route, if you like, which the rat actualizes. One may speak of concepts as being potentially present in the environment, ready to be actualized by an exploring organism. To be thoroughly consistent, then, one should say that potential food is placed on the dining table, ready to be actualized when the family arrives. If concepts seem farther removed from the concrete environment than food or paths, it is not because they are any less environmental, but because more exploring and learning are necessary to find them and make them ready for behavioral use.

Is it worth our while to raise the question whether *mathematical concepts* are present in the environment, waiting to be found by patient exploration? Roughly circular shapes can be found or constructed, but if the concept of circle were based upon these instances, it would have to state that all the radii must be *approximately* equal. The jump from *approximately* to *exactly* does take the mathematician out of the actual environment, but the concept of a perfect circle is so useful both in pure geometry and in the applications of geometry to engineering that it furnishes a tool for dealing with the environment. The same can be said of other mathematical concepts, many of which go back to the operations of counting and measuring. Like other tools they are based upon invention as well as discovery. It is a matter of discovery, for example, that strawberries vary in size; consequently no particular exact size can be included in the concept of strawberry. Another similar observation is that watermelons vary in size; consequently, no precise size can be included in the concept of watermelon. Yet it would be absurd to compare the two fruits without any reference to their different sizes. Faced with this problem, the mathematicians came up with the concepts of Average, Standard Deviation, Normal Distribution, etc., which are obviously inventions, tools devised for the accurate handling of concrete environmental data.

Concepts and their names

Since the most tangible fact about a concept, aside from the concrete instances denoted by it, is its *name,* philosophers who insist on tangibility, like the medieval nominalists or the modern behaviorists, have said that a concept *is* its name, and nothing more except for the instances. Well, a name must be the name *of* something; a combination of letters is not a name unless it designates a person or object. The object designated may be an action ("galloping") or a condition ("fever") or a quality ("sweetness"); but, however abstract the meaning, a word must have *some* meaning in order to be a name. What concerns us here is the "common noun," the name of a class of objects. What does it mean? It denotes any object belonging to a certain class. But if we question the justification for applying the same name to all these objects, the answer is that they all have the distinguishing characteristics of the class. The concept, then, is the *meaning* of the name, its connotation as well as its denotation. The connotation is the meaning, practically, for it would be impossible to list (denote) all the individual dogs in the world, though it is possible to state the characteristics an animal must possess in order to be properly called a dog.

Memory of concepts

We have been describing a concept as an environmental fact or system of facts—as a stimulus, we might say. If we ask for the response to such a stimulus, we see at once that it cannot be purely perceptual in most cases because the "stimulus" is not all present at the same time. We might help a young child to acquire the "cat" concept quickly if a whole assortment of cats were present at once; or to acquire the concept of the "cat family" if he were taken to the zoo and enabled to inspect various branches of the family in quick succession. Even so, short-time memory would be needed as he passed from cage to cage, and he would retain the concept and remember it later. If the nominalists were right, all he could retain would be the name so that if asked, "What is a cat?" he could only answer, "A cat is a cat is a cat is a cat."

More acceptable was the memory-image theory, according to which the child would retain traces of the sensory impressions received in the zoo so that later he could call up visual images of the animals—also, perhaps, auditory, olfactory, and tactual images, though the visual kind would be the most comprehensive. An objection to this theory was that the visual image, like a picture, would reproduce a momentary impression received from a single specimen, whereas the image of a concept should represent all the specimens, including what was common to all of them and nothing more. Introspective reports of such "generic images" would be hard to obtain, even from adults. Specific images, reproducing momentary impressions, are often reported, as well as numerous vague and scrappy images. Objective facts, including general characteristics, are often reported without any mention of images.

A recent theory of concept memory is based on Hull's "fractional anticipatory goal response" (our pp. 44, 113). As developed by Osgood (1952, pp. 203-204), it is stated as follows:

> Stimulus-objects elicit a complex pattern of reactions from the organism. . . . Stimuli other than the stimulus-object, but previously associated with it, . . . tend to elicit some reduced portion of the total behavior elicited by the stimulus-object. . . . Words represent things because they produce some replica of the actual behavior toward these things, as a mediation process.

For example, a child is warned not to touch a spider because spiders are dangerous. He shrinks in fear, and the associated name, "spider," will later arouse some vestige of the fear response. This "fractional" fear will stimulate in him further responses such as, perhaps, his warning other children against spiders.

In the further development of this study of *meaning* (Osgood & Suci, 1955) by the methods of factor analysis, it was possible to work out a "semantic space" of several dimensions, only three of which had much importance; these were the evaluative dimension (good versus bad), the potency dimension (strong versus weak), and the activity dimension (active versus passive). These are all in the general field of human values and quasi-emotional reactions, the system being designed to measure this sort of meanings, rather than the objective, matter-of-fact meanings characteristic of a great many concepts. We cannot suppose, for example, that the child's concept of spiders is limited to the shrinking response, and that he sees no difference between spiders and snakes since both elicit this same response.

What we would say, in accordance with what we have said before, is that in exploring and manipulating the environment the individual perceives and remembers objects and their characteristics, including characteristics that are common to a class of objects. Some objects are good or bad, helpful or harmful when he is aiming at a goal, but many other objects are interesting when he is in a playful or observant mood. He notices with interest the different gaits of a horse—walking, trotting, cantering, galloping—especially if his attention is called to them, though of course he could give only a vague description of the differences. One fact we should insist on strongly is that he learns, not merely S–R, but S–R–Rx. He learns the result of his act, the feedback, as well as the motor act itself. He learns not simply to bite an apple but also the resulting taste.

Neither the sensory "image" nor the motor "replica" tells the true story of a remembered concept. We must reiterate our insistence on the central decoding and encoding function (Chapter 1, p. 16; Chapter 6, p. 142ff; Chapter 7, p. 164ff; and Chapter 8, p. 220). Visual stimuli are decoded into the size and distance of an object in the environment, and your intention to approach and grasp that object is encoded into the appropriate muscular movements. Later you remember, not the stimuli and muscular movements, but the objective facts, actions, and results. Let us take one more example: you are asked how a golf ball compares with a ping-pong ball, and you answer from memory that they are both white and very bouncy, but the golf ball somewhat larger and much heavier. The two concepts, as you remember them, consist of objective characteristics.

Concept learning, a form of sequence learning

Is not concept learning a form of conditioning—or conditioning a form of concept learning? In spite of the apparent contrast in intellectual level, a sharp line between them would be very difficult to draw, either in respect to the environmental facts or in respect to the learning process. Pavlov's dog was presented with a series of "positive instances," each instance consisting of a signal followed by food. The dog's first response to the signal was a behavioral question, the "investigatory reflex." As the series of positive instances continued, the signal came to elicit the preparatory response of approach to the food and anticipatory salivation. The dog acquired an adjustment to a class of uniform environmental events. We symbolized such an event by the stimulus sequence $S_1 S_2$; or, since S_2 elicited the reflex eating response R_2, we can include this "unconditioned response" in the event, representing each positive instance by the sequence $S_1 S_2 R_2$. The conditioned response, R_1, we regarded as evidence that the dog learned the regular environmental sequence.

Perhaps we should not accept simple conditioning as an example of concept learning, since the dog has not yet learned to deal with "negative instances." When Pavlov went on to his experiments on differentiation, by substituting a different tone or a different beat of the metronome for the previous CS (i.e., S_1), the dog's first response to the new signal was again the "investigatory reflex" (our p. 276). This new signal was never followed by food, though the original signal continued to be reinforced, and the dog learned to respond differently to the positive and the negative instances (p. 234). He learned to distinguish two classes of events, one signal followed by food and another signal not followed by food. Can we deny, then, that conditioning is a case of concept learning?

In Chapter 9 we tried to show that "sequence learning" could account, not only for conditioning, but also for a good share, at least, of the process of getting acquainted with persons, objects and their characteristics, and the environment in general. You see a person, watch to see what he does, and so learn something about him and his characteristics. You are forming a concept, or "conception," of that person. A mere sequence of stimuli is not likely to be learned, but if S_1 arouses a question or expectant attitude and if S_2 gives a significant answer to the question, that sequence has a good chance of being learned. This question-and-answer theory is the best we have to offer toward an explanation of concept learning. The "question" will differ according to the circumstances. You may see two objects that look somewhat alike and yet rather different, and you wonder if they behave or function alike. Different objects are called by the same class name, and you ask what they have in common. You are given a collection of objects and told to divide them into classes, and you ask yourself on what basis they can be classified.

EXPERIMENTS ON CONCEPT LEARNING

In spite of the interesting variety of tests and experiments concerned with the learning of concepts, as shown in the comprehensive review by Vinacke (1951), the subject's task is usually one of only three kinds: defining, sorting, or naming. Several objects are placed before O and he is asked what they have in common. They are alike in color while differing in size and shape, or alike in shape while differing in size and color, or alike in material (wood, for example, or metal) while differing in many other respects. *Informal definitions* are accepted so long as they reveal an ability to discern the characteristic common to the otherwise diverse members of a class. This procedure as well as the sorting task goes back at least to Weigl (1927).

A *sorting* test can use the same equipment; a mixed collection of objects is placed before O and he is asked to divide the collection, "putting together those that seem to belong together." If some of them "belong together" on the dining table, at the wash basin, or in some other concrete situation, the task is easy for normal nine-year-olds and for adult feeble-minded or schizophrenic persons of the same mental age as the children. But the children, if prodded a little, can do two things which seem to be almost or quite beyond the intellectual abilities of the abnormal groups mentioned: (1) the children can disregard concrete situations and classify by *abstract* characteristics such as size or material; and (2) they can *shift* from one basis of classification to another (Bolles, 1937). They can shift, we surmise, from one *question* to another.

Baggaly (1955), using a difficult sorting task in connection with tests for Thurstone's cognitive factors, reached the conclusion that "The critical process in concept formation seems to be concentration on one aspect of the complex stimulus situation at a time."

Other experiments using some form of sorting task will be cited later.

In a *concept-naming* task *O* must learn to call every positive instance of the same concept by the same name, i.e., to call all the members of the same class by the same class name which may be a nonsense syllable or a single letter. This method goes back most definitely to the experiments of Hull (1920). Extensive use has been made of it by Heidbreder (1946-1949) and by Reed (1946, 1950). Heidbreder's instructions to her student subjects will give an idea of the task (1946, p. 181):

> This is an experiment in memorizing. You will be shown a number of drawings, for each of which you are to learn a name. The names are nonsense syllables—Rult, Brox, or something of the sort. As each drawing appears in the opening of the screen . . . the experimenter will pronounce its name. . . . The different drawings will be shown successively, and the whole series of drawings will be shown repeatedly until you can go through the entire series . . . naming each drawing correctly. Say the name of the drawing as soon as it appears or as soon as you can. If you give it the wrong name, or do not name it at all, the experimenter will prompt you. Anticipate the experimenter whenever you can.

Of the nine drawings in this first series, three represented familiar things (a tree, a building, a human face), three were nonsense shapes, and three embodied a number, 3, 5, or 6. Each drawing was an instance of a different concept. Nothing was said about concepts, however, but as soon as *O* had learned the names of these nine drawings, he was told that a second series of drawings would be shown, and that, "in order to make the learning easier, the same nonsense syllables would be used," and that he should continue to anticipate *E* whenever he could. The second series consisted of new instances of the same nine concepts (new faces, new trees, etc.); and, when this second series was mastered, a third presented still other instances of the same nine concepts; and so on for sixteen series. After a sufficient number of instances had been seen and correctly named, O could name a new instance at first sight, without any help from E. When he could do so consistently with each new instance, he had "attained" that concept. Thing concepts were attained the most quickly, number concepts the most slowly, by Heidbreder's subjects, who were inclined from the start to find things even in the nonsense drawings and in those embodying numbers (Heidbreder 1947, *J Ps* 24, pp. 99, 112). This tendency to find things and classes of things indicates, according to Heidbreder, that concept-forming is an outgrowth of the perception of things which has the function of guiding behavior in a world of things. The thing-form-number order of dominance in concept formation has been a matter of some controversy (Wenzel & Flurry, 1948; Grant, 1951; Dattman & Israel, 1951; Heidbreder, 1952; Baum, 1954; Heidbreder, 1955; Wohlwill, 1957).

The experiments of Reed (1946, 1950) were like those of Heidbreder in being based on a familiar form of memory experiment but differed entirely in the material used. His instances were groups of four familiar words with a nonsense syllable added as the name of the group; for example:

club	picnic	reaches	beet . . . . . . .Bep	(spoken by *E*)
answer	highest	airplane	red . . . . .Dax	
brook	leave	claim	precious . . . .Vor	
anywhere	green	aloud	apple . . . . . .Dax	
potato	careful	pasture	raised . . . . . .Bep	
lover	borrow	flower	point . . . . . .Vor	
berry	nickel	tomato	calm . . . . . . .Bep	
believe	cigar	owe	love . . . . .Vor	
board	beast	blue	butter . . . . .Dax	

There were six of these syllable names, each recurring with different words. Some Os were instructed as follows:

> This is an experiment in learning concepts. A concept, you know, is a word, or idea that stands for any one of a group of things. . . . I am going to show you a number of cards, one at a time. Each of these cards will be named by a nonsense syllable . . . and each nonsense syllable is a concept. Look carefully at all the words on the cards and try to learn . . . the name of each card and what it stands for.

These Os were thus given a set for finding something common to all the word-groups having the same name. To other Os nothing was said about concepts, the task being described as simply one in memory:

> I am going to show you a number of cards, one at a time. Each of these will be named by a nonsense syllable . . . Look carefully at the cards and try to learn . . . the name of each card.

The whole series of forty-two cards was repeated until *O* was able to anticipate *E* in saying the name of each card. Those *Os* who were set for finding concepts learned the names much more quickly than those approaching the task as a mere memory test. The memorizers were apt to associate the nonsense syllable with the first word in the group, disregarding the other three words; whereas the conceptualizers tried to find a significant word in each group. The difficulty of the task led any subject to try out hypotheses of various kinds, but the successful hypotheses were more quickly found by those subjects who were on the watch for some *meaningful* distinction.

Criticism and improvement of the name-learning task

In concept-learning experiments such as we have been considering, the arbitrary names are needed as a check on the attainment of the named concepts. If *O* uses a name consistently and can state its meaning, he has attained the concept. But the arbitrary names themselves have to be learned "by rote," i.e., by the same process as in ordinary memory experiments, a process possibly quite different from concept formation. So the work that *O* does on the name-learning task is partly rote learning, as was brought out forcibly by Richardson & Bergum (1954, Exp. II). Their material consisted of figures drawn on cards, differing in three respects or "dimensions": shape (circle, triangle, square); size (large, medium, small); and shade (white, gray, black). Shape and size combined gave nine two-dimensional concepts. The third dimension, shade, was irrelevant, no distinction being made between large circles that were white, gray, and black; they could all be classified as large circles and called by the same arbitrary name, the letter K. However, if the arbitrary letters were not introduced until *O* had learned to identify the nine concepts by everyday names such as "large circle," "small triangle," and "medium-sized square," only one sixth of the total time was required for this genuine concept learning, the remaining five sixths being consumed in associating the concepts with the arbitrary names. A task that calls mostly for rote learning is obviously unsuitable for the study of concept learning and its possible differences from rote learning. "Further experimentation must be done with a task in which rote learning has been either eliminated or demonstrated to be of minor importance."

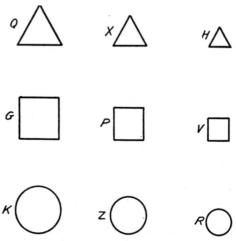

FIG. 38. Two-dimensional concepts, as used by Richardson & Bergum, 1954. Besides the relevant shape and size "dimensions," there was an irrelevant dimension of shade. Each of these nine figures appeared sometimes in white (outline only), sometimes in solid black or gray. These cards could be used in a sorting task with instructions to sort into nine piles (classes). Here each class was assigned a letter as its name, and the names had to be learned.

To minimize the amount of rote learning required by a concept-learning task, Underwood & Richardson (1956a) prepared a list of 213 familiar concrete nouns meeting these specifications: (1) many *O*s (college students) give the same verbal response to a given stimulus word when asked to indicate a sense impression received from the object mentioned, such as small, brown, heavy, noisy, odorous; (2) the same descriptive response is given to a sufficient number of the nouns to provide a basis for classification. So, if a stimulus list includes the words:

balloon   button   dome   doughnut   knob   spool

E can be sure of getting the response, "round," to some of these stimuli from many of his *O*s. And if *E* says "Right" when this response is made to any one of these particular stimuli, but "Wrong" when any other response is made to it, little rote learning will be necessary.

Every one of the 213 listed nouns elicited more than a single descriptive adjective from the original group of students. The response to "Pony," for example, was "small" from 48 percent of them, "brown" from 14 percent, "hairy" from 12 percent, the rest scattering. The higher this group frequency of a response, the more quickly it was adopted as the "Right" response in a concept-learning experiment. Another way of facilitating the formation of certain concepts was to inform O in advance what the desired concepts were, leaving to him only the decision as to which objects should go in each class. In this experiment twenty-four stimulus nouns were shown, one at a time, four of them for each of the six concepts—round, small, white, smelly, soft, and big (Underwood & Richardson, 1956b).

Concept learning in these experiments with one word as the stimulus and another word as the required response is much like a familiar type of paired-associates learning which is usually regarded as rote learning. It is like paired-associates learning also in not being slowed up by massing of the successive trials (Underwood, 1957). If "reactive inhibition" (our p. 263) were operative in this concept learning, massed trials should be especially harmful because of the frequent repetition of the same response.

The role of names in concept learning

A sorting task does not require any learning of different names for the different classes, but there is nothing to prevent the individual subject from adopting some everyday name for each class. If he is given a pack of cards with circles on some of them and squares on the rest and asked to sort them into two piles, he may very likely say to himself, "One pile for circles and one for squares." If some of both shapes are red and the rest blue, he can sort also on a color basis, probably using the color names. Being then asked to sort the same cards into *four* piles, he may name the piles: "red squares," "blue squares, "red circles," and "blue circles." The question is whether such spontaneous naming is any real help in the sorting.

Verbal sorting, as we may call it, facilitates subsequent manipulative sorting of the same materials. There were sixteen wooden blocks, each of which was either black or white and also round (cylindrical) or square, these two "dimensions" however being irrelevant. The two relevant dimensions of the same blocks were short versus tall and small versus large horizontally. In the verbal-sorting stage of the experiment, O learned through E's prompting to call each block "tall-large," "tall-small," "short-large," or "short-small," disregarding the irrelevant dimensions. In the following manipulative sorting, these four labels were no longer used (by E), but four sample blocks, one from each of the four classes, were placed on the table and O was told to place each of the remaining twelve blocks so as to match one of the samples. Matching according to the four two-dimensional categories was the usual result with the Os who had had the verbal sorting, whereas other Os matched by single dimensions, shape, color, height, and size. These results, predictable from another standpoint just as well, were by these authors predicted from the Hullian theory of internal response-produced cues: blocks which O learned to call by the same name would have their objective similarity enhanced, while blocks called by different names would have their objective differences enhanced (Fenn & Goss, 1957; see also Goss, 1955). We discussed a similar problem in cue learning on pages 269-270.

Another attempt to extend Hull's S—R theory from conditioning and rote learning into the field of concept learning and reasoning is currently being made by Kendler and his associates (Kendler & Vineberg, 1954; Kendler & D'Amato, 1955; Karaşik & Kendler, 1957). Without attempting to summarize the complex experimental evidence offered, we shall quote some of the theoretical statements from the first paper mentioned (pp. 255, 257):

> The associations underlying the process of concept formation in a card-sorting test are not between the cards and the sorting response but rather between the cards and some verbal response to them which, in turn, serves as a cue for the sorting response. . . . Our emphasis has been on response-produced cues which serve to mediate formation of the appropriate card-sorting responses. Such an analysis points to what we believe are basic mechanisms as well as to the integration of thinking behavior and simple associative learning, rather than to the creation of a hiatus between the two, as is customary by advocating a "perception-of-relationship" orientation.

Our own view on this matter is that the primary process consists in finding similarities and differences in the environment. The names, to be of any use, must fit these environmental facts; otherwise they would be wild and misleading. If O is given names for certain classes and reinforced when he uses the names correctly, he is stimulated to search for the objective facts corresponding to the different names and so may be aided in forming his concepts (Robinson, 1955). As to the "hiatus" between simple associative learning and the perception of relationships, we would point out that even in the "rote learning" of word lists or of paired associates, the learner finds whatever relationships, even fanciful ones, the material offers, and so helps himself in his difficult memorizing task (brief summary in Woodworth & Schlosberg, 1954, pp. 707-708).

The role of negative instances

A child in his third year, actively engaged in picking up new words, will learn all the common color names but will use them at first indiscriminately, answering "pink" or "brown" or "white" or "blue," apparently at random when shown an object and asked for its color. By gradual improvement during a period of several months he will come to use the names precisely. If you wished to teach the child the meaning of "red," would you use positive instances exclusively, showing him a red dress, a red hat, a red book, a red apple? Or would you introduce negative instances, a blue dress and a green apple, showing disapproval when he called them red? This particular experiment has perhaps never been tried, but negative instances have been tried out on adult subjects.

Smoke (1932, 1933) presented several positive instances of a class, asking his subjects to find the common characteristics so as to define the class and select additional specimens of the same class. A "dax," for example, was a circle with one dot inside and one dot outside, differing from specimen to specimen in size and color of the circle and exact location of the dots. In one form of the experiment, negative instances were introduced—figures marked with a minus sign to indicate that they did not conform to the definition. When the specimens were shown one at a time (1932), many Os found the negative instances useless and distracting. When the specimens of a class—all positive or some positive and some negative —were shown simultaneously (1933) most Os thought the negative instances helpful in preventing "snap judgments," i.e., in negating premature conclusions. However, there was no statistically significant difference between the two conditions (with and without negative instances) in the time required to reach a correct concept. "Thus, although negative instances may not make for rapidity in learning they tend to make for accuracy, especially in the case of difficult concepts."

Cahill (1957) finds that without some negative instances a concept is likely to be given excessive breadth—excessive denotation, that is to say, with deficient connotation—as we might expect from the principle of stimulus generalization (our p. 234).

Hovland (1952), approaching the problem of positive and negative instances from the standpoint of *information theory,* shows that two problems are really involved: (1) how much information is made available to O by a positive or a negative instance; and (2) how successful O is in utilizing the available information. When, as in many sorting or naming experiments, the instances are blocks or figures differing in several dimensions, the first problem is simplified if each dimension occurs in only two values such as circle versus square, black versus white, large versus small. O's problem is simplified if he is told in advance that the concept to be learned is two-dimensional, his task being to discover which two dimensions are revelant, and which value of each relevant dimension is positive. Let the eight figures in the pack be as follows:

Small black circle
Small black square
Small white circle
Small white square
Large black circle
Large black square
Large white circle
Large white square

And let E decide that *black circle* shall be the concept, size being irrelevant. E has two positive instances at his disposal, small black circle and large black circle. If he shows these two, informing O that both are positive, he has made all the necessary information available. There are six negative instances, but Hovland shows that only five of them need be shown (as negatives) to afford all the information required. Two negatives along with one positive will be sufficient. In other problems ten negative instances may be required to present the same information as two positives; and special problems can be arranged such that the same amount of information is presented in an equal number of positives or of negatives.

Even though five negatives embody the same information as two positives, it does not follow that the human organism can utilize the information equally well. In fact, college students succeed much better with the positive instances. This is not wholly because of the difficulty of remembering the larger number of negative instances, for the same difference, though less in degree, appears when all the required positive or negative instances are shown simultaneously. Exactly why the positive instances are easier to utilize is not perfectly clear. The authors suggest that the positive information is more directly and completely perceptible, and that the negative instances "lack an organized, unitary quality." The data, however, disprove the common assumpton that negative instances have no value, for some of the subjects attained the concept solely from negative instances (Hovland & Weiss, 1953).

Information theory, along with pretesting of the materials to be used, enables E to quantify the complexity of the task which O has to perform in attaining a concept. Without such quantification, some concepts are found empirically to be more difficult than others, but no exact relation of concept attainment to task complexity can be found. This approach has been used by one group of investigators in a study of irrelevant dimensions (Archer, Bourne & Brown, 1955; Brown & Archer 1956; Bourne, 1957). With two dimensions relevant and two values of each dimension, O's task was to sort the cards into four piles (such as black square, white square, black circle, white circle); but he had to disregard one, two, three, four, or five irrelevant dimensions (size, for example). The more irrelevant dimensions O had to disregard, the longer it took him to master the task. Rests between trials had no significant effect on O's success, as we saw once before on page 341.

The guessing game, "Twenty Questions," has considerable similarity to a concept-learning task. Each question asked, since it must be answered either "Yes" or "No," represents a two-valued "dimension" of the "universe" of possible objects. From the standpoint of information theory, a restricted universe can be prepared by E, consisting of sixteen objects differing in four independent dimensions, so that four questions can obtain all the information necessary for identification of the object—provided O makes full use of all the information. But even keen young adults, college students, do not ordinarily utilize much over 80 percent of the obtained information (Bendig, 1953, 1957).

The role of hypotheses in concept formation

The task being to discover characteristics common to the positive instances and absent from the negative instances, we can suppose O to proceed in either of two ways, or in some combination of the two. One procedure is analogous to composite photography, and the other consists in the testing of hypotheses.

In taking a *composite photograph* of ten persons, you expose the plate one tenth of the normal time for each person, taking care to get the same view of each face. The composite shows a face with the common characteristics brought out and the individual variations mostly lost. By analogy we can imagine an observer viewing one specimen after another of a class of objects and so obtaining a generalized memory image (p. 333). Without assuming a clear visual memory image, we can at least suppose that the observer would be impressed by the common characteristics of the class.

The *hypothesis-testing* procedure comes under the head of question-and-answer learning. Something common to two or three instances is found, and this "hunch" is tried out on other instances. If it holds good, it is adopted, but if it is ruled out even by a single positive instance, it should logically be rejected at once. Hypothesis testing has been prominent in all the experiments on concept formation, but there is often a lack of strict logic, a hypothesis being kept alive even after it has been ruled out. It is kept as a "working rule" which like other rules may have exceptions but which enables O to guess right in many instances (Simmel & Counts, 1957).

How hypotheses originate in the individual learner is a difficult question to approach experimentally. What Heidbreder (1924) first noticed and called *spectator behavior* was a kind of "composite photography." Having tried out all the hypotheses that occurred to him, O sat back and simply watched the specimens, hoping that a new hypothesis would emerge, as it sometimes did. In other experiments this attentive waiting has been reported at the beginning of the series of specimens, O not being in a hurry to try out a hunch till he had seen several specimens. He may wish to analyze the problem and notice the possibilities before allowing himself any hunches.

PROBLEM SOLVING

No sharp distinction can be made between the two parts of the present chapter, since concepts, as presented in the ordinary environment, or as embodied in the stimuli of an experiment, are certainly problems. The older studies of problem solution are very instructive, but we shall not review them again in this book. Rather we shall ask what there is new that increases our knowledge of this psychological field, which has always been regarded as difficult. The recent trend is toward the use of problems that are objectively simple, though they may offer difficulties to the individual. The relevant information given him may be simple but obscured by irrelevant information, "irrelevant dimensions," which he has to disregard (Hunter, 1957).

Irrelevant information

One problem is as simple as this (Adams, 1954): You have four keys in a row, numbered from 1 to 4, and are shown a pair of very different figures, say a circle and a triangle, one beside the other or else one above the other. You are told simply to press one key and find out whether you are "Right" or "Wrong," and so on for the four possible arrangements, each shown twice. Then two new figures are substituted with no further instructions. You have two positive rules to discover: (1) for a horizontal arrangement of any two given figures, use keys 1 and 2; for a vertical arrangement, keys 3 and 4; (2) one figure of any pair shown for eight trials is the important figure; if it is at the left, press key 1; if at the right, key 2; if on top, key 3; if below, key 4; disregard the other figure. If you go by these two rules you can discover the important figure in each new pair from the outcome of your first trial with the pair: if the pair is first shown horizontally, make a tentative choice of the left-hand figure as the important one; if you have guessed right, the important figure is the one you have chosen, but otherwise the other figure is the one to go by as long as the same two figures are shown. The students made slow work of this problem, though the group gained steadily during the series of twenty-four pairs of stimulus figures. They had too much irrelevance to disregard, with all the useless variety of figures. Another group of students—and here is the real point of the experiment—did not get this variety of figures but were kept on the circle and triangle throughout the training series. Their progress was much more rapid; they mastered the hidden rules of the game almost perfectly. So much we might expect, but the more significant finding was that they transferred this mastery, once gained, to new figures and did so more successfully than the group trained on various figures. It was an advantage to have the essential problem as clean as possible and free from distracting details, at least during the early stage of training. In this early stage, it should be noted, the training did not degenerate into routine drill, since O had always to make a guess and discover whether it was right. The Adams study was intended as a contribution to teaching methods.

Hypothesis testing versus "spectator behavior"

In an experiment of Goodnow & Pettigrew (1956) O's problem was to beat the system of a gambling machine; at least that is what he hoped to do, though he was told only to insert a chip and press either the left-hand or the right-hand key, one only of which would pay off on every trial so that O could always see whether he had won or lost. The machine was controlled by E behind the scenes. For one group of students, the most instructive for our purpose, the machine started by paying off always on the left, in a series LLLLLL . . . continued until O responded accordingly. Then without interruption it swung into a 50:50 series (though with some rather long RRRR and LLLL runs). Finally it shifted to a regular alternation, RLRLRL . . . which continued until O picked it up. The question was whether O's adjustment to the original LLLL . . . series would be any help in mastering the final RLRL . . . series; and the answer was that this group mastered the final series much more promptly than a control group which did not experience this initial series but started with 50:50. The LLLL . . . series led O to adopt a regular procedure of "Win-stay; lose-shift," a procedure which was not destroyed by the 50:50 series with its fairly long runs, but persisted into the final RLRL . . . series. But how could it help in this radically different series? Any regular procedure, so it seems, enables O to watch the course of events more objectively than he can while busily trying out one hypothesis after another. For example, the perfectly regular procedure of making the same choice every time would allow the stimulus alternation to stand out clearly. "This is Heidbreder's . . . spectator behavior in its most beneficial guise. . . . The slow learners . . . are the most active and participant. They form hypotheses rapidly, usually prematurely, and they test one hypothesis after another. They . . . see only the relevance of a result to the hypothesis being tested at that time" (p. 388). For much further study of the "strategies" suitable for this type of problem, see Bruner, Goodnow & Austin (1956).

Trouble shooting

A problem often encountered by the numerous class of repair and maintenance men, especially in modern electronic equipment such as radio and radar, is that of finding the cause of a breakdown. The steps in this process as mapped out by Siegel & Jensen (1955) are as follows: (1) from a survey of the situation, formulate reasonable hypotheses: (2) apply appropriate checks of these hypotheses; (3) by synthesis of the information so gained, reach a definite diagnosis of the needed replacement; and (4) make the indicated replacement (with final check). The first step calls for more than hit-or-miss hypothesizing; it calls for analysis of the situation in order not to overlook a likely hypothesis.

When many candidates for maintenance jobs are being tested and trained, as in the military services, an important question is how to instill this analytic approach to a problem. A lecture on good methods of problem solution seems to do little good unless given with actual practice. One experimenter intervened during O's work on a problem with "Socratic" questions such as, "I want you to ask yourself, 'What are the elements of my problem? What are the only ways in which a mistake [breakdown] could occur?'" If O named some of the possible sources of trouble, he was encouraged to search for more. This teaching method was much more effective than a separate lecture given in advance (Marks, 1951).

If you can half-split or dichotomize the possible sources of trouble along two dimensions and check off half of each dimension by a single test, the two tests combined will reduce the possibilities to one quarter. If someone in a guessing game is "thinking of a person," you can dichotomize repeatedly by asking whether living or dead, whether male or female, whether child or adult, and so on. As a *plan of search,* "half-split" should logically be very effective, given sufficient background knowledge of the field of operations. It is not a plan that would readily suggest itself to most people; some initiation would be necessary. When the plan was explained to a group of college students and illustrated by practice on simple problems, it still was not successfully applied to more complex trouble-shooting problems. Greater success was obtained by a more drastic initiation, with the practice closely supervised by *E* who required *O* to submit his plan of search and did not allow him to proceed until he submitted a half-split plan based on logical inference from the *symptoms* of trouble to the possible *sources* of the trouble. The advantage of this supervised practice was mostly that *O* was stimulated to start operations by inferring the possible trouble sources from the given symptoms. Some of the students, more than others, were strong in this "deductive ability" (Goldbeck, Bernstein, Hillix & Marx, 1957).

Given several possible trouble spots to be checked, their relative *probability* is an important matter for consideration. The most probable spot deserves priority, unless the *amount of work* involved (time, cost) also demands consideration. (Compare the balancing of incentive value and probability, 249.) If the most likely trouble spot happens to be the hardest to investigate, and the least likely the easiest, economy in the long run may perhaps be served by a practice of always making the easiest check first and proceeding toward the most difficult. To be sure on this matter, management would have to do some statistical balancing of work against probability. The operator himself, in solving a series of similar problems, would doubtless strike some sort of balance. According to the results of Detambel & Stolurow (1957), college students in a relatively simple trouble-shooting task tend to give too much weight to the probability factor and too little to the work or time factor. No knowledge of electronics was required in the task. The three possible trouble spots were circular holes in a table top with lids held on by screws at the edge, 7 screws for one lid, 4 for another, and only 1 for the third. To check on one of these spots, *O* had to remove its screws by finger motion and look inside to see whether it was marked "OK" or not. In each problem two spots were "OK," and the other one required a simple repair job. The location of the trouble differed from trial to trial, being under the 7-screw lid one half of the time, under the 4-screw lid one third of the time, and under the 1-screw lid one sixth of the time. The work and probability factors to be balanced against each other were:

work, 7 screws; probability, .500
"   4   "   "   .333
"   1   "   "   .167

The amounts of work required were visible to O; the probabilities or relative frequencies made themselves known, roughly at least, in the course of a long series of trials. The instructions were to "notice two things, the amount of work you must do in order to check each section and the number of times the trouble occurs in each section . . . We want you to complete this work with the least possible time and effort."

With these probabilities and work amounts, arithmetic shows that the greatest long-run economy—the fewest screws removed—would be achieved by always starting with the 1-screw lid and proceeding as far as necessary toward the more probable lids. Only one of the twelve students in the group adopted this rule; the general preference veered toward beginning with the most probable alternative. All but one of these students did more work than necessary, some of them 10 to 15 percent more than necessary. Had the work been more strenuous, preference would probably have gravitated toward the optimum rule.

Prospective research on problem solving

There are two lines of research which might be suggested by the formulas, S–O–R and R = f(S, A). The first formula suggests a tracing of the *process* that goes on in O from the presentation of the problem to the overt verbal or other solution. When the process takes considerable time, O is often able to report a succession of stages in his thinking. He saw a promising lead and followed it to a dead end before shifting to another possibility. At a more microscopic level, O's report may not be worth much, but the solution or verbal response that he gives may betray the first stage in the process. Such conditions as distraction, drowsiness, anoxia, or the influence of certain drugs, give rise to "looseness of association; . . . inability to follow a single train of thought . . . predominance of vivid imagery in thinking"—phenomena which are somewhat anal-

ogus to the first stages in the perception of an object shown only
for a small fraction of a second. This "microgenetic approach to
perception and thought" is regarded as promising by Flavell &
Draguns (1957), who give an extensive review of the literature. They
also call attention to "a rather striking similarity between micro-
genetically immature cognition" in normals "and schizophrenic
cognition." This sort of process study may therefore prove of value
in the understanding of schizophrenia and also of aphasia.

The other formula, $R = f(S, A)$, suggests *parametric* studies.
Some variable under E's control is the parameter in an experiment;
it is given different values and the resulting difference in O's performance is noted. So the dependence of R on this experimental
variable is found. For example, O's performance deteriorates with
increasing amounts of irrelevant information in the problem—an S-
variable since it is included in the problem presented. As an example of an A-variable, we can take any experiment in which O is
given different kinds or amounts of preliminary training, and the
effect on performance noted. Such studies may have a very practical bearing on the work of persons engaged in "trouble shooting"
or other problems. From the theoretical point of view the parametric studies may appear less incisive than the process studies; and
yet the question whether concept learning and problem solving
are covered by the same theory as "rote learning" comes down to
the question whether the same parametric laws hold good of all
these processes (Underwood, 1952).

Scrutinizing the relatively recent experimental literature on problem solution, with a view to further research, Ray (1955) was able
to list as many as twenty-nine problems that met some requirements, especially the requirement that O's *process* of solution
should be visible in his ways of dealing with the materials provided. Ray's conclusion, however, is in favor of the other type of
study (p. 148): "What this field needs are dimensionable independent variables, prediction of their effects on dimensionable dependent variables, and tasks especially designed to measure these effects."

Binary-choice tasks such as are used in the study of probability
learning (p. 250ff) are regarded as well suited for the study of
insightful thinking (Galanter & Gerstenhaber, 1956). When O
matches his choices to the input frequencies of the two alternatives,
he does not show insight into the operation of the gambling machine (or other environment) that he is dealing with, since his

behavior can be brought under theories of rote learning. But he shows insight if he shifts to consistent choice of the more probable alternative, as he may be induced to do by an increase of the reward. So E is provided with a quantifiable experimental variable and a corresponding measure of O's behavior.

Insight and invention

The question-and-answer procedure for getting acquainted with the environment ought to come into play in the higher intellectual processes as well as in simple learning. Sequence learning, as we conceived it, is an insightful process of a rudimentary sort at least. It may not be a seeing below the surface of things or a perception of true cause and effect. The question aroused by a stimulus may be simply, "What next?" If another striking stimulus follows, and if this sequence occurs regularly, the question is answered and the question-and-answer combination can be called insightful, provided we do not demand that insight must penetrate below the actual sequence of events. More penetrating insight depends on the asking of more penetrating questions. If the penetrating question is "Why?"—"What is the cause of an observed regular sequence of events?"—some plan of search, some "search model" (Johnson, 1955) must be invented. Some experiment must be devised, some way of simplifying the conditions, some instrument for better observation. Being provided with a microscope, you can ask questions about the movement of blood through the capillaries and obtain insight of a more penetrating sort than you get with the unaided eye.

A search model or plan of investigation takes many forms according to the object that is being sought. In the ball-in-field problem used in intelligence tests a boy is supposed to have lost his ball in a circular field. Hit-or-miss hypotheses—"Is it here?" "Is it there?" —are contrasted with planned exploration by a spiral or gridiron coverage of the field. Another problem would call for arithmetical analysis, or for the use of a yardstick, rather than for uncontrolled guessing. In general, a search model limits and organizes the exploratory, question-and-answer activity.

A search model has to be *invented;* it is not found existing in the environment. The same is true of a tool used as a means of changing the environment. How can we bring invention into our scheme of things? We can trace it back to the manipulatory drive

(p. 88) and especially to the *playful* manipulation which is so striking a characteristic of human beings from early childhood up, and also of the subhuman primates. Purposive invention is, of course, directed toward some goal. "Necessity is the mother of invention"—true enough, but the other parent is playful manipulation. Köhler's famous chimpanzee, Sultan, was faced with the problem of pulling in a banana lying on the floor outside his cage, beyond the reach of either of the two bamboo sticks in the cage. After many futile efforts he gave up and devoted himself to playful manipulation of the sticks. In the course of this play he got the sticks end to end and inserted the smaller into the hollow end of the larger. He jumped up and used his jointed stick to pull in the banana (Köhler, 1917). A human inventor must have a definite goal, but if he is too rigidly set on the goal, his invention is likely to lack originality. He does better if allowed some freedom to experiment with the possibilities. A musical composer likes to improvise idly on the piano, without any intention of remembering the little themes that turn up one after another; but if one of them seems suited for a song or for a part in some proposed composition, his playfulness gives way to serious invention. After working it out he may reject it, for *critical judgment* is one important requirement for a creative thinker in any line (Johnson, 1955; Patrick, 1955).

Index of Authors

INDEX OF AUTHORS

A

Adams, J. A. 1954. Multiple versus single problem training in human problem solving. *J exp Ps* 48, 15-18. [347]

Adelman, H. M. *See* Maatsch, J. L. 1954.

Aiken, E. G. 1957. The effort variable in the acquisition, extinction, and spontaneous recovery of an instrumental response. *J exp Ps* 53, 47-51. [262]

Allport, F. H. 1955. *Theories of perception and the concept of structure.* N. Y., Wiley. [162]

Allport, G. W. 1937. *Personality: a psychological interpretation.* N. Y., Holt. [112]

——. 1946. Effect: a secondary principle of learning. *Ps Rev* 53, 335-347. [249]

Alschuler, Rose H., Hattwick, La Berta W. 1947. *Painting and personality: a study of young children.* 2 vols. Chicago, Univ. Chicago Press. [97]

Ammons, R. B., Willig, L. 1956. Acquisition of motor skill: IV. Effects of repeated periods of massed practice. *J exp Ps* 51, 118-126. [327]

Amsel, A. 1950. The effect upon level of consummatory response of the addition of anxiety to a motivational complex. *J exp Ps* 40, 709-715. [68]

——, Maltzman, I. 1950. The effect upon generalized drive strength of emotionality as inferred from the level of consummatory response. *J exp Ps* 40, 563-569. [68]

Anastasi, A., Foley, J. P. 1949. *Differential psychology.* N. Y., Macmillan. [135]

Anderson, J. E. 1939. The development of social behavior. *Amer J sociol* 44, 839-857. [98]

Antonitis, J. J., Kish, G. B. 1955. Re actions of C57 black male mice to active and inactive social stimuli. *J genet Ps* 86, 115-130. [130]

——. *See also* Schoenfeld, W. N. 1950; Kish, G. B. 1956.

Applezweig, M. H. 1951. Response potential as a function of effort. *J comp physiol Ps* 44, 225-235. [261]

Archer, E. J., Bourne, L. E., Brown, F. G. 1955. Concept identification as a function of irrelevant information and instructions. *J exp Ps* 49, 153-164. [345]

——, Kent, G. W., Mote, F. A. 1956. Effect of long-term practice and time-on-target information feedback on a complex tracking task. *J exp Ps* 51, 103-112. [327]

Arnold, W. J. *See* Koronakos, C. 1957.

Asch, S. E. 1952. *Social psychology.* N. Y., Prentice-Hall. [112]

Atkinson, J. W. 1954. Explorations using imaginative thought to assess the strength of human motives. Jones, M. R., Ed. *Nebraska symposium on motivation 1954.* Lincoln, Univ. Nebraska Press. 56-112. [94]

——, Heyns, R. W., Veroff, J. 1954. The effect of experimental arousal of the affiliation motive on thematic apperception. *J abn soc Ps* 49, 405-410. [96]

——. *See also* McClelland, D. C. 1949, 1953.

Attneave, F. 1954. Some informational aspects of visual perception. *Ps Rev* 61, 183-193. [197]

——. 1955. Symmetry, information, and memory for patterns. *Amer J Ps* 68, 209-222. [197]

Austin, G. A. 1953. Tolman's interpre·

tation of vicarious trial and error. *Ps Rev* 60, 117-122. [271]

——. *See also* Bruner, J. S. 1956.

B

Babb, H. 1956. Proportional reinforcement of irrelevant stimuli and transfer value. *J comp physiol Ps* 49, 586-589. [288, 289]

Baer, M. *See* Buss, A. H. 1955.

Baggaly, A. R. 1955. Concept formation and its relation to cognitive variables. *J genl Ps* 52, 297-306. [337]

Bahrick, H. P. *See* Briggs, G. E. 1957.

Baldwin, R. D. 1954. Discrimination learning as a function of stimulus predifferentiation and mediated association training. *Dissertation Abstr* 14, 718-719. [269]

Ball, J. *See* Lashley, K. S. 1929.

Banks, H. P. *See* Perkins, M. J. 1954.

Barnes, R. M. 1949. *Motion and time study.* 3d ed. N. Y., Wiley. [149]

——, Mundel, M. E. 1939. A study of simultaneous symmetrical hand motions. *Univ Iowa Stud Engin Bull* 17. [150]

Baron, A. *See* Warren, J. M. 1956a, b.

Bartlett, F. C. 1932. *Remembering, a study in experimental and social psychology.* Cambridge, Eng., Cambridge Univ. Press. [196]

Bartley, S. H. 1958. *Principles of perception.* N. Y., Harper. [162]

Battig, W. F. 1956. Transfer from verbal pretraining to motor performance as a function of motor task complexity. *J exp Ps* 51, 371-378. [269]

——, Nagel, E. H., Voss, J. F., Brogden, W. J. 1957. Transfer and retention of bidimensional compensatory tracking after extended practice. *Amer J Ps* 70, 75-80. [327]

Baum, Marian H. 1954. Simple concept learning as a function of intralist generalization. *J exp Ps* 47, 89-94. [338]

Beach, F. A. 1948. *Hormones and behavior.* N. Y., Hoeber. [63]

——, Holz-Tucker, A. Marie. 1949. Effects of different concentrations of androgen upon sexual behavior in castrated white rats. *J comp physiol Ps* 42, 433-453. [63]

Beck, J., Gibson, J. J. 1955. The relation of apparent shape to apparent slant in the perception of objects. *J exp Ps* 50, 125-133. [217]

Beecroft, R. S. *See* Restle, F. 1955.

Bendig, A. W. 1953. Twenty questions: An information analysis. *J exp Ps* 46, 345-348. [346]

——. 1957. Practice effects in "twenty questions." *J genl Ps* 56, 261-268. [346]

Bergman, R. *See* Gibson, Eleanor J. 1954, 1955.

Bergum, B. O. *See* Richardson, J. 1954.

Berlyne, D. E. 1950. Novelty and curiosity as determinants of exploratory behavior. *Brit J Ps* 41, 68-80. [84]

——. 1954a. A theory of human curiosity. *Brit J Ps* 45, 180-191. [79]

——. 1954b. An experimental study of human curiosity. *Brit J Ps* 45, 256-265. [79]

——. 1955. The arousal and satiation of perceptual curiosity in the rat. *J comp physiol Ps* 48, 238-246. [83]

Bernstein, B. B. *See* Goldbeck, R. A. 1957.

Bernstein, L. 1957. The effects of variations in handling upon learning and retention. *J comp physiol Ps* 50, 162-167. [316]

Bersh, P. J. *See* Schoenfeld, W. N. 1950.

Biber, Barbara, Murphy, Lois B., Woodcock, Louise P., Black, Irma S. 1942. *Child life in school: A study of a seven-year-old group.* N. Y., Dutton. [98]

Bindra, D. *See* Falk, J. L. 1954; Sampson, H. 1954.

Birmingham, H. P. *See* Chernikoff, R. 1955.

Bitterman, M. E., Holtzman, W. H. 1952. Conditioning and extinction of the galvanic skin response as a function of anxiety. *J abn soc Ps* 47, 615-623. [74]

——, Wodinsky, J. 1953. Simultaneous and successive discrimination. *Ps Rev* 60, 371-376. [280]

——. *See also* Elam, C. B. 1954; Gottheil, E. 1951.

Black, Irma S. *See* Biber, Barbara. 1942.

Blodgett, H. C. 1929. The effect of the introduction of reward upon the maze performance of rats. *U Calif Publ Ps* 4, 113-134. [316]

Bolles, M. M. 1937. The basis of pertinence: a study of the test performance of aments, dements, and normal children of the same mental age. *Arch Ps, N. Y.* No. 212. [337]

Book, W. F. 1908. *The psychology of skill with special reference to its acquisition in typewriting.* Missoula, Univ. Montana. [325]

Boren, J. J., Sidman, M. 1957. A discrimination based upon repeated conditioning and extinction of avoidance behavior. *J comp physiol Ps* 50, 18-22. [263]

——. *See also* Sidman, M. 1955.

Boring, E. G. 1942. *Sensation and perception in the history of experimental psychology.* N. Y., Appleton-Century. [167]

——. *See also* Holway, A. H. 1941.

Boring, F. H. 1955. An experimental test of the continuity theory of discrimination learning using confounded "easy" and "hard" cues. *Dissertation Abstr* 15, 461. [288]

Bouman, H. D. *See* Stetson, R. H. 1935.

Bourne, L. E. 1957. Effects of delay of information feedback and task complexity on the identification of concepts. *J exp Ps* 54, 201-207. [345]

——, Archer, E. J. 1956. Time continuously on target as a function of distribution of practice. *J exp Ps* 51, 25-33. [327]

——. *See also* Archer, E. J. 1955.

Bowles, J. W., Jr. 1956. Electromyographic factors in aircraft control: A muscular action potential study of "conflict." *School of Aviation Medicine, USAF, Rep.* No. 55-125. [227]

Brady, J. V. *See* Sidman, M. 1955.

Brandauer, C. M. 1953. A confirmation of Webb's data concerning the action of irrelevant drives. *J exp Ps* 45, 150-152. [67]

Briggs, G. E., Fitts, P. M., Bahrick, H. P. 1957. Learning and performance

in a complex tracking task as a function of visual noise. *J exp Ps* 53, 379-387. [328]

Brogden, W. J. *See* Battig, W. F. 1957.

Brown, F. G., Archer, E. J. 1956. Concept identification as a function of task complexity and distribution of practice. *J exp Ps* 52, 316-321. [345]

——. *See also* Archer, E. J. 1955.

Brown, J. S. 1948. Gradients of approach and avoidance responses and their relation to level of motivation. *J comp physiol Ps* 41, 450-465. [89, 90]

——. 1953. Problems presented by the concept of acquired drives. *Current theory and research in motivation.* Lincoln, Univ. Nebraska Press. 1-21. [81]

Brown, W., Buel, J. 1940. Response tendencies and maze patterns as determiners of choices in a maze. *J comp Ps* 29, 337-399. [257]

Brown, W. L., Halas, E. S. 1957. Terminal extinction in a multiple-T maze within a heterogeneous environment. *J genet Ps* 90, 89-95. [261]

——, Humphrey, C. E. 1955. Generalization in spatial learning. *Amer J Ps* 68, 396-408. [307]

Brownstein, A. J. *See* Lawson, R. 1957.

Bruner, J. S., Goodnow, J. J., Austin, G. A. 1956. *A study of thinking.* N. Y., Wiley. [349]

Brunswik, E. 1939. Probability as a determiner of rat behavior. *J exp Ps* 25, 175-197. [253, 255, 256]

——. 1944. Distal focussing of perception: size-constancy in a representative sample of situations. *Ps Monogr* No. 254. [207]

——. 1956. *Perception and the representative design of psychological experiments.* Berkeley, Univ. California Press. Figure reproduced by permission. [209]

Bryan, W. L., Harter, N. 1897. Studies in the physiology and psychology of the telegraphic language. *Ps Rev* 4, 27-53. [325]

——, ——. 1899. Studies on the telegraphic language: The acquisition of a hierarchy of habits. *Ps Rev* 6, 345-375. [325]

Bucy, P. C., Klüver, H. 1955. An anatomical investigation of the temporal lobe in the monkey (Macaca mulatta). *J comp Neurol* 103, 151-252. [19]

——. *See also* Klüver, H. 1939.

Buel, J. *See* Brown, W. 1940.

Bugelski, B. R., Coyer, R. A., Rogers, W. A. 1952. A criticism of pre-acquisition and pre-extinction expectances. *J exp Ps* 44, 27-30. [261]

——, Miller, N. E. 1938. A spatial gradient in the strength of avoidance responses. *J exp Ps* 23, 494-505. [89]

Bullis, G. *See* Gesell, A. 1949.

Bullock, D. H., Smith, W. C. 1953. An effect of repeated conditioning-extinction upon operant strength. *J exp Ps* 46, 349-352. [263]

Buss, A. H., Wiener, M., Durkee, Ann, Baer, M. 1955. The measurement of anxiety in clinical situations. *J consult Ps* 19, 125-129. [73]

Buswell, G. T. 1920. An experimental study of the eye-voice span in reading. *Suppl Educ Monogr* No. 17. [146]

Butler, R. A. 1954. Incentive conditions which influence visual exploration. *J exp Ps* 48, 19-23. [81]

——. 1957. Discrimination learning by rhesus monkeys to auditory incentives. *J comp physiol Ps* 50, 239-241. [80]

——, Harlow, H. F. 1954. Persistence of visual exploration in monkeys. *J comp physiol Ps* 47, 258-263. [80]

Buxton, C. E. 1940. Latent learning and the goal gradient hypothesis. *Contr ps Theory* 2, No. 6. [317]

Buytendijk, F. J. J. 1930. Uber das Umlernen. *Arch néerl Physiol* 15, 283-310. [292]

——. 1947. La durée des mouvements de dimension variable. *Miscellanea psychologica Albert Michotte.* 297-307. [142]

C

Cacioppo, A. J. *See* Perkins, C. C., Jr. 1950.

Cahill, H. E. 1957. Discrimination and generalization effects in concept learning. *Amer Psychologist* 12, 445. [344]

Calvin, A. D. *See* Perkins, M. J. 1954.

Campbell, B. A., Sheffield, F. D. 1953. Relation of random activity to food deprivation. *J comp physiol Ps* 46, 320-322. [61]

——. *See also* Sheffield, F. D. 1954.

Campbell, R. K. *See* Hilgard, E. R. 1938.

Cannon, W. B. 1915. 1929. *Bodily changes in pain, hunger, fear and rage; an account of recent researches into the function of emotional excitement.* N. Y., Appleton. [61]

Cantor, Joan H. 1955. Amount of pretraining as a factor in stimulus predifferentiation and performance set. *J exp Ps* 50, 180-184. [269]

Capaldi, E. J., Stevenson, H. W. 1957. Response reversal following different amounts of training. *J comp physiol Ps* 50, 195-198. [295]

Carter, L. F. 1947. Psychological research on navigator training. *US AAF Aviat Psychol Prog Res Rep* No. 10. [158]

Cattell, Psyche. 1940. *The measurement of intelligence of infants and young children.* N. Y., Psychol. Corp. [202]

Chadwick, Irene. *See* French, Elizabeth G. 1956.

Chalmers, E. L., Jr. 1952. Monocular and binocular cues in the perception of size and distance. *Amer J Ps* 65, 415-423. [208]

Chernikoff, R., Birmingham, H. P., Taylor, F. V. 1955. A comparison of pursuit and compensatory tracking under conditions of aiding and no aiding. *J exp Ps* 49, 55-59. [148]

Church, R. M. 1957. Transmission of learned behavior between rats. *J abn soc Ps* 54, 163-165. [288]

Claparède, E. 1943. L'orientation lointaine. *Nouveau traité psy* 8, 337-403. [152]

Clark, R. A. *See* McClelland, D. C. 1949, 1953.

Clausen, J., Gjesvik, A., Urdal, A. 1953. Changes in galvanic skin resistance as indication of pain threshold. *J genl Ps* 49, 261-271. [10]

Conklin, J. E. 1957. Effect of control lag on performance in a tracking task. *J exp Ps* 53, 261-268. [148]

Conrad, D. G. *See* Sidman, M. 1955.

Conrad, R. 1956. The timing of signals in skill. *J exp Ps* 51, 365-370. [328]

Cook, S. W. 1947. Psychological research on radar observer training. *US AAF Aviat Psychol Prog Res Rep.* No. 12. [160]

Copelan, E. L. *See* Riopelle, A. J. 1954.

Cotton, J. W. *See* Metzger, R. 1957.

Cotzin, M. *See* Supa, M. 1944.

Counts, Sarah. *See* Simmel, Marienne L. 1957.

Cowles, J. T. 1937. Food-tokens as incentives for learning by chimpanzees. *Comp Ps Monogr* No. 71. [111]

Cox, J. W. 1934. *Manual skill: its organization and development.* N. Y., Macmillan. [151]

Coyer, R. A. *See* Bugelski, B. R. 1952.

Crawford, M. P., Sollenberger, R. T., Ward, L. B., Brown, C. W., Ghiselli, E. E. 1947. Psychological research on operational training in the Continental Air Forces. *US AAF Aviat Psychol Prog Res Rep.* No. 16. [160]

Creed, R. S., Denny-Brown, D., Eccles, J. C., Liddell, E. G. T., Sherrington, C. S. 1932. *Reflex activity of the spinal cord.* Oxford, Clarendon Press. [69]

Crespi, L. P. 1942. Quantitative variation of incentive and performance in the white rat. *Amer J Ps* 55, 467-517. [247, 248]

Cruikshank, Ruth M. 1941. The development of visual size constancy in early infancy. *J genet Ps* 58, 327-351. [203]

D

Dallenbach, K. M. *See* Supa, M. 1944; Worchel, P. 1947.

D'Amato, May F. *See* Kendler, H. H. 1955.

Danzinger, K., Mainland, Margaret. 1954. The habituation of exploratory behavior. *Austral J Ps* 6, 39-51. [84]

Dashiell, J. F. 1928. *Fundamentals of objective psychology.* Boston, Houghton Mifflin. [36]

——. 1930. Direction orientation in maze running by the white rat. *Comp Ps Monogr* No. 32. [86]

Dattman, P. E., Israel, H. E. 1951. The order of dominance among conceptual capacities: an experimental test of Heidbreder's hypothesis. *J Ps* 31, 147-160. [338]

Davis, R. C. 1935. The muscular tension reflex and two of its modifying conditions. *Indiana Univ Publ, Sci Ser* No. 3. [140]

——. 1940. Set and muscular tension. *Indiana Univ Publ, Sci Ser* No. 10. [41, 227]

——. 1942. The pattern of muscular action in simple voluntary movement. *J exp Ps* 31, 347-366. [137]

——. 1943. The genetic development of patterns of voluntary activity. *J exp Ps* 33, 471-486. [137]

——. 1950. Motor responses to auditory stimuli above and below threshold. *J exp Ps* 40, 107-120. [140]

——. 1956. Electromyographic factors in aircraft control: Response and adaptation to brief noises of high intensity. *School of Aviation Medicine, USAF Report* 55-127. [324]

——. 1957. Response patterns. *Trans N Y Acad Sci* II. 19, 731-739. [325]

De Camp, J. E. 1920. Relative distance as a factor in the white rat's selection of a path. *Psychobiology* 2, 245-253. [249]

Deese, J. 1951. The extinction of a discrimination without performance of the choice response. *J comp physiol Ps* 44, 362-366. [261]

Deiniger, R. L. *See* Fitts, P. M. 1954.

Dennis, W., Sollenberger, R. J. 1934. Negative adaptation in the maze exploration of albino rats. *J comp Ps* 18, 197-206. [87]

Denny, M. R. *See* Maatsch, J. L. 1954.

Denny-Brown, D. *See* Creed, R. S. 1932.

Detambel, M. H., Stolurow, L. M. 1957. Probability and work as determiners of multichoice behavior. *J exp Ps* 53, 73-81. [249, 350]

Deutsch, J. A. 1955. A theory of shape recognition. *Brit J Ps* 46, 30-37. [329]

Dewdney, J. C. H., McCall, J. 1954. Individual differences in size discrimination learning in rats. *Aust J Ps* 6, 71-75. [287]

Dodwell, P. C. 1957. Shape recognition in rats. *Brit J Ps* 48, 221-229. [285]

Douvan, Elizabeth. 1956. Social status and success strivings. *J abn soc Ps* 52, 219-223. [95]

Draguns, J. *See* Flavell, J. H. 1957.

Duffy, Elizabeth. 1957. The psychological significance of the concept of "arousal" or "activation." *Ps Rev* 64, 265-275. [61]

Dufort, R. H., Guttman, N., Kimble, G. A. 1954. One-trial discrimination reversal in the white rat. *J comp physiol Ps* 47, 248-249. [294]

Duncan, C. P. *See* Loess, H. B. 1952.

Durkee, Ann. *See* Buss, A. H. 1955.

E

Ebbinghaus, H. 1885. *Uber das Gedächtnis*. Leipzig, Duncker. Trans. by Ruger, H. A., Bussenius, C. E. 1913. [231, 239]

Eberhart, H. D., Inman, V. T. 1951. An evaluation of experimental procedures used in a fundamental study of human locomotion. *Ann N. Y. Acad Sci* 51, 1213-1228. [137]

Eccles, J. C. *See* Creed, R. S. 1932.

Edwards, A. S. 1946. Body sway and vision. *J exp Ps* 36, 526-535. [139]

Ehrenfreund, D. 1948. An experimental test of the continuity theory of discrimination learning with pattern vision. *J comp physiol Ps* 41, 408-422. [273]

Elam, C. B., Tyler, D. W., Bitterman, M. E. 1954. A further study of secondary reinforcement and the discrimination hypothesis. *J comp physiol Ps* 47, 381-384. [266]

Ellen, P. *See* Maier, N. R. P. 1956.

Elliott, M. H. 1929. The effect of appropriateness of reward and of complex incentives on maze performance. *Univ California Publ Ps* 4, 91-98. [67]

Eninger, M. U. 1952. Habit summation in a selective learning problem. *J comp physiol Ps* 45, 604-608. [287]

Ericksen, S. C. 1947. Specialized areas of pilot training. In Miller, N. E. Ed. *US AAF Aviat Psychol Prog Res Rep*. No. 8. p. 56. [159]

——. *See also* Youtz, R. P. 1947.

Eschenbach, A. *See* Rethlingshafer, Dorothy. 1951.

Eson, M. E., Kafka, J. S. 1952. Diagnostic implications of a study in time perception. *J genl Ps* 46, 169-183. [141]

Estes, W. K., Skinner, B. F. 1941. Some quantitative properties of anxiety. *J exp Ps* 29, 390-400. [40, 68]

F

Fairbanks, G. *See* Tiffen, J. 1937.

Falk, J. L., Bindra, D. 1954. Judgment of time as a function of serial position and stress. *J exp Ps* 47, 279-282. [141]

Farber, I. E. 1954. Anxiety as a drive state. In Jones, M. R., Ed. *Nebraska symposium on motivation*, 1-46. [74]

——. *See also* Spence, K. W. 1953.

Feldman, S. M., Underwood, B. J. 1957. Stimulus recall following paired-associate learning. *J exp Ps* 53, 11-15. [232]

Fenichel, O. 1945. *The psychoanalytic theory of neurosis*. N. Y., Norton. [106]

Fenn, J. D., Goss, A. E. 1957. The role of mediating verbal responses in the conceptual sorting behavior of normals and paranoid schizophrenics. *J genet Ps* 90, 59-67. [342]

Festinger, L. 1954. Motivations leading to social behavior. In Jones, M. R., Ed., *Nebraska symposium on motivation 1954*, 191-219. Lincoln, Univ. Nebraska Press. Quoted by permission. [79]

Fields, P. E. 1935. Studies in concept formation: II. A new multiple stimulus jumping apparatus for visual figure discrimination. *J comp Ps* 20, 183-203. [273]

——. 1953. The efficiency of the serial multiple discrimination apparatus and method with white rats. *J comp physiol Ps* 46, 69-76. [273]

——. 1954. Multiple discrimination learning by white rats. *J comp physiol Ps* 47, 472-476. [273]

Fink, J. B. 1954. Conditioning of muscle action potential increments accompanying an instructed movement. *J exp Ps* 47, 61-68. [227]

Fitts, P. M. 1947. Psychological researches on equipment design. *US AAF Aviat Psychol Prog Res Rep.* No. 19. [157]

——, Deiniger, R. L. 1954. S-R compatability: Correspondence among paired elements within stimulus and response codes. *J exp Ps* 48, 483-492. [145]

——, Seeger, C. M. 1953. S-R compatability: Spatial characteristics of stimulus and response codes. *J exp Ps* 46, 199-210. [145]

——. *See also* Briggs, G. E. 1957; Hartman, B. O. 1955.

Flavell, J. H., Draguns, J. 1957. A microgenetic approach to perception and thought. *Ps Bull* 54, 197-217. [352]

Fleishman, E. A. *See* Hempel, W. E., Jr. 1955.

Flurry, Christine. *See* Wenzel, Bernice M. 1948.

Foley, J. P. *See* Anastasi, A. 1949.

Fraenkel, G. S., Gunn, D. L. 1940. *The orientation of animals: Kineses, taxes and compass reaction.* Oxford, Clarendon Press. [152]

Freides, D. 1957. Goal-box cues and pattern of reinforcement. *J exp Ps* 53, 361-371. [266]

French, Elizabeth G., Chadwick, Irene. 1956. Some characteristics of affiliation motivation. *J abn soc Ps* 52, 296-300. [96]

Freud, S. 1900. *The interpretation of dreams.* N. Y., Macmillan. [51]

——. 1915. *Psychopathology of everyday life.* N. Y., Macmillan. [51]

——. 1923. *The ego and the id.* London, Hogarth, 1947. [105]

——. 1933. *New introductory lectures on psychoanalysis.* N. Y., Norton. [105]

——. 1935. *A general introduction to psycho-analysis.* N. Y., Liveright. Copyright 1935 Edward L. Bernays; Copyright R 1948 Susie Hoch. Quoted by permission of Liveright Publishing Corp., N. Y. [104]

——. 1938. *An outline of psychoanalysis.* N. Y., Norton. [105]

Frings, H. 1947. Biological backgrounds of the "sweet tooth." *Turtox News* 24, 133-134. [55, 120]

G

Gagné, R. M. *See* Graham, C. H. 1940.

Galambos, R. *See* Griffin, D. R. 1941.

Galanter, E., Gerstenhaber, M. 1956. On thought: The extrinsic theory. *Ps Rev* 63, 218-227. [352]

——, Shaw, W. A. 1954. "Cue" vs. "reactive inhibition" in place and response learning. *J comp physiol Ps* 47, 395-398. [312]

Galt, W. E., Grier, D. J. 1947. Evaluation and selection of flying instructors. In Miller, N. E., Ed. *US AAF Aviat Psychol Prog Res Rep.* No. 8. 289-351 [160]

Gans, Susan. *See* Waddell, D. 1955.

Gardner, R. A. 1957. Probability-learning with two and three choices. *Amer J Ps* 60, 174-185. [257]

Garvey, W. D., Knowles, W. B. 1954. Response time patterns associated with various display-control relationships. *J exp Ps* 47, 315-322. [144]

Gellhorn, E. 1954. Physiological processes related to consciousness and perception. *Brain* 77, 401-415. [62]

Gerjuoy, Irma R. *See* Schaeffer, M. S. 1955.

Gerstenhaber, M. *See* Galanter, E. 1956.

Gesell, A. 1952. *Infant development: The embryology of early human behavior.* N. Y., Harper. [141]

——, Ilg, F. L., Bullis, G. 1949. *Vision: Its development in the child.* N. Y., Harper. [165, 176]

Ghent, Lila. *See* Semmes, Josephine. 1955.

Gibson, Eleanor J., Bergman, R. 1954. The effect of training on absolute estimation of distance over the ground. *J exp Ps* 48, 473-482. [207]

——, ——, Purdy, Jean. 1955. The effect of prior training on absolute and relative judgments of distance over ground. *J exp Ps* 50, 97-105. [207]

——, Walk, R. D. 1956. The effect of prolonged exposure to visually presented patterns on learning to discriminate them. *J comp physiol Ps* 49, 239-242. [270]

——. *See also* Gibson, J. J. 1955, 1957; Purdy, Jean. 1955; Walk, R. D. 1957.

Gibson, J. J. 1947. Motion picture testing and research. *US AAF Aviat Psychol Prog Res Rep.* No. 7. [153]

——. 1950a. *The perception of the visual world.* Boston, Houghton Mifflin. [170, 174, 178]

——. 1950b. The perception of visual surfaces. *Amer J Ps* 63, 367-384. [178]

——. 1952. The relation between visual and postural determinants of the phenomenal vertical. *Ps Rev* 59, 370-375. [178]

——. 1957. Optical motions and transformations as stimuli for visual perception. *Ps Rev* 64, 288-295. [178]

——, Gibson, E. J. 1955. Perceptual learning; differentiation or enrichment? *Ps Rev* 62, 32-41. [178]

——, ——. 1957. Continuous perspective transformations and the perception of rigid motion. *J exp Ps* 54, 129-138. [178]

——, Olum, P., Rosenblatt, F. 1955. Parallax and perspective during aircraft landings. *Amer J Ps* 68, 372-385. [175]

——, Purdy, Jean, Lawrence, Lois. 1955. A method of controlling stimulation for the study of space perception: The optical tunnel. *J exp Ps* 50, 1-14. [172]

——. *See also* Beck, J. 1955.

Gilbreth, F. B. 1911. *Motion study: A method for increasing the efficiency of the workman.* N. Y., Van Nostrand. [149]

——, Gilbreth, L. M. 1916. *Fatigue study: A first step in motion study.* N. Y., Sturgis & Walton. [149]

Gilbreth, L. M. *See* Gilbreth, F. B. 1916.

Gilinsky, Alberta S. 1951. Perceived size and distance in visual space. *Ps Rev* 58, 460-482. [213]

Gillespie, J. J. 1947. *Dynamic motion and time study.* London, Elek. [151]

Gilmer, B. v. H. *See* Moyer, K. E. 1955.

Gjesvik, A. *See* Clausen, J. 1953.

Gogel, W. C., Hartman, B. O., Harker, G. S. 1957. The retinal size of a familiar object as a determiner of absolute distance. *Ps Monogr* No. 442. [169]

Goldbeck, R. A., Bernstein, B. B., Hillix, W. A., Marx, M. H. 1957. Application of the half-split technique to problem-solving tasks. *J exp Ps* 53, 330-338. [350]

Goldberger, L. *See* Goodstein, L. D. 1955.

Goldstein, K. 1939. *The organism, a holistic approach to biology derived from pathological data in man.* N. Y., American Book. [127]

——, 1940. *Human nature in the light of psychopathology.* Cambridge, Mass., Harvard Univ. Press. [126]

——. 1947. Organismic approach to the problem of motivation. *Trans. N. Y. Acad Sci* 9, 218-230. [127]

Goodell, H. *See* Hardy, J. D. 1947.

Goodnow, J. J., Pettigrew, T. P. 1956. Some sources of difficulty in solving simple problems. *J exp Ps* 51, 385-392. [248]

——. *See also* Bruner, J. S. 1956.

Goodson, F. E., Brownstein, A. 1955. Secondary reinforcing and motivating properties of stimuli contiguous with shock onset and termination. *J comp physiol Ps* 48, 381-386. [72]

Goodstein, L. D., Goldberger, L. 1955. Manifest anxiety and Rorschach performance in a chronic patient population. *J consult Ps* 19, 339-344. [73]

Goodwin, W. R. 1955. A test of the continuity hypothesis in discrimination learning. *Dissertation Abstr* 15, 1913-1914. [288]

——, Lawrence, D. H. 1955. The functional independence of two discrimination habits associated with a constant stimulus situation. *J comp physiol Ps* 48, 437-443. [288, 291]

Goss, A. E. 1955. A stimulus-response analysis of the interaction of cue-producing and instrumental responses. *Ps Rev* 62, 20-31. [342]

——, Wischner, G. J. 1956. Vicarious trial and error and related behavior. *Ps Bull* 53, 35-54. [271]

——. *See also* Fenn, J. D. 1957; Rossman, I. L. 1951.

Graham, C. H., Gagné, R. M. 1940. The acquisition, extinction, and spontaneous recovery of a conditioned operant response. *J exp Ps* 26, 251-280. [236]

Granit, A. R. 1921. A study in the perception of form. *Brit J Ps* 12, 223-247. [196]

Grant, D. A. 1951. Perceptual versus analytical responses to the number concept of a Weigl-type card sorting test. *J exp Ps* 41, 23-29. [338]

——, Hake, H. W., Hornseth, J. P. 1951. Acquisition and extinction of a verbal conditioned response with differing percentages of reinforcement. *J exp Ps* 42, 1-5. [252]

——. *See also* Morin, R. E. 1955.

Greenhut, Ann. 1954. Visual distance discrimination in the rat. *J exp Ps* 47, 148-152. [301]

Grier, D. J. *See* Galt, W. E. 1947.

Griffin, D. R. 1953. Sensory physiology and the orientation of animals. *Amer Scientist* 41, 209-244. [185]

——, Galambos, R. 1941. The sensory basis of obstacle avoidance by flying bats. *J exp Zool* 86, 481-506. [185]

Gruber, H. E. 1954. The relation of perceived size to perceived distance. *Amer J Ps* 67, 411-426. [213]

Guanella, Florence M. 1934. Block building activities of young children. *Arch Ps, N. Y.,* No. 174. [77]

Guilford, J. P., Lacey, J. I. 1947. Printed classification tests. *US AAF Aviat Psychol Prog Res Rep.* No. 5. [135, 160]

Gulliksen, H., Wolfle, D. L. 1938. A theory of learning and transfer. *Psychometrika,* 3, 128-149, 225-251. [283]

Gunn, D. L. *See* Fraenkel, G. S. 1940.

Guthrie, E. R. 1952. *The psychology of learning.* Rev. ed. N. Y., Harper. [325]

Guttman, N. 1953. Operant conditioning, extinction, and periodic reinforcement in relation to concentration of sucrose used as reinforcing agent. *J exp Ps* 46, 213-224. [119, 248]

——. *See* Dufort, R. H. 1954.

Guze, S. B. *See* Matarazzo, J. D. 1955.

H

Hake, H. W., Hyman, R. 1953. Perception of the statistical structure of a random series of binary symbols. *J exp Ps* 45, 64-74. [255, 257]

——. *See also* Grant, D. A. 1951.

Halas, E. S. *See* Brown, W. L. 1957.

Hall, J. F., Hanford, P. V. 1954. Activity as a function of a restricted feeding schedule. *J comp physiol Ps* 47, 362-363. [61]

Halverson, H. M. 1943. The development of prehension in infants. In Barker, R. G., *Child behavior and development.* N. Y., McGraw-Hill. 49-65. [141]

Hanawalt, N. G. 1937. Memory trace for figures in recall and recognition. *Arch Ps N. Y.* 216. [196]

Hanford, P. V. *See* Hall, J. F. 1954.

Hardy, J. D., Wolff, H. G., Goodell, H. 1947. Studies on pain: Discrimination of differences in intensity of a pain stimulus as a basis of a scale of pain intensity. *J clin Invest* 26, 1152-1158. [9]

Harker, G. S. *See* Gogel, W. C. 1957.

Harlow, H. F. 1944. Studies in discrimination learning by monkeys: I. The learning of discrimination series and the reversal of discrimination series. *J genl Ps* 30, 3-12. [292, 294]

——. 1949. The formation of learning sets. *Ps Rev* 56, 51-65. [273, 295, 298]

——. 1950. Learning and satiation of response in intrinsically motivated complex puzzle performance by monkeys. *J comp physiol Ps* 43, 289-294. [81]

——. 1953a. Mice, monkeys, men, and motives. *Ps Rev* 60, 23-32. [77]

——. 1953b. Motivation as a factor in

the acquisition of new responses. In Brown, J. S., *et al. Current theory and research in motivation: A symposium.* Lincoln, Univ. Nebraska Press. 24-49. [81]

——, Hicks, L. H. 1957. Discrimination learning theory: Uniprocess vs. duoprocess. *Ps Rev* 64, 104-109. [295, 297]

——, & McClearn, G. E. 1954. Object discrimination learned by monkeys on the basis of manipulation motives. *J comp physiol Ps* 47, 73-76. [81]

——. *See also* Butler, R. A. 1954; McClearn, G. E. 1954.

Harter, N. *See* Bryan, W. L. 1897.

Hartman, B. O., Fitts, P. M. 1955. Relation of stimulus and response amplitude to tracking performance. *J exp Ps* 49, 82-92. [148]

——. *See also* Gogel, W. C. 1957.

Hastorf, A. H. 1950. The influence of suggestion on the relationship between stimulus size and perceived distance. *J Ps* 29, 195-217. [169]

Hattwick, La Berta W. *See* Alschuler, Rose H. 1947.

Hayes, Catherine. *See* Hayes, K. J. 1953.

Hayes, K. J., Thompson, R., Hayes, Catherine. 1953. Discrimination learning set in chimpanzees. *J comp physiol Ps* 46, 99-107. [298, 299]

Hebb, D. O. 1949. *The organization of behavior: a neuropsychological theory.* N. Y., Wiley. [28, 62, 74, 123]

——. 1955. Drives and the C.N.S. (conceptual nervous system). *Ps Rev* 62, 243-254. [62]

Heidbreder, Edna. 1924. An experimental study of thinking. *Arch Ps* N. Y. No. 73. [346]

——. 1946-49. The attainment of concepts. *J genl Ps* 35, 173-189, 191-223; *J Ps* 24, 93-138; 25, 299-329; 26, 45-69, 193-216; 27, 3-39, 263-309. [337]

——. 1952. Experiments by Dattman and Israel on the attainment of concepts. *J Ps* 34, 115-136. [338]

——. 1955. Stimulus-discriminability and concept-attainment: a question arising from Baum's experiment. *J Ps* 39, 341-350. [338]

Helmholtz, H. v. 1850. Über die Methoden kleinste Zeitthele zu messen, und ihre Anwendung für physiologische Zwecke. Trans., On the methods of measuring very small portions of time, and their application to physiological processes. *Philos Mag* 1953 s. 4, 6, 313-325. [226]

——. 1863 & 1865, 1912. *Die Lehre von den Tonempfindungen als physiologische Grundlage für die Theorie der Musik.* Braunschweig, Vieweg. Trans., *On the sensations of tone.* N. Y., Longmans, Green. [31]

Helson, H. 1949. Design of equipment and optimal human operation. *Amer J Ps* 62, 473-497. [147]

Henneman, R. H. 1935. A photometric study of the perception of object color. *Arch Ps N. Y.,* No. 179. [219]

Hertzman, M. *See* Witkin, H. A. 1954.

Heyns, R. W. *See* Atkinson, J. W. 1954.

Hick, W. E. 1952. On the rate of gain of information. *Q J exp Ps* 4, 11-27. [145]

Hicks, L. H. *See* Harlow, H. F. 1957.

Hilden, A. H. 1937. An action current study of the conditioned hand withdrawal. *Ps Monogr* No. 217, 173-204. [232]

Hilgard, E. R. 1936. The nature of the conditioned response: I. The case for and against stimulus substitution. *Ps Rev* 43, 366-385. [232]

——. 1956. *Theories of learning.* N. Y., Appleton-Century-Crofts. [249]

——, Campbell, R. K., Sears, W. N. 1938. Conditioned discrimination: the effect of knowledge of stimulus relationships. *Amer J Ps* 51, 498-506. [278]

——, Humphreys, L. G. 1938. The retention of conditioned discrimination. *J genl Ps* 19, 111-125. [279]

Hillix, W. A. *See* Goldbeck, R. A. 1957.

Hochberg, J., McAlister, E. 1953. A quantitative approach to figural "goodness." *J exp Ps* 46, 361-364. [197]

Hollingworth, H. L. 1928. *Psychology: Its facts and principles.* N. Y., Appleton. [191]

——. 1956. Simple color discrimination in chimpanzees: effect of varying contiguity between cue and incentive. *J comp physiol Ps* 49, 492-495. [275]

Jenkin, N. 1957. Affective processes in perception. *Ps Bull* 54, 100-127. [192]

Jenkins, W. O., Stanley, J. C. 1950. Partial reinforcement: A review and critique. *Ps Bull* 47, 193-259. [265]

Jensen, J. *See* Siegel, A. I. 1955.

Jerome, E. A., Proshansky, H. 1950. Factors in the assay and use of guidance devices. In Zahl, P. E., Ed. *Blindness: modern approaches to the unseen environment,* Princeton, Princeton Univ. Press. 462-494. [185]

Jersild, A. T. 1954. Emotional development. In Carmichael, L., Ed. *Manual of child psychology,* 2d ed. N. Y., Wiley. 833-917, esp. p. 844. [128]

Johdai, K. 1956. A field theory of extinction and spontaneous recovery. *Ps Rev* 63, 243-248. [262]

Johnson, D. M. 1955. *The psychology of thought and judgment.* N. Y., Harper. [43, 353, 354]

Jones, F. N., Taylor, F. E. 1938. The relative effects of goal orientation and direction of the last turn on maze learning in the rat. *J comp Ps* 26, 19-26. [44]

Joynson, R. S. 1949. The problem of size and distance. *Q J exp Ps* 1, 119-135. [206]

K

Kafka, J. S. *See* Eson, M. E. 1952.

Kalish, D. *See* Tolman, E. C. 1946.

Kamin, L. J. *See* Solomon, R. L. 1953.

Karasik, A. D., Kendler, H. H. 1957. Concept formation as a function of competition between response produced cues. *Amer Psychologist* 12, 445. [342]

Katz, D., Künnipas, T. 1946. Propriozeptiver Reflex und Willenshandlung. *Acta paediatrica* 33, Fasc 2, 1-12. [138]

Kaufman, R. S. 1953. Effects of preventing intromission upon sexual behavior of rats. *J comp physiol Ps* 46, 209-211. [63]

Keller, F. S., Schoenfeld, W. N. 1950. *Principles of psychology, a systematic text in the science of behavior.* N. Y., Appleton-Century-Crofts. [36, 44, 114]

Kellogg, W. N., Kohler, R., Morris, H. N. 1953. Porpoise sounds as sonar signals. *Science* 117, 239-243. [185]

——. *See also* Spooner, Alice. 1947; Wolf, I. S. 1940.

Kempner, Phyllis. *See* Waddell, D. 1955.

Kendall, E. 1954. The validity of Taylor's Manifest Anxiety Scale. *J consult Ps* 18, 429-432. [73]

Kendler, H. H. 1945. Drive interaction: I. Learning as a function of the simultaneous presence of the hunger and thirst drives. *J exp Ps* 35, 96-109. [67]

——. 1946. The influence of simultaneous hunger and thirst drives upon the learning of two opposed spatial responses of the white rat. *J exp Ps* 36, 212-220. [314]

——, D'Amato, May F. 1955. A comparison of reversal shifts and nonreversal shifts in human concept formation behavior. *J exp Ps* 49, 165-174. [342]

——, Law, F. E. 1950. An experimental test of the selective principle of association of drive stimuli. *J exp Ps* 40, 299-304. [67]

——, Vineberg, R. 1954. The acquisition of compound concepts as a function of previous training. *J exp Ps* 48, 252-258. [342]

——. *See also* Karasik, A. D. 1957.

Kent, G. W. *See* Archer, E. J. 1956.

Kilpatrick, F. P. 1954. Two processes in perceptual learning. *J exp Ps* 47, 362-370. [243]

——, Ittelson, W. H. 1953. The size-distance invariance hypothesis. *Ps Rev* 60, 223-231. [208]

Kimble, G. A. *See* Dufort, R. H. 1954.

Kinsey, A. C., Pomeroy, W. B., Martin, C. E. 1948. *Sexual behavior in the human male.* Philadelphia, Saunders. [104]

Kish, G. B. 1955. Learning when the onset of illumination is used as reinforcing stimulus. *J comp physiol Ps* 48, 261-264. [129]

——, Antonitis, J. J. 1956. Unconditioned operant behavior in two homozygous strains of mice. *J genet Ps* 88, 121-129. [129, 130]

Klemm, O. 1919, 1920. Untersuchungen über die Localisation von Schallreizen. *Arch gesamte Ps* 38, 71-114; 40, 117-146. [188]

Klüver, H., Bucy, P. C. 1939. Preliminary analysis of functions of the temporal lobes in monkeys. *Arch Neurol Psychiat* 42, 979-1000. [19]

——. *See also* Bucy, P. C., 1955.

Knowles, W. B. *See* Garvey, W. D. 1954.

Koffka, K. 1935. *Principles of Gestalt psychology.* N. Y., Harcourt, Brace. [30, 194, 218]

Kohler, R. *See* Kellogg, W. N. 1953.

Köhler, W. 1917, 1924. *Intelligenzprüfungen an Menschenaffen.* Berlin, Springer. Trans., *The mentality of apes.* London, Kegan, Paul. [354]

——. 1929, 1947. *Gestalt psychology: an introduction to new concepts in modern psychology.* N. Y., Copyright; 1947, Liveright Publishing Corp., Copyright R 1956. Quoted by permission. [29, 199, 283]

Koronakos, C., Arnold, W. J. 1957. The formation of learning sets in rats. *J comp physiol Ps* 50, 11-14. [298]

Kraeling, Doris. *See* Campbell, B. A. 1954.

Krechevsky, I. 1938. A study of the continuity of the problem-solving process. *Ps Rev* 45, 107-133. [284]

Kubis, J. *See* Welch, L. 1947.

Kuhlmann, F. 1906. A study in the mental imagery and memory of meaningless visual forms. *Ps Rev* 13, 316-348. [196]

Künnipas, T. *See* Katz, D. 1946.

Kurtz, K. H. 1955. Discrimination of complex stimuli: the relationship of training and test stimuli in transfer of discrimination. *J exp Ps* 50, 283-292. [270]

L

Lacey, J. I. *See* Guilford, J. P. 1947.

Lambercier, M. *See* Piaget, J. 1951.

Landis, C., Hunt, W. A. 1939. *The startle pattern.* N. Y., Farrar, Farrar & Rinehart. [140, 324]

Langdon, J. 1953. Further studies in the perception of a changing shape. *Q J exp Ps* 5, 89-107. [218]

——. 1955a. The role of spatial stimuli in the perception of shape. *Q J exp Ps* 7, 19-36. [218]

——. 1955b. The perception of three-dimensional solids. *Q J exp Ps* 7, 133-146. [218]

Lashley, K. S. 1918. A simple maze: with data on the relation of the distribution of practice to the rate of learning. *Psychobiol* 1, 353-367. [316]

——. 1930. The mechanism of vision: I. A method for rapid analysis of pattern vision in the rat. *J genet Ps* 37, 453-460. [272]

——. 1938. The mechanism of vision: XV. Preliminary studies of the rat's capacity for detail vision. *J genl Ps* 18, 123-193. [272, 285, 287]

——. 1942. An examination of the "continuity theory" as applied to discriminative learning. *J genl Ps* 26, 241-265. [283, 284]

——, Ball, J. 1929. Spinal conduction and kinaesthetic sensitivity in the maze habit. *J comp Ps* 9, 71-105. [305]

Law, F. E. *See* Kendler, H. H. 1950.

Lawrence, D. H., Mason, W. A. 1955. Systematic behavior during discrimination reversal and change of dimensions. *J comp physiol Ps* 48, 1-7. [291]

——. *See also* Goodwin, W. R. 1955.

Lawrence, Lois. *See* Gibson, J. J. 1955.

Lawson, R., Brownstein, A. J. 1957. The effect of effort and training-test similarity on resistance to extinction. *Amer J Ps* 70, 123-125. [262]

Leeper, R. 1935. The role of motivation in learning. A study of the phenomenon of differential motivational control of the utilization of habits. *J genet Ps* 46, 3-40. [312, 313, 314]

——. 1948. A motivational theory of emotion to replace "emotion as disorganized response." *Ps Rev* 55, 5-21. [61]

Leventhal, T. *See* Witkin, H. A. 1952.

Levine, S. 1953. The role of irrelevant drive stimuli in learning. *J exp Ps* 45, 410-416. [322]

Levy, N. *See* Seward, J. P. 1949.

Lewin, K. 1922. Das Problem der Willensmessung und das Grundgesetz der Assoziation. *Ps Forsch* 1, 191-302; 2, 65-140. [49]

——. 1935. *A dynamic theory of personality.* Trans. by D. K. Adams & K. E. Zener. N. Y., McGraw-Hill. [49, 91, 195]

——. 1954. Behavior and development as a function of the total situation. In Carmichael, L., Ed. *Manual of child psychology,* 2d ed. 918-970. [91]

Lewis, D. J. *See* Metzger, R. 1957.

Lewis, H. B. *See* Witkin, H. A. 1954.

Lichten, W., Lurie, Susan. 1950. A new technique for the study of perceived size. *Amer J Ps* 63, 280-282. [208]

Liddell, E. G. T. *See* Creed, R. S. 1932.

Lincoln, R. S. 1954. Rate accuracy in handwheel cranking. *J appl Ps* 38, 195-201. [328]

Lindsley, D. B. 1951. Emotion. In Stevens, S. S., Ed. *Handbook of experimental psychology.* N. Y., Wiley. 473-516. [62]

Lippitt, R. *See* Spence, K. W. 1940, 1946.

Lissner, Käte. 1933. Die Entspannung von Bedürfnissen durch Ersatzhandlungen. *Ps Forsch* 18, 218-250. [92]

Locke, N. M. 1938. Perception and intelligence: Their phylogenetic relation. *Ps Rev* 45, 335-345. [210]

Loess, H. B., Duncan, C. P. 1952. Human discrimination learning with simultaneous and successive presentation of stimuli. *J exp Ps* 44, 215-221. [282]

Lowell, E. L. *See* McClelland, D. C. 1953.

Lurie, Susan. *See* Lichten, W. 1950.

M

Maatsch, J. L., Adelman, H. M., Denny, M. R. 1954. Effort and resistance to extinction of the bar-pressing response. *J comp physiol Ps* 47, 47-50. [262]

MacCaslin, E. F. 1954. Successive and simultaneous discrimination as a function of stimulus-similarity. *Amer J Ps* 67, 308-314. [283]

Macfarlane, D. A. 1930. The role of kinesthesis in maze learning. *Calif U Publ Ps* 4, 277-305. [305]

Machover, K. *See* Witkin, H. A. 1954.

Maddi, S. R. *See* Moltz, H. 1956.

Mahut, Helen. 1954. The effect of stimulus position on visual discrimination by the rat. *Canad J Ps* 8, 130-138. [286, 287]

Maier, N. R. F. 1956. Frustration theory: Restatement and extension. *Ps Rev* 63, 370-388. [287]

——, Ellen, P. 1956. Studies of abnormal behavior in the rat: XXIV. Position habits, position stereotypes, and abortive behavior. *J genet Ps* 89, 35-49. [287]

Mainland, Margaret. *See* Danzinger, K. 1954.

Maltzman, I. *See* Amsel, A. 1950.

Mandler, G., Sarason, S. B. 1952. A study of anxiety and learning. *J abn soc Ps* 47, 166-173. [72]

——. *See also* Sarason, S. B. 1952.

Manning, H. M. 1956. The effect of varying conditions of hunger and thirst on two responses learned to hunger and thirst alone. *J comp physiol Ps* 49, 249-253. [314]

Mansfeld, F. 1940. Die Verdunklung und die Blinden. *Arch gesamte Ps* 107, 411-436. [186]

Marks, M. R. 1951. Problem solving as a function of the situation. *J exp Ps* 41, 74-80. [349]

Martin, C. E. *See* Kinsey, A. C. 1948.

Marx, M. H. *See* Goldbeck, R. A. 1957.

Maslow, A. 1955. Deficiency motivation and growth motivation. In Jones, M. R., Ed. *Nebraska symposium on motivation 1955,* 1-30. [122]

Mason, W. A., Stone, C. P. 1953. Maze

performance of rats under conditions of surface and underwater swimming. *J comp physiol Ps* 46, 159-165. [306]

——. *See also* Lawrence, D. H. 1955.

Matarazzo, J. D., Guze, S. B., Matarazzo, R. G. 1955. An approach to the validity of the Taylor Anxiety Scale: Scores of medical and psychiatric patients. *J abn soc Ps* 51, 276-280. [73]

Matarazzo, R. G. *See* Matarazzo, J. D. 1955.

Matthews, G. V. T. 1951. The experimental investigation of navigation in homing pigeons. *J exp Biol* 28, 506-536. [152]

McAlister, E. *See* Hochberg, J. 1953.

McCall, J. *See* Dewdney, J. C. H. 1954.

McClearn, G. E., Harlow, H. F. 1954. The effect of spatial contiguity on discrimination learning by rhesus monkeys. *J comp physiol Ps* 47, 391-394. [274]

——. *See also* Harlow, H. F. 1954.

McClelland, D. C. 1955. Some social consequences of achievement motivation. In Jones, M. R., Ed. *Nebraska symposium on motivation 1955,* 41-65. [95]

——, Atkinson, J. W., Clark, R. A., Lowell, E. L. 1953. *The achievement motive.* N. Y., Appleton-Century-Crofts. [94, 123]

——, Clark, R. A., Roby, T. B., Atkinson, J. W. 1949. The projective expression of needs: IV. The effect of the need for achievement on thematic apperception. *J exp Ps* 39, 242-255. [94]

McCurdy, H. G. *See* Zener, K. 1939.

McDougall, W. 1905. *Physiological psychology.* London, Dent. [21]

——. 1908. *Introduction to social psychology.* London, Methuen. [50, 109]

——. 1930. The hormic psychology. In Murchison, C., Ed. *Psychologies of 1930.* Worcester, Mass., Clark Univ. Press. 3-36. Quoted by permission. [54]

——. 1932. *The energies of men, a study of the fundamentals of dynamic psychology.* London, Methuen. [89]

McFarland, R. A. 1953. *Human factors in air transportation: Occupational health and safety.* N. Y., McGraw-Hill. [157]

McFie, J., Piercy, M. F., Zangwill, O. L. 1950. Visual-spatial agnosia associated with lesions of the right cerebral hemisphere. *Brain,* 73, 167-190. [18]

Meissner, P. Bretnall. *See* Witkin, H. A. 1954.

Melton, A. W. 1947. Apparatus tests. *US AAF Aviat Psychol Prog Res Rep.* No. 4. [160]

Menninger, Carl. 1942. *Love against hate.* N. Y., Harcourt, Brace. Quoted by permission. [106]

Messick, S. J., Solley, C. M. 1957. Probability learning in children: Some exploratory studies. *J genet Ps* 90, 23-32. [257]

——. *See also* Solley, C. M. 1957.

Metzger, R., Cotton, J. W., Lewis, D. J. 1957. Effect of reinforcement magnitude and order of presentation of different magnitudes on runway behavior. *J comp physiol Ps* 50, 184-188. [248]

Meumann, E. 1908. *Okonomie und Technik des Gedächtnisses.* Leipzig, Klinkhardt. [224]

Meyer, D. R. *See* Miles, R. C. 1956.

Miles, R. C. 1956. Secondary-reinforcement stimulation throughout a series of spontaneous recoveries. *J comp physiol Ps* 49, 496-498. [262]

——, Meyer, D. R. 1956. Learning sets in marmosets. *J comp physiol Ps* 49, 219-222. [298, 299]

——. *See also* Wickens, D. D. 1954.

Miller, G. A. 1953a. What is information measurement? *Amer Psychologist* 8, 3-11. [198]

——. 1953b. Information theory and the study of speech. In *Current trends in information theory.* 1954. Pittsburgh, Univ. Pittsburgh Press. 119-139. [198]

Miller, N. E., Ed. 1947. Psychological research on pilot training. *US AAF Aviat Psychol Prog Res Rep.* No. 8. [153, 157, 159, 160, 161]

——. 1948. Studies of fear as an acquirable drive: I. Fear as motivation and fear-reduction as reinforcement in the learning of new responses. *J exp Ps* 38, 89-101. [52]

——. 1951. Learnable drives and rewards. In Stevens, S. S., Ed. *Handbook of experimental psychology.* N. Y., Wiley, 435-472. Quoted by permission. [114]

——. 1957. Experiments on motivation: Studies combining psychological, physiological, and pharmacological techniques. *Science* 126, 1271-1278. [62, 122]

——. *See also* Bugelski, R. 1938; Murphy, J. V. 1955; Myers, A. K. 1954; Olds, J. 1954.

Mitchell, M. J. H., Vince, M. A. 1951. The direction of movement of machine controls. *Q J exp Ps* 3, 24-35. [145]

Moltz, H. 1955. Latent extinction and the reduction of secondary reward value. *J exp Ps* 49, 395-400. [261]

——, Maddi, S. R. 1956. Reduction of secondary reward value as a function of drive strength during latent extinction. *J exp Ps* 52, 71-76. [261, 322]

Montgomery, K. C. 1952. Exploratory behavior and its relation to spontaneous alternation in a series of maze exposures. *J comp physiol Ps* 45, 50-57. [87]

——. 1953. The effect of activity deprivation upon exploratory behavior. *J comp physiol Ps* 46, 438-441. [87]

——. 1954. The role of the exploratory drive in learning. *J comp physiol Ps* 47, 60-64. [86]

——. 1955. The relation between fear induced by novel stimulation and exploratory behavior. *J comp physiol Ps* 48, 254-260. [87]

——, Segall, M. 1955. Discrimination learning based upon the exploratory drive. *J comp physiol Ps* 48, 225-228. [85]

Morgan, C. T., Stellar, E. 1950. *Physiological psychology,* 2d ed. N. Y., McGraw-Hill. [59]

Morgan, J. J. B. 1917. The speed and accuracy of motor adjustments. *J exp Ps* 2, 225-248. [142]

Morin, R. E., Grant, D. A. 1955. Learning and performance on a key-pressing task as function of the degree of spatial stimulus-response correspondence. *J exp Ps* 49, 39-47. [144]

Morris, H. N. *See* Kellogg, W. N. 1953.

Mote, F. A. *See* Archer, E. J. 1956.

Moyer, K. E., Gilmer, B. v. H. 1955. Attention spans of children for experimentally designed toys. *J genet Ps* 87, 187-201. [78]

Müller, G. E., Pilzecker, A. 1900. Experimentelle Beiträge zur Lehre vom Gedächtniss. *Z Ps Ergbd* No. 1. [231]

Mundel, M. E. *See* Barnes, R. N. 1939.

Murdock, B. B., Jr. 1956. "Backward" learning in paired associates. *J exp Ps* 51, 213-215. [232]

Murphy, J. V., Miller, R. E. 1955. The effect of spatial contiguity of cue and reward in the object-quality learning of rhesus monkeys. *J comp physiol Ps* 48, 221-224. [274]

Murphy, Lois B. *See* Biber, Barbara. 1942.

Murray, H. A. 1938. *Explorations in personality.* N. Y., Oxford Univ. Press. Quoted by permission. [94, 107, 108f]

Myers, A. K., Miller, N. E. 1954. Failure to find a learned drive based on hunger; evidence for learning motivated by "exploration." *J comp physiol Ps* 47, 428-436. [79, 81, 86]

N

Nagel, E. H., *See* Battig, W. F. 1957.

Newman, E. B. *See* Stevens, S. S. 1936.

Nielsen, J. M. 1951. *A textbook of clinical neurology,* 3d ed. N. Y., Hoeber. [139]

Nissen, H. W. 1951. Motivational aspects of behavior. In Stevens, S. S., Ed. *Handbook of experimental psychology.* N. Y., Wiley, 355-364. [61]

——. 1954. The nature of the drive as innate determinant of behavioral organization. In Jones, M. R., Ed.

Nebraska symposium on motivation. Lincoln, Univ. Nebraska Press. 281-321. Quoted by permission. [61, 81, 125]

——. *See also* Warden, C. J. 1928.

North, A. J. 1950a. Improvement in successive discrimination reversals. *J comp physiol Ps* 43, 442-460. [293]

——. 1950b. Performance during an extended series of discrimination reversals. *J comp physiol Ps* 43, 461-470. [292]

Nowlis, Helen H. 1941. The influence of success and failure on the resumption of an interrupted task. *J exp Ps* 28, 304-325. [93]

Nowlis, V. 1953. The development and modification of motivational systems in personality. *Current theory and research in motivation: A symposium.* Lincoln, Univ. Nebraska Press. [66]

Nuttin, J. 1953. *Tâche, réussite et échec: theorie de la conduite humaine.* Louvain, Publications Universitaries. [259]

O

Olds, J. 1956. A preliminary mapping of electrical reinforcing effects in the rat brain. *J comp physiol Ps* 49, 281-285. [121]

——. 1958. Self-stimulation of the brain. *Science* 127, 315-324. [62, 121]

——, Milner, P. 1954. Positive reinforcement produced by electrical stimulation of septal area and other regions of rat brain. *J comp physiol Ps* 47, 419-427. [121]

Olum, P. *See* Gibson, J. J. 1955.

Orlansky, J. 1948. *The human factor in the design of stick and rudder controls for aircraft.* N. Y., Psychological Corp. [157]

Osgood, C. E. 1952. The nature and measurement of meaning. *Ps Bull* 49, 197-237. [333]

——, Suci, G. J. 1955. Factor analysis of meaning. *J exp Ps* 50, 325-338. [334]

Ovsiankina, Maria. 1928. Die Wiederaufnahme unterbrochener Handlungen. *Ps Forsch* 11, 302-379. [91]

P

Page, H. A. 1955. The facilitation of experimental extinction by response prevention as a function of the acquisition of a new response. *J comp physiol Ps* 48, 14-16. [261]

Parducci, A. 1957. Alternative measures for the discrimination of shift in reinforcement-ratio. *Amer J Ps* 60, 194-202. [257]

Pastore, N. 1954. Discrimination learning in the canary. *J comp physiol Ps* 47, 389-390. [298]

——. 1955. Discrimination and delayed response learning in the canary. *Ps Rep* 1, 307-315. [298]

Patrick, Catharine. 1955. *What is creative thinking?* N. Y., Philosophical Library. [354]

Pavlov, I. P. 1927. *Conditioned reflexes: an investigation of the physiological activity of the cerebral cortex.* N. Y., Oxford Univ. Press. [34, 39, 228, 235, 261, 276, 277]

Peak, Helen, 1955. Attitude and motivation. In Jones, M. R., Ed. *Nebraska symposium on motivation 1955.* Lincoln, Univ. Nebraska Press, 149-188. [74, 249]

Pereboom, A. C. 1957. An analysis and revision of Hull's Theorem 30. *J exp Ps* 53, 234-238. [248]

Perkins, C. C., Jr., Cacioppo, A. J. 1950. The effect of intermittent reinforcement on the change in extinction rate following successive reconditionings. *J exp Ps* 40, 794-801. [262, 265]

Perkins, M. J., Banks, H. P., Calvin, A. D. 1954. The effect of delay on simultaneous and successive discrimination in children. *J exp Ps* 48, 416-418. [282]

Pettigrew, T. P. *See* Goodnow, J. J. 1956.

Piaget, J. 1932. *The moral judgment of the child.* N. Y., Harcourt, Brace. [100]

——. 1937. *La construction du réel chez l'enfant.* Neuchatel, Delachaux & Niestlé. [176, 202]

——, Inhelder, B. 1948. *La représenta-*

tion de l'espace chez l'enfant. Paris, Presses universitaries de France. [168]

——, Lambercier, M. 1951. La comparison des grandeurs projectives chez l'enfant et chez l'adulte. *Arch Ps, Geneva* 33, 81-130. [204, 205, 206, 208]

Piercy, M. F. *See* McFie, J. 1950.

Piéron, H. 1920. Recherches comparatives sur la mémorie des formes et celle des chiffres. *Année ps* 21, 119-148. [196]

Pilzecker, A. *See* Müller, G. E. 1900.

Poffenberger, A. T. 1942. 1952. *Principles of applied psychology.* N. Y., Appleton-Century. [150]

Pomeroy, W. B. *See* Kinsey, A. C. 1948.

Poulton, E. C. 1952a. Perceptual anticipation with two-pointer and one-pointer displays. *Brit J Ps* 43, 222-229. [148]

——. 1952b. The basis of perceptual anticipation in tracking. *Brit J Ps* 43, 295-302. [148]

——. 1957. Learning the statistical properties of the input in pursuit tracking. *J exp Ps* 54, 28-32. [328]

Pratt, Cornelia H. *See* Schlosberg, H. 1956.

Prentice, W. C. H. 1949. Continuity in human learning. *J exp Ps* 39, 187-194. [286]

Proshansky, H. *See* Jerome, E. A. 1950.

Pubols, B. H., Jr. 1956. The facilitation of visual and spatial discrimination reversal by overlearning. *J comp physiol Ps* 49, 243-248. [294]

Purdy, Jean, Gibson, Eleanor J. 1955. Distance judgment by the method of fractionation. *J exp Ps* 50, 374-380. [213]

——. *See also* Gibson, Eleanor J. 1955; Gibson, J. J. 1955.

R

Raben, Margaret W. 1949. The white rat's discrimination of differences in intensity of illumination measured by a running response. *J comp physiol Ps* 42, 254-272. [280]

Ratner, S. C. 1956. Effect of extinction of dipper-approaching on subsequent extinction of bar-pressing and dipper-approaching. *J comp physiol Ps* 49, 576-581. [260]

Ray, W. S. 1955. Complex tasks for use in human problem-solving research. *Ps Bull* 52, 134-149. [352]

Razran, G. 1955. Conditioning and perception. *Ps Rev* 62, 83-95. [229]

——. 1956. Backward conditioning. *Ps Bull* 53, 55-69. [231]

Reed, H. B. 1918. Associative aids. *Ps Rev* 25, 128-155, 257-285, 378-400. Esp. p. 276. [225]

——. 1946, 1950. The learning and retention of concepts: I. The influence of set. II. The influence of length of series. III. The origin of concepts. IV. The influence of the complexity of the stimuli. V. The influence of form of presentation. *J exp Ps* 36, 71-87, 166-179, 252-261; 40, 504-511. [337, 338]

Reichlin, B. *See* Taylor, J. G. 1951.

Reid, L. S. 1953. The development of noncontinuity behavior through continuity learning. *J exp Ps* 46, 107-112. [294]

Reinhold, Margaret. 1950. A case of auditory agnosia. *Brain* 73, 203-223. [19]

Restle, F. 1957. Discrimination of cues in mazes: A resolution of the "place-vs.-response" question. *Ps Rev* 64, 217-228. [305]

——, Beecroft, R. S. 1955. Anxiety, stimulus generalization, and differential conditioning: A comparison of two theories. *Ps Rev* 62, 433-437. [74]

Rethlingshafer, Dorothy, Eschenbach, A., Stone, J. T. 1951. Combined drives in learning. *J exp Ps* 41, 226-231. [314]

Richardson, J., Bergum, B. O. 1954. Distributed practice and rote learning in concept formation. *J exp Ps* 47, 442-446. [339, 340]

——. *See also* Underwood, B. J. 1956a, 1956b.

Riley, D. A., Rosenzweig, M. R. 1957. Echolocation in rats. *J comp physiol Ps* 50, 323-328. [303]

Riopelle, A. J. 1953. Transfer suppres-

set in preschool children. *J comp physiol Ps* 50, 15-17. [299]

Sherrington, C. S. 1906, 1948. *The integrative action of the nervous system.* N. Y., Scribner; New Haven, Yale Univ. Press. [69, 138]

——. *See also* Creed, R. S. 1932.

Shipley, T. E., Jr., Veroff, J. 1952. A projective measure of need for affiliation. *J exp Ps* 43, 349-356. [96]

Shuford, E. H., Jr. *See* Young, P. T. 1954, 1955.

Sidman, M., Brady, J. V., Boren, J. J., Conrad, D. G., Schulman, A. 1955. Reward schedules and behavior maintained by intercranial self-stimulation. *Science* 122, 830-831. [122]

——. *See also* Boren, J. J. 1957.

Sidowski, J. B. *See* Wyckoff, L. B. 1955.

Siegel, A. I., Jensen, J. 1955. The development of a job sample trouble-shooting performance examination. *J appl Ps* 39, 343-347. [349]

Simmel, Marienne L., Counts, Sarah. 1957. Some stable response determinants of perception, thinking, and learning: A study based on the analysis of a single test. *Genet Ps Monogr* 56, 3-157. [346]

Simon, J. R., Smader, R. C. 1955. Dimensional analysis of motion: VIII. The role of visual discrimination in motion cycles. *J appl Ps* 39, 5-10. [151]

Skinner, B. F. 1938. *The behavior of organisms.* N. Y., Appleton-Century. [6, 8, 34, 40, 229, 236, 239, 264, 280]

——. 1950. Are theories of learning necessary? *Ps Rev* 57, 193-216. [237]

——. 1953. *Science and human behavior.* N. Y., Macmillan. Quoted by permission. [6, 238]

——. *See also* Estes, W. K. 1941.

Slater-Hammel, A. T. 1948. Action current study of contraction-movement relationships in golf stroke. *Res Q Amer Assoc Health* 19, 164-177. [138]

——. 1949. An action current study of contraction-movement relationships in the tennis stroke. *Res Q Amer Assoc Health* 20, 424-431. [138]

Smith, W. C. *See* Bullock, D. H. 1953.

Smoke, K. L. 1932. An objective study of concept formation. *Ps Monogr* No. 191. [343]

——. 1933. Negative instances in concept learning. *J exp Ps* 16, 583-588. [343]

Sollenberger, R. J. *See* Dennis, W. 1934.

Solley, C. M., Messick, S. J. 1957. Probability-learning, the statistical structure of concepts, and the measurement of meaning. *Amer J Ps* 60, 161-173. [257]

——. *See also* Messick, S. J. 1957.

Solomon, L. M. *See* Thompson, W. R. 1954.

Solomon, R. L. 1943. Latency of response as a measure of learning in a "single-door" discrimination. *Amer J Ps* 56, 422-432. [279]

——, Kamin, L. J., Wynne, L. C. 1953. Traumatic avoidance learning: The outcomes of several extinction procedures with dogs. *J abn soc Ps* 48, 291-302. [69]

——, Wynne, L. C. 1953. Traumatic avoidance learning: Acquisition in normal dogs. *Ps Monogr* No. 354. [69]

——. *See also* Wynne, L. C. 1955.

Spence, K. W. 1936. The nature of discrimination learning in animals. *Ps Rev* 43, 427-449. [285, 287, 289]

——. 1937. Analysis of the formation of visual discrimination habits in chimpanzee. *J comp Ps* 23, 77-100. [289]

——. 1951. Theoretical interpretations of learning. In Stevens, S. S., Ed. *Handbook of experimental psychology.* N. Y., Wiley. 690-729. [285]

——. 1952. The nature of response in discrimination learning. *Ps Rev* 59, 89-93. [281]

——, Farber, I. E. 1953. Conditioning and extinction as a function of anxiety. *J exp Ps* 45, 116-119. [74]

——, Lippitt, R. 1940. "Latent" learning of a simple maze problem with relevant needs satiated. *Ps Bull* 37, 429. [67, 319, 320]

——, ——. 1946. An experimental test of the sign-Gestalt theory of trial-and-error learning. *J exp Ps* 36, 491-502. [67]

Spooner, Alice, Kellogg, W. N. 1947. The backward conditioning curve. *Amer J Ps* 60, 321-334. [230]

Spragg, S. D. S. 1933. Anticipation as a factor in maze errors. *J comp Ps* 15, 313-329. [44]

——. 1934. Anticipatory responses in the maze. *J comp Ps* 18, 51-73. [44]

Stanley, J. C. *See* Jenkins, W. O. 1950.

Stavrianos, Bertha K. 1945. The relation of shape perception to explicit judgments of inclination. *Arch Ps, N. Y.* No. 296. [215, 216, 217]

Stellar, E. *See* Morgan, C. T. 1950.

Stetson, R. H., Bouman, H. D. 1935. The coördination of simple skilled movements. *Arch néerl Physiol* 20, 177-254. [138]

Stevens, S. S., Newman, E. B. 1936. The localization of actual sources of sound. *Amer J Ps* 48, 297-306. [189]

Stevenson, H. W. *See* Capaldi, E. J. 1957.

Stolurow, L. M. *See* Detambel, M. H. 1957.

Stone, C. P. 1932. Sexual drive. In Allen, E., Ed. *Sex and internal secretions.* Baltimore, Williams & Wilkins. 828-879. [58]

——. 1939. Sex drive. In Allen, E., Ed. *Sex and internal secretions,* 2d ed. Baltimore, Williams & Wilkins. 1213-1262. [63]

——. *See also* Mason, W. A. 1953.

Stone, J. T. *See* Rethlingshafer, Dorothy. 1951.

Suci, G. J. *See* Osgood, C. E. 1955.

Supa, M., Cotzin, M., Dallenbach, K. M. 1944. "Facial vision:" the perception of obstacles by the blind. *Amer J Ps* 57, 133-183. [185]

Sutherland, N. S. 1957. Spontaneous alternation and stimulus avoidance. *J comp physiol Ps* 50, 358-362. [86]

Swartz, P. 1953. A new method for scaling pain. *J exp Ps* 45, 288-293. [10]

Sweet, W. H. *See* White, J. C. 1955.

Switzer, St. C. A. 1934. Anticipatory and inhibitory characteristics of delayed conditioned reactions. *J exp Ps* 17, 603-620. [40]

T

Taylor, F. E. *See* Jones, F. N. 1938.

Taylor, F. V. *See* Chernikoff, R. 1955.

Taylor, J. G., Reichlin, B. 1951. Vicarious trial and error. *Ps Rev* 58, 389-402. [271, 272]

Taylor, Janet A. 1953. A personality scale of manifest anxiety. *J abn soc Ps* 48, 285-290. [73]

——. 1956. Drive theory and manifest anxiety. *Ps Bull* 53, 303-320. [74]

Taylor, W. S. 1933. A critique of sublimation in males: A study of forty superior single men. *Genet Ps Monogr* 13, 1-115. [104]

Teuber, H. L. *See* Semmes, J. 1955.

Thompson, M. E. 1944. Learning as a function of the absolute and relative amounts of work. *J exp Ps* 34, 506-515. [249]

Thompson, R. 1953. Approach-avoidance in an ambivalent object discrimination problem. *J exp Ps* 45, 341-344. [298]

——. *See also* Hayes, K. J. 1953.

Thompson, W. R., Solomon, L. M. 1954. Spontaneous pattern discrimination in the rat. *J comp physiol Ps* 47, 104-107. [84]

Thorndike, E. L. 1898. Animal intelligence: an experimental study of the associative processes in animals. *Ps Rev Monogr* No. 8. [236, 238, 239]

——. 1931. *Human learning.* N. Y., Century. [225]

——. 1932. *The fundamentals of learning.* N. Y., Teachers College, Columbia Univ. [225]

——. 1935a. *Adult interests.* N. Y., Macmillan. Quoted by permission. [115]

——. 1935b. *The psychology of wants, interests, and attitudes.* N. Y., Appleton-Century. [115]

Thouless, R. H. 1932. Individual differences in phenomenal regression. *Brit J Ps* 22, 216-241. [211]

Thurstone, L. L. 1923. The stimulus-response fallacy in psychology. *Ps Rev* 30, 354-369. [36]

——. 1924. *The nature of intelligence.* N. Y., Harcourt, Brace. [36]

Tiffen, J., Fairbanks, G. 1937. An eye-voice camera for clinical and research studies. *Ps Monogr* No. 215. [146]

Tighe, T. J. *See* Walk, R. D. 1957.

Tolman, E. C. 1932. *Purposive behavior in animals and men.* N. Y., Century. Reprinted, 1949, Univ. California Press. [3, 22, 43, 241, 242]

——. 1938. The determiners of behavior at a choice point. *Ps Rev* 45, 1-41. [3]

——. 1955. Principles of performance. *Ps Rev* 62, 315-326. [3, 5, 241, 243, 249]

——, Honzik, C. H. 1930. Degrees of hunger, reward and non-reward, and maze learning in rats; Introduction and removal of reward, and maze performance in rats. *Univ Calif Publ Ps* 4, 241-275. [308, 309]

——, Ritchie, B. F., Kalish, D. 1946. Studies in spatial learning: II. Place learning versus response learning. *J exp Ps* 36, 221-229. [310]

Towe, A. L. 1955. Visual figure discrimination and the mediation of equivalence responses. *Ps Rev* 62, 287-289. [287]

Troland, L. T. 1928. *The fundamentals of human motivation.* N. Y., Van Nostrand. [33]

Tyler, D. W. *See* Elam, C. B. 1954.

U

Underwood, B. J. 1952. An orientation for research on thinking. *Ps Rev* 59, 209-220. [352]

——. 1957. Studies of distributed practice: XV. Verbal concept learning as a function of intralist interference. *J exp Ps* 54, 33-40. [341]

——, Richardson, J. 1956a. Some verbal materials for the study of concept formation. *Ps Bull* 53, 84-95. [340]

——, ——. 1956b. Verbal concept learning as a function of instructions and dominance level. *J exp Ps* 51, 229-238. [340, 341]

——. *See also* Feldman, S. M. 1957.

Urdal, A. *See* Clausen, J. 1953.

V

Varley, Margaret A. *See* Wodinsky, J. 1954.

Vernon, M. D. 1952. *A further study of visual perception.* Cambridge, Cambridge Univ. Press. [196]

——. 1955. The functions of schemata in perceiving. *Ps Rev* 62, 180-192. [196]

Vernon, P. E. 1951. *The structure of human abilities.* N. Y., Wiley. [135]

Veroff, J. *See* Atkinson, J. W. 1954; Shipley, T. E., Jr. 1952.

Verplanck, W. S. 1942. The development of discrimination in a simple motor habit. *J exp Ps* 31, 441-464. [280]

——. 1955. The operant, from rat to man: An introduction to some recent experiments on human behavior. *Trans N. Y. Acad Sci,* Ser. II, 17, 594-601. [36]

——. 1956. The operant conditioning of human motor behavior. *Ps Bull* 53, 70-83. [237]

Viaud, G. 1953. Problemes psychophysiologiques posés par les migrations des animaux. *J Ps norm path* 46, 12-48. [152]

Vinacke, W. E. 1951. The investigation of concept formation. *Ps Bull* 48, 1-31. [336]

Vince, M. A. *See* Mitchell, M. J. H. 1951.

Vinci, Leonardo da. 1585. *Trattato della Pittura.* Napoli. (Edition used, 1733.) German trans., 1882 V. 2. *Das Buch von der Malerei.* Wein. [168]

Vineberg, R. *See* Kendler, H. H. 1954.

Viteles, M. S. 1953. *Motivation and morale in industry.* N. Y., Morton. [100]

Voss, J. F. *See* Battig, W. F., 1957.

W

Waddell, D., Gans, Susan, Kempner, Phyllis, Williams, Ann. 1955. A comparison of place and response learning in very young rats. *J comp physiol Ps* 48, 375-377. [310]

Walk, R. D., Gibson, Eleanor J.,

Tighe, T. J. 1957. Behavior of light- and dark-reared rats on a visual cliff. *Science* 126, 80-81. [302]

——. *See also* Gibson, Eleanor J. 1956.

Walshe, F. M. R. 1952. *Diseases of the nervous system*, 7th ed. Baltimore, Williams & Wilkins. [139]

Wapner, S. *See* Witkin, H. A. 1952, 1954.

Warden, C. J., Nissen, H. W. 1928. An experimental analysis of the obstruction method of measuring animal drives. *J comp Ps* 8, 325-342. Reprinted in Warden, C. J., 1931. *Animal motivation*. N. Y., Columbia Univ. Press. 34-49. [249]

Warner, L. H. 1932. The association span of the white rat. *J genet Ps* 41, 57-90. [52, 53]

Warren, J. M. 1954a. An analysis of the formation of visual discriminative habits of rhesus monkeys. *Amer J Ps* 67, 517-520. [298]

——. 1954b. Reversed discrimination as a function of the number of reinforcements during pre-training. *Amer J Ps* 67, 720-722. [294]

——, Baron, A. 1956a. The formation of learning sets by cats. *J comp physiol Ps* 49, 227-231. [298]

——, ——. 1956b. Acquisition of successive and simultaneous discrimination habits by cats. *J genet Ps* 89, 61-64. [282]

Washburn, Margaret Floy. 1936. *The animal mind: A textbook of comparative psychology*, 4th ed. N. Y., Macmillan. [120]

Watson, J. B. 1907. Kinesthetic and organic sensations: their role in the reactions of the white rat to the maze. *Ps Monogr* No. 33. [303]

——. 1913. Psychology as a behaviorist views it. *Ps Rev* 20, 158-177. [8, 11]

——. 1914. *Behavior, an introduction to comparative psychology*. N. Y., Holt. [8, 11, 27, 303]

——. 1919. *Psychology from the standpoint of a behaviorist*. Philadelphia, Lippincott. [27]

——. *See also* Yerkes, R. M. 1911.

Webb, W. B. 1949. The motivational aspect of an irrelevant drive in the behavior of the white rat. *J exp Ps* 39, 1-14. [67]

Wechsler, I. S. 1952. *A textbook of clinical neurology*, 7th ed. Philadelphia, Saunders. [139]

Weigl, E. 1927. Zur Psychologie sogennanter Abstraktionsprozesse: I. Untersuchungen über das "Ordnen." *Z Ps* 103, 2-45. Trans. by Rioch, Margaret J. 1941. On the psychology of so-called processes of abstraction. *J abn soc Ps* 36, 3-33. [336]

Weinstein, S. *See* Semmes, Josephine. 1955.

Weinstock, S. 1954. Resistance to extinction of a running response following partial reinforcement under widely spaced trials. *J comp physiol Ps* 47, 318-322. [265]

Weiss, W. *See* Hovland, C. I. 1953.

Weisz, P. B. 1954. *Biology*. N. Y., McGraw-Hill. [38]

Welch, L., Kubis, J. 1947. The effect of anxiety on the conditioning rate and stability of the PGR. *J Ps* 23, 83-91. [74]

Welker, W. I. 1956. Some determinants of play and exploration in chimpanzees. *J comp physiol Ps* 49, 84-89. [81, 82]

Wenzel, Bernice M., Flurry, Christine. 1948. The sequential order of concept attainment. *J exp Ps* 38, 547-557. [338]

Wertheimer, M. 1923. Untersuchungen zur Lehre von der Gestalt. *Ps Forsch* 4, 301-350. [193]

——. *See also* Hornbostel, E. M. v. 1920.

White, J. C., Sweet, W. H. 1955. *Pain: Its mechanisms and neurosurgical control*. Springfield, Ill., Thomas. [10]

Wickens, D. D. 1954. Stimulus-response theory as applied to perception. *Kentucky symposium: Learning theory, personality theory, and clinical research.* N. Y., Wiley. 22-35. [288]

——, Miles, R. C. 1954. Extinction changes during a series of reinforcement-extinction sessions. *J comp physiol Ps* 47, 315-317. [262]

Wiener, M. *See* Buss, A. H. 1955.

Williams, Ann. *See* Waddell, D. 1955.

Williams, H. *See* Seeman, W. 1952.

Willig, L. *See* Ammons, R. B. 1956.

Wischner, G. J. *See* Goss, A. E. 1956.

Witkin, H. A. 1949. Perception of bodily position and of the position of the visual field. *Ps Monogr* No. 302. [180]

——. 1952. Further studies of perception of the upright when the direction of the force acting on the body is changed. *J exp Ps* 43, 9-20. [181]

——, Lewis, H. B., Hertzman, M., Machover, K., Meissner, P. Bretnall, Wapner, S. 1954. *Personality through perception: An experimental and clinical study.* N. Y., Harper. [180, 181, 182]

——, Wapner, S., Leventhal, T. 1952. Sound localization with conflicting visual and auditory cues. *J exp Ps* 43, 58-67. [189]

Wodinsky, J., Varley, Margaret A., Bitterman, M. E. 1954. Situational determinants of the relative difficulty of simultaneous and successive discrimination. *J comp physiol Ps* 47, 337-340. [275]

——. *See also* Bitterman, M. E. 1953.

Wohlwill, J. F. 1957. The abstraction and conceptualization of form, color, and number. *J exp Ps* 53, 304-309. [338]

Wolf, I. S., Kellogg, W. N. 1940. Changes in general behavior during flexion conditioning and their importance for the learning process. *Amer J Ps* 53, 384-396. [245]

Wolfe, J. B. 1936. Effectiveness of token-rewards for chimpanzees. *Comp Ps Monogr* No. 60. [111]

Wolff, H. G. *See* Hardy, J. D. 1947.

Wolfle, D. L. *See* Gulliksen, H. 1938.

Woodcock, Louise P. *See* Biber, Barbara. 1942.

Woodworth, R. S. 1899. 1939. The accuracy of voluntary movement. *Ps Rev Monogr Suppl* No. 13.

——. 1908. *Psychology* (a lecture). N. Y., Columbia Univ. Press. [22]

——. 1915. A revision of imageless thought. *Ps Rev* 22, 1-27. Reprinted in *Psychological Issues.* N. Y., Columbia Univ. Press, 1939, 103-127, esp. pp. 118-119. [224]

——. 1918. *Dynamic psychology.* N. Y., Columbia Univ. Press. [50]

——. 1929. *Psychology.* Rev. ed. N. Y., Holt. [22]

——. 1937. Situation-and-goal set. *Amer J Ps* 50, 130-140. Reprinted in *Psychological Issues.* N. Y., Columbia Univ. Press, 1939, 149-160. [47]

——. 1938. *Experimental psychology.* N. Y., Holt. [307]

——. 1939. *Psychological issues. Selected papers.* N .Y., Columbia Univ. Press.

——. 1947. Reënforcement of perception. *Amer J Ps* 60, 119-124. [193]

——. 1948. *Contemporary schools of psychology,* N. Y., Ronald. [2]

——, Schlosberg, H. 1954. *Experimental psychology.* Rev. ed. N. Y., Holt. [9, 43, 46, 47, 61, 94, 141, 196, 265, 343]

Worchel, P. 1951. Space perception and orientation in the blind. *Ps Monogr* No. 332. [185]

——, Dallenbach, K. M. 1947. "Facial vision:" perception of obstacles by the deaf-blind. *Amer J Ps* 60, 502-553. [185]

Wulf, F. 1922. Über die Veränderung von Vorstellungen (Gedächtnis und Gestalt). *Ps Forsch* 1, 333-373. [196]

Wyckoff, L. B., Sidowski, J. B. 1955. Probability discrimination in a motor task. *J exp Ps* 50, 225-231. [257]

Wynne, L. C., Solomon, R. L., 1955. Traumatic avoidance learning: acquisition and extinction in dogs deprived of normal peripheral autonomic function. *Genet Ps Monogr* 52, 241-284. [69]

——. *See also* Solomon, R. L. 1953.

Y

Yerkes, R. M. 1907. *The dancing mouse.* N. Y., Macmillan. [276]

——, Watson, J. B. 1911. Methods of studying vision in animals. *Beh Monogr* 1, No. 2. [276]

Young, P. T. 1948. Studies of food preference, appetite and dietary habit: VIII. Food-seeking drives, palatability and the law of effect. *J comp physiol Ps* 41, 269-300. [120]

——. 1949. Food-seeking drive, affective process, and learning. *Ps Rev* 56, 98-121. [121]

——. 1955. The role of hedonic processes in motivation. In Jones, M. R., Ed. *Nebraska symposium on motivation 1955.* Lincoln, Nebraska Univ. Press. 193-238. [121]

——, Shuford, E. H., Jr., 1954. Intensity, duration, and repetition of hedonic processes as related to acquisition of motives. *J comp physiol Ps* 47, 298-305. [121]

——, ——. 1955. Quantitative control of motivation through sucrose solutions of different concentrations. *J comp physiol Ps* 48, 114-118. [121]

Youtz, R. P., Ericksen, S. C. 1947. Analysis of the pilot's task. In Miller, N. E., Ed. *US AAF Aviat Psychol Prog Res Rep* No. 8. 25-71. [153, 157, 159]

Z

Zangwill, O. L. *See* McFie, J. 1950.

Zeaman, D. 1949. Response latency as a function of the amount of reinforcement. *J exp Ps* 39, 466-483. [248]

Zeigarnik, Bluma. 1927. Über das Behalten von erledigten und unerledigten Handlungen. *Ps Forsch* 9, 1-85. [93]

Zener, K. 1937. The significance of behavior accompanying conditioned salivary secretion for theories of the conditioned response. *Amer J Ps* 50, 384-403. [231]

——, McCurdy, H. G. 1939. Analysis of motivational factors in conditioned behavior. *J Ps* 8, 321-350. [231]

Ziegler, H. P. 1957. Electrical stimulation of the brain and the psychophysiology of learning and motivation. *Ps Bull* 54, 363-382. [122]

Subject Index

SUBJECT INDEX

A

Ability, 5
  learning, 51, 325ff
Absorption, 132
Achievement, 88ff, 94, 116, 123, 127, 132
  desire, 119
  ego-involved, 89, 131
  goal, 124
  indicators, 94f, 123
  need, 94
Activation, 60ff, 66, 72ff, 93
Activity cage or wheel, 61, 87
Adjustment, 46
Advance information, 146ff, 257
A-factor, A-variables, 33, 351
Affiliation, 95
Age curves for perceptual constancy, 209
Agnosia, 18ff
Airplane, 152ff
  controls, 155ff
  cues, 153ff, 157, 175
  landing, 154
  landmarks, 158f
  maps, 158
  navigation, 157ff
  pilot, 152ff, 175
  radar, 159
  spatial environment, 156f
  steering, 153
  turning, 155f
All-or-none law, 136
Ameliorative tendency, 259
Animal subjects, 12, 79ff, 125, 164, 267ff, 301ff
Anticipation, 44, 113, 257
  behavioral, 13, 41ff, 227
  expectancy, 240ff
  memory method, 232
  reification, 242

Anticipatory
  error, 44f
  goal reaction, 27, 44ff, 113, 117, 146, 333
Anxiety
  animal, 40, 68ff, 81, 87, 90f
  human, 72
  questionnaire, 73
  redirected, 72
  Taylor scale, 73
Aphasia, 19
Approach, 55, 140
Apraxia, 19
Association
  areas, 17ff
  backward, 231
  contiguity, 224ff, 231, 319
  controlled, 42
  force, 49
  frequency, 341
  law, 49
  learning, 224ff
  mediating, 269, 333, 342
  specific, 143f, 163
Ataxia, 139
Ataxiameter, 139
Attention, 42, 271, 273ff, 284, 286, 327
Attitude
  acquired, 115
  scientific, 102, 238
Auditory space perception, 183ff
Aviation, 152ff, 202
  tests, 160
Avoidance
  conditioned, 60, 70
  emotion, 69
  extinction, 70, 113
  gradient, 89f
  motivation, 52f, 70f, 103
  place learning, 318
  theory, 70ff